ENDANGERED SPECIES
PROTECTING BIODIVERSITY

ISSN 1930-3319

ENDANGERED SPECIES
PROTECTING BIODIVERSITY

Kim Masters Evans

INFORMATION PLUS® REFERENCE SERIES
Formerly Published by Information Plus, Wylie, Texas

GALE
CENGAGE Learning·

Farmington Hills, Mich • San Francisco • New York • Waterville, Maine
Meriden, Conn • Mason, Ohio • Chicago

Endangered Species: Protecting Biodiversity

Kim Masters Evans

Kepos Media, Inc.: Steven Long and Janice Jorgensen, Series Editors

Project Editors: Laura Avery, Tracie Moy

Rights Acquisition and Management: Ashley M. Maynard

Composition: Evi Abou-El-Seoud, Mary Beth Trimper

Manufacturing: Rita Wimberley

For product information and technology assistance, contact us at
Gale Customer Support, 1-800-877-4253.
For permission to use material from this text or product,
submit all requests online at **www.cengage.com/permissions.**
Further permissions questions can be e-mailed to
permissionrequest@cengage.com

Cover photograph: © cdelacy/Shutterstock.com.

Gale
27500 Drake Rd.
Farmington Hills, MI 48331-3535

ISBN-13: 978-0-7876-5103-9 (set)
ISBN-13: 978-1-57302-698-7

ISSN 1930-3319

This title is also available as an e-book.
ISBN-13: 978-1-57302-710-6 (set)
Contact your Gale sales representative for ordering information.

Printed in the United States of America
1 2 3 4 5   20 19 18 17 16

TABLE OF CONTENTS

PREFACE

Endangered Species: Protecting Biodiversity is part of the *Information Plus Reference Series*. The purpose of each volume of the series is to present the latest facts on a topic of pressing concern in modern American life. These topics include the most controversial and studied social issues of the 21st century: abortion, capital punishment, care for the elderly, crime, the environment, health care, immigration, race and ethnicity, social welfare, women, youth, and many more. Although this series is written especially for high school and undergraduate students, it is an excellent resource for anyone in need of factual information on current affairs.

By presenting the facts, it is the intention of Gale, Cengage Learning, to provide its readers with everything they need to reach an informed opinion on current issues. To that end, there is a particular emphasis in this series on the presentation of scientific studies, surveys, and statistics. These data are generally presented in the form of tables, charts, and other graphics placed within the text of each book. Every graphic is directly referred to and carefully explained in the text. The source of each graphic is presented within the graphic itself. The data used in these graphics are drawn from the most reputable and reliable sources, such as from the various branches of the U.S. government and from private organizations and associations. Every effort has been made to secure the most recent information available. Readers should bear in mind that many major studies take years to conduct and that additional years often pass before the data from these studies are made available to the public. Therefore, in many cases the most recent information available in 2016 is from 2013 or 2014. Older statistics are sometimes presented as well, if they are landmark studies or of particular interest and no more-recent information exists.

Although statistics are a major focus of the *Information Plus Reference Series*, they are by no means its only content. Each book also presents the widely held positions and important ideas that shape how the book's subject is discussed in the United States. These positions are explained in detail and, where possible, in the words of their proponents. Some of the other material to be found in these books includes historical background, descriptions of major events related to the subject, relevant laws and court cases, and examples of how these issues play out in American life. Some books also feature primary documents, or have pro and con debate sections that provide the words and opinions of prominent Americans on both sides of a controversial topic. All material is presented in an evenhanded and unbiased manner; readers will never be encouraged to accept one view of an issue over another.

HOW TO USE THIS BOOK

The status of endangered species is an issue of concern both for many Americans and for people around the world. In particular, balancing biodiversity with economics has led to much controversy. This book looks at what has been done to protect endangered species in the United States and around the world and examines the debate over what future actions are warranted.

Endangered Species: Protecting Biodiversity consists of 10 chapters and three appendixes. Each chapter is devoted to a particular aspect of endangered species. For a summary of the information that is covered in each chapter, please see the synopses that are provided in the Table of Contents. Chapters generally begin with an overview of the basic facts and background information on the chapter's topic, then proceed to examine subtopics of particular interest. For example, Chapter 8: Birds begins by describing how birds are classified by scientists and the important roles that birds play in their ecosystems. It then presents data regarding the dozens of U.S. bird species listed under the Endangered Species Act. Imperiled species within particular classes—woodpeckers, passerines (songbirds), raptors, and waterbirds—are discussed in terms of the conservation measures taken to protect them from extinction. The general threats to birds, such as pesticides, oil, and invasive species, are then reviewed. Several success stories are presented to highlight bird species that have been recovered from the brink of extinction. The chapter ends with a brief overview of the hundreds of foreign bird species that are endangered and threatened. Readers can find their way through a chapter by looking for the section and subsection headings, which are clearly set off from the text. They can also refer to the book's extensive Index if they already know what they are looking for.

Statistical Information

The tables and figures featured throughout *Endangered Species: Protecting Biodiversity* will be of particular use to readers in learning about this issue. The tables and figures represent an extensive collection of the most recent and important statistics on endangered species, as well as related issues—for example, graphics cover the number of endangered species, foreign endangered and threatened plant species, and the life cycle of Pacific salmon. The photographs illustrate some of the most threatened species on the earth, such as the red wolf. Gale, Cengage Learning, believes that making this information available to readers is the most important way to fulfill the goal of this book: to help readers understand the issues and controversies surrounding endangered species and reach their own conclusions.

Each table or figure has a unique identifier appearing above it, for ease of identification and reference. Titles for the tables and figures explain their purpose. At the end of each table or figure, the original source of the data is provided.

To help readers understand these often complicated statistics, all tables and figures are explained in the text. References in the text direct readers to the relevant statistics. Furthermore, the contents of all tables and figures are fully indexed. Please see the opening section of the Index at the back of this volume for a description of how to find tables and figures within it.

Appendixes

Besides the main body text and images, *Endangered Species: Protecting Biodiversity* has three appendixes. The first is the Important Names and Addresses directory. Here, readers will find contact information for a number of government and private organizations that can provide further information on aspects of endangered species. The second appendix is the Resources section, which can also assist readers in conducting their own research. In this section, the author and editors of *Endangered Species: Protecting Biodiversity* describe some of the sources that were most useful during the compilation of this book. The final appendix is the detailed Index. It has been greatly expanded from previous editions and should make it even easier to find specific topics in this book.

COMMENTS AND SUGGESTIONS

The editors of the *Information Plus Reference Series* welcome your feedback on *Endangered Species: Protecting Biodiversity*. Please direct all correspondence to:

Editors
Information Plus Reference Series
27500 Drake Rd.
Farmington Hills, MI 48331-3535

CHAPTER 1
EXTINCTION AND ENDANGERED SPECIES

The earth is richly supplied with different types of living organisms that coexist in their environments, forming complex, interrelated communities. Living organisms depend on one another for nutrients, shelter, and other benefits. The extinction of any one species can set off a chain reaction that affects many other species, particularly if the loss occurs near the bottom of the food chain. For example, the extinction of a particular insect or plant might seem inconsequential. Small animals, however, may feed on that resource. The loss can threaten the survival of these creatures and the larger predators that prey on them. Extinction can have a ripple effect that spreads throughout nature.

Besides its biological consequences, extinction poses a moral dilemma for humans. The presence of humans on the planet has affected all other life-forms. Human lifestyles have proven incompatible with the survival of some other species. Purposeful efforts have eliminated animals that prey on people, livestock, and crops or pose any threat to human livelihoods. Some wild animals have been decimated by human desire for meat, hides, fur, and other body parts. Likewise, the demand for land, water, timber, and other natural resources has left many wild plants and animals with little to no suitable habitat. Humans have also affected nature by introducing non-native species and producing pollutants that negatively impact the environment and climate. The combination of these anthropogenic (human-related) effects with natural obstacles that limit survival, such as disease or low birth-rates, have proven to be too much for some species to overcome. They have no chance of survival without human help.

Societies have difficult choices to make about the amount of effort and money they are willing to spend to keep imperiled species from becoming extinct. Will people accept limits on their property rights, recreational activities, and means of livelihood to save a plant or animal? Should saving popular species such as whales and dolphins take priority over saving annoying or feared species? Is it the responsibility of humans to save every life-form from disappearing, or is extinction an inevitable part of nature, in which the strong survive and the weak perish? These are some of the difficult questions that people face as they ponder the fate of other species living on this planet.

DEFINING AND NAMING LIFE ON THE EARTH

Living organisms are named and categorized according to a taxonomy, a hierarchical system of order that is based on the natural relationships among life-forms. Table 1.1 shows the taxonomic chart for blue whales, the largest creatures on the earth. They are described by eight taxonomic levels ending with "species." A species is a group of organisms that are capable of interbreeding with one another. A subspecies (abbreviated ssp.) ranks immediately below species and is a population of a particular geographical region that is genetically different from other populations of the same species, but can still interbreed with them.

Plants and animals are identified by their common names and by unique scientific names. Some organisms have more than one common name. For example, the mountain lion is also called a puma or cougar. To avoid confusion, scientific bodies have established a nomenclature (naming) system for life-forms. This system is based on the example set by Carolus Linnaeus (1707–1778), a Swedish naturalist who published classifications for thousands of plants and animals. Linnaeus popularized a binary naming system in which the first word names an organism's genus (a group of closely related species). This is followed by a specific epithet (a descriptive word or phrase) that differentiates one species from another. Linnaeus used Latin words in his nomenclature because Latin was the preferred language for scientific publications during the 18th century.

TABLE 1.1

Taxonomic chart for blue whales

Classification	Blue whale example	Explanation
Kingdom	Animalia	Whales belong to the kingdom Animalia because whales have many cells, ingest food, and are formed from a "blastula" (from a fertilized egg).
Phylum	Chordata	An animal from the phylum Chordata has a spinal cord and gill pouches.
Class	Mammalia	Whales and other mammals are warm blooded, have glands to provide milk for their offspring, and have a four-chambered heart.
Order	Cetacea	Cetaceans are mammals that live completely in the water.
[Suborder]	Mysticeti	Whales that belong to the suborder Mysticeti have baleen plates (big filters in their mouths) rather than teeth.
Family	Balaenidae	The family Balaenidae, also called rorqual whales. They have pleats around their throat that allow them to hold lots of water (which contains their food).
Genus	*Balaenoptera*	A genus is a group of species that are more closely related to one another than any group in the family. *Balaenoptera* refers to the genus.
Species	*Musculus*	A species is a grouping of individuals that interbreed successfully. The blue whale species name is *musculus*.

SOURCE: "The Chart below Is a Sample Taxonomic Chart for Blue Whales," in *What Is Taxonomy?* National Oceanic and Atmospheric Administration, Alaska Fisheries Science Center, National Marine Mammal Laboratory, undated, http://www.afsc.noaa.gov/nmml/education/taxonomy.php (accessed April 18, 2016)

Modern convention dictates that the scientist who first describes an organism in a scholarly publication chooses the organism's scientific name. The latter must be in Latin or contain words that have been rendered to appear Latin. Scientific names are either italicized or underlined in print. The first letter of the genus is capitalized; the specific epithet is in lower case.

Subspecies are indicated in scientific nomenclature with an additional term. For example, the scientific name of the blue whale is *Balaenoptera musculus*. A subspecies, the pygmy blue whale, is called *Balaenoptera musculus brevicauda*. Genus reassignments are indicated with the "=" sign in a scientific name. When the royal snail was discovered in 1977, it was assigned to the genus *Marstonia*. Ten years later biologists decided the snail was more properly a member of the genus *Pyrgulopsis*. Thus, the scientific name of the royal snail is written as *Pyrgulopsis (=Marstonia) ogmorhaphe*. When the species is not known for an organism of known genus, the scientific name is written with sp. (indicating a single species) or spp. (indicating multiple species) as the specific epithet. The latter format is also used when referring to all species in a genus. For example, *Pyrgulopsis* spp. refers to all species within the genus *Pyrgulopsis*.

The rules governing scientific names for animals are overseen by the International Commission on Zoological Nomenclature, which is headquartered in London, England. The International Code of Botanical Nomenclature for plants is managed by the International Botanical Congress, a meeting of botanists from around the world that is held every six years. The most recent meeting took place in Australia in 2011, and the next will be in China in 2017.

ASSESSING SPECIES

The question of how many different species exist on the earth is hotly debated by scientists. Estimates range from 3 million to more than 100 million. Based in Switzerland, the International Union for Conservation of Nature (IUCN) is the world's largest conservation organization. According to the IUCN (http://cms.iucn.org/about/union/members/index.cfm), in February 2016 it had more than 1,200 members and 11,000 scientific experts working in over 160 countries "to help the world find pragmatic solutions to our most pressing environment and development challenges."

Since 1960 the IUCN has compiled the *Red List of Threatened Species* (http://www.iucnredlist.org/), which examines the status of species worldwide. The IUCN indicates in *Red List of Threatened Species Version 2015.4* (http://www.iucnredlist.org/about/summary-statistics) that as of November 2015 more than 1.7 million species had been officially described. The largest groups were insects (1 million), flowering plants (268,000), arachnids (e.g., spiders; 102,248), and mollusks (e.g., clams; 85,000). Mammals, which are probably the best-studied group—and the one that includes humans—had 5,515 described organisms.

EXTINCTION

A species is described as extinct when no living members remain. Scientists know from the study of fossils that dinosaurs, mammoths, saber-toothed cats, and countless other animal and plant species that once lived on the earth no longer exist. These species have "died out," or become extinct.

Mass Extinctions

In the billions of years since life began on the earth, species have formed, existed, and then become extinct. Scientists call the natural extinction of a few species per million years a background, or normal, rate. When the extinction rate doubles for many different groups of plants and animals at the same time, this is described as a mass extinction. Mass extinctions have occurred infrequently and, in general, have been attributed to major cataclysmic geological or astronomical events. Five mass extinctions have occurred during the last 600 million years. These episodes, known as the Big Five, occurred at the end of five geologic periods:

- Ordovician (505 million to 440 million years ago)
- Devonian (410 million to 360 million years ago)
- Permian (286 million to 245 million years ago)
- Triassic (245 million to 208 million years ago)
- Cretaceous (146 million to 65 million years ago)

After each mass extinction the floral (plant) and faunal (animal) composition of the earth changed drastically. The largest mass extinction on record occurred at the end of the Permian, when an estimated 90% to 95% of all species became extinct. The Cretaceous extinction, which is hypothesized to have resulted from the collision of an asteroid with the earth, saw the demise of many species of dinosaurs.

The Sixth Mass Extinction?

Scientists estimate that hundreds, or even thousands, of species are being lost annually worldwide. This suggests that another mass extinction is taking place. However, the current extinction is not associated with a cataclysmic physical event. Rather, the heightened extinction rate has coincided with the success and spread of human beings. Researchers predict that as humans continue to destroy and alter natural habitats, create pollution, introduce nonnative species, and contribute to global climate change, the extinction rate will continue to rise. The United Nations (UN) concludes in *Global Biodiversity Outlook 4* (2014, https://www.cbd.int/gbo/gbo4/publication/gbo4-en-hr.pdf) that "although actions to support particular threatened species have proven effective in preventing extinctions, these have not been enough to reverse the overall trend towards extinction for many species groups."

RECENT EXTINCTION STATISTICS. In *IUCN Red List Categories and Criteria, Version 3.1 Second Edition* (2012, http://jr.iucnredlist.org/documents/redlist_cats_crit_en.pdf), the IUCN notes that it considers a species extinct "when there is no reasonable doubt that the last individual has died." As of November 2015, the IUCN (http://cmsdocs.s3.amazonaws.com/summarystats/2015-4_Summary_Stats_Page_Documents/2015_4_RL_Stats_Table_3a.pdf) counted 732 animal species as extinct. Another 32 animal species were classified as extinct in the wild, meaning that no individuals were believed to exist in the wild, but some individuals were being cultivated, kept in captivity, or otherwise maintained "well outside the past range." Of the extinct animal species, the largest numbers were gastropods, such as snails (281 species), birds (140 species), and mammals (78 species). The IUCN (November 2015, http://cmsdocs.s3.amazonaws.com/summarystats/2015-4_Summary_Stats_Page_Documents/2015_4_RL_Stats_Table_3b.pdf) also counted 102 plant species as extinct and 37 plant species as extinct in the wild.

One recent extinction noted by the IUCN is an unnamed snail (*Plectostoma sciaphilum*) that was found exclusively in and around a small limestone hill in Malaysia. The organization (http://www.iucnredlist.org/details/168180/0) states that the hill was mined away by the first decade of the 21st century and "recent survey work has confirmed that this species [is] now extinct." Thus, the IUCN categorized the species as extinct in 2014.

Resurrecting Extinct Species?

In the 1993 film *Jurassic Park* scientists use ancient deoxyribonucleic acid (DNA) that was preserved in amber to clone dozens of prehistoric dinosaur species. (A clone is a later-born identical twin.) With the advent of modern genetic science, the possibility of resurrecting extinct species has received considerable attention. According to Charles Q. Choi, in "First Extinct-Animal Clone Created" (NationalGeographic.com, February 10, 2009), in 2003 scientists conducted the first-known cloning of an extinct subspecies: *Capra pyrenaica pyrenaica*—commonly called the Pyrenean ibex. Ibex are wild goats. The Pyrenean ibex went extinct in 2000. Choi indicates that hundreds of clone embryos were created using frozen skin cells taken from the last living Pyrenean ibex. They were implanted in Spanish ibex and ibex-goat hybrids. Only seven of the embryos developed into fetuses, and only one of the fetuses survived to full term, but it died "immediately after birth" because of lung abnormalities. Choi notes that "such abnormalities are common in cloning" due to irregularities that arise during DNA transfer.

Resurrecting extinct species is fraught with technical challenges and is highly controversial. There are also ethical questions involved, such as the morality of treating animals as objects for genetic experimentation. Scientists note that many nonclosely related members of a species would have to be reproduced for the species as a whole to survive. The resurrection of long-extinct species, such as the wooly mammoth, is especially daunting because of DNA deterioration over time and the lack of suitable surrogate mothers.

It is considered more feasible to produce hybrids of extinct and extant (still in existence) species. In 2015 researchers at Harvard University genetically manipulated elephant cells to contain a few fragments of wooly mammoth DNA. The last living mammoths died out thousands of years ago. Scientists have been able to decode the animal's DNA sequence by studying well-preserved corpses found in thawing Arctic ice. The creation of hybrid elephant-mammoth cells in the laboratory led to much speculation in the press that mammoths (or at least mammoth-like elephants) can be genetically manufactured. In "Could We 'De-extinctify' the Woolly Mammoth?" (Guardian.com, April 26, 2015), Beth Shapiro acknowledges the scientific value of the endeavor but cautions, "Elephants should be provided with the opportunity to make more elephants, and not be subjected to scientific manipulation for what seems like a far-fetched and unrealistic goal."

U.S. HISTORY: SOME EXTINCTIONS AND SOME CLOSE CALLS

The colonization of the North American continent by European settlers severely depleted the ranks of some native wild species. The introduction of livestock brought new animal diseases that devastated some native animals. Widespread hunting and trapping led to the demise of other species. During the early 1800s the United States was home to millions, perhaps billions, of passenger pigeons. These migratory birds traveled in enormous flocks and were extremely popular with hunters. By the beginning of the 20th century the species was virtually exterminated. The last known passenger pigeon died in the Cincinnati Zoo in 1914. The heath hen, a small wild fowl native to the United States and once very abundant, was wiped out of existence by 1932. Stocks of other animals—beaver, elk, wild turkey, and bison (American buffalo; see Figure 1.1)—were driven to the brink of extinction, but saved by conservation efforts.

The U.S. Fish and Wildlife Service (USFWS) tracks imperiled animal and plant species under mandates set out in the Endangered Species Act (ESA), which was passed in 1973 and is described in detail in Chapter 2. Through February 2016, 10 U.S. species had officially been declared extinct under the act, as shown in Table 1.2.

In March 2011 USFWS researchers recommended in *Eastern Puma (=Cougar) (Puma concolor couguar): 5-Year Review: Summary and Evaluation* (http://ecos.fws .gov/docs/five_year_review/doc3611.pdf) that the eastern puma (*Puma concolor couguar*), a terrestrial mammal, be declared extinct under the ESA. In June 2015 the agency (https://www.gpo.gov/fdsys/pkg/FR-2015-06-17/pdf/2015-14931.pdf) officially proposed the delisting, noting that there had not been a confirmed sighting of the animal since 1938. As of April 2016, the designation had not yet become final.

CONSEQUENCES OF EXTINCTION: LOSS OF BIODIVERSITY

In general, the major consequence of extinction is the loss of biodiversity. The term *biodiversity* is short for biological diversity, and it refers to the variability among all living organisms. In 1992 representatives from dozens of nations around the world met in Rio de Janeiro, Brazil, at the UN Conference on Environment and Development. One of the outcomes was the Convention on Biological Diversity, an international agreement devoted to protecting the earth's biodiversity. The Convention on Biological Diversity (http://www.cbd.int/convention/articles/ default.shtml?a=cbd-02) notes that biodiversity encompasses three interconnected realms: ecosystems, species, and genetics.

Biodiversity Realms

Ecosystems are natural areas that include communities of living organisms. The earth contains a wide variety of ecosystem types including forests, swamps, deserts, and oceans. Different ecosystems provide different habitats for different types of plants and animals that have evolved to thrive in their environments. Ecosystem variety is important to maintaining a rich array of species across the planet.

The organisms within an ecosystem are affected by the physical environment in which they live, such as the weather, the climate (weather conditions over the long term), and the air, water, and soil conditions. In addition, the organisms interact with each other. Scientists have shown that habitats with species diversity are more stable—that is, better able to adjust to and recover from disturbances. This is because different species may perform overlapping functions in a biologically diverse ecosystem. Ecosystems with a great variety of species tend to best support sustainable food sources. Dramatic declines in one or more species in the ecosystem can greatly stress the remaining species. This is true at multiple levels of the food chain. For example, the disappearance of prey species (e.g., deer) harms predator species (e.g., wolves) that depend on them for food.

FIGURE 1.1

Bison (or American buffalo) are the largest terrestrial animals in North America. ©*Steve Degenhardt/Shutterstock.com.*

TABLE 1.2

Species delisted due to extinction as of February 2016

Common name	Scientific name	Species group	Date first listed	Date delisted	U.S. or U.S./foreign listed	Historic distribution and status
Amistad gambusia	*Gambusia amistadensis*	Fishes	04/30/80	12/04/87	US	TX; believed to be extinct
Blue pike	*Stizostedion vitreum glaucum*	Fishes	03/11/67	09/02/83	US/foreign	MI, NY, OH, PA; believed to be extinct
Caribbean monk seal	*Monachus tropicalis*	Mammals	04/10/79	10/28/08	US/foreign	FL, PR, VI; no known populations in the wild; presumed extinct
Dusky seaside sparrow	*Ammodramus maritimus nigrescens*	Birds	03/11/67	12/12/90	US	FL; believed to be extinct
Guam broadbill	*Myiagra freycineti*	Birds	08/27/84	02/23/04	US	GU; possibly extinct
Longjaw cisco	*Coregonus alpenae*	Fishes	03/11/67	02/23/04	US/foreign	IL, IN, MI, NY, OH, PA, WI; believed to be extinct
Mariana mallard	*Anas oustaleti*	Birds	12/08/77	02/23/04	US	GU, MP; possibly extinct
Sampson's pearlymussel	*Epioblasma sampsoni*	Clams	06/14/76	01/09/84	US	IL, IN; believed to be extinct
Santa Barbara song sparrow	*Melospiza melodia graminea*	Birds	06/04/73	10/12/83	US	CA; believed to be extinct
Tecopa pupfish	*Cyprinodon nevadensis calidae*	Fishes	10/13/70	01/15/82	US	CA; extinct

SOURCE: Adapted from "Generate Species List," and "Delisting Report," in *Environmental Conservation Online System Species Reports*, U.S. Department of the Interior, U.S. Fish and Wildlife Service, February 2016, http://ecos.fws.gov/tess_public/pub/adHocSpeciesForm.jsp (accessed February 19, 2016)

In contrast, a dramatic decline in predator populations can allow prey to overpopulate to the point that the available food is not sufficient to sustain them.

Biodiversity is also important at the genetic level. There are natural genetic differences between members of the same species that affect individual characteristics, such as coloring, resistance to disease, and behavioral traits. Genetic variation within a species is desirable because it increases the chances that at least some members will survive environmental changes or other stressors. For example, if all members of a species are equally susceptible to a disease, then the entire population can be decimated by the sickness. If the members have varying resistance levels, then some will succumb, but others will survive to perpetuate the species.

High genetic variation also lowers the chances that problems associated with inbreeding will occur. Inbreeding is mating between closely related individuals with extremely similar genetic material. It is almost certain that if one of these individuals has a gene disorder, the other individual will also have it. This disorder might not cause any notable problems in the parents, but it could become concentrated in the offspring and cause serious health problems for them. Many animal and plant species naturally avoid inbreeding. For example, studies show that humans and some other animal species appear to rely on genetic markers (such as the major histocompatibility complex—a group of molecules built into the immune system) to avoid mating with individuals that are genetically similar to themselves. In addition, humans have social and cultural taboos against inbreeding with their closest relatives. However, some animal species—particularly those in isolated and/or small populations—may engage in inbreeding when there are no other viable mating choices.

There is a certain lower limit to the population of some species, particularly those that are isolated in location. If the population falls too low, the remaining individuals will be so closely related that any inherent gene problems can kill off the resulting offspring and ultimately wipe out the entire species.

Extinction Consequences for Specific Species

It is difficult to quantify the consequences of the extinction of a particular species. Every species plays some kind of role in its particular ecosystem. In some cases, these roles are quite evident and easily identified as beneficial. For example, as described in Chapter 7, elephants dig water holes, keep forest growth in check, and open up grasslands that support other species. These activities are important to maintaining the savanna habitats. As such, elephants are called a "keystone species" because other species in their ecosystems are highly dependent on them and would suffer major impacts if they disappeared. As explained in Chapter 6, the desert tortoise is another keystone species because the burrows it makes for itself provide habitat for multiple other desert animals. Some actions by one species indirectly benefit other species. Chapter 3 notes that sea otters prey on sea urchins, an aquatic creature that consumes seaweed such as kelp. Keeping the sea urchins from overpopulating allows kelp forests to spread, providing valuable habitat and sustenance to many other aquatic species.

In addition, there are a multitude of complex interactions between species of different types. For example, many plants depend on animals to propagate. Bees visit flowers for nourishment and in the process help flowers reproduce by transferring pollen from one location to another. Birds and other animals that consume berries and seeds and then expel them in their waste unwittingly help plants spread. Losing any of the species involved in these interactions harms the other species involved.

HOW MANY SPECIES ARE ENDANGERED?

As noted earlier, the IUCN compiles the annual *Red List of Threatened Species*, in which it examines the status of species worldwide. The so-called Red List categorizes species based on the level of risk of their extinction in the wild as follows:

- Critically endangered—extremely high risk
- Endangered—very high risk
- Vulnerable—high risk

The IUCN refers to species in all three of these categories as "threatened" species.

Determining how many species of plants and animals are imperiled is difficult. In fact, only a small fraction of the species in existence have even been identified and named, let alone studied in detail. In *Red List of Threatened Species Version 2015.4*, the IUCN designated 23,250 species as threatened in 2015. Nearly 80,000 species were examined out of the 1.7 million species that the IUCN considers "described species." Thus, less than 5% of all known species were evaluated. Further study will likely result in many more species being added to the Red List.

In the United States imperiled species are identified and listed as either endangered or threatened in accordance with the ESA. Endangered species are at risk of extinction through all or a significant portion of their natural habitats. Threatened species are likely to become endangered in the future. Management at the federal level of listed species is handled by the USFWS and the National Marine Fisheries Service (NMFS). The USFWS is an agency of the U.S. Department of the Interior (DOI) and oversees terrestrial (land-based) and freshwater species. The NMFS is an agency of the National Oceanic and Atmospheric Administration under the U.S. Department of Commerce and has jurisdiction for marine (ocean-dwelling) species and those that are anadromous (migrate between the ocean and freshwater).

Table 1.3 tabulates the number of ESA-listed species as of February 2016. Of the 1,346 animal species, 693 were found in the United States. Among these, 493 were endangered and 200 were threatened. Among animals, the greatest numbers of endangered and threatened species occurred among fish, birds, and clams. Of the 900 plant species, 897 were found in the United States. Among these, 732 were endangered and 165 were threatened. Nearly all the endangered plants were flowering plants.

Figure 1.2 shows the number of U.S. species listed per calendar year between 1967 and 2015. The peak year was 1994, when 127 species were listed. Within the United States, endangered and threatened species are not evenly distributed but are clustered in specific geographical areas. Table 1.4 shows the number of listed species in each state.

Note that some species are found in multiple states. Four states (Hawaii, California, Alabama, and Florida) each had over 100 listed species. Despite its small size, Hawaii harbored 435 listed species, more than any other state. This is because a significant proportion of Hawaiian plant and animal life is endemic (found nowhere else on the earth). Endemism is dangerous for imperiled species for a variety of reasons. A single calamitous event, such as a hurricane, earthquake, or disease epidemic, could wipe out the entire population at one time. The likelihood of inbreeding and resulting genetic problems is also higher for species that are geographically isolated.

SAVING ENDANGERED SPECIES: BENEFITS AND COSTS TO SOCIETY

As described earlier, saving endangered species and preventing their extinction has numerous benefits to the ecosystems in which they live. Extinction can also negatively affect human society both directly and indirectly in areas such as aesthetics (e.g., the beauty of nature), education, and scientific study. Wildlife also has practical value to society in terms of recreation and tourism.

This is evidenced by the popularity of hunting, fishing, and wildlife viewing. Later in this chapter, national programs will be described that have designated millions of acres across the country as national parks, wilderness areas, and wildlife refuges. They are visited by millions of people each year that help support local economies. Other wildlife ventures with economic value include zoos, safaris, and bird-watching tours. Wild plants and animals have commercial uses in other industries as well. Plants provide the genetic diversity that is used to breed new strains of agricultural crops, and many plants have been used to develop pharmaceutical products. For example, during the 1960s scientists discovered a cancer-fighting chemical called taxol in Pacific yew trees in northwestern forests. At the time, the trees were considered a nuisance species and were destroyed as weeds. If the species had disappeared, then humans would likely not have discovered taxol, which became a major component of the chemotherapy treatments used against some types of cancer.

As explained in Chapter 2, saving endangered species does have costs. Taxpayer dollars are used to fund agencies that carry out the ESA and state-level laws devoted to imperiled species. In addition, the laws put certain restrictions on what property owners are allowed to do on their own land. Some people believe that humans have a moral obligation to attempt to preserve species in decline regardless of the costs or the potential benefits to humans. This might be called "saving nature for nature's sake." The lawmakers who crafted the ESA in 1973 seemed to have this idealistic viewpoint. The original law did not require economic analyses or consideration of the costs

TABLE 1.3

Count of endangered and threatened species and U.S. species with recovery plans, February 8, 2016

Group	United States[a]			Foreign			Total listings (US and foreign)	US listings with active recovery plans[b]
	Endangered	Threatened	Total listings	Endangered	Threatened	Total listings		
Annelid worms	0	0	0	0	0	0	0	0
Flatworms and roundworms	0	0	0	0	0	0	0	0
Sponges	0	0	0	0	0	0	0	0
Corals	0	6	6	0	16	16	22	0
Snails	38	12	50	1	0	1	51	29
Fishes	92	70	162	19	3	22	184	104
Amphibians	20	15	35	8	1	9	44	21
Reptiles	15	24	39	69	20	89	128	36
Mammals	75	25	100	255	21	276	376	64
Clams	75	13	88	2	0	2	90	71
Insects	64	11	75	4	0	4	79	42
Arachnids	12	0	12	0	0	0	12	12
Crustaceans	22	3	25	0	0	0	25	18
Birds	80	21	101	217	17	234	335	86
Millipedes	0	0	0	0	0	0	0	0
Hydroids	0	0	0	0	0	0	0	0
Animal totals	**493**	**200**	**693**	**575**	**78**	**653**	**1,346**	**483**
Conifers and cycads	2	2	4	0	2	2	6	3
Ferns and allies	29	2	31	0	0	0	31	26
Lichens	2	0	2	0	0	0	2	2
Flowering plants	699	161	860	1	0	1	861	645
Plant totals	**732**	**165**	**897**	**1**	**2**	**3**	**900**	**676**
Grand totals	**1,225**	**365**	**1,590**	**576**	**80**	**656**	**2,246**	**1,159**

[a]United States listings include those populations in which the United States shares jurisdiction with another nation.
[b]There are a total of 603 distinct active (draft and final) recovery plans. Some recovery plans cover more than one species, and a few species have separate plans covering different parts of their ranges. This count includes only plans generated by the U.S. Fish and Wildlife Services (USFWS) (or jointly by the USFWS and National Marine Fisheries Service), and only listed species that occur in the United States.

SOURCE: "Summary of Listed Species Listed Populations and Recovery Plans as of Mon, 08 Feb 2016 19:30:34 GMT," in *Environmental Conservation Online System Species Reports*, U.S. Department of the Interior, U.S. Fish and Wildlife Service, February 8, 2016, http://ecos.fws.gov/tess_public/pub/Boxscore.do (accessed February 8, 2016)

FIGURE 1.2

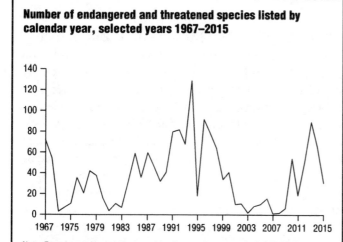

Number of endangered and threatened species listed by calendar year, selected years 1967–2015

Note: Experimental populations, and foreign species are not included. Distinct population segments (DPS) are included, as are species listed due to similarity of appearance and joint U.S./foreign listings (those that are listed in the U.S. and an adjacent country). Species listed by National Marine Fisheries Service (NMFS) (which has authority under the Endangered Species Act to list marine species) are also included. The effective date (as given in the Federal Register notice) is used to determine in which Calendar Year a species is counted.a

SOURCE: Adapted from "U.S. Federal Endangered and Threatened Species by Calendar Year," in *Environmental Conservation Online System Species Reports*, U.S. Department of the Interior, U.S. Fish and Wildlife Service, 2016, http://ecos.fws.gov/tess_public/reports/species-listings-count-by-year-report (accessed February 8, 2016)

versus the benefits of saving endangered species. Over time, Congress has amended the law to add a few mechanisms for weighing costs against benefits in certain situations. Overall, however, the ESA as it exists in the 21st century continues to reflect the principle that nature should be saved for nature's sake. This makes the law extremely controversial and subject to harsh criticism that it is impractical and favors the welfare of plants and animals over the welfare of human beings. Throughout this book numerous battles are described in which conflicts have arisen over the well-being of an imperiled species versus the interests (chiefly economic) of humans.

Although the overall value of wildlife to society is well recognized, the relative value of specific species to humans is highly variable. In general, the public places high value on some species and not on others. For example, whales and seals are popular animals for which protection measures receive widespread support. By contrast, several species listed under the ESA are considered pests or predators because they pose a threat to human livelihoods or safety. For example, Utah prairie dogs are burrowing animals that produce networks of underground tunnels. The resulting holes and dirt mounds can ruin cropland and trip and injure livestock.

TABLE 1.4

Number of endangered and threatened species, by state or territory, 2016

Alabama	128 listings
Alaska	12 listings
Arizona	65 listings
Arkansas	34 listings
California	307 listings
Colorado	33 listings
Connecticut	12 listings
Delaware	11 listings
District of Columbia	2 listings
Florida	125 listings
Georgia	69 listings
Hawaii	435 listings
Idaho	15 listings
Illinois	31 listings
Indiana	25 listings
Iowa	17 listings
Kansas	18 listings
Kentucky	39 listings
Louisiana	24 listings
Maine	12 listings
Maryland	18 listings
Massachusetts	16 listings
Michigan	25 listings
Minnesota	18 listings
Mississippi	48 listings
Missouri	39 listings
Montana	15 listings
Nebraska	14 listings
Nevada	39 listings
New Hampshire	11 listings
New Jersey	17 listings
New Mexico	53 listings
New York	22 listings
North Carolina	60 listings
North Dakota	10 listings
Ohio	25 listings
Oklahoma	22 listings
Oregon	57 listings
Pennsylvania	14 listings
Rhode Island	10 listings
South Carolina	38 listings
South Dakota	15 listings
Tennessee	93 listings
Texas	99 listings
Utah	42 listings
Vermont	5 listings
Virginia	69 listings
Washington	48 listings
West Virginia	20 listings
Wisconsin	21 listings
Wyoming	12 listings
American Samoa	2 listings
Guam	20 listings
Northern Mariana Islands	20 listings
Puerto Rico	71 listings
Virgin Islands	12 listings
Outlying Caribbean Islands	0 listings
Outlying Pacific Islands	0 listings

SOURCE: "Listed Species Believed to or Known to Occur in Each State," in *Environmental Conservation Online System Species Reports*, U.S. Department of the Interior, U.S. Fish and Wildlife Service, 2016, http://ecos.fws.gov/tess_public/reports/species-listed-by-state-totals-report? (accessed February 8, 2016)

The protection of Utah prairie dogs and other imperiled rodents is a source of contention for people who believe that the ESA puts animal interests above human interests. The same debate rages over predators such as wolves and mountain lions that may prey on livestock, pets, and even people.

Under the ESA species are listed for protection based on their biological status (e.g., population, health, and well-being) and the threats against them, not for their importance to humans or the potential costs of protecting them. This does not mean, however, that the ESA process is immune from economic influences. As explained in Chapter 2, financial considerations do come into play. Although the number of species eligible for protection under the ESA skyrocketed from around 100 during the early 1970s to more than 2,000 in 2016, federal funding for the agencies responsible for administering the act has not increased sufficiently to allow them to handle the expansion in the workload. There is a lack of political and public will to fund the activities needed to pursue the very optimistic (and some say unrealistic) goals laid out in the ESA to save all endangered species.

Public Opinion

The Gallup Organization conducts an annual poll on environmental issues. Table 1.5 shows the results from March 2015, when participants were asked to express their level of worry about various environmental problems. Thirty-six percent of those asked expressed a "great deal" of concern and 28% expressed a "fair amount" of concern regarding the extinction of plant and animal species. This placed extinction fourth in terms of the amount of worry about the various environmental problems. As shown in Table 1.6, concern over extinction has generally declined since 2000, when Gallup first polled people about the issue. In 2000, 45% of respondents expressed a "great deal" of concern and 33% expressed a "fair amount" of concern.

THE ROLE OF THE FEDERAL GOVERNMENT

As noted earlier, the USFWS and the NMFS conserve endangered and threatened species through the authority of the ESA, which allows them to issue rules and regulations that govern how imperiled species are managed. They also educate the public by maintaining websites and publishing fact sheets and other documents about the issue. Since 2006 Congress has annually declared an Endangered Species Day on which the agencies work with private partners to raise awareness about species conservation. In 2016 the day was set for May 20 and was to include events around the country.

Federal Lands

According to Carol Hardy Vincent et al. of the Congressional Research Service, in *Federal Land Ownership: Acquisition and Disposal Authorities* (May 19, 2015, https://www.fas.org/sgp/crs/misc/RL34273.pdf), the federal government owns approximately 640 million acres (259 million ha) of U.S. land. This is more than a quarter of the nation's land area. The vast majority of federally owned lands are in western states and are managed by the

Bureau of Land Management (BLM), the National Park Service (NPS) within the DOI, or the USFWS.

Protecting natural ecosystems and habitats helps ensure that imperiled species (and other native plants and animals) have places to flourish. The USFWS manages the National Wildlife Refuge System, the only network of federal lands and waters that is managed principally for the protection of fish and wildlife. In 2016 the National Wildlife Refuge System (http://www.fws.gov/refuges/refugeLocatorMaps/index.html) included 561 refuges and thousands of small natural wetlands and grasslands around the country. Fifty-nine of the refuges were established specifically for endangered species. (See Table 1.7.) Protected species include a variety of plants and animals. Many other listed animal species use refuge lands on a temporary basis for breeding or migratory rest stops.

The USFWS, the U.S. Forest Service, the NPS, and the BLM oversee the National Wilderness Preservation System of undeveloped federal land. According to Wilderness.net, in "Creation and Growth of the National Wilderness Preservation System" (http://www.wilderness.net/NWPS/fastfacts), as of 2016, 765 so-called wilderness areas had been designated across the country covering approximately 109 million acres (44 million ha). Alaska, California, and other western states are home to most of the wilderness areas.

The NPS (2016, http://www.nps.gov/aboutus/faqs.htm) notes that in 2016 there were 410 units in the National Park System covering more than 84 million acres (34 million ha). The units include national parks, monuments, preserves, lakeshores, seashores, wild and scenic rivers, trails, historic sites, military parks, battlefields, historical parks, recreation areas, memorials, and parkways. Besides preserving habitats that range from Arctic tundra to tropical rain forest, the system protects many imperiled plant and animal species.

The national parks have played a significant role in the return of several species, including wolves and peregrine falcons. The national parks also contain designated

TABLE 1.5

Poll respondents expressing their level of worry regarding environmental problems, March 2015

I'M GOING TO READ YOU A LIST OF ENVIRONMENTAL PROBLEMS. AS I READ EACH ONE, PLEASE TELL ME IF YOU PERSONALLY WORRY ABOUT THIS PROBLEM A GREAT DEAL, A FAIR AMOUNT, ONLY A LITTLE, OR NOT AT ALL. FIRST, HOW MUCH DO YOU PERSONALLY WORRY ABOUT—[RANDOM ORDER]?

2015 Mar 5–8 (sorted by "a great deal")	Great deal	Fair amount	Only a little/ not at all
Pollution of drinking water	55	22	23
Pollution of rivers, lakes, and reservoirs	47	32	21
Air pollution	38	33	29
Extinction of plant and animal species	36	28	36
The loss of tropical rain forests	33	30	37
Global warming/global warming or climate change	32	23	45

SOURCE: Jeff Jones and Lydia Saad, "I'm going to read you a list of environmental problems. As I read each one, please tell me if you personally worry about this problem a great deal, a fair amount, only a little, or not at all. First, how much do you personally worry about—[RANDOM ORDER]?" in *Gallup Poll Social Series: Environment—Final Topline*, The Gallup Organization, March 5–8 2015, http://www.gallup.com/file/poll/182111/150325EnviroWorries.pdf (accessed February 8, 2016). Copyright © 2015 Gallup, Inc. All rights reserved. The content is used with permission; however, Gallup retains all rights of republication.

TABLE 1.6

Poll respondents expressing their level of worry regarding extinction of plant and animal species, various dates, selected years 2000–15

	Great deal	Fair amount	Only a little	Not at all	No opinion
2015 Mar 5–8	36	28	22	14	*
2014 Mar 6–9	41	24	24	10	1
2013 Mar 7–10	35	29	22	13	*
2012 Mar 8–11	36	29	23	12	1
2011 Mar 3–6	34	30	23	13	1
2010 Mar 4–7	31	30	24	15	*
2009 Mar 5–8	37	28	22	12	*
2008 Mar 6–9	37	31	20	11	*
2007 Mar 11–14	39	30	19	12	*
2006 Mar 13–16	34	29	23	14	1
2004 Mar 8–11	36	26	23	15	*
2003 Mar 3–5	34	32	21	12	1
2002 Mar 4–7	35	30	22	12	1
2001 Mar 5–7	43	30	19	7	1
2000 Apr 3–9	45	33	14	8	*

*Less than 0.5%.

SOURCE: Jeff Jones and Lydia Saad, "I'm going to read you a list of environmental problems. As I read each one, please tell me if you personally worry about this problem a great deal, a fair amount, only a little, or not at all. First, how much do you personally worry about extinction of plant and animal species?" in *Gallup Poll Social Series: Environment—Final Topline*, The Gallup Organization, March 5–8, 2015, http://www.gallup.com/file/poll/182111/150325EnviroWor-ries.pdf (accessed February 8, 2016). Copyright © 2015 Gallup, Inc. All rights reserved. The content is used with permission; however, Gallup retains all rights of republication.

TABLE 1.7

National wildlife refuges established for endangered species

State	Unit name	Species of concern	Unit acreage
Alabama	Sauta Cave NWR	Indiana bat, gray bat	264
	Fern Cave NWR	Indiana bat, gray bat	199
	Key Cave NWR	Alabama cavefish, gray bat	1,060
	Watercress Darter NWR	Watercress darter	7
Arkansas	Logan Cave NWR	Cave crayfish, gray bat, Indiana bat, Ozark cavefish	124
Arizona	Buenos Aires NWR	Masked bobwhite quail	116,585
	Leslie Canyon	Gila topminnow, Yaqui chub, Peregrine falcon	2,765
	San Bernardino NWR	Gila topminnow, Yaqui chub, Yaqui catfish, Beautiful shiner, Huachuca water umbel	2,369
California	Antioch Dunes NWR	Lange's metalmark butterfly, Antioch Dunes evening-primrose, Contra Costa wallflower	55
	Bitter Creek NWR	California condor	14,054
	Blue Ridge NWR	California condor	897
	Castle Rock NWR	Aleutian Canada goose	14
	Coachella Valley NWR	Coachello Valley fringe-toed lizard	3,592
	Don Edwards San Francisco Bay NWR	California clapper rail, California least tern, Salt marsh harvest mouse	21,524
	Ellicott Slough NWR	Santa Cruz long-toed salamander	139
	Hopper Mountain NWR	California condor	2,471
	Sacramento River NWR	Valley elderberry longhorn beetle, Bald eagle, Least Bell's vireo	7,884
	San Diego NWR	San Diego fairy shrimp, San Diego mesa mint, Otay mesa mint, California orcutt grass, San Diego button-celery	1,840
	San Joaquin River NWR	Aleutian Canada goose	1,638
	Seal Beach NWR	Light-footed clapper rail, California least tern	911
	Sweetwater Marsh NWR	Light-footed clapper rail	316
	Tijuana Slough NWR	Light-footed clapper rail	1,023
Florida	Archie Carr NWR	Loggerhead sea turtle, Green sea turtle	29
	Crocodile Lake NWR	American crocodile	6,686
	Crystal River NWR	West Indian manatee	80
	Florida Panther NWR	Florida panther	23,379
	Hobe Sound NWR	Loggerhead sea turtle, Green sea turtle	980
	Lake Wales Ridge NWR	Florida scrub jay, Snakeroot, Scrub blazing star, Carter's mustard, Papery whitlow-wort, Florida bonamia, Scrub lupine, Highlands scrub hypericum, Garett's mint, Scrub mint, Pygmy gringe-tree, Wireweed, Florida ziziphus, Scrub Plum, Eastern indigo snake, Bluetail mole skink, Sand skink	659
	National Key Deer Refuge	Key deer	8,542
	St. Johns NWR	Dusky seaside sparrow	6,255
Hawaii	Hakalau Forest NWR	Akepa, Akiapolaau, 'O'u, Hawaiian hawk, Hawaiian creeper	32,730
	Hanalei NWR	Hawaiian stilt, Hawaiian coot, Hawaiian moorhen, Hawaiian duck	917
	Huleia NWR	Hawaiian stilt, Hawaiian coot, Hawaiian moorhen, Hawaiian duck	241
	James C. Campbell NWR	Hawaiian stilt, Hawaiian coot, Hawaiian moorhen, Hawaiian duck	164
	Kakahaia NWR	Hawaiian stilt, Hawaiian coot	45
	Kealia Pond NWR	Hawaiian stilt, Hawaiian coot	691
	Pearl Harbor NWR	Hawaiian stilt	61
Iowa	Driftless Area NWR	Iowa Pleistocene snail	521
Massachusetts	Massasoit NWR	Plymouth red-bellied turtle	184
Michigan	Kirtland's Warbler WMA	Kirtland's warbler	6,535
Mississippi	Mississippi Sandhill Crane NWR	Mississippi sandhill crane	19,713
Missouri	Ozark Cavefish NWR	Ozark cavefish	42
	Pilot Knob NWR	Indiana bat	90
Nebraska	Karl E. Mundt NWR	Bald eagle	19
Nevada	Ash Meadows NWR	Devil's hole pupfish, Warm Springs pupfish, Ash Meadows amargosa pupfish, Ash Meadows speckled dace, Ash Meadows naucorid, Ash Meadows blazing star, Amargosa niterwort, Ash Meadows milk-vetch, Ash Meadows sunray, Spring-loving centaury, Ash Meadows gumplant, Ash Meadows invesia	13,268
	Moapa Valley NWR	Moapa dace	32
Oklahoma	Ozark Plateau NWR	Ozark big-eared bat, gray bat	2,208
Oregon	Bear Valley NWR	Bald eagle	4,200
	Julia Butler Hansen Refuge for Columbian White-tail deer	Columbian white-tailed deer	2,750
	Nestucca Bay NWR	Aleutian Canada goose	457
South Dakota	Karl E. Mundt NWR	Bald eagle	1,044
Texas	Attwater Prairie Chicken NWR	Attwater's greater prairie chicken	8,007
	Balcones Canyonlands NWR	Black-capped vireo, Golden-cheeked warbler	14,144
Virgin Islands	Green Cay NWR	St. Croix ground lizard	14
	Sandy Point NWR	Leatherback sea turtle	327

critical habitat for many listed species. However, not all of these are publicly disclosed, to protect rare species from collectors, vandals, or curiosity seekers.

In 2016 the U.S. Forest Service (2016, http://www .fs.fed.us/about-agency) managed 154 national forests and 20 national grasslands. National Forest lands also

TABLE 1.7

National wildlife refuges (NWR) established for endangered species [CONTINUED]

State	Unit name	Species of concern	Unit acreage
Virginia	James River NWR	Bald eagle	4,147
	Mason Neck NWR	Bald eagle	2,276
Washington	Julia Butler Hansen Refuge for Columbian white-tail deer	Columbian white-tailed deer	2,777
Wyoming	Mortenson Lake NWR	Wyoming toad	1,776

NWR = National wildlife refuge.

SOURCE: "National Wildlife Refuges Established for Endangered Species," in *National Wildlife Refuge System*, U.S. Department of the Interior, U.S. Fish and Wildlife Service, August 15, 2015, http://www.fws.gov/Refuges/whm/EndSpRefuges.html (accessed February 8, 2016)

include many lakes and ponds. National Forest lands are, in general, not conserved to the same degree as NPS lands. For example, much logging occurs within these forests. Endangered, threatened, and sensitive species on National Forest lands are subjected to biological evaluations to determine the effects of management activities on them. Conservation measures are also incorporated to preserve these species.

THE DEBATE OVER USE OF FEDERALLY PROTECTED LANDS. Ever since federal conservation lands were first set aside, a national debate has raged over how they should be used. Many of these lands contain natural resources of great value in commercial markets, including timber, oil, gas, and minerals. Political and business interests that wish to harvest these resources are pitted against environmentalists, who want to preserve the lands. The debate is particularly intense in the West, where the federal government owns and manages hundreds of millions of acres of land.

During the 1990s a political battle raged over the issue of logging in old-growth forests of the Pacific Northwest—the same forests that provided habitat for endangered northern spotted owls. A similar controversy has been brewing for decades over the drilling of oil and gas in the Arctic National Wildlife Refuge.

OIL DRILLING IN THE ARCTIC NATIONAL WILDLIFE REFUGE. The Arctic National Wildlife Refuge (ANWR) is located in northern Alaska. (See Figure 1.3.) Covering 19 million acres (7.7 million ha), it is the largest national wildlife refuge in the United States. The ANWR was established in 1980 by passage of the Alaska National Interest Lands Conservation Act. In Section 1002 of the act, Congress deferred a decision on the future management of 1.5 million acres (607,000 ha) of the ANWR because of conflicting interests between potential oil and gas resources thought to be located there and the area's importance as a wildlife habitat. This disputed area of coastal plain came to be known as the 1002 area.

There has been interest in tapping the oil deposits in northern Alaska since the mid-1900s. In 2002 and 2010

the U.S. Geological Survey (USGS) estimated the volumes of oil and natural gas potentially available in the National Petroleum Reserve in Alaska. In "2010 Updated Assessment of Undiscovered Oil and Gas Resources of the National Petroleum Reserve in Alaska" (October 2010, http://pubs.usgs.gov/fs/2010/3102/pdf/FS10-3102 .pdf), the USGS estimates that 896 million barrels of oil and 52.8 trillion cubic feet (1.5 trillion cubic meters) of natural gas are available in "conventional undiscovered accumulations."

Environmentalists argue that USFWS studies suggest that oil drilling in the refuge will harm many Arctic species by taking over habitat, damaging habitats through pollution, interfering with species' activities directly, or increasing opportunities for invasive species. The ANWR harbors the greatest number of plant and animal species of any park or refuge in the Arctic, including unique species such as arctic foxes, caribou, musk oxen, polar bears, and snow geese.

The protected status of the ANWR has been challenged by large oil companies and their political supporters, particularly Republicans. However, bills seeking to lift the protections have failed to pass Congress. Thus, as of April 2016 federal legislation had not been passed that allowed drilling in the ANWR.

Federal Funding for Private Land Conservation

The U.S. Department of Agriculture contains a branch called the Natural Resources Conservation Service (NRCS). The Federal Agriculture Improvement and Reform Act of 1996 established the Wildlife Habitat Incentive Program. It was a voluntary program for farmers, ranchers, forest landowners, and Native American tribes. The NRCS provided technical and financial assistance to qualified applicants who agreed to manage their land to develop or improve wildlife habitat. The Wildlife Habitat Incentive Program ended in 2014; however, financial incentives for wildlife habitat conservation have continued under the NRCS's Environmental Quality Incentives Program (http://www.nrcs.usda.gov/wps/portal/ nrcs/detail/national/programs/financial/eqip/?cid=stelprdb 1242633).

FIGURE 1.3

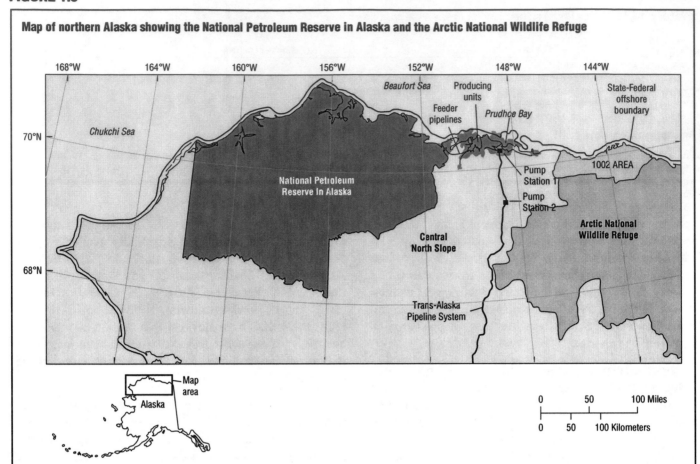

Map of northern Alaska showing the National Petroleum Reserve in Alaska and the Arctic National Wildlife Refuge

SOURCE: Emil D. Attanasi and Philip A. Freeman, "Figure 1. Map Showing the National Petroleum Reserve in Alaska (NPRA), the 1002 Area of the Arctic National Wildlife Refuge, and Oil-Producing Units near Prudhoe Bay in the Central North Slope," in *Economic Analysis of the 2010 U.S. Geological Survey Assessment of Undiscovered Oil and Gas in the National Petroleum Reserve in Alaska*, U.S. Department of the Interior, U.S. Geological Survey, 2011, http://pubs.usgs.gov/of/2011/1103/ofr2011-1103.pdf (accessed February 19, 2016)

Meanwhile, the DOI and the NRCS launched the Working Lands for Wildlife (WLFW) program in 2012. According to the agencies (March 8, 2012, http://www.nrcs.usda.gov/wps/portal/nrcs/detail/national/newsroom/?cid=STELPRDB1047050), "Federal, state and local wildlife experts jointly identify at-risk species that would benefit from targeted habitat restoration investments on private lands." Farmers, ranchers, forest landowners, and tribes can voluntarily agree to conserve habitat for the at-risk species. In exchange, they receive technical and financial assistance from the NRCS. The NRCS (2016, http://www.nrcs.usda.gov/wps/portal/nrcs/detail/national/programs/initiatives/?cid=stelprdb1046975) notes that the "WLFW also gives peace of mind to participating producers that as long as they maintain the conservation practices and systems that benefit the targeted species, they can continue their farming, ranching and forest operations and remain compliant with the ESA regulatory responsibilities for up to 30 years." As of April 2016, the WLFW program covered seven targeted species: the bog turtle, the golden-winged warbler, the gopher tortoise, the greater sage grouse, the lesser prairie chicken, the New England cottontail, and the southwestern willow flycatcher.

THE ROLE OF STATE GOVERNMENTS

Every state has its own agency that is charged with managing and overseeing land and wildlife conservation. The USFWS (January 5, 2016, http://www.fws.gov/offices/statelinks.html) maintains a database of website links to agencies in all 50 states, the District of Columbia, and U.S. territories, such as Guam and the U.S. Virgin Islands.

Most states maintain their own lists of endangered, threatened, or "special concern" species. For example, as of April 2016 the New York Department of Environmental Conservation (http://www.dec.ny.gov/animals/7494.html) listed 53 animal species as endangered, 36 as threatened, and 58 as special concern. It should be noted that state lists of imperiled species often include species that are not federally listed.

Some states have become proactive in working to prevent species from being listed under the ESA. The Western Association of Fish and Wildlife Agencies (http://www.wafwa.org/) coordinates multistate strategies and plans for conserving and managing land to benefit imperiled species, particularly official candidates for ESA listing. As of 2016, the Western Association of Fish and Wildlife Agencies represented 23 western states and Canadian provinces. As described in Chapter 2, the organization has played a key role in the USFWS listing decisions for candidate species inhabiting prairie lands in the interior west.

THE ROLE OF PRIVATE ORGANIZATIONS AND INDIVIDUALS

Federal and state governments are not the only entities involved in land conservation and conserving imperiled species. Increasingly, environment-minded private organizations and citizens are purchasing land with the intent of preserving it for wildlife. National environmental groups such as the Nature Conservancy participate in these endeavors. The Nature Conservancy (2016, http://www.nature.org/about-us/index.htm) notes that it helps protect more than 120 million acres (49 million ha) worldwide. Other major groups engaged in private land conservation include the Conservation Fund, the Land Trust Alliance, the Rocky Mountain Elk Foundation, the Society for the Protection of New Hampshire Forests, and the Trust for Public Land.

Every five years the Land Trust Alliance conducts a census on lands that are held for private conservation. As of April 2016, the most recent census available was from 2010. The alliance states in *2010 National Land Trust Census Report: A Look at Voluntary Land Conservation in America* (November 16, 2011, http://s3.amazonaws.com/landtrustalliance.org/page/files/2010LandTrustCensus.pdf) that approximately 47 million acres (19 million ha) of land were held in local, regional, or national land trusts in 2010. Land trusts either purchase land outright or develop private, voluntary agreements called conservation easements or restrictions that limit future development of the land.

As explained in Chapter 2, the ESA allows private organizations and individuals to participate directly in the federal listing of endangered and threatened species by petitioning the USFWS or the NMFS on behalf of particular species. In addition, private parties can file lawsuits against the government for alleged failures to abide by the ESA.

CONSERVATION BANKING

Conservation (or habitat) banking is a relatively new mechanism for protecting imperiled species. A landowner sets aside a large tract of land with appropriate habitat as a bank (refuge) for one or more species. In "Conservation Banking: Incentives for Stewardship" (August 2012, http://www.fws.gov/endangered/esa-library/pdf/conservation_banking.pdf), the USFWS explains that conservation banking began during the 1990s. Private, tribal, state, and local government lands may qualify as conservation banks. Bank landowners must maintain and manage their banks in accordance with ESA rules. This means they may not be allowed to put up new buildings or otherwise develop the land in a way that would minimize its habitat value. In exchange, they are granted "habitat or species credits" that they can sell to other landowners who want to develop properties that contain imperiled species.

Imagine a landowner whose property contains a threatened species. The landowner wishes to develop the property, but faces restrictions under the ESA. The USFWS might forbid the development outright or it might agree to a smaller development so long as the landowner sets aside part of the land for species conservation. If the latter approach is taken across multiple properties in an area, the species winds up with a fragmented habitat. Conservation banking provides another alternative. The USFWS can agree to let affected landowners proceed with their development plans in exchange for buying habitat or species credits. The species benefits overall because a large bank is set aside for it, and the bank is managed to ensure its well-being.

Conservation banking is a market-based system designed to help both species and landowners. As explained in Chapter 2, it is increasingly being used to keep species from being listed under the ESA in the first place.

INTERNATIONAL EFFORTS AT CONSERVATION

The UN Environment Programme (UNEP) was established to address diverse environmental issues on an international level. The UNEP and the IUCN maintain the World Database on Protected Areas (http://www.protectedplanet.net/), a database of terrestrial and marine conservation areas around the globe. In addition, many UNEP conventions have been extremely valuable in protecting global biodiversity and natural resources. The UNEP has also helped regulate pollution and the use of toxic chemicals.

Convention on International Trade in Endangered Species of Wild Fauna and Flora

The Convention on International Trade in Endangered Species of Wild Fauna and Flora (CITES) is an international agreement administered under the UNEP that regulates international trade in wildlife. CITES is perhaps the single most important international agreement relating to endangered species and has contributed critically to the protection of many threatened species. The international wildlife trade is estimated to involve hundreds of millions of specimens annually.

CITES was first drafted in 1963 at a meeting of the IUCN and went into effect in 1975. Protected plant and animals are listed in three separate CITES appendixes, depending on the degree of endangerment. Appendix I includes species that are in immediate danger of extinction. CITES generally prohibits international trade of these species. Appendix II lists species that are likely to become in danger of extinction without strict protection from international trade. Permits may be obtained for the trade of Appendix II species only if trade will not harm the survival prospects of the species in the wild. Appendix III lists species whose trade is regulated in one or more nations. Any member nation can list a species in Appendix III to request international cooperation to prevent unsustainable levels of international trade. Nations agree to abide by CITES rules voluntarily. In 2016 there were 182 nations participating in the agreement (https://cites.org/eng/disc/parties/chronolo.php).

Convention on Biological Diversity

The Convention on Biological Diversity, which was mentioned earlier in this chapter, was set up to conserve biodiversity and to promote the sustainable use of biological resources. The convention supports national efforts in the documentation and monitoring of biodiversity, the establishment of refuges and other protected areas, and the restoration of degraded ecosystems. It also supports goals that are related to the maintenance of traditional knowledge of sustainable resource use, the prevention of invasive species introductions, and the control of invasive species that are already present. Finally, it funds education programs that promote public awareness of the value of natural resources.

Convention on the Conservation of Migratory Species of Wild Animals

The Convention on the Conservation of Migratory Species of Wild Animals (CMS) recognizes that certain migratory species cross national boundaries and require protection throughout their range. The convention (2016, http://www.cms.int/en/legalinstrument/cms) "provides a global platform for the conservation and sustainable use of migratory animals and their habitats." It was originally signed in Bonn, Germany, in 1979 and went into force in November 1983. According to the CMS (http://www.cms.int/en/parties-range-states), as of October 2015, 122 nations were involved in the agreement. The United States and several other nations were not official parties to the agreement but nonetheless abide by its rules.

The CMS provides two levels of protection to migratory species. Appendix I species are endangered and strictly protected. Appendix II species are less severely threatened but would nonetheless benefit from international cooperative agreements.

FACTORS THAT CONTRIBUTE TO SPECIES ENDANGERMENT

Wildlife populations can be harmed by extreme weather events and other natural phenomena, such as floods, droughts, storms, disease, and wild fires. For example, Chapter 6 describes the adverse effects in 2005 of Hurricane Katrina on imperiled baby sea turtles. The strong tides and waves impeded the tiny creatures from crawling from their nesting beaches to the sea. Natural stressors have always existed, and animal and plant species have evolved to avoid or survive them. In addition, society takes certain actions to minimize the negative impacts of natural stressors on imperiled species. For example, people helped the baby sea turtles reach the sea safely. Government agencies at the federal, state, and local levels work in concert with private organizations and citizen volunteers to carry out activities such as these when natural disasters occur. The USFWS is a major player in this respect. In "Natural Disasters and Other Emergencies" (2016, http://refugeassociation.org/advocacy/funding/refuge-system/emergency-and-natural-disasters/), the National Wildlife Refuge Association notes that "baby sea turtles, nesting birds and many endangered animals are often in the path of natural disasters. The ability of the U.S. Fish and Wildlife Service ... to respond quickly to these disasters can determine the fate of these vulnerable creatures."

Natural phenomena can play a role in species loss, particularly when a species is isolated and/or low in number. However, experts suggest the primary cause of wildlife loss is the destructive effect of human activities. For example, Navjot S. Sodhi, Barry W. Brook, and Corey J. A. Bradshaw state in "Causes and Consequences of Species Extinctions" (S. A. Levin, ed., *The Princeton Guide to Ecology*, 2009) that "the major 'systematic drivers' of modern species loss are changes in land use (habitat loss degradation and fragmentation), overexploitation, invasive species, disease, climate change (global warming) connected to increasing concentration of atmospheric carbon dioxide, and increases in nitrogen deposition." Anthropomorphic (human-linked) activities can also cause or allow natural stressors to be more damaging to wildlife than they would be otherwise. For example, exposure to pollution can weaken a species and make it more susceptible to disease or drought.

The major anthropomorphic factors mentioned by Sodhi, Brook, and Corey that contribute to species loss are described in the following sections.

Changes in Land Use

For millennia humans have been changing the land to meet their needs and in the process destroying natural habitat. Raising crops, grazing livestock, logging, filling swamps, building dams, mining, and developing land for housing and commerce are major types of land use changes that greatly impact wildlife populations. Many of these activities produce negative secondary impacts as well. For example, agricultural activity can result in soil erosion, pollution from pesticides and fertilizers, and runoff into aquatic habitats. Finally, human recreational activity, particularly the use of off-road vehicles, results in the destruction of natural habitat and stresses wildlife populations.

HABITAT FRAGMENTATION. Human land-use patterns often result in the fragmentation of natural habitat areas that are available to species. For example, building a road through a forest or converting part of a meadow into a farm or subdivision fragments the large area that used to be available to species into smaller separated pieces. Habitat fragmentation can have significant effects on species. Small populations can become isolated, so that dispersal from one habitat patch to another is impossible. Smaller populations are also more likely to become extinct. Finally, because there are more "edges" when habitats are fragmented, there can be increased exposure to predators and vulnerability to disturbances that are associated with human activity.

Overexploitation

The National Wildlife Federation (2016, http://www.nwf.org/wildlife/threats-to-wildlife/overexploitation.aspx) defines overexploitation as "the over use of wildlife and plant species by people for food, clothing, pets, medicine, sport and many other purposes." As noted earlier, overhunting led to the extinction of several U.S. species including passenger pigeons and heath hens. Numerous cases will be presented in this book of endangered species in decline due to overuse by humans. As with other stressors, overexploitation can indirectly harm ecosystems and human interests. For example, Sodhi, Brook, and Bradshaw describe the unexpected consequences of overfishing of large pelagic sharks, such as great white sharks. Lowering the population of this superpredator "resulted in an increase in rays and skates that eventually suppressed commercially important scallop populations."

Invasive Species

Invasive species are also known as exotic, nuisance, or nonnative species. Basically, they are species that have been introduced directly or indirectly by humans into a new environment. Invasive species that thrive disrupt their new ecosystems in multiple ways. They compete with the established species for food, shelter, and other resources. They may also carry "new" diseases or other pathogens to which the existing species do not have natural resistance. Predatory invasive species are particularly harmful. As is described in Chapter 8, some endangered island bird populations have been decimated by nonnative predators. Nearly all of Guam's native birds have been wiped out by the brown tree snake, an invasive species that likely arrived on the island decades ago via cargo ships. Introduced species that are genetically similar to established species can wreak havoc if interbreeding produces sterile offspring or offspring with a predominantly exotic genetic makeup. Over time, the native species can disappear completely as its unique genetic blueprint fades out of existence.

Disease

Disease has always posed a threat to wildlife, but its scope and hazard have greatly increased due to human interference in ecosystems. Plants and animals have evolved defense and immunity mechanisms that naturally help protect them from diseases to which they have been regularly exposed. Nevertheless, "new" diseases (e.g., from introduced species) can be devastating because the victims have no natural resistance. Likewise, wildlife already stressed by habitat changes, pollution, or other human-induced problems are more susceptible to disease.

Climate Change

The earth's temperature is regulated by many factors, including energy inputs and outputs, chemical processes, and physical phenomena. Radiation from the sun passes through the earth's atmosphere and warms the planet. In turn, the earth emits infrared radiation. Some of this outgoing infrared radiation does not escape into outer space but is trapped beneath the atmosphere to provide a warm "blanket" for the planet. The amount of trapped energy depends on several variables, including the composition of the atmosphere. Certain gases, such as carbon dioxide and methane, naturally trap heat beneath the atmosphere in the same way that glass panels keep heat from escaping from a greenhouse. This natural greenhouse effect keeps the earth warm and habitable for life. Scientists believe massive combustion (burning) of fossil fuels, such as oil and natural gas, introduced large amounts of carbon dioxide, methane, and other heat-trapping gases into the atmosphere over the last century. This buildup has been increasing the earth's temperature above that expected from the natural greenhouse effect, an effect known as global warming. Global warming is bringing about climate change, which has numerous consequences to the planet's environment, ecosystems, and inhabitants.

Continued warming of the earth would alter habitats drastically, with serious consequences for many species. The Intergovernmental Panel on Climate Change (IPCC) is an international body of scientists and policy makers that publishes reports on climate change. In *Climate Change 2014: Synthesis Report: Summary for Policymakers* (March 2015, https://www.ipcc.ch/pdf/assessment-report/ar5/syr/AR5_SYR_FINAL_SPM.pdf), the IPCC explains, "A large fraction of species faces increased extinction risk due to climate change during and beyond the 21st century, especially as climate change interacts with other stressors."

Michelle D. Staudinger et al. describe in *Impacts of Climate Change on Biodiversity, Ecosystems, and Ecosystem Services: Technical Input to the 2013 National Climate Assessment* (July 2012, https://downloads.globalchange.gov/nca/technical_inputs/Biodiversity-Ecosystems-and-Ecosystem-Services-Technical-Input.pdf) observed and projected impacts to U.S. ecosystems. Thirty case studies are reviewed involving impacts to specific animal and plant species or habitats around the country. For example, warmer temperatures have allowed pests and diseases to flourish and kill conifers (evergreen trees, such as spruce and pine) in northwestern forests. Subsequent chapters in this book address the role of climate change in stressing some endangered and threatened U.S. species.

Increases in Nitrogen Deposition

Nitrogen is a key nutrient for plant growth. Human activities, however, such as use of nitrogen-rich fertilizers and the combustion of fossil fuels have introduced massive amounts of nitrogen into the environment. Excessive nitrogen concentrations in soils and water bodies upset the natural chemical balance needed to maintain healthy ecosystems. Rivers, lakes, and streams can become too acidic, putting wildlife at risk. This is especially problematic for species such as fish and amphibians (e.g., frogs) that are highly sensitive to acid content. Overenrichment of soils with nitrogen can greatly change the mix of plants growing in a particular ecosystem as some species respond with vigorous growth and others falter. Such alterations disrupt the existing food webs further and stress the ecosystem inhabitants.

CHAPTER 2
THE ENDANGERED SPECIES ACT

The Endangered Species Act (ESA) of 1973 is considered to be one of the most far-reaching laws ever enacted by any nation for the preservation of wildlife. The passage of the act resulted from alarm at the decline of many species worldwide, as well as from recognition of the importance of preserving species diversity. The purpose of the ESA is to identify species that are either endangered (at risk of extinction throughout all or a significant portion of their range) or threatened (likely to become endangered in the future). Except for recognized insect pests, all animals and plants are eligible for listing under the ESA. Listed species are protected without regard to either commercial or sport value.

The ESA is also one of the most controversial and contentious laws ever passed. It affects the rights of private landowners and how they manage their property if endangered species are found there. It also allows private individuals and groups to sue federal agencies for alleged failures in carrying out the law. The result has been a flood of litigation since the 1990s by conservation organizations. They believe that full and effective implementation of the ESA will help ensure the survival of imperiled species. However, critics charge that the ESA has saved virtually no species, puts too many restrictions on land and water development projects, and is too expensive for the results that it achieves.

THE ESA: A LANDMARK LAW

The roots of the ESA lie in the Endangered Species Preservation Act, which was passed in 1966. This act established a process for listing species as endangered and provided some measure of protection. The first species to be listed are shown in Table 2.1. The Endangered Species Conservation Act of 1969 provided protection to species facing worldwide extinction, prohibiting their import and sale within the United States.

Passed by Congress in 1973, the ESA was substantially amended in 1978, 1982, and 1987. The law is administered by the U.S. Department of the Interior (DOI) through the U.S. Fish and Wildlife Service (USFWS). The U.S. Department of Commerce, through the National Marine Fisheries Service (NMFS), is responsible for most marine (ocean-based) species and those that are anadromous (migrate between freshwaters and marine waters). The two agencies are often referred to collectively as the "ESA agencies." It should be noted, however, that other federal agencies have input into the ESA process. For example, the Biological Resources Division of the U.S. Geological Survey conducts research on species for which the USFWS has management authority. Federal agencies that administer federally owned lands also play a role. The Bureau of Land Management (BLM), the National Park Service, and the U.S. Forest Service include measures to protect imperiled species in their management plans.

Citizen Involvement

One of the hallmarks of the ESA is the broad latitude that it provides U.S. citizens to participate in the implementation and enforcement of the law. Individuals and groups can petition the ESA agencies to list specific species under the law. So long as the petitions meet defined screening criteria, the agencies must take further action on them. During the 1990s private groups devoted to conservation and animal protection began flooding the agencies with listing petitions for hundreds of imperiled species. The law includes specific time deadlines for completion of certain tasks by the ESA agencies. For example, they must make a decision on each new listing petition within 90 days. As will be explained throughout this chapter, the agencies have struggled (and often failed) to meet the legally required deadlines because their workload has greatly outpaced their resources.

Section 11 (http://www.fws.gov/endangered/laws-policies/section-11.html) of the ESA allows private citizens

TABLE 2.1

First list of endangered species, 1967

In accordance with section 1(c) of the Endangered Species Preservation Act of October 15, 1966 (80 Stat. 926; 16 U.S.C. 668aa(c) I [the Secretary of the Interior] find after consulting the states, interested organizations, and individual scientists, that the following listed native fish and wildlife are threatened with extinction.

Mammals

- Indiana bat—*Myotis sodalis*
- Delmarva Peninsula fox squirrel—*Sciurus niger cinereus*
- Timber wolf—*Canis lupus lycaon*
- Red wolf—*Canis niger*
- San Joaquin kit fox—*Vulpes macrotis mutica*
- Grizzly bear—*Ursus horribilis*
- Black-footed ferret—*Mustela nigripes*
- Florida panther—*Felis concolor coryi*
- Caribbean monk seal—*Monachus tropicalis*
- Guadalupe fur seal—*Arctocephalus philippi townsendi*
- Florida manatee or Florida sea cow—*Trichechus manatus latirostris*
- Key deer—*Odocoileus virginianus clavium*
- Sonoran pronghorn—*Antilocapra americana sonoriensis*

Birds

- Hawaiian dark-rumped petrel—*Pterodroma phaeopygia sandwichensis*
- Hawaiian goose (nene)—*Branta sandvicensis*
- Aleutian Canada goose—*Branta canadensis leucopareia*
- Tule white-fronted goose—*Anser albifrons gambelli*
- Laysan duck—*Anas laysanensis*
- Hawaiian duck (or koloa)—*Anas wyvilliana*
- Mexican duck—*Anas diazi*
- California condor—*Gymnogyps californianus*
- Florida Everglade kite (Florida Snail Kite)—*Rostrhamus sociabilis plumbeus*
- Hawaiian hawk (or ii)—*Buteo solitarius*
- Southern bald eagle—*Haliaeetus t. leucocephalus*
- Attwater's greater prairie chicken—*Tympanuchus cupido attwateri*
- Masked bobwhite—*Colinus virginianus ridgwayi*
- Whooping crane—*Grus americana*
- Yuma clapper rail—*Rallus longirostris yumanensis*
- Hawaiian common gallinule—*Gallinula chloropus sandvicensis*
- Eskimo curlew—*Numenius borealis*
- Puerto Rican parrot—*Amazona vittata*
- American ivory-billed woodpecker—*Campephilus p. principalis*
- Hawaiian crow (or alala)—*Corvus hawaiiensis*
- Small Kauai thrush (puaiohi)—*Phaeornia pulmeri*
- Nihoa millerbird—*Acrocephalus kingi*
- Kauai oo (or oo aa)—*Moho braccatus*
- Crested honeycreeper (or akohekohe)—*Palmeria dolei*
- Akiapolaau—*Hemignathus wilsoni*
- Kauai akialoa—*Hemignathus procerus*
- Kauai nukupuu—*Hemignathus lucidus hanapepe*

- Laysan finchbill (Laysan finch)—*Psittirostra c. cantans*
- Nihoa finchbill (Nihoa finch)—*Psittirostra cantans ultima*
- Ou—*Psittirostra psittacea*
- Palila—*Psittirostra bailleui*
- Maui parrotbill—*Pseudonestor xanthophyrys*
- Bachman's warbler—*Vermivora bachmanii*
- Kirtland's warbler—*Dendroica kirtlandii*
- Dusky seaside sparrow—*Ammospiza nigrescens*
- Cape Sable sparrow—*Ammospiza mirabilis*

Reptiles and Amphibians

- American alligator—*Alligator mississippiensis*
- Blunt-nosed leopard lizard—*Crotaphytus wislizenii silus*
- San Francisco garter snake—*Thamnophis sirtalis tetrataenia*
- Santa Cruz long-toed salamander—*Ambystoma macrodactylum croceum*
- Texas blind salamander—*Typhlomolge rathbuni*
- Black toad, Inyo County toad—*Bufo exsul*

Fishes

- Shortnose sturgeon—*Acipenser brevirostrum*
- Longjaw Cisco—*Coregonus alpenae*
- Paiute cutthroat trout—*Salmo clarki seleniris*
- Greenback cutthroat trout—*Salmo clarki stomias*
- Montana Westslope cutthroat trout—*Salmo clarki*
- Gila trout—*Salmo gilae*
- Arizona (*Apache*) trout—*Salmo sp.*
- Desert dace—*Eremichthys acros*
- Humpback chub—*Gila cypha*
- Little Colorado spinedace—*Lepidomeda vittata*
- Moapa dace—*Moapa coriacea*
- Colorado River squawfish—*Ptychocheilus lucius*
- Cui-ui—*Chasmistes cujus*
- Devils Hole pupfish—*Cyprinodon diabolis*
- Commanche Springs pupfish—*Cyprinodon elegans*
- Owens River pupfish—*Cyprinodon radiosus*
- Pahrump killifish—*Empetrichythys latos*
- Big Bend gambusia—*Gambusia gaigei*
- Clear Creek gambusia—*Gambusia heterochir*
- Gila topminnow—*Poeciliopsis occidentalis*
- Maryland darter—*Etheostoma sellare*
- Blue pike—*Stizostedion vitreum glaucum*

SOURCE: Stewart L. Udall, "Native Fish and Wildlife Endangered Species," in *Federal Register*, vol. 32, no. 48, March 11, 1967

or groups to file lawsuits against the ESA agencies for any alleged failures to carry out the law, including failing to meet the mandated deadlines. Conservation groups have seized on the so-called citizen suit provision and filed numerous lawsuits against the agencies. The USFWS, in particular, has found itself mired in litigation since the 1990s. As a consequence, the agency's ESA scope of work and future planning are driven in large part by legal agreements that it has reached with plaintiffs that have sued it in court. Some critics complain that the ESA process has been hijacked by private groups with their own agendas. The groups respond that they are simply exercising the rights of citizen involvement that were built into the law. Many critics blame Congress for not changing the law to be more flexible or for not funding the agencies sufficiently so that they can better meet the ever-mounting demands placed on them under the ESA.

Cost Considerations

Another remarkable feature of the ESA is the relative lack of consideration it requires for the economic consequences of protecting endangered and threatened species. For example, it does not require the agencies to consider costs when they determine whether a species should be listed under the law. As noted in Chapter 1, this "saving nature for nature's sake" stance is highly controversial and deeply criticized by people who believe the financial costs of protecting imperiled plants and animals should be considered. As this chapter will explain, there are provisions in the law for assessment of the economic impacts of some ESA-related actions, such as the designation of critical habitat. Overall, however, the law requires that science rather than economics underlie many of the decisions regarding imperiled species.

LISTING SPECIES UNDER THE ESA

Definition of Species

The original ESA defined the word *species* to include species, subspecies, or "smaller taxa." Taxa is the plural of taxon, which is a grouping on the taxonomic table. In 1978 the ESA was amended to define a smaller taxon for vertebrates (animals with a backbone) as a distinct population segment (DPS). A DPS is a distinct population of vertebrates capable of interbreeding with each other that live in a specific geographical area. A DPS is usually described using geographical terms, such as northern or southern, or by a given latitude or longitude. In 1991 the NMFS developed a policy defining the DPS for Pacific salmon populations. Salmon are anadromous, and most salmon migrate in groups at particular times of the year (e.g., during the fall or spring). Each of these groups is called a stock. The NMFS developed the term *evolutionarily significant unit* (ESU) to refer to a distinct stock of Pacific salmon.

In summary, the word *species* as used in the ESA can mean a species, a subspecies, a DPS (vertebrates only), or an ESU (Pacific salmon only).

Listing Considerations

According to the USFWS, in "Listing a Species as Threatened or Endangered: Section 4 of the Endangered Species Act" (January 2015, http://www.fws.gov/endangered/esa-library/pdf/listing.pdf), the ESA stipulates five considerations for listing a species:

- The present or threatened destruction, modification, or curtailment of its habitat or range

- Overutilization for commercial, recreational, scientific, or educational purposes

- Disease or predation

- The inadequacy of existing regulatory mechanisms

- Other natural or manmade factors affecting its survival

For example, Table 2.2 shows the ESA listing considerations for the Sonoran pronghorn, an endangered antelope-like species found in the Arizona desert. Section 4 (http://www.fws.gov/endangered/laws-policies/section-4.html) of the law requires the agencies to base their listing determinations "solely on the basis of the best scientific and commercial data available." Thus, the ESA does not require economic factors to be considered during the listing process.

As of February 2016, there were 1,590 U.S. species (693 animals and 897 plants) listed under the ESA. (See Table 1.3 in Chapter 1.) Most (493) of the animals were endangered, while 200 were threatened. Likewise, 732 of the plants were endangered, while 165 were threatened. In addition, there were 656 foreign species on the list, including 575 animals and one plant listed as endangered and 78 animals and two plants listed as threatened.

The Listing Process

The procedure by which a species becomes listed under the ESA is a legal process with specifically defined steps. Successful listing results in regulations that are legally enforceable within all U.S. jurisdictions. At various stages of the listing process, the USFWS or the NMFS publishes its actions in the *Federal Register* (https://www.federalregister.gov/), an official document that is compiled daily by the National Archives and Records Administration in Washington, D.C., and printed/published digitally by the U.S. Government Printing Office. The *Federal Register* details specific legal actions of the federal government, such as rules, proposed rules, notices from federal agencies, executive orders, and miscellaneous presidential documents.

There are three ways for the ESA listing process to be initiated:

- Submittal of a petition to the USFWS or the NMFS

- Initiative of the USFWS or the NMFS

- Emergency designation by the USFWS or the NMFS

Figure 2.1 diagrams the most common listing process under the ESA, one that begins with a petition submittal. The listing process is described in detail by Joy Nicholopoulos in "Endangered Species Listing Program" (*Endangered Species Bulletin*, vol. 24, no. 6, November–December 1999) and by the USFWS in "Listing a Species as Threatened or Endangered: Section 4 of the Endangered Species Act" (February 2001, http://library.fws.gov/Pubs9/listing.pdf).

PETITION SUBMITTAL. The process for listing a new species under the ESA begins with a formal petition from a person, organization, or government agency. This petition is submitted to the USFWS for terrestrial and freshwater species or to the NMFS for marine and anadromous species. All listing petitions must be backed by published scientific data supporting the need for listing the species under the ESA. Within 90 days of petition receipt, the USFWS or the NMFS is supposed to determine whether there is "substantial information" to suggest that a species might require listing. If so, the species undergoes a status review.

STATUS REVIEW. A status review is a detailed biological assessment of a particular species. During the petition process a status review helps the agencies determine whether a species should be listed and, if so, what its listing should be (endangered or threatened).

In *Endangered Species Petition Management Guidance* (July 1996, http://www.nmfs.noaa.gov/pr/pdfs/laws/petition_management.pdf), the USFWS and the NMFS define a status review as "the act of reviewing all the available information on a species to determine if it should be provided protection under the ESA. A status review should also use the knowledge of experts; the greater the extent to which Service biologists can build an external consensus using the expertise of various parties

TABLE 2.2

Summary of threats to Sonoran pronghorn

ESA listing factor	Stressor	Source
A: Present or threatened destruction, modification, or curtailment of its habitat or range	Habitat loss	Mining
		Agriculture
		Livestock grazing
		Renewable energy
	Habitat fragmentation	Habitat conversion
		Physical barriers
		Human disturbance
	Multiple stressors and sources	Climate change
	Reduced access to water	Physical barriers
		Human disturbance
		Inadequate distribution
	Reduced availability of water	Low annual rainfall
		Increased frequency and severity of drought
		Altered runoff patterns
	Reduced forage quality	Low annual rainfall
		Increased frequency and severity of drought
		Livestock grazing
		Extreme heat
		Altered hydrology
		Altered fire regimes
		Increased cover of creosotebush
		Invasive plants
		Erosion
		Lack of pollination
	Altered habitat structure	Fire
		Livestock grazing
		Military training
		Renewable energy
		Mining
		Illegal extraction
B: Overutilization for commercial, recreational, scientific, or educational Purposes	None	N/A
	Predation	N/A
C: Disease or predation	Disease	N/A
	Lack of genetic diversity	N/A
	None	N/A
D: Inadequacy of existing regulatory mechanisms	Human disturbance	Border activities
E: Other natural or manmade factors affecting its continued existence		Recreation
		Military activities
		Land management activities
		Mining, ranching, and agriculture
	High mortality rates	Drowning in canals
		Entanglement in fences
		Vehicle collision
		Thermal stress
		Poaching
		Capture myopathy
		Military activities
	Catastrophic events	Lack of redundancy of populations
		Small population size

Note: N/A = Not applicable.

SOURCE: "Table 3. Summary of Threats (Stressors and Sources) to Sonoran Pronghorn by ESA Listing Factor," in *Draft Recovery Plan for Sonoran Pronghorn (Antilocapra Americana Sonoriensis), Second Revision*, U.S. Department of the Interior, U.S. Fish and Wildlife Service, 2015, http://ecos.fws.gov/docs/recovery_plan/Sonoran%20Pronghorn%20-%20draft%20revised%20recovery%20plan%204.8.15.pdf (accessed February 17, 2016)

(e.g., Federal, State, Tribal, University, Heritage programs), the better." Comments and information are also requested from the general public through publication of a notice in the *Federal Register*.

In general, a status review covers the following elements:

• Biology, life history, and reproductive factors of the species

• Genetic information

• Habitat characteristics

• Abundance and population trends

• Threats to species survival and well-being

• Conservation measures

• Existing regulatory mechanisms protecting the species

The ESA does not require the agencies to consider economic factors during status reviews. Each status review is supposed to be completed within 12 months. There are three possible determinations from a status review:

• Listing is not warranted

• Listing is warranted but precluded

• Listing is warranted

FIGURE 2.1

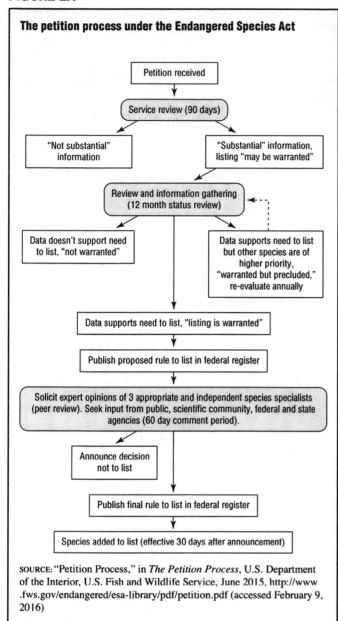

The petition process under the Endangered Species Act

Petition received

↓

Service review (90 days)

↙ ↘

"Not substantial" information   "Substantial" information, listing "may be warranted"

↓

Review and information gathering (12 month status review)

↙ ↓ ↘

Data doesn't support need to list, "not warranted"   Data supports need to list but other species are of higher priority, "warranted but precluded," re-evaluate annually

↓

Data supports need to list, "listing is warranted"

↓

Publish proposed rule to list in federal register

↓

Solicit expert opinions of 3 appropriate and independent species specialists (peer review). Seek input from public, scientific community, federal and state agencies (60 day comment period).

↙ ↓

Announce decision not to list

↓

Publish final rule to list in federal register

↓

Species added to list (effective 30 days after announcement)

SOURCE: "Petition Process," in *The Petition Process*, U.S. Department of the Interior, U.S. Fish and Wildlife Service, June 2015, http://www.fws.gov/endangered/esa-library/pdf/petition.pdf (accessed February 9, 2016)

LISTING IS NOT WARRANTED. A finding that listing is not warranted must be accompanied by information explaining why the data presented do not support the petitioned action or why there are not enough data to make an appropriate determination.

LISTING IS WARRANTED BUT PRECLUDED—CANDIDATE SPECIES. The ESA agencies may decide that a species should be proposed for listing, but must wait while they deal with higher priorities. In other words, they acknowledge that a species deserves protection under the ESA, but they choose to devote their resources to what they consider to be more pressing needs. The on-hold species are officially called "candidate species."

The USFWS indicates in "Candidate Species: Section 4 of the Endangered Species Act" (December 2014,

http://www.fws.gov/endangered/esa-library/pdf/candidate_species.pdf) that candidate species are assigned a listing priority number ranging from 1 to 12, with lower numbers (1 to 3) indicating greater priority compared with other candidates. Priority is determined based on three considerations:

- The magnitude of the threats facing the species
- The immediacy of the threats facing the species
- The taxonomic uniqueness of the species

Candidate species are reevaluated annually to confirm that their listing status and listing priority number remain appropriate. The USFWS describes the reevaluation of each of the candidate species under its jurisdiction in a publication called a Candidate Notice of Review (CNOR). CNORs are published (typically annually) in the *Federal Register*. CNORs dating back to 1994 are available at http://www.fws.gov/endangered/what-we-do/cnor.html.

The candidate reevaluations continue until the species is proposed for listing or until its status improves sufficiently to remove it from consideration for listing. Because they are not officially listed, candidate species do not enjoy the protection mechanisms of the ESA. Nonetheless, the ESA agencies work with state wildlife agencies and other groups to help preserve and improve the status of candidate species, hoping that populations will recover sufficiently such that the species will not require listing in the future.

As of April 2016, the most recent CNOR was published in December 2015 (http://www.fws.gov/endangered/what-we-do/pdf/2015_CNOR_2015_12_24.pdf) and included 60 candidate species. (See Table 2.3.) Most of the USFWS candidates were flowering plants. In addition, the NMFS (http://www.nmfs.noaa.gov/pr/species/esa/candidate.htm) had 15 candidate species as of January 2016. (See Table 2.4.) Most of the NMFS candidates were fish species.

LISTING IS WARRANTED: THE PROPOSAL PROCESS. If a status review indicates that listing is warranted, the agency with jurisdiction officially proposes the species for listing under the ESA. This declaration is made in the *Federal Register*. The agency first asks at least three independent biological experts to verify that the petitioned species requires listing. After that, input from the public, other federal and state agencies, and the scientific community is welcomed. The period of public comment typically lasts 60 days, but may be extended in some cases. Within 45 days of proposal issuance interested parties can request that public hearings be held on the issues involved with listing. Such hearings are also held in cases where public interest is high in the listing outcome.

TABLE 2.3

U.S. Fish and Wildlife Service candidate species by group type as of December 2015

Category	Status Priority	Lead region	Scientific name	Family	Common name
Mammals					
C*	6		Tamias minimus atristriatus		Chipmunk, Peñasco least
C*	3		Vulpes vulpes necator		Fox, Sierra Nevada red (Sierra Nevada DPS)
C*	5		Urocitellus washingtoni		Squirrel, Washington ground
C*	9		Arborimus longicaudus		Vole, Red (north Oregon coast DPS)
C*	9		Odobenus rosmarus divergens		Walrus, Pacific
Birds					
C*	3		Porzana tabuensis		Crake, spotless (American Samoa DPS)
C*	5		Synthliboramphus hypoleucus		Murrelet, Xantus's
C*	2		Amazona viridigenalis		Parrot, red–crowned
C*	8		Anthus spragueii		Pipit, Sprague's
Reptiles					
C*	5		Pituophis ruthveni		Snake, Louisiana pine
C*	8		Gopherus polyphemus		Tortoise, gopher (eastern population)
C*	6		Kinosternon sonoriense longifemorale		Turtle, Sonoyta mud
Amphibians					
C*	8		Lithobates onca		Frog, relict leopard
C*	8		Notophthalmus perstriatus		Newt, striped
C*	8		Gyrinophilus gulolineatus		Salamander, Berry Cave
C	3		Hyla wrightorum		Treefrog, Arizona (Huachuca/Canelo DPS)
C*	2		Necturus alabamensis		Waterdog, black warrior (=Sipsey Fork)
Fishes					
C*	11		Etheostoma cragini		Darter, Arkansas
C*	8		Percina aurora		Darter, Pearl
C*			Moxostoma sp.		Redhorse, sicklefin
C*			Spirinchus thaleichthys		Smelt, longfin (San Francisco Bay—Delta DPS)
Clams					
C*	2		Lampsilis bracteata		Fatmucket, Texas
C*	2		Truncilla macrodon		Fawnsfoot, Texas
C*	8		Popenaias popei		Hornshell, Texas
C*	8		Quadrula aurea		Orb, golden
C*	8		Quadrula houstonensis		Pimpleback, smooth
C*	2		Quadrula petrina		Pimpleback, Texas
Snails					
C*	8		Elimia melanoides		Mudalia, black
C*	2		Planorbella magnifica		Ramshorn, magnificent
C*	11		Pyrgulopsis thompsoni		Springsnail, Huachuca
Insects					
C*	5		Lycaena hermes		Butterfly, Hermes copper
C*	2		Atlantea tulita		Butterfly, Puerto Rican harlequin
C*	5		Pseudanophthalmus caecus		Cave beetle, Clifton
C*	5		Pseudanophthalmus frigidus		Cave beetle, icebox
C*	5		Pseudanophthalmus troglodytes		Cave beetle, Louisville
C*	5		Pseudanophthalmus parvus		Cave beetle, Tatum
C*	8		Papaipema eryngii		Moth, rattlesnake-master borer
C*	11		Heterelmis stephani		Riffle beetle, Stephan's
C*	5		Arsapnia (= Capnia) arapahoe		Snowfly, Arapahoe
C*	5	R6	Lednia tumana	Nemouridae	Stonefly, meltwater lednian
C*	5	R4	Cicindela highlandensis	Cicindelidae	Tiger beetle, highlands
Crustaceans					
C	8	R5	Stygobromus kenki	Crangonyctidae	Amphipod, Kenk's
Flowering plants					
C*	3	R1	Artemisia borealis var. wormskioldii	Asteraceae	Wormwood, northern
C*	8	R6	Astragalus microcymbus	Fabaceae	Milkvetch, skiff
C*	8	R6	Astragalus schmolliae	Fabaceae	Milkvetch, Chapin Mesa
C*	8	R6	Boechera (Arabis) pusilla	Brassicaceae	Rockcress, Fremont County or small
C*	12	R4	Chamaesyce deltoidea pinetorum	Euphorbiaceae	Sandmat, pineland
C*	6	R8	Chorizanthe parryi var. fernandina	Polygonaceae	Spineflower, San Fernando Valley
C*	8	R2	Cirsium wrightii	Asteraceae	Thistle, Wright's

As shown in Table 2.5, there were 71 species under USFWS jurisdiction proposed for listing under the ESA as of December 2015. Most were flowering plants or insects. In addition, 28 marine or anadromous species under NMFS jurisdiction were proposed for listing. (See Table 2.6.)

TABLE 2.3

U.S. Fish and Wildlife Service candidate species by group type as of December 2015 [CONTINUED]

Category	Priority	Lead region	Scientific name	Family	Common name
	Status				
Flowering pants					
C*	3		*Dalea carthagenensis var. floridana*		Prairie-clover, Florida
C*	2		*Dichanthelium hirstii*		Panic grass, Hirst Brothers'
C*	5		*Digitaria pauciflora*		Crabgrass, Florida pineland
C*	8		*Eriogonum soredium*		Buckwheat, Frisco
C*	11		*Festuca ligulata*		Fescue, Guadalupe
C*	8		*Lepidium ostleri*		Peppergrass, Ostler's
C*	8		*Pinus albicaulis*		Pine, whitebark
C	12		*Sideroxylon reclinatum austrofloridense*		Bully, Everglades
C*	2		*Solanum conocarpum*		Bacora, marron
C*	8		*Streptanthus bracteatus*		Twistflower, bracted
C*	8		*Trifolium friscanum*		Clover, Frisco

Notes: C = Candidate species. C* = Candidate species for which a petition was submitted.

SOURCE: Adapted from "Table 1. Candidate Notice of Review (Animals and Plants)," in "Endangered and Threatened Wildlife and Plants; Review of Native Species That Are Candidates for Listing as Endangered or Threatened; Annual Notice of Findings on Resubmitted Petitions; Annual Description of Progress on Listing Actions," *Federal Register*, vol. 80, no. 247, December 24, 2015, http://www.fws.gov/endangered/what-we-do/pdf/2015_CNOR_2015_12_24.pdf (accessed February 9, 2016)

TABLE 2.4

National Marine Fisheries Service candidate species by group type as of January 2016

Species	Year	Federal Register (FR) notice
Fishes		
Cusk (*Brosme brosme*)	2007	72 FR 10710
Ray, Caribbean electric (*Narcine bancroftii*)	2014	79 FR 4877
Seahorse, dwarf (*Hippocampus zosterae*)	2012	77 FR 26478
Shad, Alabama (*Alosa alabamae*)	2013	78 FR 57611
Shark, bigeye thresher (*Alopias superciliosus*)	2015	80 FR 48061
Shark, common thresher (*Alopias vulpinus*)	2015	80 FR 11379
Shark, oceanic whitetip (*Carcharhinus longimanus*)	2016	81 FR 1376
Shark, porbeagle (*Lamna nasus*)	2015	80 FR 16356
Shark, smooth hammerhead (*Sphyrna zygaena*)	2015	80 FR 48053
2 Guitarfish species	2014	79 FR 10104
• Guitarfish (*Rhinobatos rhinobatos*)		
• Guitarfish, blackchin (*Rhinobatos cemiculus*)		
Skate, thorny (*Amblyraja radiata*)	2015	80 FR 65175
Marine mammals		
Dolphin, Hector's (*Cephalorhynchus hectori*)	2014	79 FR 9880
Seal, Pacific harbor (1 candidate DPS) (*Phoca vitulina richardii*)	2013	78 FR 29098
• Iliamna Lake		
Whale, Bryde's (1 candidate DPS) (*Balaenoptera edeni*)	2015	80 FR 18343
• Gulf of Mexico		

SOURCE: Adapted from "Candidates for Listing (15 Candidate "Species")," in *Candidate and Proposed Species under the Endangered Species Act (ESA)*, U.S. Department of Commerce, National Oceanic and Atmospheric Administration, National Marine Fisheries Service, January 29, 2016, http://www.nmfs.noaa.gov/pr/species/esa/candidate.htm (accessed February 9, 2016)

FINAL DECISION ON LISTING. Once a species begins the proposal process, the USFWS or the NMFS must ultimately take one of three possible actions:

- Withdraw the proposal—the biological information is found not to support listing the species

- Extend the proposal period—there is substantial disagreement within the scientific community regarding the listing; only one six-month extension is allowed, and then a final decision must be made

- Publish a final listing rule in the *Federal Register*—the listing becomes effective 30 days after publication, unless otherwise indicated

EMERGENCY LISTING. The ESA authorizes the USFWS or the NMFS to issue temporary emergency listings for species when evidence indicates an immediate and significant risk to the well-being of a species (e.g., following a natural disaster). Two designations are possible: endangered emergency listing and threatened emergency listing. The listing must be published in the *Federal Register* and is effective for only 240 days. During this time the normal status review procedure continues.

Petitioners also have the right under the ESA to ask the USFWS or the NMFS for an emergency listing for a species.

The USFWS (http://ecos.fws.gov/tess_public/pub/ad HocSpeciesCountForm.jsp) indicates that as of April 2016 there were no emergency listings in effect for endangered or threatened species.

PROTECTIONS AND ACTIONS TRIGGERED BY LISTING

In "Threatened and Endangered Species" (January 12, 2015, http://www.fws.gov/carlsbad/TEspecies/Recovery/5YearReview.htm) and "Listing and Critical Habitat: Overview" (December 8, 2015, http://www.fws.gov/endangered/what-we-do/listing-overview.html), the USFWS describes the protections and actions that are triggered when a species is listed under the ESA.

TABLE 2.5

U.S. Fish and Wildlife Service proposed species by group type as of December 2015

Category	Priority	Scientific name	Common name
Mammals			
PE	3	Emballonura semicaudata semicaudata	Bat, Pacific sheath-tailed (American Samoa DPS)
PT	6	Martes pennanti	Fisher (west coast DPS)
Birds			
PE	9	Gallicolumba stairi	Ground-dove, friendly (American Samoa DPS)
PE	2	Gymnomyza samoensis	Ma'oma'o
PE	3	Oceanodroma castro	Storm-petrel, band-rumped (Hawaii DPS)
PT	11	Dendroica angelae	Warbler, elfin-woods
Reptiles			
PT	8	Sistrurus catenatus	Massasauga (= rattle-snake), eastern
Fishes			
PT	8	Gila nigra	Chub, headwater
PT	9	Gila robusta	Chub, roundtail (Lower Colorado River Basin DPS)
PE	2	Crystallaria cincotta	Darter, diamond
PT	2	Etheostoma spilotum	Darter, Kentucky arrow
PSAT	N/A	Salvelinus malma	Trout, Dolly Varden
Clams			
PT	—	Medionidus walkeri	Moccasinshell, Suwannee
Snails			
PE	2	Eua zebrina	Snail, no common name
PE	2	Ostodes strigatus	Snail, no common name
Insects			
PE	2	Hylaeus anthracinus	Bee, Hawaiian yellow-faced
PE	2	Hylaeus assimulans	Bee, Hawaiian yellow-faced
PE	2	Hylaeus facilis	Bee, Hawaiian yellow-faced
PE	2	Hylaeus hilaris	Bee, Hawaiian yellow-faced
PE	2	Hylaeus kuakea	Bee, Hawaiian yellow-faced
PE	2	Hylaeus longiceps	Bee, Hawaiian yellow-faced
PE	2	Hylaeus mana	Bee, Hawaiian yellow-faced
PE	8	Megalagrion xanthomelas	Damselfly, orangeblack Hawaiian.
Crustaceans			
PE	—	Cambarus callainus	Crayfish, Big Sandy
PE	—	Cambarus veteranus	Crayfish, Guyandotte River
PE	5	Procaris hawaiana	Shrimp, anchialine pool
Flowering plants			
PT	11	Argythamnia biodgettii	Silverbush, Blodgett's
PE	2	Calamagrostis expansa	Reedgrass, Maui
PE	9	Chamaecrista lineata var. keyensis	Pea, Big Pine partridge
PE	9	Chamaesyce deltoidea serpyllum.	Spurge, wedge
PE	2	Cyanea kauaulaensis	No common name
PE	2	Cyperus neokunthianus	No common name
PE	2	Cyrtandra hematos	Haiwale
PE	2	Exocarpos menziesii	Heau
PE	2	Festuca hawaiiansis	No common name
PE	2	Gardenia remyi	Nanu
PE	3	Joinvillea ascendens ascendens.	Ohe
PE	2	Kadua (=Hedyotis) fluviatilis	Kampuaa
PE	2	Kadua haupuensis	No common name
PE	2	Labordia lorenciana	No common name
PE	2	Lepidium orbiculare	Anaunau
PE	—	Lepidium papilliferum	Peppergrass, slickspot
PE	5	Linum arenicola	Flax, sand
PE	2	Myrsine fosbergii	Kolea
PE	2	Nothocestrum latifolium	Aiea

TABLE 2.5

U.S. Fish and Wildlife Service proposed species by group type as of December 2015 [CONTINUED]

Category	Priority	Scientific name	Common name
PE	2	Ochrosia haleakalae	Holei
PE	2	Phyllostegia brevidens	No common name
PE	2	Phyllostegia helleri	No common name
PE	2	Phyllostegia stachyoides	No common name
PT	8	Platanthera integrilabia	Orchid, white fringeless
PE	2	Portulaca villosa	Ihi
PE	2	Pritchardia bakeri	Loulu (=Loulu lelo)
PE	3	Pseudognaphalium (=Gnaphalium) sandwicensium var. molokaiense.	Enaena
PE	2	Ranunculus hawaiensis	Makou
PE	2	Ranunculus mauiensis	Makou
PE	2	Sanicula sandwicensis	No common name
PE	2	Santalum involutum	Iliahi
PE	3	Schiedea diffusa ssp. diffusa.	No common name
PE	2	Schiedea pubescens	Maolioli
PE	2	Sicyos lanceoloideus	Anunu
PE	2	Sicyos macrophyllus	Anunu
C	12	Sideroxylon reclinatum austrofloridense.	Bully, Everglades
C*	2	Solanum conocarpum	Bacora, marron
PE	8	Solanum nelsonii	Popolo
PE	3	Stenogyne kaalae ssp. sherffii.	No common name
C*	8	Streptanthus bracteatus	Twistflower, bracted
C*	8	Trifolium friscanum	Clover, Frisco
PE	2	Wikstroemia skottsbergiana.	Akia
Ferns and allies			
PE	2	Asplenium diellaciniatum	No common name
PE	8	Cyclosorus boydiae	Kupukupu makalii
PE	2	Deparia kaalaana	No common name
PE	3	Dryopteris glabra var. pusilla.	Hohiu
PE	3	Hypolepis hawaiiensis var. mauiensis.	Olua
PE	2	Huperzia (=Phlegmariurus) stemmermanniae.	No common name
PE	3	Microlepia strigosa var. mauiensis (=Microlepia mauiensis)	No common name

Notes: PE = Proposed Endangered. PT = Proposed Threatened. PSAT = Proposed Similarity of Appearance to a Threatened Taxon. C = Candidate; warranted but precluded. C* = Continued warranted but precluded.

SOURCE: Adapted from "Table 1. Candidate Notice of Review (Animals and Plants)," in "Endangered and Threatened Wildlife and Plants; Review of Native Species That Are Candidates for Listing as Endangered or Threatened; Annual Notice of Findings on Resubmitted Petitions; Annual Description of Progress on Listing Actions," *Federal Register*, vol. 80, no. 247, December 24, 2015, http://www.fws.gov/endangered/what-we-do/pdf/2015_CNOR_2015_12_24.pdf (accessed February 9, 2016)

Five-Year Status Reviews

Section 4(c)(2)(A) of the ESA requires a status review of the condition and situation of a listed species at least every five years to determine whether it still requires government protection. As the number of listed species has increased over the years so has the number of required five-year reviews, greatly stressing agency resources.

USFWS records indicate that the so-called five-year reviews are seldom performed on time. They are frequently

TABLE 2.6

National Marine Fisheries Service proposed species by group type as of January 2016

Species	Year proposed	Status
Fishes		
6 elasmobranch species	2015	Proposed endangered
• Guitarfish, Brazilian *(Rhinobatos horkelii)*		
• Shark, Argentine angel *(Squatina argentina)*		
• Shark, daggernose *(Isogomphodon oxyrhynchus)*		
• Shark, striped smoothhound *(Mustelus fasciatus)*		
• Shark, narrownose smoothhound *(Mustelus schmitti)*		Proposed threatened
• Shark, spiny angel *(Squatina guggenheim)*		
Coelacanth, African (1 DPS) *(Latimeria chalumnae)*	2015	Proposed threatened
• Tanzanian DPS		
Grouper, gulf *(Mycteroperca jordani)*	2015	Proposed endangered
Grouper, island *(Mycteroperca fusca)*	2015	Proposed threatened
Grouper, Nassau *(Epinephelus striatus)*	2014	Proposed threatened
Shark, common angel *(Squatina squatina)*	2015	Proposed endangered
Shark, sawback angel *(Squatina aculeata)*		
Shark, smoothback angel *(Squatina oculata)*		
Marine mammals		
Whale, humpback (4 DPSs) *(Megaptera novaeangliae)*	2015	Proposed threatened
• Central America		
• Western North Pacific		
• Arabian Sea		Proposed endangered
• Cape Verde Islands/Northwest Africa		
Marine reptiles		
Sea turtle, green (11 DPSs) *(Chelonia mydas)*	2015	Proposed threatened
• Central North Pacific		
• East Indian-West Pacific		
• East Pacific		
• North Atlantic		
• North Indian		
• South Atlantic		
• Southwest Indian		
• Central South Pacific		Proposed endangered
• Central West Pacific		
• Mediterranean		

Note: DPS = Distinct population segment.

SOURCE: "Proposed for Listing (28 Proposed "Species")," in *Candidate and Proposed Species under the Endangered Species Act (ESA)*, U.S. Department of Commerce, National Oceanic and Atmospheric Administration, National Marine Fisheries Service, January 29, 2016, http://www.nmfs.noaa.gov/pr/species/esa/candidate.htm (accessed February 9, 2016)

late by several years or even decades. This chronic tardiness has spurred substantial litigation against the agency. Development and industry groups are keen to have five-year reviews performed for listed species that they believe have recovered sufficiently to be delisted or downlisted (reclassified from endangered to threatened). By contrast, conservation groups want five-year status reviews conducted in a timely manner for threatened species that they believe should be uplisted from threatened to endangered status.

Taking, Possessing, or Trading Listed Species

The ESA makes illegal the taking of listed species. For animal species, taking is defined as killing, harming, harassing, pursuing, or removing the species from the wild. For plants, taking means collecting or "maliciously" damaging endangered plants on federal lands. The ESA also outlaws removing or damaging listed plants on state and private lands "in knowing violation of State law or in the course of violating a State criminal trespass law." The USFWS notes that some state laws specifically prohibit the taking of federally listed plants and animals.

The USFWS explains in "Permits for Native Species under the Endangered Species Act" (March 2013, http://www.fws.gov/endangered/esa-library/pdf/permits.pdf) that it is also illegal under the ESA to possess, ship, deliver, carry, transport, sell, or receive any listed species that was taken in violation of the law. Likewise, the import, export, and interstate or foreign sales of listed species are prohibited except for permitted conservation purposes.

Civil and criminal penalties can be levied for violations of these provisions; exemptions, however, are allowed under certain sections of the ESA.

SECTION 4(D) EXEMPTIONS. Section 4(d) of the ESA (http://www.fws.gov/endangered/laws-policies/section-4.html) allows the USFWS to issue regulations governing the conservation of threatened species and those listed as experimental populations. As a result, "special" rules have been issued that grant exemptions from the taking, possession, and import/export/sales provisions for some threatened species and experimental populations. For example, grizzly bears can be harmed "in self-defense or in defense of others." However, such taking has to be reported to authorities within a specified period. An updated listing of species with section 4(d) exemptions is available at http://ecos.fws.gov/tess_public/reports/species-with-fourd-special-rules-report.

INCIDENTAL TAKE PERMITS AND HABITAT CONSERVATION PLANS. When the original ESA was passed, it included exceptions that allowed the taking of listed species only for scientific research or other conservation activities authorized by the act. In 1982 Congress added a provision in section 10 of the ESA that allows "incidental take" of listed species of wildlife by nonfederal entities. Incidental take is defined as take that is incidental to, but not the purpose of, an otherwise lawful activity. Incidental taking cannot appreciably reduce the likelihood of the survival and recovery of listed species in the wild. The incidental take provision was added to allow private landowners some freedom to develop their land even if it provides habitat to listed species.

To obtain an incidental take permit, an applicant has to prepare a Habitat Conservation Plan (HCP). The HCP process is described by the USFWS in "Habitat Conservation Plans under the Endangered Species Act" (April 2011, http://www.fws.gov/endangered/esa-library/pdf/hcp.pdf). An HCP describes the impacts that are likely to result from the taking of the species and the measures the applicant will take to minimize and mitigate the impacts. HCPs are generally partnerships drawn up by people at the local level who are working with officials from the USFWS or the NMFS. The plans frequently represent compromises between developers and environmentalists.

Included in the agreement is a "no surprise" provision that assures landowners that the overall cost of species protection measures will be limited to what has been agreed to under the HCP. In return, landowners make a long-term commitment to conservation as negotiated in the HCP. Many HCPs include the preservation of significant areas of habitat for endangered species.

ENHANCEMENT OF SURVIVAL PERMITS. Another type of permit issued under the ESA is the enhancement of survival permit. This permit applies to species that are candidate species or are likely to become candidate species. It authorizes future incidental take (should the species become listed) by nonfederal landowners in exchange for proactive management of the species on their property. Permit applicants must agree to participate in a Candidate Conservation Agreement with Assurances (CCAA) or a Safe Harbor Agreement (SHA). These agreements provide assurances to landowners that no additional future regulatory restrictions will be imposed.

SUBSISTENCE TAKING. Besides the previously mentioned taking exemptions offered by the ESA, the native peoples of Alaska who rely on certain endangered or threatened animals for food or other products needed for subsistence are exempt from the taking rule under the Marine Mammal Protection Act. This act is described in detail in Chapter 3.

Critical Habitat

Under the ESA, the USFWS or the NMFS must decide whether critical habitat should be designated for a listed species. Critical habitat is specific geographical areas of land, water, and/or air space that contain features essential for the conservation of a listed species and that may require special management and protection. For example, these could be areas that are used for breeding, resting, and feeding. If the agency decides that critical habitat should be designated, a proposal notice is published in the *Federal Register* for public comment. If it is decided that critical habitat is needed, then the final boundaries are published in the *Federal Register*.

The role of critical habitat is often misunderstood by the public. Critical habitat designation does not set up a refuge or sanctuary for a species in which no development can take place. It can provide additional protection for a specific geographical area that might not occur without the designation. For example, if the USFWS determines that an area not currently occupied by a species is needed for species recovery and designates that area as critical habitat, any federal actions involving that area have to avoid adverse modifications. Critical habitat designation has no regulatory impact on private landowners unless they wish to take actions on their land that involve federal funding or permits.

The original ESA did not provide a time limit for the setting of critical habitat. In 1978 the law was amended to require that critical habitat be designated at the same time a species is listed. However, the designation is required only "when prudent." For example, the USFWS or the NMFS can refuse to designate critical habitat for a species if doing so would publicize the specific locations of organisms known to be targets for illegal hunting or collection. Historically, both agencies have broadly used the "when prudent" clause to justify not setting critical habitat for many listed species. This has been a contentious issue between the government and conservation groups.

Notices regarding proposed new or revised critical habitat designations must be placed in the *Federal Register* so that public comment can be obtained and considered before a designation is finalized.

Section 4(b)(2) of the ESA requires the ESA agencies to consider economic and other impacts when designating critical habitat. In August 2013 the USFWS (http://www.gpo.gov/fdsys/pkg/FR-2013-08-28/html/2013-20994.htm) indicated that beginning in October 2013 the economic analyses reports would be completed and published for public comment at the same time that critical habitat is proposed.

As of February 2016, the USFWS (http://ecos.fws.gov/tess_public/pub/criticalHabitat.jsp?nmfs=0) indicated that critical habitat had been designated for 709 U.S. species under its jurisdiction. Likewise, the NMFS (http://ecos.fws.gov/tess_public/pub/criticalHabitat.jsp?nmfs=2) had designated critical habitat for five species under its jurisdiction. Together, these 714 species represented 45% of the 1,590 U.S. species listed under the ESA at that time. (See Table 1.3 in Chapter 1.)

Experimental Populations

For some species, primarily mammals, birds, fish, and aquatic invertebrates, recovery efforts include the introduction of individuals into new areas. Typically, this is accomplished by moving a small group of imperiled animals from an established area to one or more other locations within the species' historical range of distribution.

Experimental populations of a species are not subject to the same rigorous protections under the ESA as other members of the species. Experimental populations can be considered threatened, even if the rest of the species is listed as endangered. In addition, the USFWS can designate an experimental population as essential or nonessential. A nonessential designation indicates that the survival of this population is not believed essential to the survival of the species as a whole. A nonessential experimental population is treated under the law as if it is proposed for listing, not already listed. This results in less protection under the ESA.

As of April 2016, the USFWS (http://ecos.fws.gov/tess_public/pub/experimentalPopulations.jsp) indicated there were 64 experimental populations listed under the ESA, all nonessential. It should be noted that some species have multiple experimental populations.

Actions by Federal Agencies

Section 7 of the ESA includes restrictions on federal agencies (and their nonfederal agency permit applicants) regarding endangered and threatened species. These restrictions are described by the USFWS in "Consultations with Federal Agencies: Section 7 of the Endangered Species Act" (April 2011, http://www.fws.gov/endangered/esa-library/pdf/consultations.pdf). Specifically, the federal agencies must "aid in the conservation of listed species" and "ensure that their activities are not likely to jeopardize the continued existence of listed species or adversely modify designated critical habitats." This applies to any activities that are funded, authorized, or permitted by these federal agencies or carried out on lands or waters managed by them.

According to the USFWS, there are two processes through which federal agencies (known as action agencies) comply with section 7 of the ESA as they plan projects or activities that might impact listed species: informal consultation or formal consultation. In either case, the first step is for the action agency to coordinate with the USFWS or the NMFS early in the process to determine which, if any, listed species are within the project area and to determine whether the project might affect the listed species or its critical habitat. If the action agency and the USFWS or the NMFS (whichever has jurisdiction) agree that the project will not jeopardize the listed species, then the project may proceed. The same is true if the project can be easily modified to prevent adverse effects. In either case, an informal consultation is said to have taken place.

If the action agency makes a preliminary determination that the project is likely to adversely affect listed species, then it may initiate a formal consultation. The action agency provides detailed information about the project and the listed species to the USFWS or the NMFS.

The governing agency then issues a report called a "biological opinion" that determines whether the proposed action is likely to have an adverse effect, and if so, recommends "reasonable and prudent alternatives that could allow the project to move forward."

Recovery Plans

The ESA requires that a recovery plan be developed and implemented for every listed species unless "such a plan will not promote the conservation of the species." The USFWS and the NMFS are directed to give priority to those species that are most likely to benefit from having a plan in place. The recovery potential of a species is ranked from 1 to 18 by the USFWS. Low rankings indicate a greater likelihood that the species can be recovered. Priority is based on the degree of threat, the potential for recovery, and taxonomy (genetic distinctiveness). In addition, rankings can be appended with the letter C when species recovery is in conflict with economic activities. Species with a C designation have higher priority than other species within the same numerical ranking. The NMFS uses a different rating system that ranges from 1 (highest recovery potential) to 12 (lowest recovery potential).

Each recovery plan must include the following three elements:

- Site-specific management actions to achieve the plan's goals

- Objective and measurable criteria for determining when a species is recovered

- Estimates of the amount of time and money that will be required to achieve recovery

The USFWS describes in "Endangered Species Recovery Program" (June 2011, http://www.fws.gov/endangered/esa-library/pdf/recovery.pdf) a recovery plan as "a road map with detailed site-specific management actions for private, Federal, and State cooperation in conserving listed species and their ecosystems." Recovery plans include precisely defined milestones for recovery achievement. For example, recovery may be considered accomplished when a certain number of individuals is reached and specifically named threats are eliminated. The USFWS notes, however, that a recovery plan is not a regulatory document.

As of February 2016, most (1,159, or 73%) of the 1,590 listed species in the United States at that time had recovery plans in place. (See Table 1.3 in Chapter 1.)

TRACKING RECOVERY PLANS. Notices regarding proposed new or revised recovery plans must be placed in the *Federal Register* so that public comment can be obtained and considered before a plan is finalized. A searchable database of recovery plans is available at the

USFWS website (http://ecos.fws.gov/tess_public/pub/speciesRecovery.jsp?sort=1). The database also includes some information about the implementation and scheduling of recovery plan activities. Information on the progress (or lack thereof) toward recovery is provided in the five-year status review reports on a species-by-species basis; however, as noted earlier, many of the five-year reviews are not conducted in a timely manner.

DELISTING UNDER THE ESA

Delisting occurs when a species is removed from the candidate list, the proposed list, or the final list of endangered and threatened species. Delisting takes place for a variety of reasons. In general, delisting occurs when the USFWS or the NMFS finds that a species has recovered or become extinct, or on various procedural grounds, including discovery of additional habitats or populations. As of February 2016, the USFWS (http://ecos.fws.gov/tess_public/reports/delisting-report) indicated that 19 species had been delisted on procedural grounds. Another 10 species

were delisted due to extinction. (See Table 1.2 in Chapter 1). In addition, 31 entities (entire species or subpopulations) were delisted due to recovery. U.S. entities that have been delisted due to recovery as of February 2016 are shown in Table 2.7. Foreign species that have been delisted due to recovery are shown in Table 2.8.

Recovered Species

The USFWS notes in "Delisting a Species: Section 4 of the Endangered Species Act" (April 2011, http://www.fws.gov/endangered/esa-library/pdf/delisting.pdf) that the delisting process for a species believed recovered is similar to the listing process. The agency assesses population data, recovery achievements, and threats to the species. A proposal for delisting is published in the *Federal Register* for review and comment by scientists and the public. Expert opinions are obtained from three independent species specialists. All the collected information is analyzed and a final decision on delisting is published in the *Federal Register*. Under the ESA, the USFWS or the NMFS (in cooperation with state agencies)

TABLE 2.7

Species delisted due to recovery as of February 2016

Common name	Scientific name	Species group	Date first listed	Date delisted	U.S. or U.S./foreign listed	Population or range delisted
Aleutian Canada goose	*Branta canadensis leucopareia*	Birds	03/11/67	03/20/01	US/Foreign	Entire range
American peregrine falcon	*Falco peregrinus anatum*	Birds	06/02/70	08/25/99	US/Foreign	Entire range
Arctic peregrine falcon	*Falco peregrinus tundrius*	Birds	06/02/70	10/05/94	US/Foreign	Entire range
Bald eagle	*Haliaeetus leucocephalus*	Birds	03/11/67	08/08/07	US	U.S.A., conterminous (lower 48) States
Brown pelican	*Pelecanus occidentalis*	Birds	06/02/70	02/04/85	US/Foreign	U.S. Atlantic coast, FL, AL
Brown pelican	*Pelecanus occidentalis*	Birds	06/02/70	12/17/09	US/Foreign	Entire range, except U.S. Atlantic coast, FL, AL
Columbian white-tailed deer	*Odocoileus virginianus leucurus*	Mammals	07/24/03	07/24/03	US	Douglas County, Oregon
Concho water snake	*Nerodia paucimaculata*	Reptiles	09/03/86	11/28/11	US	Entire range
Delmarva Peninsula fox squirrel	*Sciurus niger cinereus*	Mammals	03/11/67	12/16/15	US	Entire range, except where experimental
Eggert's sunflower	*Helianthus eggertii*	Flowering Plants	05/22/97	08/18/05	US	Entire range
Gray whale	*Eschrichtius robustus*	Mammals	06/16/94	06/16/94	US/Foreign	Eastern North Pacific Ocean–coastal and Bering, Beaufort, and Chukchi Seas
Gray wolf	*Canis lupus*	Mammals	03/09/78	05/05/11	US	Northern Rocky Mountain DPS: Montana, Wyoming, Idaho, eastern Washington, eastern Oregon, and north central Utah
Island night lizard	*Xantusia riversiana*	Reptiles	09/12/77	04/01/14	US	Entire range
Johnston's frankenia	*Frankenia johnstonii*	Flowering Plants	08/07/84	02/11/16	US/Foreign	Entire range
Lake Erie water snake	*Nerodia sipedon insularum*	Reptiles	08/30/99	09/15/11	US/Foreign	Lake Erie offshore islands and their adjacent waters (located more than 1 mile from mainland) OH, Canada (Ontario)
Magazine Mountain shagreen	*Inflectarius magazinensis*	Snails	04/17/89	06/14/13	US	Entire range
Maguire daisy	*Erigeron maguirei*	Flowering Plants	09/05/85	02/18/11	US	Entire range
Modoc sucker	*Catostomus microps*	Fishes	06/11/85	01/07/16	US	Entire range
Oregon chub	*Oregonichthys crameri*	Fishes	10/18/93	03/23/15	US	Entire range
Robbins' cinquefoil	*Potentilla robbinsiana*	Flowering Plants	09/17/80	08/27/02	US	Entire range
Steller sea lion	*Eumetopias jubatus*	Mammals	04/05/90	12/04/13	US/Foreign	Eastern DPS—Entire range, except the population segment west of 1440 West Longitude
Tennessee purple coneflower	*Echinacea tennesseensis*	Flowering Plants	07/05/79	09/02/11	US	Entire range
Tinian monarch (old world flycatcher)	*Monarcha takatsukasae*	Birds	06/02/70	09/21/04	US	Entire range
Virginia northern flying squirrel	*Glaucomys sabrinus fuscus*	Mammals	07/31/85	03/04/13	US	Entire range

DPS = Distinct Population Segment.

SOURCE: Adapted from "Generate Species List," and "Delisting Report," in *Environmental Conservation Online System Species Reports*, U.S. Department of the Interior, U.S. Fish and Wildlife Service, February 2016, http://ecos.fws.gov/tess_public/pub/adHocSpeciesForm.jsp (accessed February 19, 2016)

TABLE 2.8

Foreign species delisted due to recovery as of February 2016

Common name	Scientific name	Date first listed	Date delisted	Species group	Current distribution	Where delisted
Eastern gray kangaroo	*Macropus giganteus*	12/30/74	03/09/95	Mammals	Australia	Entire range
Morelet's crocodile	*Crocodylus moreletii*	06/02/70	05/23/12	Reptiles	Belize, Guatemala, Mexico	Entire range
Palau fantail flycatcher	*Rhipidura lepida*	06/02/70	09/12/85	Birds	Palau, West Pacific Ocean	Entire range
Palau ground dove	*Gallicolumba canifrons*	06/02/70	09/12/85	Birds	Palau, West Pacific Ocean	Entire range
Palau owl	*Pyrroglaux podargina*	06/02/70	09/12/85	Birds	Palau, West Pacific Ocean	Entire range
Red kangaroo	*Macropus rufus*	12/30/74	03/09/95	Mammals	Australia	Entire range
Western gray kangaroo	*Macropus fuliginosus*	12/30/74	03/09/95	Mammals	Australia	Entire range

SOURCE: Adapted from "Generate Species List," and "Delisting Report," in *Environmental Conservation Online System Species Reports*, U.S. Department of the Interior, U.S. Fish and Wildlife Service, February 2016, http://ecos.fws.gov/tess_public/pub/adHocSpeciesForm.jsp (accessed February 19, 2016)

is required to monitor for at least five years any species that has been delisted due to recovery. This is accomplished through a post-delisting monitoring strategy that goes through peer review (review by qualified scientists) and public comment before being finalized.

PRIVATE-PARTY PETITIONS

The ESA allows private parties (e.g., individuals and nongovernmental organizations [NGOs]) to submit listing petitions to the federal government. The NGOs are typically environmental or conservation groups that have the funding and expertise to develop petitions containing the required scientific data supporting the need for listing. Since the passage of the law in 1973, some NGOs have flooded the USFWS and the NMFS with listing petitions. According to D. Noah Greenwald, Kieran Suckling, and Martin Taylor, in "The Listing Record" (Dale D. Goble, J. Michael Scott, and Frank W. Davis, eds., *The Endangered Species Act at Thirty: Renewing the Conservation Promise*, 2006), the vast majority of the listings that occurred between 1996 and 2004 were driven by private-party petitions. Since 2004 private parties have submitted petitions covering hundreds of additional species.

The USFWS or the NMFS must determine within 90 days whether a petition contains "substantial information" suggesting that a species may require listing under the ESA. If listing is found to be warranted, the responsible agency is supposed to complete a status review for the species within 12 months. These time constraints have proven infeasible given the large number of petitions coming into the agencies and the large number of species involved. As a result, NGOs have filed numerous lawsuits against the agencies for failing to comply with ESA-mandated deadlines.

Since the 1990s the USFWS has repeatedly complained that many of its decisions and activities are driven by court orders, rather than by scientific priorities. The agency has also suggested that NGOs have taken advantage of ESA provisions that allow citizen lawsuits. Critics claim the groups flood the USFWS

with petitions so that lawsuits can be brought when the agency is unable to respond in a timely manner. Deborah Zabarenko notes in "Deal Aims to Cut Endangered Species Red Tape" (Reuters.com, May 10, 2011) that between 1994 and 2006 the USFWS received an average of approximately 17 petitions annually; however, between 2007 and May 2011 the agency received 1,230 petitions.

Environmentalists argue that the lawsuits are necessary because the USFWS fails to do the job assigned to it under the ESA.

CANDIDATE SPECIES BACKLOG

The USFWS has also been repeatedly sued for designating species as candidate species. As noted earlier, this designation means the USFWS acknowledges that the species deserves protection under the ESA, but believes that more pressing priorities must come first. The agency's September 1997 CNOR (http://www.gpo.gov/fdsys/pkg/FR-1997-09-19/html/97-24805.htm) included 207 candidate species. Subsequent annual CNORs (http://www.fws.gov/endangered/what-we-do/earlier-notices.html) continued to include 200 or more candidate species, much to the displeasure of conservation and wildlife NGOs.

In "Improving ESA Implementation" (February 17, 2016, http://www.fws.gov/endangered/improving_ESA/listing_workplan.html), the USFWS notes that multiple lawsuits dealing with candidate species were bundled together and resolved in late 2011 through legal settlements that were reached separately with the suing NGOs. Overall, the agency agreed to make listing decisions by 2017 for over 250 species included in the November 2010 CNOR (http://www.fws.gov/endangered/what-we-do/cnor-2010.html) and to make critical habitat determinations for any of these species that become listed. The agency also set a timetable for reviewing previously submitted petitions for hundreds of species. In exchange, the NGOs involved in the settlements agreed to restrictions on their ESA petitioning and litigation activities through 2017.

The USFWS (http://www.fws.gov/endangered/improving _esa/pdf/20151113_MDL_Listing_Accomplishments.pdf) maintains a database of its listing decision accomplishments under the legal agreements. For example, the Kentucky arrow darter (a fish) was on the November 2010 CNOR as a candidate species. In October 2015 it was given a new status of proposed threatened. (See Table 2.5.) The USFWS CNOR published in November 2015 included only 60 candidates. (See Table 2.3.) Thus, the agency has made considerable progress in reducing the number of candidate species.

Equal Access to Judgment Act

Critics assert that NGOs benefit financially from ESA-related lawsuits at the taxpayers' expense because of the Equal Access to Judgment Act (EAJA). The EAJA, passed by Congress in 1980 and signed into law by President Ronald Reagan (1911–2004), requires the federal government to pay the attorneys' fees of eligible individuals, nonprofit organizations, and other entities when these parties sue the federal government and prevail in court. NGOs have filed and won so many ESA-related lawsuits that they are believed to have collected many millions of dollars in legal fees from the government. The exact figures are unknown because the government does not compile or disclose the information.

Critics claim that litigious NGOs abuse the EAJA by submitting numerous ESA listing petitions and then suing when the government is unable to meet the mandated deadlines. The groups then collect attorneys' fees that fund additional listing petitions and lawsuits.

Overprotection Lawsuits

Overprotection lawsuits are typically filed by private parties whose economic interests are threatened by ESA measures. Examples include farmers, ranchers, landowners and developers, industry groups and associations, and the operators or users of natural resources, such as water and irrigation districts. The parties may be opposed to listings or designation of critical habitat for particular species or they may attempt to compel the federal government to delist or downlist species.

One of the most famous overprotection cases in ESA history concerns the polar bear, which was proposed in 2007 for listing as threatened. As is explained in Chapter 3, the listing is unique because the most significant threat to the species' survival is believed to be climate change, specifically the loss of habitat due to continuing global warming. The Pacific Legal Foundation (PLF) notes in "PLF Challenges Unwarranted Polar Bear Listing" (2015, http://www.pacificlegal.org/cases/PLF-challenges-unwarranted-polar-bear-listing) that it sued the government in 2008 on behalf of the California Cattlemen's Association and other groups on various legal grounds. In June 2011 a

federal court ruled against the PLF. The organization appealed, but lost. In October 2013 the U.S. Supreme Court refused to consider the case, which essentially settled the matter.

As noted earlier, the USFWS has historically been late in completing five-year reviews that are required by the ESA. Groups that allege the ESA is overprotective use legal action to force the agency to conduct the reviews for species they believe have recovered or improved in population. In 2005 the PLF (http://www .pacificlegal.org/document.doc?id=761) entered into a settlement agreement with the agency over the latter's failure to conduct status reviews for nearly 100 listed species, most in California. By 2009 the reviews resulted in recommendations for six of the species: the delisting of the Inyo California towhee (a bird) and the downlisting of the arroyo toad, the Indian Knob mountain balm (a plant), the Lane Mountain milk-vetch (a plant), the Modoc sucker (a fish), and the Santa Cruz cypress (a plant). However, the agency did not finalize the decisions over the following year, spurring a petition from the PLF.

In 2013 the PLF (http://www.pacificlegal.org/document .doc?id=760) sued the USFWS for failing to finalize the decisions. The agency responded as follows:

- Arroyo toad—officially proposed in March 2014 for downlisting from endangered to threatened. However, the USFWS (http://ecos.fws.gov/tess_public/profile/ speciesProfile?spcode=D020) withdrew its proposal in December 2015 following receipt of additional information about the species.

- Indian Knob mountain balm—the USFWS (http:// ecos.fws.gov/tess_public/profile/speciesProfile?spcode =Q1W5) decided in December 2013 that downlisting from endangered to threatened was not warranted.

- Inyo California towhee—officially proposed in November 2013 for delisting due to recovery. As of April 2016, however, this decision had not been finalized by the USFWS (http://ecos.fws.gov/tess_public/ profile/speciesProfile?spcode=B07Q).

- Lane Mountain milk-vetch—the USFWS (http://ecos .fws.gov/tess_public/profile/speciesProfile?spcode= Q064) decided in May 2014 that downlisting from endangered to threatened was not warranted.

- Modoc sucker—officially proposed in February 2014 by the USFWS (http://ecos.fws.gov/tess_public/profile/ speciesProfile?spcode=E053) to be delisted due to recovery. This designation became final in January 2016 as shown in Table 2.7.

- Santa Cruz cypress—the USFWS (http://ecos.fws .gov/tess_public/profile/speciesProfile?spcode=R005) officially proposed in September 2013 that this species be downlisted from endangered to threatened.

The final rule on the reclassification was published in February 2016 and was scheduled to take effect in March 2016.

Environment and Natural Resources Division

The U.S. Department of Justice's Environment and Natural Resources Division (ENRD) handles litigation cases that are associated with the nation's environmental and conservation laws, including the ESA. The ENRD provides in *Overview of the Endangered Species Act and Highlights of Recent Litigation* (January 2004, http://www.abanet.org/environ/committees/endangered/Overviewof theESA.pdf) a brief summary of the several hundred ESA-related lawsuits that had reached the courts as of early 2004. The ENRD notes that some ESA litigation involved broad issues, such as the function of the law and the scope of the duties of the USFWS and the NMFS under the law. However, the vast majority of lawsuits focused on particular species. ENRD-litigation summaries for individual years since 2004 are available at http://www.justice.gov/enrd/Current_topics.html.

U.S. Supreme Court Cases

One of the foremost legal cases in ESA history involved a tiny fish called the snail darter in the Little Tennessee River. The ENRD reports in *"Tennessee Valley Authority v. Hill"* (May 15, 2015, http://www.justice.gov/enrd/Tennessee_Valley_Authority_vs_Hill.html) that a biologist discovered the fish in the river in 1973, the same year that the ESA became law. At that time the Tennessee Valley Authority (TVA; a federally owned corporation) was building the Tellico Dam near Knoxville, Tennessee. The dam was to provide hydroelectric power and flood control by backing up the river into a 30-mile (48-km) reservoir. In 1975 the USFWS declared the snail darter an endangered species and designated the Little Tennessee River as its critical habitat. Completion of the nearly finished dam—on which $78 million of tax money had already been spent—was put on hold while a massive legal battle was fought.

In 1978 the U.S. Supreme Court ruled in *Tennessee Valley Authority v. Hill* (437 U.S. 153) that protection of the snail darter outweighed the economic loss of abandoning the dam. The ENRD notes that the Supreme Court acknowledged "the perceived absurdity in forfeiting tens of millions of dollars of public funds for a small fish," but points out that the ESA did not include any provisions for cost-benefit analysis. In other words, the apparent intent of the ESA was to protect imperiled species regardless of the cost.

The decision was hailed as a great victory by environmental and conservation groups, but was extremely unpopular otherwise. Congress added new language to section 7 of the ESA allowing costs to be considered when federally funded or managed projects conflict with the needs of imperiled species. In addition, a separate bill was passed exempting the Tellico Dam from the ESA requirements for the snail darter. In 1979 the dam was completed, and the tiny fish was presumed exterminated. However, during the early 1980s more populations of the snail darter were discovered in Tennessee rivers and streams. In 1984 the USFWS downlisted the species from endangered to threatened and rescinded its critical habitat designation. As of April 2016, the snail darter remained on the list of threatened species.

In "ESA in the Supreme Court" (May 15, 2015, https://www.justice.gov/enrd/supreme-court), the ENRD notes that four other notable ESA-related cases have reached the U.S. Supreme Court:

- *Babbitt v. Sweet Home Chapter of Communities for a Better Oregon* (515 U.S. 687 [1985])—the court affirmed the DOI's interpretation of taking under the ESA to include "significant modification or degradation where it actually kills or injures wildlife."

- *Bennett v. Spear* (520 U.S. 154 [1997])—the court broadened the right of individuals (and groups) to sue the federal government over ESA issues.

- *National Association of Home Builders v. Defenders of Wildlife* (551 U.S. 644 [2007])—the court affirmed that only specific types of federal actions fall under section 7 of the ESA.

- *Winter v. Natural Resources Defense Council* (555 U.S. 7 [2008])—the court overruled lower court decisions that had placed restrictions on the U.S. Navy's use of sonar during submarine training exercises off the coast of California. The lower courts had found in favor of plaintiffs, which argued that the sonar harmed marine mammals protected by federal laws, including the ESA.

ESA SPENDING

Various federal agencies spend money to uphold the ESA. The primary agencies are the USFWS and the NMFS. For accounting purposes, the federal government operates on a fiscal year (FY) that runs from October through September. Thus, FY 2016 covers October 1, 2015, through September 30, 2016. Each year by the first Monday in February the U.S. president must present a proposed budget to the U.S. House of Representatives. This is the amount of money that the president estimates will be required to operate the federal government during the next fiscal year. It should be noted that Congress can take many months, even more than a year, to finalize and enact a federal budget. This has been particularly true during the 21st century due to fierce disagreements within Congress about government spending.

TABLE 2.9

U.S. Fish and Wildlife Service budgetary amounts devoted to ecological services, fiscal years 2015–17

[Dollars in thousands]

Appropriation: resource management	2015 actual	2016 enacted	2017 president's budget
Ecological services			
Listing	20,515	20,515	22,901
Listing			
Planning and consultation	98,336	99,079	105,650
Gulf Coast restoration			
General program activities			
Conservation and restoration	29,146	32,396	34,562
National Wetlands inventory			
Sagebrush Steppe ecosystem			
Recovery	77,916	82,016	89,180
Aquatic species conservation delivery			
Cooperative recovery			
Multi-partner recovery actions			
(aplomado falcon, condor)			
Wolf livestock demonstration program			
General program activities			
Ecological services total	225,913	234,006	252,293

SOURCE: Adapted from "2017 Budget at a Glance," in *The United States Department of the Interior: Budget Justifications and Performance Information Fiscal Year 2017*, U.S. Department of the Interior, February 2016, http://www.fws.gov/budget/2016/FY2017_FWS_Greenbook.pdf (accessed February 10, 2016)

The USFWS has many responsibilities in addition to administering the Endangered Species Program; however, many of the program's tasks are covered under the agency's ecological services appropriation. As shown in Table 2.9, this appropriation includes money for listing activities, planning and consultation, conservation and restoration, and species recovery. The funding for FY 2015 for this appropriation was $225.9 million. The agency received slightly more ($234 million) for FY 2016. The president's FY 2017 request for this appropriation was $252.3 million.

The NMFS does not provide a breakdown of its ESA activities for the budget process.

Species Expenditures

Section 18 of the ESA requires the USFWS to file an annual report detailing certain expenditures that were made for the conservation of threatened and endangered species under the act. As of March 2016, the USFWS (http://www.fws.gov/endangered/esa-library/index.html) noted that the report for FY 2014 was the most recent one available. In *Federal and State Endangered and Threatened Species Expenditures: Fiscal Year 2014* (March 2016, http://www.fws.gov/endangered/esa-library/pdf/20160302_final_FY14_ExpRpt.pdf), the USFWS indicates that more than $1.4 billion was spent by federal and state agencies during FY 2014 to protect more than

1,300 listed species under the ESA. This includes both domestic and foreign species. Federal agencies accounted for nearly all (95%) of the total. Around $121 million of the total was spent on land acquisition.

Overall, the 10 species with the highest spending during FY 2104, excluding land acquisition costs, were:

- Pallid sturgeon—$68.8 million
- Steelhead (Snake River basin DPS)—$52.2 million
- Chinook salmon (Snake River spring/summer-run ESU)—$49.2 million
- Steelhead (Middle Columbia River DPS)—$48.5 million
- Chinook salmon (Lower Columbia River ESU)—$42.5 million
- Chinook salmon (Snake River fall-run ESU)—$35.4 million
- Bull trout (lower 48 states)—$35.2 million
- Chinook salmon (Upper Columbia spring-run ESU)—$33.8 million
- Desert tortoise (Entire population, except in Sonoran desert)—$33.7 million
- Steelhead (Upper Columbia River DPS)—$31.7 million

Subsequent chapters provide spending data for particular species groups.

Grants to State, Territory, and Local Governments

The ESA is a federal law and is implemented and enforced by federal agencies. However, the federal government cooperates with state, territorial, and local governments to carry out ESA measures. As of 2016, listed species were found in every state and most U.S. territories. (See Table 1.4 in Chapter 1.) Some species are found in more than one state. However, each species (or DPS) is regulated under the ESA by range (the geographical area a species is known or believed to occupy). Thus, a range can cover two or more states. For example, Figure 2.2 shows that the range of the Preble's meadow jumping mouse extends across portions of both Wyoming and Colorado.

Primarily the federal ESA agencies coordinate with state agencies (such as fish and wildlife agencies) in carrying out conservation programs. Section 6 of the ESA authorizes the federal government to operate the Cooperative Endangered Species Conservation Fund to provide grants to states to support their conservation efforts. The USFWS indicates in "Cooperative Endangered Species Conservation Fund Grants" (August 2015, http://www.fws.gov/endangered/esa-library/pdf/section6-aug2015.pdf) that $48.7 million in grants were awarded in 2015 to states and territories as follows:

FIGURE 2.2

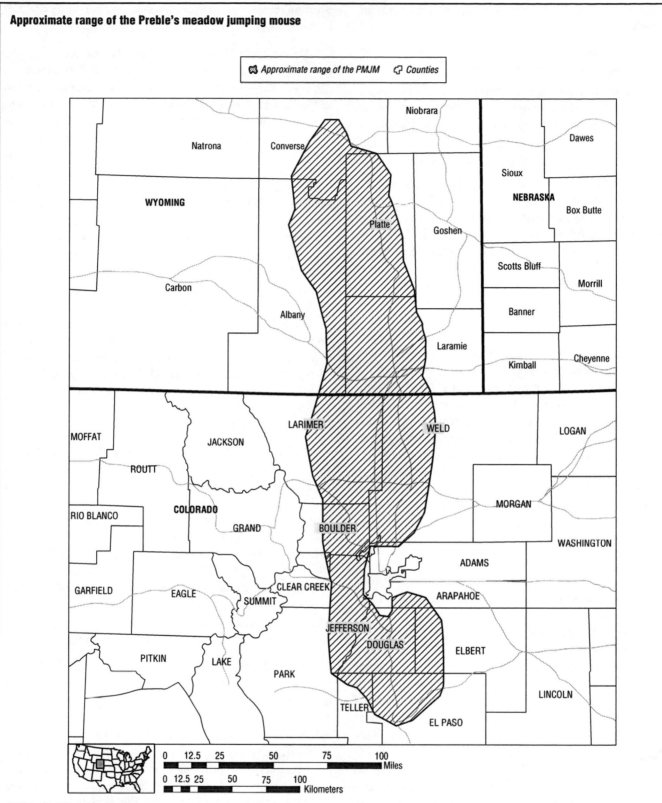

Approximate range of the Preble's meadow jumping mouse

Approximate range of the PMJM   Counties

PMJM = Preble's Meadow jumping mouse.

SOURCE: "Figure 1. Approximate Range of the Preble's Meadow Jumping Mouse," in "Endangered and Threatened Wildlife and Plants; 12-Month Finding on Two Petitions to Delist the Preble's Meadow Jumping Mouse," *Federal Register*, vol. 78, no. 101, May 24, 2013, https://www.gpo.gov/fdsys/pkg/FR-2013-05-24/pdf/2013-12387.pdf (accessed February 17, 2016)

- Conservation grants ($11.5 million)—implement conservation projects for listed species and at-risk species

- Habitat conservation planning assistance grants ($4.7 million)—support the development of HCPs through support of baseline surveys and inventories, document preparation, outreach, and similar planning activities

- HCP land acquisition grants ($20.3 million)—acquire land associated with approved HCPs
- Recovery land acquisition grants ($12.2 million)— acquire habitat for endangered and threatened species in support of draft and approved recovery plans

THE POLITICAL HISTORY OF THE ESA

The ESA has become one of the most controversial, litigious, and politically polarizing laws in U.S. history. Interestingly, it did not start out that way. According to J. Michael Scott, Frank W. Davis, and Dale D. Goble, in "Introduction" (Dale D. Goble, J. Michael Scott, and Frank W. Davis, eds., *The Endangered Species Act at Thirty: Renewing the Conservation Promise*, 2006), the original act enjoyed broad bipartisan support from members of both major political parties. The bills establishing the ESA were passed unanimously by the U.S. Senate and almost unanimously in the House of Representatives. Although Congress had a Democratic majority at the time, the Republican president Richard M. Nixon (1913–1994) supported the ESA and signed the final bill into law in 1973. Environmental issues were a high priority during the early 1970s, and numerous sweeping environmental laws were passed during this time. Scott, Davis, and Goble describe passage of the ESA as "an idealistic and perhaps naive attempt to preserve humanity by preserving other species in the ecological support system that makes life possible." Certainly, its original supporters did not foresee the bitter contention that this law would later arouse.

The original law was very restrictive, in that it prohibited taking under almost all circumstances. The controversial snail darter court case and other litigation prompted Congress to make the ESA more permissive and flexible via amendments in 1978 and 1982. The 1982 amendment was particularly striking because it allowed for incidental take under certain circumstances, a concession that bothered environmentalists. The amendment was also notable for ending the possibility of using economic considerations in listing species. In 1981 President Reagan signed Executive Order 12291 (http://www.archives.gov/federal-register/codification/executive-order/12291.html) to "reduce the burdens of existing and future regulations." One requirement of this broad executive order was that federal agencies had to weigh the economic costs against the benefits of regulations. Reagan was a conservative Republican who opposed what he viewed as the overregulation of business and private interests. Congress responded by adding language in the 1982 ESA amendment that listing determinations would be made "solely on the basis of the best scientific and commercial data available." Thus, economic costs are not a consideration during the ESA listing process. This decision remains highly controversial and is bitterly opposed by many industrial and commercial interests.

By the early 1990s conservative Republicans enjoyed much greater political power in the United States. In general, Republicans believe the ESA violates private property rights and stifles economic growth by curbing development. They charge that environmental protection often results in the loss of jobs and business profits. During the spring of 1995 the Republican-controlled Congress imposed a moratorium on new ESA listings, and the law itself was in jeopardy. The authorization for funding the ESA had expired at the end of FY 1992. In 1993 and 1994 the Democratic-controlled Congress appropriated annual funds to keep the ESA going; however, the Republican-controlled Congress that took power in 1995 refused to do so. According to Scott, Davis, and Goble, this open congressional "hostility" toward the ESA spurred Bruce Babbitt (1938–), the U.S. secretary of the interior, to make changes. He added so-called incentive-based strategies "to try and reconcile endangered species conservation with economic development." These reforms included the HCPs, CCAAs, and SHAs described earlier in this chapter for private landowners. During the spring of 1996 funding was restored for the ESA, and the listing moratorium ended.

In 2000 the Republican George W. Bush (1946–) was elected president. Bush favored less government regulation of business and industry. He espoused a so-called new environmentalism that promoted conservation and cooperation at the local level over federal government prohibitions. During his eight years in office only 61 new listings were made under the ESA. (See Figure 1.2 in Chapter 1.) This historically low number was criticized and hailed as proof that the administration tried to undermine the intent of the law. There were also many accusations of political bullying of DOI scientists by administration officials.

The Bush administration supported legislative efforts to amend the ESA to change its scientific process and be less restrictive on private property owners, businesses, and industry. However, these legislative efforts failed to pass. The administration also attempted to reform the ESA through procedural policy changes and rule interpretations. For example, in December 2008, the last full month of the Bush administration, the DOI issued a rule relaxing the mandatory requirement that federal agencies consult with the ESA agencies as required by section 7 of the law. These consultations became optional under certain circumstances. The rule was greeted positively by business interests and negatively by environmentalists, who considered it a last-ditch effort by the Bush administration to weaken the ESA.

In January 2009 Bush was succeeded by the Democrat Barack Obama (1961–). Months later, Obama reversed the Bush administration's rule regarding section 7 consultations under the ESA. Conservation and animal protection groups were further pleased in 2011, when the USFWS forged a legal agreement to move forward with listing decisions for hundreds of candidate species that had languished on hold for years. However, many of these same groups expressed displeasure when the USFWS eventually chose not to list some of those species under the act.

Republicans gained majority control in the House of Representatives after the November 2010 elections and in the Senate after the November 2014 elections. As a result, the Obama administration has faced fierce congressional battles related to ESA funding and implementation. The Great Recession (which lasted from late 2007 to mid-2009) and the boom in the U.S. energy industry focused sharp attention on the economic ramifications of the ESA.

Congressional Actions

The Center for Biological Diversity is a conservation group that strongly favors the ESA. The organization (http://www.biologicaldiversity.org/campaigns/esa_attacks/table.html) maintains a listing of what it calls congressional "attacks" on the ESA. These are proposed laws or amendments that the Center for Biological Diversity believes are designed to weaken ESA restrictions. As of April 2016, the organization indicated that 250 "attacks" had taken place. The majority of them occurred between 2011 and 2016 (during Obama's time in office) and were led by Republican lawmakers.

Riders to Appropriations Bills

The House of Representatives and Senate each have separate processes for deliberating a bill. Amendments can be added or stripped away during these deliberations. When the two bodies reach a compromise and settle on one version of a bill, it is then sent to the president. The president can either sign the bill into law or veto (refuse to sign) it, in which case the bill does not become law.

Congress is supposed to pass several individual appropriations bills each year in which it sets funding for federal government agencies for the upcoming fiscal year. Since the 1990s political feuding over budget priorities has upset the traditional appropriations process. As a result, Congress began bundling most or all appropriations bills for a year into one giant piece of legislation called an omnibus bill. Omnibus appropriations bills are massive in scope and vitally important to pass to fund the federal government. They are often referred to as "must-pass" legislation.

Some congressional members have used riders (amendments added to bills that have little relation to the actual subject of the bills) to thwart or bypass ESA actions. In 2011 two western legislators—Senator Jon Tester (1956–; D-MT) and Representative Mike Simpson (1950–; R-ID)—added a rider to an omnibus bill that was signed into law. Chapter 7 explains how the rider forced the USFWS to delist a population of gray wolves known as the Rocky Mountain DPS. In other words, Congress circumvented (found a way around) the normal ESA procedures regarding delisting decisions. Although the Obama administration did not agree with the rider, passage of the overall bill was so vital that the president signed it. Some conservation groups were outraged and filed lawsuits over the matter; however, they were unsuccessful in court.

In 2014 Representative Rob Bishop (1950–; R-UT) added a rider to an omnibus bill. The rider forbade the USFWS from making listing decisions for various populations of sage grouse, a ground-dwelling bird found in the western United States. The Republican and Democratic governors of the affected states were also keenly interested in preventing the sage grouse from being listed under the ESA. The rider survived Senate scrutiny and was in the final version of the bill that President Obama signed into law in December 2014 as the Consolidated and Further Continuing Appropriations Act of 2015.

Not all rider attempts have been successful. In May 2015 the House of Representatives passed its version of the National Defense Authorization Act (NDAA) for 2016 to fund the U.S. Department of Defense (DOD). The House's bill included riders added by Representative Frank Lucas (1960–; R-OK). They would have continued the listing prohibitions on the sage grouse and delisted the lesser prairie chicken (another western ground-dwelling bird) and the American burying beetle. The Senate stripped out the riders when it deliberated the bill. Thus, they were not in the final version that was sent to the president. In October 2015 Obama vetoed the NDAA. As a result, the DOD appropriations were included in another omnibus bill that was signed into law in December 2015 as the Consolidated Appropriations Act of 2016, which included a species rider. Section 117 of the law forbids the DOI from spending money during FY 2016 on proposing for ESA listing the greater sage grouse or the Columbia basin DPS of greater sage grouse.

The use of riders to compel ESA listing and delisting actions is strongly criticized by some conservation groups. They decry it as politically motivated interference that overrules the science-based processes that are supposed to guide ESA decisions. Advocates for the riders defend them as protective measures against what they see as unreasonable and economically damaging regulation by the federal government.

State Governments Fight for Their Interests

There is growing political pressure for the federal government to give greater power to state governments under the ESA. This is a major goal for Republican lawmakers, because they favor decreasing the power of the federal government. It is also a popular objective in many western states, even those governed by Democrats. Western states with oil, gas, and mining industries are very keen to avoid listings under the ESA that could hamper these industries and have negative economic consequences.

POLAR BEAR. Chapter 3 describes Alaska's bitter opposition to the USFWS decision in 2008 to list the polar bear as threatened. The state's leaders feared the listing would threaten oil and natural gas development and filed a lawsuit arguing that the listing was not justified. The lawsuit was rejected by a federal court. In 2010 the USFWS designated a huge swath of Alaskan land and coastal waters/ice as critical habitat for the polar bear. The state sued again, arguing that the designation was improper. It was joined in the suit by oil and gas industry groups and by corporations representing Alaskan Natives. In 2013 a federal court ruled in their favor; however, the decision was overturned on appeal in early 2016.

GRAY WOLF. Wolf management is a long-running source of conflict in some western states. In 2003 the USFWS (https://www.gpo.gov/fdsys/pkg/FR-2012-09-10/pdf/2012-21988.pdf) proposed delisting a gray wolf DPS in Idaho, Montana, and Wyoming. The delisting was contingent on the three states developing wolf management plans acceptable to the federal government. The plans from Idaho and Montana were approved. Wyoming's plan would have allowed wolves outside of national park lands to be "trophy hunted" or shot as predators. It was rejected by the USFWS, prompting a lawsuit by the state. After years of court battles, Wyoming revised its plan, and in 2008 the USFWS delisted the northern Rocky Mountain DPS of wolves. Environmental groups challenged the decision in court and prevailed. The USFWS relisted gray wolves and was again sued by Wyoming. As noted earlier, a congressional rider to an omnibus bill finally forced the USFWS to delist the northern Rocky Mountain DPS of wolves.

PRAIRIE-DWELLING SPECIES. Recent state-federal clashes have occurred over imperiled species found in the vast arid prairies of the interior west. The 2010 CNOR included several prairie dwellers, mainly the lesser prairie chicken, the dunes sagebrush lizard, and various sage grouse populations. A settlement agreement requires the USFWS to make listing decisions by 2017 for the species on the 2010 CNOR. States with candidate species have worked aggressively to prevent such listings from occurring. They fear economic harm, primarily to their oil, natural gas, and mining industries. The USFWS decided to list the lesser prairie chicken. However, it eventually decided not to list the dunes sagebrush lizard and the sage grouse.

In December 2010 the USFWS (http://www.gpo.gov/fdsys/pkg/FR-2010-12-14/pdf/2010-31140.pdf#page=1) officially proposed listing the dunes sagebrush lizard under the ESA as endangered. The lizard is found in southeastern New Mexico and western Texas, areas with extensive oil and natural gas exploration activities. In 2012 the USFWS (https://www.gpo.gov/fdsys/pkg/FR-2012-06-19/pdf/2012-14818.pdf) announced that it would not finalize the proposed listing under the ESA. In large part, this decision was based on conservation plans that had been developed by New Mexico and Texas. In "Obama Administration Cancels Endangered Species Listing for Lizard" (HumanEvents.com, June 13, 2012), Audrey Hudson explains that the conservation plans commit "oil and gas developers and other stakeholders to protect 650,000 acres of land as habitat for the creature in Texas and New Mexico." Obama administration officials praised the agreement as a means for balancing economic and conservation interests. According to Hudson, "The unprecedented agreement commits the states and other stakeholders to decades of conservation efforts estimated to cost millions of dollars, thereby avoiding a certain shutdown of all oil and gas development near the lizard's habitat and save thousands of jobs." However, conservation groups were unhappy with the decision. Hudson notes that "environmentalists accused the Obama administration of selling out to energy companies and criticized the decision."

An even fiercer political battle has raged over the sage grouse. Western lawmakers in Congress added riders to federal appropriations bills to prohibit the USFWS from listing the birds under the ESA during FYs 2015 and 2016. State wildlife agencies have acted individually and through the Western Association of Fish and Wildlife Agencies to develop conservation plans for the species. They have recruited industry partners and private landowners to voluntarily agree to the plans. In March 2015 the first conservation bank for sage grouse was established. (Chapter 1 explains the concepts of conservation banking.) The USFWS states in the press release "U.S. Fish and Wildlife Service, State of Wyoming, Sweetwater River Conservancy Launch Nation's First Greater Sage-Grouse Conservation Bank" (March 18, 2015, http://www.fws.gov/news/ShowNews.cfm?ID=2EA1ED88-F89B-76F0-9D79A5EB32AB6E61) that "the bank will manage a vast expanse of central Wyoming for sage-grouse, mule deer and other wildlife, allowing energy development and other economic activities to proceed on lands elsewhere in the state."

The federal government owns huge tracts of land in the West that are overseen by agencies, such as the BLM within the DOI and the U.S. Forest Service within the

U.S. Department of Agriculture (USDA). These federal agencies have initiated conservation measures on behalf of the sage grouse. In "Hard Questions Presage Challenges to Federal Grouse Plans" (EENews.net, June 16, 2015), Scott Streater notes that the BLM amended its resource management plans for lands with sage grouse habitat. Chapter 1 describes the Working Lands for Wildlife program of the USDA's Natural Resources Conservation Service. One of the program's target species is the sage grouse. According to the USFWS, in "Historic Conservation Campaign Protects Greater Sage-Grouse" (September 22, 2015, https://www.doi.gov/pressreleases/historic-conservation-campaign-protects-greater-sage-grouse), the Natural Resources Conservation Service's Sage Grouse Initiative signed up more than 1,100 ranchers who have "restored or conserved approximately 4.4 million acres of key habitat" for the bird.

All of these efforts proved convincing. In September 2015 the USFWS decided not to list the greater sage grouse under the ESA. In "Decision Not to List Sage Grouse as Endangered Is Called Life Saver by Some, Death Knell by Others" (WashingtonPost.com, September 22, 2015), Darryl Fears notes that some wildlife groups, such as the Audubon Society, welcomed the news, whereas others were critical of it. A spokesperson for WildEarth Guardians complained, "The sage grouse faces huge problems from industrial development and livestock grazing across the West, and now the Interior Department seems to be squandering a major opportunity to put science before politics and solve these problems."

Although western states were pleased by the USFWS decision, not all of them agreed with the federal plans for conserving sage grouse habitat. Idaho sued over the issue. The Idaho Governor's Office of Species Conservation complains in "Sage-Grouse" (2016, http://species.idaho.gov/list/sagegrouse.html) that "the federal agencies in Washington D.C. deviated from Idaho's local, scientifically-based collaborative agreement and unilaterally adopted additional and unnecessary restrictions for land use activities in key sage-grouse habitat." According to the article "Groups Sue over Sage Grouse Plan" (MtExpress.com, March 2, 2016), the suit had not been settled as of March 2016. That same month four conservation groups also sued the federal government. Their argument is that the conservation plans for the sage grouse are not comprehensive enough.

OTHER ESA CRITICISMS
Private Property Rights

The issue of private property rights is a prime concern among ESA critics, particularly industry and development groups. One measure they strongly support is compensation for the loss of use of land. For example, the National Stone, Sand, and Gravel Association states in "Endangered Species Act Reform" (September 2014, http://www.nssga.org/endangered-species-act-reform/), "ESA mandates have severely restricted the use and value of privately owned property. When severe restrictions occur without compensation by the federal government, the Act shifts to individual citizens costs and burdens that should be shared by all citizens. The ESA must be modified to justly compensate landowners in a timely fashion when private property is preserved in a habitat conservation plan."

Evading the ESA

ESA critics also complain that the law provides no incentive for private landowners to participate in the conservation process. In fact, there is evidence that some people actively evade the law to prevent government restrictions on their land use. This claim is supported by Dean Lueck and Jeffrey A. Michael in "Preemptive Habitat Destruction under the Endangered Species Act" (*Journal of Law and Economics*, vol. 46, no. 1, 2003). The researchers examined land-use data between 1984 and 1990 for approximately 1,000 forest plots in North Carolina. As is described in Chapter 8, the red-cockaded woodpecker is an endangered bird found in scattered forested habitats in the Southeast. It has been listed under the ESA since 1970. Lueck and Michael find that landowners with forest plots near areas known to contain the imperiled birds were much more likely to harvest and sell their timber than landowners with plots located farther from the birds. In addition, the plots closest to the birds were harvested when the trees were younger (and subsequently smaller and worth less). The researchers surmise that landowners with plots close to the birds rushed to harvest their trees before the trees became home to the imperiled species. Lueck and Michael call this "preemptive habitat destruction." The landowners evaded potential future ESA restrictions on their land use by destroying the very habitat that might attract and harbor the birds.

A more dire evasion technique allegedly used by some landowners is described by the colorful phrase "shoot, shovel, and shut up." The phrase was supposedly coined by Ralph R. Reiland, an economics professor known for his conservative views, in a column for the *Pittsburgh Tribune-Review*. In "Shoot, Shovel & Shut Up" (PittsburghLive.com, April 5, 2005), Reiland discusses the Lueck and Michael study and provides anecdotal stories about private landowners he claims have been economically harmed by ESA land-use restrictions. Reiland, like many ESA opponents, asserts that preemptive habitat destruction and shoot, shovel and shut up strategies are practiced by private landowners to avoid government interference with how they manage their land. As a result, these strategies thwart the preservation of the very species that the ESA is supposed to protect. This is presented as evidence that the ESA is a failed law.

Recovery Rate Controversy

One of the most frequent criticisms leveled against the ESA is that it has achieved recovery for few species since its passage in 1973. As shown in Table 2.7 and discussed earlier, only 24 U.S. entities (species or DPS) had been delisted due to recovery under the ESA as of February 2016. (Some of the recovered mammal entities are not entire species, but subpopulations of the wider population.) Considering that 1,590 species were listed under the ESA as of February 2016, the recovery rate was around 1.5%. (See Table 1.3 in Chapter 1.) This low recovery rate is often touted by ESA opponents as proof that the act has failed.

ESA proponents take a different stance on this issue. For example, Verlyn Klinkenborg asks in "Last One" (NationalGeographic.com, January 2009): "How many species might have vanished without it?" Conservation groups maintain that rates of full recovery and delisting are not adequate measures of ESA success because it can take many decades for a species to recover after being listed under the ESA.

THE FUTURE OF THE ESA

The ESA agencies struggle under intense legal and political pressures to carry out the law. Its general lack of consideration for the economic consequences of listing species exposes it to constant criticism. Although the law has been tweaked occasionally since its inception, Congress has failed to make overwhelming changes to it. Traditionally, the ESA has pitted conservation groups against developers, industry, and landowners. In the early 21st century the struggle is growing more complicated with federal legislators and states demanding (and sometimes getting) much greater say in how the ESA is administered.

The sage grouse story described earlier highlights the rising use of voluntary and incentive-based conservation measures (such as conservation banking). They provide landowners, developers, ranchers, and industries a way to influence ESA outcomes outside of the courtroom. Furthermore, they played a major role in the USFWS decision in 2015 not to list the bird. Some conservation groups are skeptical of voluntary measures, believing the measures will not be adequately implemented. Instead, they advocate strengthening and better funding the ESA agencies to strictly enforce the law.

Some observers believe the ESA cannot continue in its current form with listing decisions prodded back and forth by political maneuvers and constant lawsuits. The growing impacts of global warming and climate change likely mean that many more animal and plant species will qualify for ESA listing in the future. At some point the United States may have to limit ESA protections to selected species. Erica Goode discusses this controversial topic in "A Shifting Approach to Saving Endangered Species" (NYTimes.com, October 5, 2015). She quotes Daniel M. Ashe, the director of the USFWS, who said, "We have to prepare ourselves to make better choices about what is going to come along for the ride with us and where and in what numbers."

CHAPTER 3
MARINE MAMMALS

Marine mammals live in and around the ocean. They are warm-blooded, breathe air, have hair at some point during their life, give birth to live young (as opposed to laying eggs), and nourish their young by secreting milk. Whales, dolphins, porpoises, seals, sea lions, sea otters, manatees, dugongs (manatee relatives), polar bears, and walruses fall into this category.

In "Research Themes—Role of Marine Mammals in Marine Ecosystems" (2016, http://www.dfo-mpo.gc.ca/science/coe-cde/cemam/themes/ecosystem-eng.html), Fisheries and Oceans Canada notes that marine mammals play a crucial role in the oceanic food web, particularly in the predator-prey balance. Some species, such as killer whales and polar bears, are called apex predators, meaning they are at the top of their respective food chains and as healthy adults are not preyed on by any other animals (except humans). Killer whales and polar bears do prey on lesser marine mammals, including seals. These two apex predators and many other marine mammals consume massive amounts of fish, which often puts them into conflict with humans over the valuable food source. Some marine mammal species prey on aquatic invertebrates (animals lacking a backbone) such as shrimp, crabs, and krill. Whatever their position in the food web, marine mammals are important to their ecosystems. Fisheries and Oceans Canada explains, "In some cases marine mammals play a very clear role in structuring marine ecosystems. For example sea otter predation on sea urchins reduces grazing pressure, which allows the proliferation of kelp bed forests. This leads to the development of new ecosystems and an increase in marine fauna density and diversity."

For centuries, marine mammals of interest to humans for food, fur, or other commodities were hunted without restraint. As will be explained in this chapter, some species were driven to the brink of extinction by overhunting. Although modern restrictions and protections have largely eliminated that particular threat to marine mammals, much damage has already been done. In addition, new threats have arisen, including climate change due to global warming, entanglement of the animals in fishing gear and marine debris, and strikes from ships and boats in the world's busy waterways.

Marine mammals enjoy a relatively high level of public support and legal protection. During the 1960s the television show *Flipper* entertained U.S. audiences with stories about a highly intelligent and loveable dolphin that befriended and helped a family. Tourist attractions such as Marineland in Florida and SeaWorld in California began featuring acrobatic dolphins and whales in popular shows. The growing environmental movement seized on the public interest in marine mammals and lobbied for measures to protect animals that many people believed to be extremely smart and sociable.

At the time, purse-seine fishing was widely practiced by commercial tuna fishers in the eastern tropical Pacific Ocean. This fishing method involved the use of enormous nets, often hundreds of miles long, that were circled around schools of tuna. Many dolphins were inadvertently captured because they tend to mingle with fleets of tuna in that part of the ocean. Nontargeted animals that are captured during commercial fishing activities are called bycatch. Dolphin bycatch became a major public issue. Hauling in the enormous tuna-filled nets was a long process. As a result, the air-breathing dolphins were trapped for long periods underwater and often drowned. Public outcry over these killings and general concern for the welfare of marine mammals led Congress to pass the Marine Mammal Protection Act of 1972.

THE MARINE MAMMAL PROTECTION ACT

The Marine Mammal Protection Act (MMPA) was passed in 1972 and was substantially amended in 1994. The original act noted that "certain species and population stocks of marine mammals are, or may be, in danger of extinction or depletion as a result of man's activities." However, it was acknowledged that "inadequate" information was available concerning the population dynamics of the animals being protected.

The MMPA prohibits the taking (hunting, killing, capturing, and harassing) of marine mammals. The act also bars the importation of most marine mammals or their products. Exceptions are occasionally granted for scientific research, public display in aquariums, traditional subsistence hunting by Alaskan Natives, and some incidental capture during commercial fishing operations. The goal of the MMPA is to maintain marine populations at or above "optimum sustainable" levels.

Whales, dolphins, seals, and sea lions were put under the jurisdiction of the National Marine Fisheries Service (NMFS), an agency of the National Oceanic and Atmospheric Administration (NOAA) in the U.S. Department of Commerce. Polar bears, sea and marine otters, manatees, dugongs, and walruses were placed under the jurisdiction of the U.S. Fish and Wildlife Service (USFWS), an agency of the U.S. Department of the Interior.

The MMPA requires the NMFS and the USFWS to conduct periodic surveys to estimate populations and to predict population trends for marine mammals in three regions of U.S. waters: the Pacific Ocean coast (excluding Alaska), the Atlantic Ocean coast (including the Gulf of Mexico), and the Alaskan coast. The survey results are published in an annual *Stock Assessment Report* (*SAR*) by the NMFS (http://www.nmfs.noaa.gov/pr/sars/) and the USFWS (http://www.fws.gov/alaska/fisheries/mmm/reports.htm).

The MMPA was passed a year before the Endangered Species Act (ESA). The MMPA was driven largely by public affection for marine mammals, rather than by specific knowledge about impending species extinction. Eugene H. Buck and Harold F. Upton of the Congressional Research Service explain in *Fishery, Aquaculture, and Marine Mammal Issues in the 112th Congress* (November 4, 2011, http://www.fas.org/sgp/crs/misc/R41613.pdf) that "while some critics assert that the MMPA is scientifically irrational because it identifies one group of organisms for special protection unrelated to their abundance or ecological role, supporters note that the MMPA has accomplished much by way of promoting research and increased understanding of marine life as well as encouraging attention to incidental bycatch mortalities of marine life by commercial fishing and other maritime industries."

THE ENDANGERED SPECIES ACT

As shown in Table 2.1 in Chapter 2, the first list of native endangered species issued in 1967 included only three marine mammal species: the Caribbean monk seal,

the Guadalupe fur seal, and the Florida manatee (or Florida sea cow). Over the following decades additional marine mammals were added as information became available on their population status. As of February 2016, there were 19 species of marine mammals listed as endangered or threatened in the United States. (See Table 3.1.) In addition, there were 20 foreign species listed as endangered or threatened. (See Table 3.2.) As of February 2016, one marine mammal—the Caribbean monk seal—had been delisted under the ESA due to extinction. (See Table 1.2 in Chapter 1.) Two species— the gray whale (1994) and the eastern population of the Steller sea lion (2013)—have been delisted due to recovery, as explained later in this chapter.

In *Federal and State Endangered and Threatened Species Expenditures: Fiscal Year 2014* (March 2016, http://www.fws.gov/endangered/esa-library/pdf/20160302 _final_FY14_ExpRpt.pdf), the USFWS provides spending data under the ESA for fiscal year (FY) 2014. Table 3.3 shows the 10 marine mammals with the highest ESA spending during FY 2014.

As of February 2016, ESA-listed endangered and threatened marine mammals fell into six main categories: whales, dolphins and porpoises, seals and sea lions, sea otters, manatees and dugongs, and polar bears.

WHALES

Whales are in the order Cetacea (along with dolphins and porpoises). Cetaceans are marine mammals that live in the water all the time and have torpedo-shaped nearly hairless bodies. (See Figure 3.1.) There are approximately 70 known whale species. The so-called great whales are the largest animals on the earth. In general, the great whale species range in size from 30 to 100 feet (9.1 to 30.5 m) in length. There are 13 whale species normally considered to be great whales. The blue whale is the largest of these species.

Whales are found throughout the world's oceans; however, many species are concentrated in cold northern waters. Although they are warm-blooded and do not have fur, whales can survive in cold waters because they have a thick layer of dense fat and tissue known as blubber lying just beneath the skin. This blubber layer can be up to 1 foot (30.5 centimeters) thick in larger species.

Most whales have teeth and are in the suborder Odontoceti. By contrast, the handful of whales in the suborder Mysticeti filter their food through strong flexible plates called baleen. (See Figure 3.2.) Baleen is informally known as "whalebone." It is composed of a substance similar to human fingernails. Baleen whales strain large amounts of water to obtain their food, mostly zooplankton, tiny fish, and crustaceans. Nearly all the great whales are baleen whales.

TABLE 3.1

Endangered and threatened marine mammals, February 2016

Common name	Scientific name	Federal listing status*	U.S. or U.S./foreign listed	Listing note
Beluga whale	Delphinapterus leucas	E	US/foreign	Cook Inlet DPS
Blue whale	Balaenoptera musculus	E	US/foreign	Entire range
Bowhead whale	Balaena mysticetus	E	US/foreign	Entire range
False killer whale	Pseudorca crassidens	E	US/foreign	Main Hawaiian Islands Insular DPS
Finback whale	Balaenoptera physalus	E	US/foreign	Entire range
Guadalupe fur seal	Arctocephalus townsendi	T	US/foreign	Entire range
Hawaiian monk seal	Monachus schauinslandi	E	US	Entire range
Humpback whale	Megaptera novaeangliae	E	US/foreign	Entire range
Killer whale	Orcinus orca	E	US/foreign	Southern Resident DPS
North Atlantic right whale	Eubalaena glacialis	E	US/foreign	Entire range
North Pacific right whale	Eubalaena japonica	E	US/foreign	Entire range
Northern sea otter	Enhydra lutris kenyoni	T	US	Southwest Alaska, from Attu Island to Western Cook Inlet, including Bristol Bay, the Kodiak Archipelago, and the Barren Islands
Polar bear	Ursus maritimus	T	US/foreign	Entire range
Ringed seal	Phoca (=Pusa) hispida hispida	T	US	Arctic subspecies
Sei whale	Balaenoptera borealis	E	US/foreign	Entire range
Southern sea otter	Enhydra lutris nereis	T	US/foreign	Entire range
Sperm whale	Physeter catodon (=macrocephalus)	E	US/foreign	Entire range
Steller sea lion	Eumetopias jubatus	E	US/foreign	Western DPS
West Indian manatee	Trichechus manatus	E	US/foreign	Entire range

*T = Threatened. E = Endangered.
DPS = Distinct Population Segment.

SOURCE: Adapted from "Generate Species List," in *Environmental Conservation Online System Species Reports*, U.S. Department of the Interior, U.S. Fish and Wildlife Service, February 2016, http://ecos.fws.gov/tess_public/pub/adHocSpeciesForm.jsp (accessed February 17, 2016)

TABLE 3.2

Foreign endangered and threatened marine mammals, February 2016

Common name	Scientific name	Federal listing status*	Current distribution
Amazonian manatee	Trichechus inunguis	E	South America (Amazon River Basin)
Bearded seal (Okhotsk DPS)	Erignathus barbatus nauticus	T	Okhotsk Sea
Cameroon clawless otter	Aonyx congicus (=congica) microdon	E	Nigeria, Cameroon
Chinese river dolphin	Lipotes vexillifer	E	China
Cochito	Phocoena sinus	E	Mexico (Gulf of California)
Dugong	Dugong dugon	E	East Africa to southern Japan; Palua
Giant otter	Pteronura brasiliensis	E	South America
Gray whale (Western North Pacific DPS)	Eschrichtius robustus	E	North Pacific Ocean-coastal and Bering Sea, formerly North Atlantic Ocean; Western North Pacific Ocean only
Long-tailed otter	Lontra (=Lutra) longicaudis (incl. platensis)	E	South America
Marine otter	Lontra (=Lutra) felina	E	Peru south to Straits of Magellan
Mediterranean monk seal	Monachus monachus	E	Mediterranean, Northwest African Coast and Black Sea
Ringed seal (Baltic subspecies)	Phoca (=Pusa) hispida botnica	T	Baltic Sea
Ringed seal (Ladoga subspecies)	Phoca (=Pusa) hispida ladogensis	E	Russia (Lake Ladoga)
Ringed seal (Okhotsk subspecies)	Phoca (=Pusa) hispida ochotensis	T	Okhotsk Sea
Ringed seal (Saimaa subspecies)	Phoca hispida saimensis	E	Finland (Lake Saimaa)
South Asian river dolphin (Indus River subspecies)	Platanista gangetica minor	E	Pakistan (Indus River and tributaries)
Southern right whale	Eubalaena australis	E	Oceanic
Southern river otter	Lontra (=Lutra) provocax	E	Chile, Argentina
Spotted seal (Southern DPS)	Phoca largha	T	China and Russia
West African manatee	Trichechus senegalensis	T	West Coast of Africa from Senegal River to Cuanza River

*T = Threatened. E = Endangered.
DPS = Distinct Population Segment.

SOURCE: Adapted from "Generate Species List," in *Environmental Conservation Online System Species Reports*, U.S. Department of the Interior, U.S. Fish and Wildlife Service, February 2016, http://ecos.fws.gov/tess_public/pub/adHocSpeciesForm.jsp (accessed February 17, 2016)

Imperiled Whale Populations

As of February 2016, 11 whale species had been listed for protection under the ESA in U.S. waters: beluga whales, blue whales, bowhead whales, false killer whales, fin (or finback) whales, humpback whales, killer whales, North Atlantic right whales, North Pacific

TABLE 3.3

The 10 listed marine mammal species with the highest expenditures under the Endangered Species Act, fiscal year 2014

Ranking	Species	Population	Expenditure
1	Sea lion, steller (*Eumetopias jubatus*)	Western DPS	$30,472,348
2	Whale, North Atlantic right (*Eubalaena glacialis*)	Entire	$10,207,748
3	Seal, Hawaiian monk (*Monachus schauinslandi*)	Entire	$5,272,505
4	Manatee, West Indian (*Trichechus manatus*)	Entire	$4,948,295
5	Whale, humpback (*Megaptera novaeangliae*)	Entire	$4,745,649
6	Bear, polar (*Ursus maritimus*)	Entire	$3,761,287
7	Whale, blue (*Balaenoptera musculus*)	Entire	$2,560,771
8	Whale, killer (*Orcinus orca*)	Southern Resident DPS	$2,408,118
9	Whale, beluga (*Delphinapterus leucas*)	Cook Inlet DPS	$2,142,015
10	Whale, finback (*Balaenoptera physalus*)	Entire	$1,666,456

Note: DPS = Distinct Population Segment.

SOURCE: Adapted from "Table 2. Species Ranked in Descending Order of Total FY 2014 Reported Expenditures, Not Including Land Acquisition Costs," in *Federal and State Endangered and Threatened Species Expenditures: Fiscal Year 2014*, U.S. Department of the Interior, U.S. Fish and Wildlife Service, March 2, 2016, http://www.fws.gov/endangered/esa-library/pdf/20160302_final_FY14_ExpRpt.pdf (accessed March 9, 2016)

FIGURE 3.1

Humpback whales. ©*Jan Kratochvila/Shutterstock.com.*

right whales, sei whales, and sperm whales. (See Table 3.1.) Most of these species have baleen plates. In 1994 the NMFS delisted a stock of the gray whale due to recovery. (See Table 2.7 in Chapter 2.) According to the agency, in "Gray Whale (*Eschrichtius robustus*)" (May 13, 2013, http://www.nmfs.noaa.gov/pr/species/mammals/cetaceans/graywhale.htm), the species as a whole was first listed in 1970 under a precursor law to the ESA. In 1994 the eastern North Pacific (California) population was delisted because the whales "had recovered to near their estimated original population size."

FIGURE 3.2

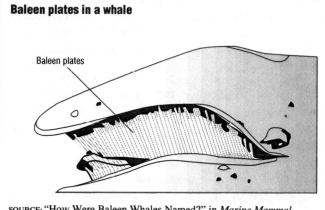

Baleen plates in a whale

Baleen plates

SOURCE: "How Were Baleen Whales Named?" in *Marine Mammal Education Web: Baleen Whales*, National Oceanic and Atmospheric Administration, Alaska Fisheries Science Center, National Marine Mammal Laboratory, undated, http://www.afsc.noaa.gov/nmml/education/cetaceans/baleen1.php (accessed February 9, 2016)

The right whale is the most endangered of the great whales. It was once the "right" whale to hunt because it swims slowly, prefers shallow coastal waters, and floats when it dies. According to the NMFS, in "North Atlantic Right Whales (*Eubalaena glacialis*)" (January 27, 2016, http://www.nmfs.noaa.gov/pr/species/mammals/cetaceans/rightwhale_northatlantic.htm), right whales first received international protection from whaling during the 1930s. In 1973 the right whale was listed as endangered under the ESA. Since then, three distinct species have been determined: the North Atlantic right whale (*E. glacialis*) and the North Pacific right whale (*E. japonica*) in the Northern Hemisphere and the southern right whale (*E. australis*) in the Southern Hemisphere. The NMFS reports that the North Atlantic right whale can be further subdivided into two geographical populations: western and eastern. The latter is believed to be "nearly extinct." The NMFS estimates its population in the "low tens of animals." The western North Atlantic right whale population includes an estimated 450 individuals and is considered "critically" endangered.

Threats to Whales

Whale populations are imperiled due to a long history of hunting by humans. As early as the eighth century humans hunted whales for meat and baleen. Whales were relatively easy for fishermen to catch because the animals spend a great deal of time at the surface of the ocean and provide a large target for harpoons. Advances in shipbuilding and the invention of the steam engine allowed fishermen greater access to whale populations, even those in Arctic areas that had previously been out of reach. By the 19th century large numbers of whales were being killed for blubber and baleen. Blubber was rendered to extract whale oil, which was used to light lamps. Baleen was valued for making fans, corsets, and other consumer goods.

On December 2, 1946, the representatives of 14 nations signed the International Convention for the Regulation of Whaling (http://iwc.int/convention), which formed the International Whaling Commission (IWC). The signatory nations were Argentina, Australia, Brazil, Canada, Chile, Denmark, France, the Netherlands, New Zealand, Peru, South Africa, the Soviet Union, the United Kingdom, and the United States. The IWC was formed as a means to regulate the industry and limit the number and type of whales that could be killed. The MMPA banned commercial whaling in U.S. waters.

Centuries of whaling severely depleted whale populations. Low birthrates and high mortality rates due to a variety of factors have prevented many species from recovering. Like other marine animals, whales are endangered by water pollution and loss or degradation of habitat. However, the NMFS notes that the biggest threats to the right whale and other imperiled whale species are entanglement in fishing gear and ship strikes. For example, Allison G. Henry et al. report in *Serious Injury Determinations for Baleen Whale Stocks along the Gulf of Mexico, United States East Coast and Atlantic Canadian Provinces, 2009–2013* (August 2015, http://nefsc.noaa.gov/publications/crd/crd1510/crd1510.pdf) on their investigation of the causes of death for 288 baleen whales known to have died in U.S. and Canadian waters between 2009 and 2013. The researchers indicate that for 215 of the animals the cause of death could not be determined with certainty. Another 14 whales were found to have died from causes other than vessel strike or entanglement, such as natural causes. The remaining whales died from human interactions: 30 from entanglement and 29 from ship strikes.

ENTANGLEMENT IN FISHING GEAR. In "What Kinds of Fishing Gear Most Often Entangle Right Whales?" (*Right Whale News*, vol. 12, no. 4, November 2005), the NMFS describes a study by researchers at Duke University that found that lobster pot gear, mostly buoy lines, were particularly problematic. It was concluded "that any line rising vertically in the water column poses a significant entanglement risk" to North Atlantic right whales.

The Woods Hole Oceanographic Institution (WHOI) indicates in the press release "Study Reveals How Fishing Gear Can Cause Slow Death of Whales" (May 21, 2013, https://www.whoi.edu/news-release/rightwhale_dtag) that approximately 75% of known North Atlantic right whales "bear scars of fishing lines that cut into their flesh." Whales that drag gear, particularly buoyant equipment, have trouble getting food and migrating. In addition, they expend large amounts of energy due to the extra weight they are pulling. Together, these problems can contribute to what the WHOI calls "slow death."

WHOI scientists participate in the Marine Mammal Health and Stranding Response Program, which includes the Atlantic Large Whale Entanglement Response Program. Under the latter program rescue teams approach whales entangled in gear, sedate the animals if necessary, and cut away the gear. For example, in 2010 the WHOI reports that aerial survey teams spotted an emaciated whale with gear tangled around its mouth and fins and trailing behind it. A rescue team sedated the animal and cut away almost all the gear. Data provided by a monitoring chip placed on the whale indicated it dived to much greater depths and for longer durations after the removal. In 2011, however, the whale was found dead. A necropsy (animal autopsy) revealed "that effects of the chronic entanglement were the cause of death."

In "Drag from Fishing Gear Entanglements Quantified" (December 9, 2015, http://www.whoi.edu/news-release/drag), the WHOI describes an investigation it sponsored in which researchers towed various kinds of fishing gear behind a boat to measure their drag forces (the forces opposing forward movement). The results were used to calculate the additional energy costs to whales that are encumbered by fishing gear, such as ropes, buoys, and crab and lobster traps. The WHOI notes, "Entangled whales can tow fishing gear for tens to hundreds of miles over months or even years, before either being freed, shedding the gear on their own, or succumbing to their injuries."

SHIP STRIKES. As noted earlier, Henry et al. find that 29 baleen whales died from ship strikes during the study period of 2009 through 2013. The actual number could be much higher because of the difficulties involved in detecting, confirming, and documenting the events.

The NMFS states in "Ship Strike Reduction" (2016, http://www.greateratlantic.fisheries.noaa.gov/protected/

shipstrike/) that "collision with vessels is the leading human-caused source of mortality for the endangered North Atlantic right whale." The animals are particularly vulnerable because they move rather slowly and spend a lot of time in coastal waters at or near the surface.

The Right Whale Sighting Advisory System (RWSAS) is a notification system operated by NOAA to reduce collisions between ships and right whales. Whale sightings and other detects are reported to the RWSAS and alerts are passed on to mariners in the area. In addition, there is an interactive RWSAS website (http://www.nefsc.noaa.gov/psb/surveys/) at which the public can access the survey data. As of April 2016, the database included 2,075 whale sightings reported in 2015. The largest number of sightings was associated with aerial whale search surveys. During calving season (from November through April) the NMFS performs aerial surveys and alerts ships about whales in their vicinity. In addition, federal law (http://www.greateratlantic.fisheries.noaa.gov/Protected/mmp/viewing/regs/) requires that ships remain 500 yards (457 m) from right whales. There are also routing requirements and speed limits for large vessels traveling in U.S. coastal waters that are frequented by right whales. Any sightings of dead, injured, or entangled whales must be reported to authorities.

Whale Recovery Plans

Table 3.4 provides information about 10 U.S. whale species listed as endangered under the ESA in U.S. waters as of February 2016. Recovery plans had been developed or were under development for almost all the listed whales. The populations of humpback and North Atlantic right whales were believed to be increasing,

TABLE 3.4

Status of endangered whale species, February 2016

Species/DPS	Date listed/ reclassified	ESA status	Trend	Recovery priority number	Status of recovery plan	Date 5-year status review completed*
Beluga whale—Cook Inlet DPS	10/22/2008	E	Decreasing	1	Under development	In progress
Blue whale	06/02/1970	E	Stable	7	Completed 7/1998; Notice to revise 4/2012	In progress
False killer whale—Main Hawaiian Islands Insular	11/28/2012	E	Unknown	3	Not started	N/A
Fin whale	06/02/1970	E	Unknown	9	Completed 7/2010	12/2011
Humpback whale	06/02/1970	E	Increasing	9	Completed 11/1991	03/2015
Killer whale—Southern resident DPS	11/18/2005	E	Decreasing	1	Completed 1/2008	03/2011
North Atlantic right whale	06/02/1970; 03/06/2008	E	Increasing	3	Completed 5/2005	09/2012
North Pacific right whale	06/02/1970; 03/06/2008	E	Unknown	3	Completed 6/2013	07/2012
Sei whale	06/02/1970	E	Unknown	11	Completed 12/2011	06/2012
Sperm whale	06/02/1970	E	Unknown	7	Completed 12/2010	01/2009; Review initiated 9/2014

*For species listed within 5 years, N/A (not applicable) is applied to the 5-year review status.
DPS = Distinct Population Segment. E = Endangered. ESA = Endangered Species Act. NMFS = National Marine Fisheries Service.

SOURCE: Adapted from "Table 1. ESA-Listed Species under NMFS Jurisdiction," in *Species in the Spotlight: Survive to Thrive: Recovering Threatened and Endangered Species FY 2013–2014 Report to Congress*, U.S. Department of Commerce, National Oceanic and Atmospheric Administration, National Marine Fisheries Service, May 2015, http://www.nmfs.noaa.gov/pr/laws/esa/final_biennial_report_2012-2014.pdf (accessed February 19, 2016)

whereas the populations of beluga whale (Cook Inlet distinct population segment [DPS]) and killer whale (southern resident DPS) were believed to be decreasing. The blue whale population was believed stable. Information was inadequate to determine population trends for the other whale species.

Table 3.4 also shows the recovery priority numbers assigned by the NMFS to each endangered whale species. Priority numbers can range from a value of 1 (highest priority) to 12 (lowest priority). The beluga and killer whale DPSs had a priority level of 1, indicating strong concern about their abundance and chances for survival as a species.

Imperiled Whales around the World

The International Union for Conservation of Nature (IUCN) indicates in *Red List of Threatened Species Version 2015.4* (http://www.iucnredlist.org/about/summary-statistics) that as of late 2015 the following whale species were threatened:

- Antarctic blue whale

- Blue whale

- North Atlantic right whale

- North Pacific right whale

- Sperm whale

- Fin whale

- Sei whale

The IUCN notes that it lacked sufficient data to determine the status of more than two dozen other whale species.

The southern right whale and one DPS of the gray whale were listed under the ESA as foreign endangered species as of February 2016. (See Table 3.2.)

INTERNATIONAL WHALING CONTROVERSIES. As noted earlier, the IWC was formed in 1946 to regulate the commercial whaling industry and limit the number and type of whales that can be killed. In 1986 the IWC banned commercial whaling after most whale populations were placed under Appendix I of the Convention on International Trade in Endangered Species of Wild Fauna and Flora (CITES) agreement. In 1991 Iceland dropped out of the IWC over the commercial whaling ban. It rejoined in 2002, but as of April 2016 it refused to abide by the ban. Norway also does not adhere to the ban. Commercial whalers and some scientists argue that some whale species are not imperiled and thus can be hunted, assuming that reasonable catch limits are employed.

The IWC (http://iwc.int/members.htm) indicates that as of 2016 it had 89 member nations. The commission allows whaling for "subsistence" purposes by native peoples, for example, Alaskan Eskimos. It also allows whaling for "scientific purposes." Conservation and wildlife groups have complained for decades that some IWC member countries, particularly Japan, kill many whales under this loophole and sell the meat commercially. In addition, Iceland and Norway openly hunt whales for commercial purposes and sell the meat primarily in Japanese markets.

DOLPHINS AND PORPOISES

Dolphins and porpoises are toothed cetaceans. They are similar in shape; however, dolphins are generally larger than porpoises and prefer shallower, warmer waters. Dolphins tend to have long bottlenoses and cone-shaped teeth, whereas porpoises have flatter noses and teeth. As of April 2016, there were no U.S. species of dolphins or porpoises listed under the ESA.

Imperiled Foreign Dolphins and Porpoises

Most dolphin and porpoise populations around the world are hardy and not in danger of extinction. However, there are several species that are in trouble due to limited geographical distribution. According to the IUCN, in *Red List of Threatened Species Version 2015.4*, 16 dolphin and porpoise species were considered threatened in 2016. The most imperiled (those with a critically endangered rating) were the baiji (also known as the Chinese river dolphin), the cochito (or vaquita, which is found in Mexico), the North Island Hector's dolphin (which is found in New Zealand), and the Yangtze finless porpoise (which is found in China). The Chinese river dolphin and cochito, along with the Indus River dolphin of Pakistan, were on the ESA list of foreign species as of February 2016. (See Table 3.2.)

SEALS AND SEA LIONS

Seals and sea lions are considered pinnipeds. This designation comes from the Latin word *pinnipedia*, which means "feather or fin foot." Pinnipeds have finlike flippers. Although they spend most of their time in the ocean, pinnipeds come on shore to rest, breed, give birth, and nurse their young. Areas preferred for breeding, birthing, and nursing are called rookeries. Pinnipeds not yet of reproductive age congregate at shore areas known as haul-outs.

Seals and sea lions were hunted extensively through the early 1900s for their blubber, fur, and meat. They continue to be imperiled by human encroachment of haul-out beaches, entanglement in marine debris and fishing nets, incidental catches, disease, and lack of food due to competition from humans for prey species.

Imperiled Seal and Sea Lion Populations

As of February 2016, there were four U.S. species of seals and sea lions listed under the ESA. (See Table 3.1.) Another U.S. species, the Caribbean monk seal, was formerly listed, but is now believed to be extinct. It was officially delisted in 2008. (See Table 1.2 in Chapter 1.) The species that were listed were as follows:

- Guadalupe fur seal—found in U.S. and Mexican waters west of Baja, California. (See Figure 3.3.) It was on the first list of endangered species published in 1967. (See Table 2.1 in Chapter 2.) According to the NMFS, in "Guadalupe Fur Seal (*Arctocephalus townsendi*)" (January 15, 2015, http://www.fisheries .noaa.gov/pr/species/mammals/seals/guadalupe-fur-seal .html), the species was heavily hunted during the 1700s and 1800s and is imperiled by fishing gear entanglement. The agency notes that the species "is slowly recovering from the brink of extinction."

- Hawaiian monk seal—native to the waters around Hawaii and found only there. In "Hawaiian Monk Seal (*Neomonachus schauinslandi*)" (February 10, 2016, http://www.fisheries.noaa.gov/pr/species/mammals/ seals/hawaiian-monk-seal.html), the NMFS notes that the species is "one of the rarest marine mammals in the world." It was hunted almost to extinction during the 1800s. Between 2003 and 2012 its population declined at about 3.3% annually, as shown in Figure 3.4. The species is imperiled due to low genetic diversity, food limitations, and a host of human-related causes, including entanglement in marine debris and bycatch in fishing gear.

- Ringed seal—the Arctic subspecies (*Phoca hispida hispida*) is found in U.S. waters around Alaska. According to the NMFS, in "Ringed Seal (*Phoca hispida*)" (March 23, 2016, http://www.nmfs.noaa .gov/pr/species/mammals/seals/ringed-seal.html), the subspecies numbers more than 300,000 individuals. Like other Arctic pinnipeds, the ringed seal is dependent on sea ice for habitat. Global warming is considered the primary threat to its existence, but bycatch in fishing gear is also a problem.

- Steller sea lion—there are two DPSs within U.S. waters along the West Coast and around Alaska and the Aleutian Islands. (See Figure 3.5.) In "Steller Sea Lion (*Eumetopias jubatus*)" (January 15, 2015, http:// www.fisheries.noaa.gov/pr/species/mammals/sealions/ steller-sea-lion.html), the NMFS indicates that the entire species was classified as threatened when it was first listed in 1990. By then, historic stocks had been depleted by hunting and intentional killing by fisherman due to competition for food fish. In 1997 the western DPS was uplisted to endangered, a listing it maintained in 2016. By contrast, the eastern DPS was delisted in 2013 due to recovery. Continuing

FIGURE 3.3

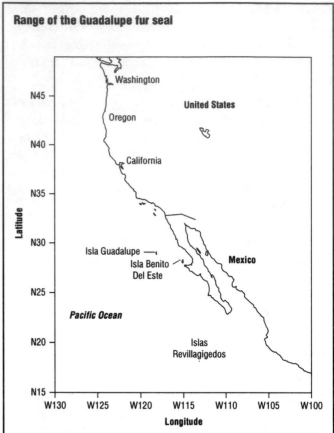

Range of the Guadalupe fur seal

SOURCE: James V. Carretta et al., "Figure 1. Geographic Range of the Guadalupe Fur Seal, Showing Location of Two Rookeries at Isla Guadalupe and Isla Benito Del Este," in *U.S. Pacific Marine Mammal Stock Assessments: 2014*, U.S. Department of Commerce, National Oceanic and Atmospheric Administration, National Marine Fisheries Service, August 2015, http://www.nmfs.noaa.gov/pr/sars/pdf/pacific_ sars_2014_final_noaa_swfsc_tm_549.pdf (accessed February 19, 2016)

threats to the Steller sea lion include fishing impacts (such as entanglement), boat and ship strikes, pollution and habitat degradation, offshore oil and gas exploration, and poaching (illegal hunting). During FY 2014 species-specific expenditures under the ESA for the western DPS of Steller sea lions totaled $30.5 million. (See Table 3.3.)

Imperiled Foreign Seals and Sea Lions

According to the IUCN, in *Red List of Threatened Species Version 2015.4*, 11 seal and sea lion species were considered threatened in 2016. Nearly all of them had decreasing population trends. As of February 2016, seven exclusively foreign seal species or DPSs were listed under the ESA. (See Table 3.2.)

SEA OTTERS

Sea otters are the smallest marine mammals in North America. They are furry creatures that grow to be about 4 feet (1.2 m) in length and weigh up to 65 pounds (30 kg). Otters are related to weasels and mink and are members

FIGURE 3.4

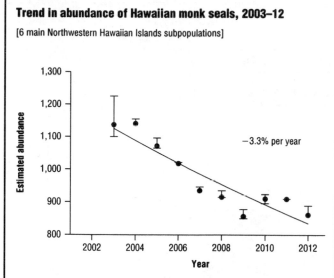

Trend in abundance of Hawaiian monk seals, 2003–12

[6 main Northwestern Hawaiian Islands subpopulations]

−3.3% per year

SOURCE: James V. Carretta et al., "Figure 1. Geographic Range of California Sea Lions Showing Stock Boundaries and Locations of Major Rookeries," in *U.S. Pacific Marine Mammal Stock Assessments: 2014*, U.S. Department of Commerce, National Oceanic and Atmospheric Administration, National Marine Fisheries Service, August 2015, http://www.nmfs.noaa.gov/pr/sars/pdf/pacific_sars_2014_final_noaa_swfsc_tm_549.pdf (accessed February 19, 2016)

of the Mustelidae family. Sea otters are almost entirely aquatic and inhabit relatively shallow waters along the rocky coasts of the North Pacific Ocean. They eat a wide variety of marine invertebrates. They use rocks and other objects to smash open the hard shells of clams and crabs to get the meat inside.

Although they inhabit cold waters, sea otters do not have a blubber layer to keep them warm. Instead, they have extremely dense fur coats and high metabolism rates. Their fur coats are waterproof, but only if kept clean. This makes sea otters susceptible to water contaminants, such as oil.

Imperiled Otter Populations

At one time sea otters were populous along the entire U.S. West Coast from Southern California to Alaska. Their thick and lustrous fur, however, made them a target of intensive hunting for many centuries. By the dawn of the 20th century sea otters were on the brink of extinction. In 1911 they became protected under the International Fur Seal Treaty, and their numbers began to increase.

Biologists recognize two distinct populations: the northern sea otter and the southern sea otter. The northern sea otter extends from Russia across the Aleutian Islands and the coast of Alaska south to the state of Washington. As shown in Figure 3.6, there are three stocks: Southwest Alaska, Southcentral Alaska, and Southeast Alaska. Only the Southwest Alaska stock is listed under the ESA. (See Table 3.1.) It had a listing of threatened as of February

2016. The southern sea otter is found only off the California coast, as shown in Figure 3.7. It was also listed as threatened under the ESA. (See Table 3.1.)

NORTHERN SEA OTTERS. As of February 2016, the most recently published *SAR* for northern sea otters was a draft report dated April 2013. The USFWS indicates in *Draft Revised Northern Sea Otter (*Enhydra lutris kenyoni*): Southwest Alaska Stock* (http://www.fws.gov/alaska/fisheries/mmm/seaotters/pdf/Draft%20Southwest%20Alaska%20Sea%20Otter%20April%202013.For%20Surname.pdf) that the southwestern stock includes nearly 55,000 individuals. Although this number has increased slightly in recent years, the long-term trend is negative, as this stock has declined by more than 50% since the 1980s. The USFWS notes that "there is no evidence of recovery"; however, the overall population trend appears to have stabilized.

The causes of the huge population decline since the 1980s are hotly debated by scientists. In *Southwest Alaska Distinct Population Segment of the Northern Sea Otter (*Enhydra lutris kenyoni*) Recovery Plan* (July 2013, http://ecos.fws.gov/docs/recovery_plan/Recovery%20Plan%20SW%20AK%20DPS%20Sea%20Otter%20Aug13.pdf), the USFWS fingers predation by killer whales as the main cause. The agency rates this threat of moderate to high importance to the future recovery of the southwestern stock. Numerous other threats of low to moderate importance are also named, including oil spills, subsistence harvest (harvest by Alaska's native peoples), infectious disease, and poaching.

SOUTHERN SEA OTTERS. Southern (or California) sea otters were designated as a threatened species in 1977. (See Figure 3.8.) At that time, the animals inhabited a small stretch of coastline in central California. Scientists feared that this isolated population was in grave danger of being wiped out by a single catastrophe, such as an oil spill. In 1987 the USFWS decided to establish an "experimental population" of sea otters at another location. Over the next few years more than 100 sea otters were moved, a few at a time, to San Nicolas Island. (See Figure 3.9.) It was hoped that these translocated animals would thrive and develop an independent growing colony. The venture, however, achieved only limited success. Many of the otters swam back to their original habitat; others died, apparently from the stress of moving. During the early 1990s the transport effort was abandoned. In December 2012 the USFWS (http://www.fws.gov/Ventura/docs/frnotices/77%20FR%2075266.pdf) officially ended the program. The agency indicates that the program resulted in a small colony of approximately 50 otters at the island, but "its ability to become established and persist is uncertain."

The USFWS states in *Final Revised Recovery Plan for the Southern Sea Otter (*Enhydra lutis nereis*)* (February 24, 2003, http://ecos.fws.gov/docs/recovery_plans/

FIGURE 3.5

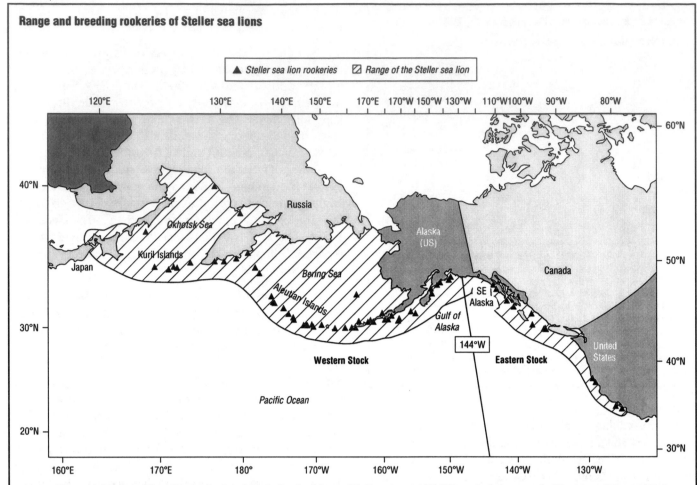

Range and breeding rookeries of Steller sea lions

SOURCE: "Figure 1. Range and Breeding Rookeries of the Steller Sea Lion and Delineation at 144° W Longitude between the Western and Eastern Distinct Population Segments," in *Status Review of the Eastern Distinct Population Segment of Steller Sea Lion (Eumetopias jubatus)*, U.S. Department of Commerce, National Oceanic and Atmospheric Administration, National Marine Fisheries Service, Alaska Region, 2013, https://alaskafisheries.noaa.gov/sites/default/files/statusreview071813.pdf (accessed February 19, 2016)

2003/030403.pdf) that the primary recovery objective is to manage human activities that can damage or destroy habitat. Specifically, the agency sets a goal to "protect the population and reduce or eliminate the identified potential limiting factors related to human activities, including: managing petroleum exploration, extraction, and tankering to reduce the likelihood of a spill along the California coast to insignificant levels; minimizing contaminant loading and infectious disease; and managing fishery interactions to reduce sea otter mortality incidental to commercial fishing to insignificant levels." The USFWS indicates that southern sea otters can be considered for delisting under the ESA when the average population level over a three-year period exceeds 3,090 animals.

The U.S. Geological Survey conducts annual surveys for southern sea otters during the springtime counting both independent otters and pups in mainland waters and at San Nicolas Island. According to the USFWS, in *Featured Story: Slowly Swimming towards Recovery, California's*

Sea Otter Numbers Holding Steady (September 22, 2014, http://www.fws.gov/ventura/newsroom/release.cfm?item=309), the mainland population has generally increased since the early 1990s, reaching more than 2,700 individuals (a three-year average) in 2014. In addition, more than 60 otters were counted at San Nicolas Island in 2014. Absent any catastrophic events, the southern sea otter could achieve delisting within the next decade.

Foreign Species of Otters

According to the IUCN, in *Red List of Threatened Species Version 2015.4*, two sea otter species—the marine otter (*Lontra felina*) and the sea otter (*Enhydra lutris*)—were considered threatened in 2016. Two other otter species that are not truly sea-dwelling, but typically inhabit coastal areas, are also considered threatened.

As of February 2016, five foreign otter species were listed as endangered under the ESA. (See Table 3.2.) They populate areas of Africa and South America.

FIGURE 3.6

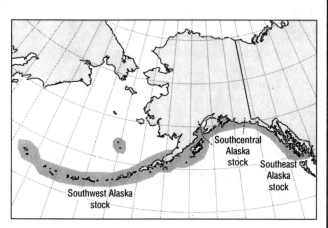

Approximate distribution of northern sea otters in Alaska waters

SOURCE: B. M. Allen and R. P. Angliss, "Figure 1. Approximate Distribution of Northern Sea Otters in Alaska Waters (Shaded Area)," in *Alaska Marine Mammal Stock Assessments, 2012*, U.S. Department of Commerce, National Oceanic and Atmospheric Administration, National Marine Fisheries Service, Alaska Fisheries Science Center, March 2013, http://www.nmfs.noaa.gov/pr/sars/pdf/ak2012.pdf (accessed February 9, 2016)

FIGURE 3.7

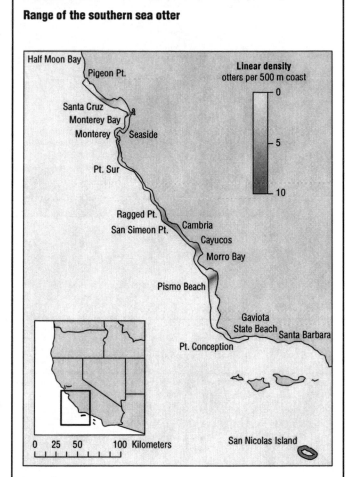

Range of the southern sea otter

m = meters.

SOURCE: James V. Carretta et al., "Figure 1. Current Range of the Southern Sea Otter (2013 Census)," in *U.S. Pacific Marine Mammal Stock Assessments: 2014*, U.S. Department of Commerce, National Oceanic and Atmospheric Administration, National Marine Fisheries Service, August 2015, http://www.nmfs.noaa.gov/pr/sars/pdf/pacific_sars_2014_final_noaa_swfsc_tm_549.pdf (accessed February 19, 2016)

MANATEES AND DUGONGS

Manatees are large stout mammals that inhabit freshwaters and coastal waterways. (See Figure 3.10.) They are from the Sirenian order, along with dugongs. There are only five Sirenian species, and all are endangered or extinct. Scientists believe Steller's sea cow, the only species of cold-water manatee, was hunted to extinction during the 1700s.

The West Indian manatee, also known as the Florida manatee, primarily swims in the rivers, bays, and estuaries of Florida and surrounding states. As of February 2016, this species was listed as endangered under the ESA. (See Table 3.1.)

Manatees are often called sea cows and can weigh up to 2,000 pounds (900 kg). They swim just below the surface of the water and feed on vegetation. West Indian manatees migrate north during the summer, though generally no farther than the North Carolina coast. During the winter many manatees huddle around warm-water discharges from power plants and other industrial facilities. Although this can keep them warm, scientists worry that overcrowding in small areas makes the animals more susceptible to sickness.

Imperiled Manatee Populations

In most years biologists conduct surveys during cold weather to determine the number of Florida manatees remaining in the wild. The Florida Fish and Wildlife Research Institute explains in "Population Monitoring" (2016, http://myfwc.com/research/manatee/projects/population-monitoring/) that surveys were not conducted in 2008, 2012, and 2013 due to "warmer than average weather." The survey results are estimates based on surveys conducted at known wintering habitats. According to the Florida Fish and Wildlife Research Institute, in "Manatee Synoptic Surveys" (2016, http://myfwc.com/research/manatee/research/population-monitoring/synoptic-surveys/), the February 2016 survey found 6,250 manatees living along the Florida coast. This number compares with 1,267 reported in 1991 (the first year of the survey) and 5,077 reported in 2010.

Many manatees have scars on their backs from motorboat propellers. In fact, motorboat strikes are the major documented cause of manatee mortalities. Manatees are large and swim slowly at the surface of the water.

FIGURE 3.8

Southern sea otter. ©*U.S. Fish and Wildlife Service.*

They often cannot move away from boats quickly enough to avoid being hit. As a result, several Florida waterways have been declared boat-free zones to protect manatees from boat collisions. There are also areas where boaters are required to lower their speed.

Other threats to manatee survival include disease, natural pathogens, and cold-water temperatures. Although the animals can live up to 50 to 60 years, they have naturally low birthrates, which makes it difficult for their population to rebound.

Regulating Water Activities

The Florida manatee was on the first list of endangered species published in 1967. (See Table 2.1 in Chapter 2.) According to the USFWS (August 26, 2011, http://

FIGURE 3.9

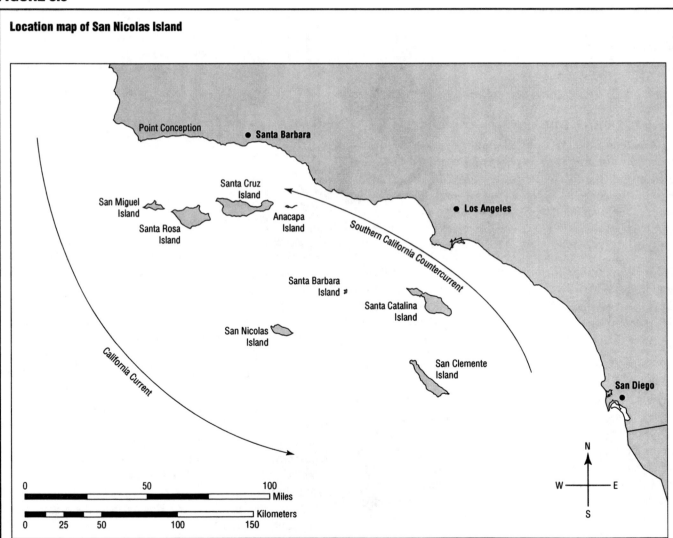

Location map of San Nicolas Island

SOURCE: "Figure 4-1. Main Surface Currents of the Southern California Bight," in *Final Supplemental Environmental Impact Statement: Translocation of Southern Sea Otters*, vol. 1, U.S. Department of the Interior, U.S. Fish and Wildlife Service, November 2012, http://www.fws.gov/ventura/docs/species/sso/fseis/Final%20Supplemental%20EIS%20on%20the%20Translocation%20of%20Southern%20Sea%20Otters%20-%20Volume%201.pdf (accessed February 9, 2016)

FIGURE 3.10

West Indian manatee (Florida manatee). ©*Kipling Brock/Shutterstock.com.*

www.fws.gov/northflorida/Manatee/Documents/MPA Rules/June11_KB_Proposed_Rule/20110621_frn_Federal _Register_Notice_for_Proposed_Kings_Bay_Manatee _Rule.html), in 1979 the agency "adopted a regulatory process to provide a means for establishing manatee protection areas in waters under the jurisdiction of the United States where manatees were taken by waterborne activities." The regulatory process is codified at 50 Code of Federal Regulations (http://www.ecfr.gov/cgi-bin/text-idx?tpl=/ ecfrbrowse/Title50/50tab_02.tpl), part 17, subpart J.

As noted earlier, the MMPA and the ESA prohibit taking of marine mammals and listed species, respectively. Between 1980 and 1998 the USFWS designated seven manatee protection areas in and around Crystal River/Kings Bay on the western coast of Florida. The bay is fed by warm spring waters and is a major manatee habitat, both during cold and warm weather. However, the bay is also used for commercial boating and is a popular recreation area that features an active "manatee viewing industry." As a result, the USFWS reports that the bay has suffered increasing problems with manatee harassment and fatal boat strikes.

In 2000 a coalition of 18 environmental and wildlife groups and three individuals sued the USFWS and the state of Florida over manatee protection measures. In 2001 a settlement with the federal government was reached in *Save the Manatee Club v. Ballard.* According to the USFWS, in the press release "Settlement Reached in Manatee Lawsuit" (January 4, 2001, http://www.fws.gov/ southeast/news/2001/r01-001.html), the agency agreed to a timetable for completing the following actions:

- Designate additional manatee protection areas

- Revise the manatee recovery plan

- Develop regulations allowing manatee taking under the MMPA

- Coordinate with the U.S. Army Corps of Engineers to improve procedures for reviewing permit applications for the construction of boating facilities in manatee habitat and improve the related consultation process required under the ESA

As of February 2016, the USFWS (http://www.fws .gov/northflorida/Manatee/Documents/MPARules/index-federal-mpa-maps.htm) had established 19 manatee protection areas (five sanctuaries and 14 refuges) in 12 counties along the central western coast of Florida. In addition, the Florida Fish and Wildlife Conservation Commission (2016, http://myfwc.com/wildlifehabitats/managed/manatee/ protection-zones/) had designated dozens of "manatee protection zones" with specific watercraft speed limit restrictions.

Foreign Manatee and Dugong Species

According to the IUCN, in *Red List of Threatened Species Version 2015.4,* the dugong, the South American manatee (also known as the Amazonian manatee), the West Indian manatee, and the West African manatee—the only remaining dugong and manatee species—were considered threatened in 2016.

As of February 2016, the species found in western Africa and in and around the Amazon River in South America were listed under the ESA and were in grave danger of extinction due to illegal hunting, deforestation, habitat destruction, and water pollution. (See Table 3.2.) The only remaining dugongs live in the coastal waters of the Indian Ocean and the Pacific Ocean. Their populations are also considered imperiled. Dugongs around East Africa to southern Japan and around the tiny island of Palau in the western Pacific Ocean were listed as endangered under the ESA.

POLAR BEARS

Polar bears are the largest of the bear species. They are believed to have evolved from grizzly bears hundreds of thousands of years ago. Polar bears have stocky bodies and can weigh up to 1,400 pounds (635 kg) when fully grown. They are relatively long lived and have small litters, typically only a cub or two per litter. Their fur includes water-repellent guard hairs and a dense undercoat that is white to pale yellow in color. They have large paddle-like paws that help make them excellent swimmers.

Polar bears are considered a marine mammal because sea ice is their primary habitat. They are found throughout the Arctic and near-Arctic regions of the Northern Hemisphere. The bears prefer coastal sea ice and other areas in which water conditions are conducive to providing prey. Seals are their primary food source, particularly ringed seals. As described earlier, the Arctic subspecies of the ringed seal was listed under the ESA with a status of threatened as of February 2016. (See Table 3.1.)

The USFWS notes in the fact sheet "Polar Bear: Threatened under Endangered Species Act" (November 2014, http://www.fws.gov/alaska/fisheries/endangered/pdf/polarbear_factsheet_v2.pdf) that there are 20,000 to 25,000 bears worldwide. There are two stocks of polar bears in the United States; both are in and around Alaska: the southern Beaufort Sea stock and the Chukchi/Bering Sea stock. (See Figure 3.11.) There is extensive overlap between the two stocks. According to the USFWS, in *Polar Bear (Ursus maritimus): Southern Beaufort Sea Stock* (January 1, 2010, http://alaska.fws.gov/fisheries/mmm/stock/final_sbs_polar_bear_sar.pdf), scientists estimate that the southern Beaufort population consists of approximately 1,500 individuals. The bears are found mostly in areas that have at least 50% ice cover.

The USFWS notes that after passage of the MMPA in 1972 the populations of both stocks increased, due to hunting restrictions. Nevertheless, the southern Beaufort Sea population showed "little or no growth" during the 1990s and declined by approximately 3% per year between 2001 and 2005. Reduced sea ice, particularly during the summer and fall, is believed to be a factor in the decline.

In *Polar Bear (Ursus maritimus): Chukchi/Bering Seas Stock* (January 1, 2010, http://alaska.fws.gov/fisheries/mmm/stock/final_cbs_polar_bear_sar.pdf), the USFWS indicates that the Chukchi/Bering Sea stock population is roughly estimated at 2,000 bears. However, the number is uncertain due to logistical challenges (e.g., the vast and difficult terrain) and the passage of the animals into Russian territory. The USFWS notes that this stock faces "different stressors" than those affecting the southern Beaufort Sea stock. In particular, the Chukchi/Bering Sea stock endures "increased harvest in Russia" and a greater loss of sea ice during the summer. The population of the stock is believed to be declining.

Listing Controversy

In 2005 the USFWS was petitioned by the Center for Biological Diversity (later joined by the Natural Resources Defense Council and Greenpeace) to list the polar bear as threatened throughout its range. Due to a heavy workload, the agency failed to issue a 90-day finding to the petition. The organizations sued, and in February 2006 the agency issued its 90-day finding, noting that there was sufficient scientific information to warrant the listing. In January 2007 the polar bear was officially proposed for listing as a threatened species.

Following a legal challenge, the USFWS was forced to make a decision by May 15, 2008. On that date the agency officially listed the polar bear as threatened. The USFWS also issued a "special rule" under section 4(d) of the ESA adopting the existing conservation regulatory requirements for polar bears under the MMPA and the CITES agreement. In other words, activities already authorized in these regulations would take precedence over the general prohibitions under U.S. law that apply to threatened species. Such activities include take, import and export, and shipment in interstate or foreign commerce for commercial purposes.

The USFWS notes in "Endangered and Threatened Wildlife and Plants; 12-Month Petition Finding and Proposed Rule to List the Polar Bear (*Ursus maritimus*) as Threatened throughout Its Range" (*Federal Register*, vol. 72, no. 5, January 9, 2007) that melting and thinning sea ice have already stressed polar bear populations. Computer models indicate these conditions are expected to worsen in the future as temperatures continue to warm. Polar bears have evolved to move on ice. They have special suckers on their paws to help them walk on the ice. They are poorly suited to walking on ground and expend a great deal of energy when they are forced to do so because of a lack of sea ice. In addition, warmer temperatures are degrading the snowy birthing dens of ringed seals, the major prey of the polar bears, and endangering seal pup survival. Thus, both populations face problems due to the warming of their icy ecosystems.

Following the USFWS listing of the polar bear in 2008, the state of Alaska sued the USFWS arguing that the listing was not justified. The article "Alaska Sues to Overturn Polar Bear Protection" (WashingtonPost.com, November 16, 2009) explains that Alaska feared the listing would threaten oil development in the state, particularly of offshore reserves. In June 2011 a federal judge rejected the suit and ruled that the USFWS followed proper procedures in listing the polar bear.

Environmentalists hoped the listing status granted to polar bears under the ESA would facilitate legal restrictions on oil and gas exploration in Alaska and on U.S. emissions of carbon dioxide (a suspected cause of global warming). However, the 4(d) rule issued for the polar bear specifically noted that the incidental take of the species due to oil and gas exploration is already allowed under regulations of the MMPA. In addition, the administration of President Barack Obama (1961–) decided not

FIGURE 3.11

Map of polar bear stocks near Alaska

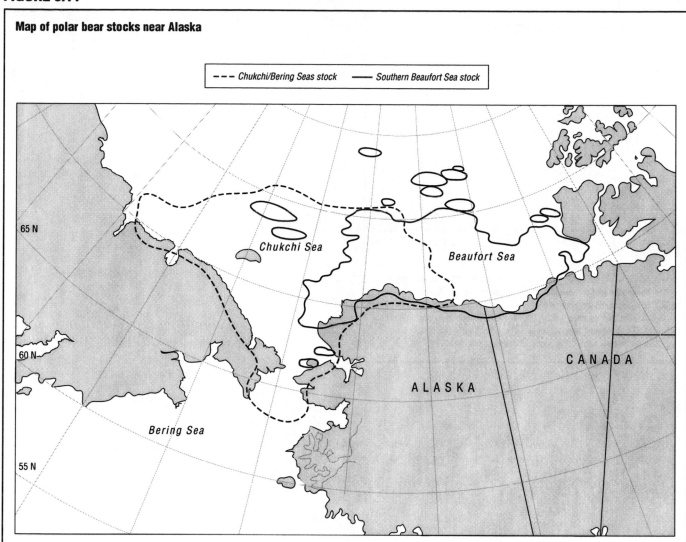

– – – Chukchi/Bering Seas stock   —— Southern Beaufort Sea stock

SOURCE: B. M. Allen and R. P. Angliss, "Figure 1. Map of the Southern Beaufort Sea and the Chukchi/Bering Seas Polar Bear Stocks," in *Alaska Marine Mammal Stock Assessments, 2009*, U.S. Department of Commerce, National Oceanic and Atmospheric Administration, National Marine Fisheries Service, Alaska Fisheries Science Center, rev. January 2010, http://www.nmfs.noaa.gov/pr/pdfs/sars/fws2009_polarbear-chbe.pdf (accessed February 9, 2016)

to use the ESA listing as a mechanism for restricting carbon dioxide emissions. Instead, those efforts have focused on legislation dealing with air pollution.

ARCTIC SEA ICE DECLINES. The National Snow and Ice Data Center (NSIDC) in Boulder, Colorado, monitors ice coverage in the Arctic Sea. As shown in Figure 3.12, the average areal extent of Arctic sea ice declined dramatically between the late 1970s and 2012 due to the effects of global warming and climate change.

The NSIDC website (http://nsidc.org/arcticseaicenews/charctic-interactive-sea-ice-graph/) includes an interactive chart that shows Arctic Sea ice extent, which it defines as the area of the ocean with at least 15% sea ice. The ice extent varies seasonally throughout the year peaking around March and declining to its lowest level around

September. According to the NSIDC, the average minimum ice extent between 1981 and 2010 was 2.4 million square miles (6.3 million square km). In 2012 the ice extent reached a new record low of 1.4 million square miles (3.6 million square km). In 2015 the minimum was higher at 1.8 million square miles (4.6 million square km), but still below the historical average minimum.

Scientists worry that continued global warming will further diminish the ice extent and seriously stress polar bear populations. In "Polar Bears: Time to Prepare for the Worst" (Discovery.com, February 8, 2013), Kieran Mulvaney describes the findings of various studies showing the negative effects of a smaller ice extent, such as polar bears are increasingly suffering from malnourishment and having to expend more energy to swim greater distances between ice floes.

FIGURE 3.12

Summer Arctic sea ice extent, 1979–2012

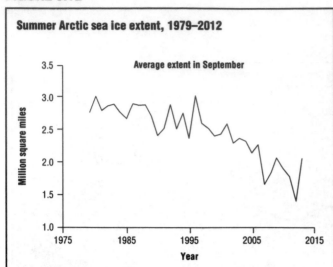

SOURCE: Adapted from J. D. Walsh et al., "Figure 2.28. Summer Arctic sea ice has declined dramatically since satellites began measuring it in 1979," in *Climate Change Impacts in the United States*, U.S. Global Change Research Program, 2014, http://s3.amazonaws.com/nca2014/high/NCA3_Climate_Change_Impacts_in_the_United%20States_HighRes.pdf?download=1 (accessed February 19, 2016)

CHAPTER 4
FISH

Fish are cold-blooded vertebrates with fins. They occur in nearly all permanent water environments, from deep oceans to remote alpine lakes and desert springs. Marine fish inhabit the salty waters of oceans and seas, whereas freshwater fish inhabit inland rivers, lakes, and ponds. Some fish species migrate between fresh- and marine waters. These include species called anadromous fish that are born in freshwater, migrate to the ocean to spend their adulthood, and then return to freshwater to spawn.

Fish are the most diverse vertebrate group on the planet and include thousands of different species. The largest known fish are the whale sharks, which can grow to be more than 50 feet (15.2 m) long and weigh several tons. At the other end of the spectrum is *Paedocypris progenetica*, a tiny fish discovered in Sumatra, Indonesia, that is less than 0.3 of an inch (0.8 cm) in length.

FishBase (http://www.fishbase.org/search.php) is a comprehensive online database of scientific information about fish. It was developed by the WorldFish Center of Malaysia in collaboration with the United Nations Food and Agriculture Organization and is supported by many government and research institutions. As of April 2016, FishBase contained information on 33,200 fish species around the world. Scientists report that only a small fraction of these species have been assessed for their conservation status.

Historically, imperiled fish species have drawn far less public attention than other species, such as marine mammals. The disappearance of large food fish species does garner concern because of their commercial importance to humans. Every fish species, however, plays some role in its respective ecosystem and food web. The U.S. Fish and Wildlife Service (USFWS) makes this point in "The Pallid Sturgeon, a Missouri River 'Dinosaur'" (2016, http://www.fws.gov/mountain-prairie/feature/sturgeon.html), which discusses the pallid sturgeon, an endangered species once

common to midwestern rivers. The agency notes, "Species interact in complex ways, and survival of all native species in a given region is an indicator of a healthy ecosystem. If one species declines, others can become negatively affected. Recovery programs for any species, such as the pallid sturgeon, aim to restore the critical balance that exists between all members of a healthy ecosystem."

As of February 2016, there were 162 fish species listed under the Endangered Species Act (ESA) in the United States. (See Table 1.3 in Chapter 1.) Four fish species have been delisted because of extinction: Tecopa pupfish (1982), blue pike (1983), Amistad gambusia (1987), and longjaw cisco (2004). (See Table 1.2 in Chapter 1.) All were freshwater fish. The Tecopa pupfish and the Amistad gambusia were found in isolated habitats in springs in California and Texas, respectively. The blue pike and the longjaw cisco were once plentiful fish in the Great Lakes region and disappeared because of overfishing and other stresses. As shown in Table 2.7 in Chapter 2, as of February 2016, two fish species had been delisted because of recovery: the Modoc sucker and the Oregon chub, both freshwater fish.

In *Federal and State Endangered and Threatened Species Expenditures: Fiscal Year 2014* (March 2016, http://www.fws.gov/endangered/esa-library/pdf/20160302 _final_FY14_ExpRpt.pdf), the USFWS indicates that $721.9 million was spent under the ESA during fiscal year (FY) 2014 on listed fish.

GENERAL THREATS TO FISH

Fish species have become endangered and threatened in the United States for a variety of reasons, both natural and anthropogenic (caused by humans). Most fish are not imperiled by a single threat to their survival, but by multiple threats that combine to produce daunting challenges to recovery. Some scientists believe natural threats, such as disease, have been aggravated by human actions that stress fish populations. Dams and other structures that are used for power generation, flood control, irrigation, and navigation have dramatically changed water flow patterns in many rivers. These impediments disrupt migration patterns and affect water temperature and quality. Likewise, the dredging of river and stream beds to produce channels and the filling of wetlands and swamps have changed water habitats.

Dams

Dams affect rivers, the lands abutting them, the water bodies they join, and aquatic wildlife throughout the United States. Water flow is reduced or stopped altogether downstream of dams, altering aquatic habitats and drying wetlands. Arthur C. Benke and Colbert E. Cushing, the editors of *Rivers of North America* (2005), note that it is difficult to find any river in the United States that has not been dammed or channeled. According to Benke and Cushing, "All human alterations of rivers, regardless of whether they provide services such as power or drinking water supply, result in degradation."

The U.S. Army Corps of Engineers maintains the National Inventory of Dams (http://nid.usace.army.mil/ cm_apex/f?p=838:5:0::NO). As of April 2016, the inventory included more than 87,000 dams throughout the country. To be included in this inventory, dams have to be at least 6 feet (1.8 m) tall or hold back a minimum of 15 acre-feet (4.9 million gallons [18.5 million L]) of water. Dams are built for a variety of purposes. The most frequent purposes listed in the National Inventory of Dams are recreation, fire protection, and flood control.

Although only a small percentage of the dams listed with the National Inventory of Dams produce hydroelectric power, these dams tend to be the largest in size and affect large watersheds. These structures provide many challenges to aquatic species, besides impeding water flow and migration paths. Turbines operate like massive underwater fans. Passage through running turbine blades can result in the death of many small aquatic creatures that are unable to escape their path. Some modern hydroelectric dams include stairlike structures called fish ladders that provide migrating fish a watery path to climb up and over the dams.

SNAIL DARTERS. The snail darter, a small fish species related to perch, was at the center of a dam-building controversy during the 1970s. The USFWS listed the snail darter as endangered in 1975. At the time it was believed to exist only in the Little Tennessee River, and this area was designated as critical habitat for the species. That same year the Tellico Dam was near completion on the Little Tennessee River, and the filling of the Tellico Reservoir would have destroyed the entire habitat of the snail darter. A lawsuit was filed to prevent this from happening. The case went all the way to the U.S. Supreme Court, which ruled in *Tennessee Valley Authority v. Hill* (437 U.S. 153 [1978]) that under the ESA species protection must take priority over economic and developmental concerns. One month after this ruling Congress amended the ESA to allow for exemptions under certain circumstances.

In late 1979 the Tellico Dam received an exemption, and the Tellico Reservoir was filled. The snail darter is now extinct in that habitat. However, snail darter populations were later discovered in other river systems. In addition, the species has been introduced into several other habitats. Because of an increase in numbers, the snail darter was reclassified as threatened in 1984.

Entrainment and Impingement

Entrainment occurs when fish are pulled or diverted away from their natural habitat by mechanical equipment or other nonnatural structures in water bodies. A prime example is a freshwater intake structure in a river or lake. Small fish, in particular, are susceptible to being sucked into pipes through which water is being pumped out of a water body. Even if the pipe end is screened, the force of the suction can impinge (crush) fish against the screen, causing serious harm. In a more general sense entrainment refers to diversions that occur when fish accidentally feed through artificial water structures, such as gates, locks, or dams, and cannot return to their original location.

Excessive Sediment

Many river and stream banks and adjacent lands have been stripped of vegetation by timber harvesting, crop growing, and excessive grazing of livestock. This eliminates habitat for insects and other tiny creatures that serve as foodstuff for fish. It also aggravates erosion problems and allows large amounts of dirt to enter water bodies. Once in the water, this dirt is known as silt or sediment. Most of these particles settle to the bottom. However, sediment is easily stirred up by the movement of fish and other aquatic creatures, many of which spawn or lay eggs at the bed of their habitat. The dirt that remains in suspension in the water is said to make water turbid. The measure of the dirtiness (lack of clarity) of a water body is called its turbidity.

Freshwater aquatic creatures are sensitive to turbidity levels and choose their habitats based in part on their sediment preferences. Some fish prefer waters with large amounts of sediment. It provides cover that prevents predator fish from seeing them. Other species prefer clean waters with low turbidity levels. Excessive sediment may clog their gills or smother their eggs. (See Figure 4.1.)

FIGURE 4.1

Effects of siltation on aquatic life

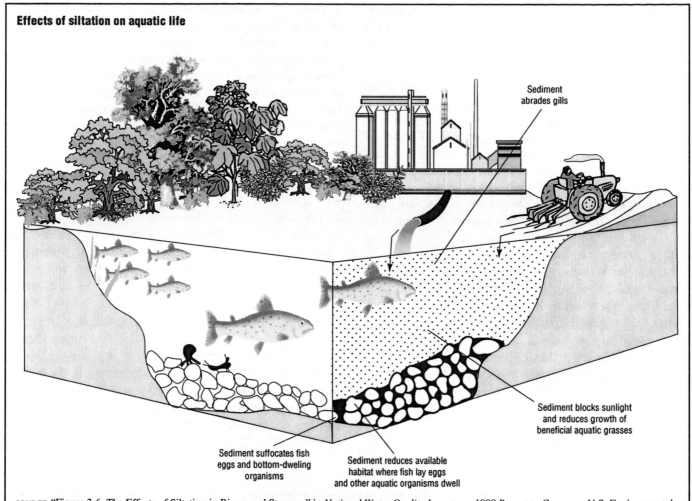

Sediment abrades gills

Sediment blocks sunlight and reduces growth of beneficial aquatic grasses

Sediment suffocates fish eggs and bottom-dweling organisms

Sediment reduces available habitat where fish lay eggs and other aquatic organisms dwell

SOURCE: "Figure 3-6. The Effects of Siltation in Rivers and Streams," in *National Water Quality Inventory: 1998 Report to Congress*, U.S. Environmental Protection Agency, June 2000, http://www.epa.gov/sites/production/files/2015-09/documents/1998_national_water_quality_inventory_report_to_congress .pdf (accessed February 10, 2016)

Forestry and agricultural practices can drastically affect the sediment levels in a water system through the deforestation of banks and nearby lands. Excessive grazing of livestock along riverbanks can strip vegetation and permit large amounts of dirt to enter the water. Likewise, timber harvesting and crop production can expose loosened dirt to wind and rain that carry it into water bodies. Dams and diversion structures trap sediments behind them, interrupting the natural downstream flow of sediments that takes place in moving waters.

Chemical and Biological Pollutants

Water pollution poses a considerable threat to many aquatic species. Industrial pollution introduces metal and organic chemicals to water bodies. In agricultural areas there is runoff of manure, fertilizers, and pesticides. U.S. pesticide use during the 1960s centered around chlorine-containing organic compounds, such as dichlorodiphenyl-trichloroethane (DDT) and chlordane. Scientists eventually learned that these chemicals are extremely persistent in the

environment and have damaging effects on wildlife, particularly fish and bird species. DDT was banned in the United States in 1972 and chlordane in 1983; however, nearly four decades later both pesticides continue to show up in water, sediment, and fish samples.

In general, aquatic creatures are not killed outright by water contamination. A major exception is an oil spill, which can kill many creatures through direct contact. The more widespread and common threat is overall degradation of water quality and habitats because of pollutants. Exposure to contaminants can weaken the immune systems of aquatic animals and make them more susceptible to disease and to other health and reproductive problems.

Bioaccumulative contaminants are those that accumulate in the tissues of aquatic organisms at much higher concentrations than are found in the water body itself. This biomagnification effect occurs with mercury (a metal), the pesticides DDT and chlordane, and dioxins. Dioxins are a category of several hundred chlorinated organic compounds. Polychlorinated biphenyls are dioxins that were widely used to cool and lubricate electrical equipment before a 1977 ban on their manufacture. Bioaccumulative contaminants are a particular concern for fish at the higher end of the aquatic food chain, such as salmon and large freshwater species.

WATER QUALITY RATINGS. Federal law requires the states to regularly assess their water bodies for quality and rate them as good, threatened, or impaired. Because of budget and resource limitations not all water bodies are assessed. The U.S. Environmental Protection Agency (EPA) summarizes in *National Summary of State Information* (April 12, 2016, http://iaspub.epa.gov/tmdl_waters10/attains_nation_cy.control) state water assessment data through 2014 for designated uses important to humans. One use relevant to fish well-being is fish, shellfish, and wildlife protection and propagation. As shown in Table 4.1, state water bodies showed differing levels of water quality for this use. Nearly all (98.5%) of the Great Lakes open water that was assessed was rated as impaired. By contrast, 44.4% of rivers and streams were considered impaired. Another relevant use is aquatic life harvesting. More than 70% of all the water bodies assessed were rated as impaired for this use. (See Table 4.2.) The worst water bodies were the open waters and shorelines of the Great Lakes. All (100%) of them were considered impaired.

FISH CONSUMPTION ADVISORIES. The states issue advisories to protect residents from the adverse health risk of eating fish that are contaminated with certain pollutants. The EPA provides a website (http://fishadvisoryonline.epa.gov/General.aspx) with an interactive map at which visitors can find the most recent fish advisory notices by state or water body. Although the purpose of fish advisories is to protect human health, the underlying data illustrate that toxic pollutants pose a worrisome threat to the nation's fish species.

Unwelcome Guests: Injurious Invasive Fish

Historically, fish were generally geographically limited in their habitats, such as to streams, rivers, or lakes in a particular area. However, human intervention has allowed species to move into new habitats, sometimes thousands of miles from where they originated. Many fish species have been purposely introduced to new water bodies to improve sport and recreational fishing. Some species that are popular in aquariums have been intentionally dumped into the environment. Other species have been introduced unintentionally by migrating through human-built canals and locks, stowing away in the ballast water of ships, or escaping from research, breeding, and aquaculture (fish farming) facilities. Some introduced species are not problematic in their new habitats, but others

TABLE 4.1

Percentage of waterbodies supporting fish, shellfish, and wildlife protection and propagation, 2014

Waterbody type	Amount assessed	Percent good	Percent threatened	Percent impaired
Rivers and streams	886,372 miles	55.0	0.5	44.4
Lakes, reservoirs, and ponds	11,242,453 acres	55.7	1.1	43.2
Bays and estuaries	21,002 square miles	39.1	0.0	60.9
Coastal shoreline	916 miles	45.6	0.0	54.4
Ocean and near coastal	919 square miles	40.5	0.0	59.5
Wetlands	1,235,391 acres	51.7	0.0	48.3
Great Lakes shoreline	865 miles	33.1	0.0	66.9
Great Lakes open water	14,300 square miles	1.5	0.0	98.5

SOURCE: Adapted from "Water Quality by Waterbody Type," in *National Summary of State Information*, Environmental Protection Agency, 2016, http://ofmpub.epa.gov/waters10/attains_nation_cy.control (accessed February 12, 2016)

TABLE 4.2

Percentage of waterbodies supporting aquatic life harvesting, 2014

Waterbody type	Amount assessed	Percent good	Percent threatened	Percent impaired
Rivers and streams	280,278 miles	29.0	0.9	70.2
Lakes, reservoirs, and ponds	9,935,340 acres	22.0	1.3	76.8
Bays and estuaries	25,423 square miles	17.3	0.0	82.7
Coastal shoreline	7,157 miles	6.7	0.0	93.3
Ocean and near coastal	888 square miles	7.0	0.0	93.0
Wetlands	121,882 acres	0.8	0.0	99.2
Great Lakes shoreline	4,064 miles	0.0	0.0	100.0
Great Lakes open water	39,184 square miles	0.0	0.0	100.0

SOURCE: Adapted from "Water Quality by Waterbody Type," in *National Summary of State Information*, Environmental Protection Agency, 2016, http://ofmpub.epa.gov/waters10/attains_nation_cy.control (accessed February 12, 2016)

cause ecological or economic harm by competing with native species for habitat and food, preying on them, or breeding with them. Injurious nonnative species are commonly called invasive species. Invasive species have played a role in the decline of some endangered and threatened species. For example, the threatened bull trout has become imperiled, in part, because of the introduction of nonnative brook trout to bull trout habitats. Because brook trout are an extremely popular sport and food fish, they are not considered by the public to be injurious.

Overcrowding

The overcrowding of stressed fish populations into smaller and smaller areas has contributed to hybridization (uncharacteristic mating between closely related species resulting in hybrid offspring). According to the USFWS, environmental degradation appears to inhibit natural reproductive instincts that historically prevented fish from mating outside their species. In addition, a shortage of suitable space for spawning has resulted in more mating between species. Cross-mating can be extremely detrimental to imperiled species because the offspring can be sterile.

IMPERILED FRESHWATER FISH

Freshwater fish listed under the ESA fall within the jurisdiction of the USFWS. They include a wide variety of species and are found all over the country. As of February 2016, there were 117 freshwater fish species listed under the ESA for U.S. waters. (See Table 4.3.) It should be noted that some species included experimental populations considered nonessential. As noted in Chapter 2, an experimental population is achieved by introducing a species to an area in which it is not currently found. The nonessential designation means that the survival of the experimental population is not believed essential to the survival of the species as a whole. Thus, the experimental population receives less protection under the ESA than does the species as a whole. Most of the imperiled fish species had recovery plans in place. In general, imperiled freshwater fish are small in size and are associated with flowing (lotic) waters, such as rivers and streams, rather than with still (lentic) waters, such as lakes and ponds.

Table 4.4 shows the 10 freshwater species with the highest expenditures under the ESA during FY 2014. Nearly $104 million was spent on only two of the fish: pallid sturgeon ($68.8 million) and bull trout ($35.2 million).

Pallid Sturgeon

The pallid sturgeon is a unique and rare freshwater fish that is sometimes called the "swimming dinosaur." It is descended from fish that were common more than 50 million years ago. The pallid sturgeon has a long flat snout and a slender body that ends with a pronounced tail fin. (See Figure 4.2.) Adults range in size from 3 to 5 feet (0.9 to 1.5 m) and typically weigh 25 to 50 pounds (11.3 to 22.7 kg). The fish is a bottom-feeder and prefers large rivers of relatively warm free-flowing water with high turbidity (high mud content).

Historically, the pallid sturgeon was found throughout the Mississippi and Missouri River systems from Montana and North Dakota south to the Gulf of Mexico. (See Figure 4.3.) During the early 1900s specimens as large as 85 pounds (38.6 kg) and 6 feet (1.8 m) long were reported. Over the next century the fish virtually disappeared. In 1990 it was listed as endangered under the ESA. Three years later the USFWS published the first recovery plan for the species. In *Pallid Sturgeon Recovery Plan* (Scaphirhynchus albus) (November 1993, http://ecos.fws.gov/docs/recovery_plans/1993/931107.pdf), the agency blames human destruction and modification of habitat as the two primary causes for the pallid sturgeon's decline.

Pallid sturgeon are believed to be extremely sensitive to changes in the velocity and volume of river flows. They are nearly blind and forage along muddy river bottoms feeding on tiny fish and other creatures that prefer turbid waters. Dams and channelization have reduced the erosion of riverbank soil into the Missouri and Mississippi Rivers, their last remaining primary habitat. This has given other fish species with better eyesight an advantage over the pallid sturgeon at finding small prey. In addition, mating between the pallid sturgeon and the shovelnose sturgeon in the lower Mississippi River has produced a population of hybrid sturgeon that is thriving compared with their imperiled parents. In 2007 the USFWS completed a five-year review on the pallid sturgeon and decided to maintain its listing as endangered. The species was given a recovery priority number of 2c. The USFWS ranks recovery priority on a scale from 1 to 18, with lower numbers indicating higher priority. The "c" designation means the recovery of this species is in conflict with economic activities in its region.

The USFWS published an updated recovery plan in January 2014. In *Revised Recovery Plan for the Pallid Sturgeon* (Scaphirhynchus albus) (http://ecos.fws.gov/docs/recovery_plan/Pallid%20Sturgeon%20Recovery%20Plan%20First%20Revision%20signed%20version%2001 2914_3.pdf), the agency summarizes the information collected about the pallid sturgeon and notes, "Since listing, the status of the species has improved and is currently stable." The USFWS has a short-term goal to downlist the pallid sturgeon from endangered to threatened. This status change will be initiated when "a self-sustaining genetically diverse population of 5,000 adult Pallid Sturgeon is realized and maintained within each management unit for 2 generations (20–30 years)." The USFWS estimates that full recovery of the species could be achieved by 2047 at a cost of approximately $239 million if all the

TABLE 4.3

Endangered and threatened freshwater fish species, February 2016

Common name	Scientific name	Federal listing status[a]	U.S. or U.S./foreign listed	Recovery plan date	Recovery plan stage[b]
Alabama cavefish	*Speoplatyrhinus poulsoni*	E	US	10/25/90	RF(2)
Alabama sturgeon	*Scaphirhynchus suttkusi*	E	US	07/08/13	F
Amber darter	*Percina antesella*	E	US	06/20/86	F
Apache trout	*Oncorhynchus apache*	T	US	09/03/09	RF(2)
Arkansas River shiner	*Notropis girardi*	T	US	None	—
Ash Meadows Amargosa pupfish	*Cyprinodon nevadensis mionectes*	E	US	09/28/90	F
Ash Meadows speckled dace	*Rhinichthys osculus nevadensis*	E	US	09/28/90	F
Bayou darter	*Etheostoma rubrum*	T	US	07/10/90	RF(1)
Beautiful shiner	*Cyprinella formosa*	T	US/foreign	03/29/95	F
Big Bend gambusia	*Gambusia gaigei*	E	US	09/19/84	F
Big Spring spinedace	*Lepidomeda mollispinis pratensis*	T	US	01/20/94	F
Blackside dace	*Phoxinus cumberlandensis*	T	US	08/17/88	F
Blue shiner	*Cyprinella caerulea*	T	US	08/30/95	F
Bluemask (=jewel) darter	*Etheostoma sp.*	E	US	07/25/97	F
Bonytail chub	*Gila elegans*	E	US	08/01/02	RF(1)
Borax Lake chub	*Gila boraxobius*	E	US	02/04/87	F
Boulder darter	*Etheostoma wapiti*	E; EXPN	US	07/27/89	F
Bull trout	*Salvelinus confluentus*	E; EXPN	US	09/30/15	F
Cahaba shiner	*Notropis cahabae*	E	US	04/23/92	F
Cape Fear shiner	*Notropis mekistocholas*	E	US	10/07/88	F
Cherokee darter	*Etheostoma scotti*	T	US	11/17/00	F
Chihuahua chub	*Gila nigrescens*	T	US/foreign	04/14/86	F
Chucky Madtom	*Noturus crypticus*	E	US	None	—
Clear Creek gambusia	*Gambusia heterochir*	E	US	01/14/82	F
Clover Valley speckled dace	*Rhinichthys osculus oligoporus*	E	US	05/12/98	F
Colorado pikeminnow (=squawfish)	*Ptychocheilus lucius*	E; EXPN	US	08/28/02	RF(2)
Comanche Springs pupfish	*Cyprinodon elegans*	E	US	09/02/81	F
Conasauga logperch	*Percina jenkinsi*	E	US	06/20/86	F
Cui-ui	*Chasmistes cujus*	E	US	05/15/92	RF(2)
Cumberland darter	*Etheostoma susanae*	E	US	None	—
Delta smelt	*Hypomesus transpacificus*	T	US	11/26/96	F
Desert dace	*Eremichthys acros*	T	US	05/27/97	F
Desert pupfish	*Cyprinodon macularius*	E	US/foreign	12/08/93	F
Devils Hole pupfish	*Cyprinodon diabolis*	E	US	09/28/90	F
Devils River minnow	*Dionda diaboli*	T	US/foreign	09/13/05	F
Diamond darter	*Crystallaria cincotta*	E	US	None	—
Duskytail darter	*Etheostoma percnurum*	E; EXPN	US	03/30/94	F
Etowah darter	*Etheostoma etowahae*	E	US	11/17/00	F
Foskett speckled dace	*Rhinichthys osculus ssp.*	T	US	04/27/98	F
Fountain darter	*Etheostoma fonticola*	E	US	02/14/96	RF(1)
Gila chub	*Gila intermedia*	E	US/foreign	None	—
Gila topminnow (incl. Yaqui)	*Poeciliopsis occidentalis*	E	US/foreign	03/05/99	RD(1)
Gila trout	*Oncorhynchus gilae*	T	US	09/10/03	RF(3)
Goldline darter	*Percina aurolineata*	T	US	11/17/00	F
Greenback cutthroat trout	*Oncorhynchus clarki stomias*	T	US	03/01/98	RF(2)
Grotto sculpin	*Cottus specus*	E	US	None	—
Hiko White River springfish	*Crenichthys baileyi grandis*	E	US	05/26/98	F
Humpback chub	*Gila cypha*	E	US	09/19/90	RF(2)
Hutton tui chub	*Gila bicolor ssp.*	T	US	04/27/98	F
Independence Valley speckled dace	*Rhinichthys osculus lethoporus*	E	US	05/12/98	F
June sucker	*Chasmistes liorus*	E	US	06/25/99	F
Kendall Warm Springs dace	*Rhinichthys osculus thermalis*	E	US	10/14/15	RF(1)
Lahontan cutthroat trout	*Oncorhynchus clarkii henshawi*	T	US	01/30/95	F
Laurel dace	*Chrosomus saylori*	E	US	01/14/15	D
Leon Springs pupfish	*Cyprinodon bovinus*	E	US	08/14/85	F
Leopard darter	*Percina pantherina*	T	US	05/03/93	RD(1)
Little Colorado spinedace	*Lepidomeda vittata*	T	US	01/09/98	F
Little Kern golden trout	*Oncorhynchus aguabonita whitei*	T	US	None	—
Loach minnow	*Tiaroga cobitis*	E	US/foreign	09/30/91	F
Lost River sucker	*Deltistes luxatus*	E	US	04/16/13	RF(1)
Maryland darter	*Etheostoma sellare*	E	US	10/17/85	RF(1)
Moapa dace	*Moapa coriacea*	E	US	05/16/96	RF(1)
Mohave tui chub	*Gila bicolor ssp. mohavensis*	E	US	09/12/84	F
Neosho madtom	*Noturus placidus*	T	US	09/30/91	F
Niangua darter	*Etheostoma nianguae*	T	US	07/17/89	F
Okaloosa darter	*Etheostoma okaloosae*	T	US	10/26/98	RF(1)
Owens pupfish	*Cyprinodon radiosus*	E	US	09/30/98	F
Owens tui chub	*Gila bicolor ssp. snyderi*	E	US	09/30/98	F
Ozark cavefish	*Amblyopsis rosae*	T	US	11/14/89	F
Pahranagat roundtail chub	*Gila robusta jordani*	E	US	05/26/98	F

TABLE 4.3

Endangered and threatened freshwater fish species, February 2016 [CONTINUED]

Common name	Scientific name	Federal listing status[a]	U.S. or U.S./foreign listed	Recovery plan date	Recovery plan stage[b]
Pahrump poolfish	*Empetrichthys latos*	E	US	03/17/80	F
Paiute cutthroat trout	*Oncorhynchus clarkii seleniris*	T	US	09/10/04	RF(1)
Palezone shiner	*Notropis albizonatus*	E	US	07/07/97	F
Pallid sturgeon	*Scaphirhynchus albus*	E	US	03/04/14	RF(1)
Pecos bluntnose shiner	*Notropis simus pecosensis*	T	US	09/30/92	F
Pecos gambusia	*Gambusia nobilis*	E	US	05/09/83	F
Pygmy madtom	*Noturus stanauli*	E; EXPN	US	09/27/94	F
Pygmy sculpin	*Cottus paulus (=pygmaeus)*	T	US	08/06/91	F
Railroad Valley springfish	*Crenichthys nevadae*	T	US	03/15/97	F
Razorback sucker	*Xyrauchen texanus*	E	US/foreign	08/28/02	RF(1)
Relict darter	*Etheostoma chienense*	E	US	07/31/94	D
Rio Grande silvery minnow	*Hybognathus amarus*	E; EXPN	US/foreign	02/22/10	RF(1)
Roanoke logperch	*Percina rex*	E	US	03/20/92	F
Rush Darter	*Etheostoma phytophilum*	E	US	None	—
San Marcos gambusia	*Gambusia georgei*	E	US	02/14/96	RF(1)
Santa Ana sucker	*Catostomus santaanae*	T	US	11/24/14	D
Scioto madtom	*Noturus trautmani*	E	US	None	—
Sharpnose shiner	*Notropis oxyrhynchus*	E	US	03/04/15	O
Shortnose sucker	*Chasmistes brevirostris*	E	US	04/16/13	RF(1)
Shovelnose sturgeon	*Scaphirhynchus platorynchus*	SAT	US	None	—
Slackwater darter	*Etheostoma boschungi*	T	US	03/08/84	F
Slender chub	*Erimystax cahni*	T; EXPN	US	07/29/83	F
Smalleye shiner	*Notropis buccula*	E	US	03/04/15	O
Smoky madtom	*Noturus baileyi*	E; EXPN	US	08/09/85	F
Snail darter	*Percina tanasi*	T	US	05/05/83	F
Sonora chub	*Gila ditaenia*	T	US/foreign	09/30/92	F
Spikedace	*Meda fulgida*	E	US/foreign	09/30/91	F
Spotfin chub	*Erimonax monachus*	E; EXPN	US	11/21/83	F
Spring pygmy sunfish	*Elassoma alabamae*	T	US	None	—
Tidewater goby	*Eucyclogobius newberryi*	E	US	12/07/05	F
Topeka shiner	*Notropis topeka (=tristis)*	E; EXPN	US	None	—
Unarmored threespine stickleback	*Gasterosteus aculeatus williamsoni*	E	US	12/26/85	RF(1)
Vermilion darter	*Etheostoma chermocki*	E	US	08/06/07	F
Virgin River chub	*Gila seminuda (=robusta)*	E	US	04/19/95	RF(2)
Waccamaw silverside	*Menidia extensa*	T	US	08/11/93	F
Warm Springs pupfish	*Cyprinodon nevadensis pectoralis*	E	US	09/28/90	F
Warner sucker	*Catostomus warnerensis*	T	US	04/27/98	F
Watercress darter	*Etheostoma nuchale*	E	US	03/29/93	RF(2)
White River spinedace	*Lepidomeda albivallis*	E	US	03/28/94	F
White River springfish	*Crenichthys baileyi baileyi*	E	US	05/26/98	F
White sturgeon	*Acipenser transmontanus*	E	US/foreign	09/30/99	F
Woundfin	*Plagopterus argentissimus*	E; EXPN	US	04/19/95	RF(2)
Yaqui catfish	*Ictalurus pricei*	T	US/foreign	03/29/95	F
Yaqui chub	*Gila purpurea*	E	US/foreign	03/29/95	F
Yellowcheek darter	*Etheostoma moorei*	E	US	None	—
Yellowfin madtom	*Noturus flavipinnis*	T; EXPN	US	06/23/83	F
Zuni bluehead sucker	*Catostomus discobolus yarrowi*	E	US	None	—

[a]E = Endangered. T = Threatened. EXPN = Experimental population, non-essential.
[b]F = Final. RF = Final revision. D = Draft.

SOURCE: Adapted from "Generate Species List," in *Environmental Conservation Online System Species Reports*, U.S. Department of the Interior, U.S. Fish and Wildlife Service, February 2016, http://ecos.fws.gov/tess_public/pub/adHocSpeciesForm.jsp (accessed February 12, 2016), and "Listed FWS/Joint FWS and NMFS Species and Populations with Recovery Plans (Sorted by Listed Entity)," in *Recovery Plans Search*, U.S. Department of the Interior, U.S. Fish and Wildlife Service, February 2016, http://ecos.fws.gov/tess_public/pub/speciesRecovery.jsp?sort=1 (accessed February 12, 2016)

recovery tasks are completed and the recovery criteria are met. The recovery tasks cover a wide variety of activities, including data collection, habitat restoration, and a propagation and stocking program (raising pallid sturgeon in a hatchery and releasing them into the wild).

Bull Trout

Bull trout are relatively large fish that live in streams, lakes, and rivers. They can weigh more than 20 pounds (9.1 kg); however, those that inhabit small streams seldom exceed 4 pounds (1.8 kg) in weight. Bull trout are members of the char subgroup of the salmon family (Salmonidae). (See Figure 4.4.) Their backs are dark in color (green to brown) with small light-colored spots (crimson to yellow), and their undersides are pale. The fish prefer cold and clean inland waters in the Northwest.

Historically, bull trout were found throughout much of the northwestern United States and as far north as Alaska. Large populations have disappeared from major rivers, leaving mostly isolated pockets of smaller-sized fish in headwater streams. A variety of factors have

TABLE 4.4

The 10 listed freshwater fish species with the highest expenditures under the Endangered Species Act, fiscal year 2014

Ranking	Species	Population	Expenditure
1	Sturgeon, pallid (*Scaphirhynchus albus*)	Entire	$68,778,575
2	Trout, bull (*Salvelinus confluentus*)	Lower 48 states	$35,194,738
3	Chub, humpback (*Gila cypha*)	Entire	$13,409,098
4	Smelt, delta (*Hypomesus transpacificus*)	Entire	$11,960,799
5	Sturgeon, white (*Acipenser transmontanus*)	Idaho, Montana, and British Columbia, Kootenai River system	$10,544,074
6	Sucker, razorback (*Xyrauchen texanus*)	Entire	$9,539,766
7	Minnow, Rio Grande silvery (*Hybognathus amarus*)	Entire, except where listed as an experimental population	$9,223,652
8	Chub, bonytail (*Gila elegans*)	Entire	$6,249,048
9	Trout, Lahontan cutthroat (*Oncorhynchus clarkii henshawi*)	Entire	$4,639,473
10	Pikeminnow (=squawfish), Colorado (*Ptychocheilus lucius*)	Entire, except EXPN	$3,065,764

Note: EXPN = Experimental Population, Non-essential.

SOURCE: Adapted from "Table 2. Species Ranked in Descending Order of Total FY 2014 Reported Expenditures, Not Including Land Acquisition Costs," in *Federal and State Endangered and Threatened Species Expenditures: Fiscal Year 2014*, U.S. Department of the Interior, U.S. Fish and Wildlife Service, March 2, 2016, http://www.fws.gov/endangered/esa-library/pdf/20160302_final_FY14_ExpRpt.pdf (accessed March 9, 2016)

FIGURE 4.2

Pallid sturgeon

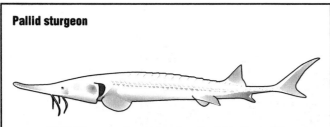

SOURCE: "Pallid Sturgeon (Scaphirhynchus albus)," in *Revised Recovery Plan for the Pallid Sturgeon (Scaphirhynchus albus)*, U.S. Department of the Interior, U.S. Fish and Wildlife Service, January 2014, http://ecos.fws.gov/docs/recovery_plan/Pallid%20Sturgeon%20Recovery%20Plan%20First%20Revision%20signed%20version%20012914_3.pdf (accessed February 12, 2016)

contributed to the decline of the bull trout. The species is extremely sensitive to changes in water temperature and purity. Its survival is threatened by water pollution, degraded habitat, and dams and other diversion structures. In addition, the introduction of brook trout, a nonnative game fish, has been devastating. The two species are able to mate, but produce mostly sterile offspring, which is a genetic dead end for the imperiled bull trout.

The legal history of the bull trout is extensive. In 1992 three environmental groups petitioned the USFWS to list the fish as an endangered species under the ESA. In 1993 the agency concluded that listing the species was warranted, but low in priority. This set off a long series of court battles that culminated in 1999, when all bull trout in the coterminous United States (the lower 48 states) were listed as threatened under the ESA. In 2001 the Alliance for the Wild Rockies and Friends of the Wild Swan (two of the original petitioners) filed a lawsuit against the USFWS for failing to designate critical habitat for the bull trout. The following year the agency published a draft recovery plan for the species. In 2005

the USFWS designated critical habitat for the bull trout, but that designation was challenged by the Alliance for the Wild Rockies and Friends of the Wild Swan. In 2010 the USFWS designated revised critical habitat, this time consisting of 19,729 miles (31,751 km) of stream/coastal shoreline and 488,252 acres (197,589 ha) of lakes and reservoirs in five states: Idaho, Montana, Nevada, Oregon, and Washington.

In 2015 the USFWS (http://ecos.fws.gov/docs/five_year_review/doc4654.pdf) published the results of a five-year status review for the bull trout and recommended that it retain a threatened listing under the ESA.

Also in 2015 the agency published an updated recovery plan for the species. In *Recovery Plan for the Coterminous United States Population of Bull Trout (Salvelinus confluentus)* (September 2015, http://ecos.fws.gov/docs/recovery_plan/Final_Bull_Trout_Recovery_Plan_092915-corrected.pdf), the USFWS designates six recovery units: coastal, Columbia headwaters, mid-Columbia, Saint Mary, Upper Snake, and Klamath. (See Figure 4.5.) There are four key requirements (called the four Cs) for the bull trout's recovery: cold water temperatures, clean streambed substrates (such as gravel), complex stream habitat features, and connectivity between different but important habitats, such as spawning and foraging areas. Each recovery unit has different recovery criteria. For example, recovery will be achieved in the Columbia headwaters unit when primary threats affecting 75% of the population are "effectively managed." The USFWS estimates that it could take as long as 50 to 70 years to achieve recovery across all the recovery units. The projected total cost is approximately $1.6 billion.

Recovery Plans for Freshwater Fish

As of February 2016, there were recovery plans for the vast majority of listed freshwater fish populations. (See Table 4.3.) Most of the plans were finalized. The

FIGURE 4.3

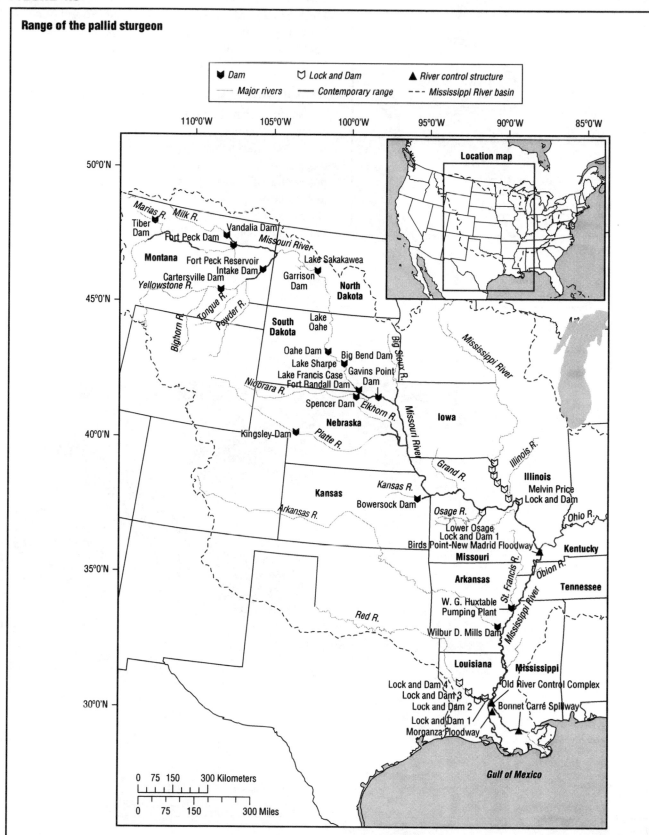

Range of the pallid sturgeon

⬻ Dam	⬯ Lock and Dam	▲ River control structure
⋯ Major rivers	— Contemporary range	--- Mississippi River basin

SOURCE: "Figure 3. Post-Development Map of Prominent Rivers in the Mississippi River Basin," in *Revised Recovery Plan for the Pallid Sturgeon (Scaphirhynchus albus)*, U.S. Department of the Interior, U.S. Fish and Wildlife Service, January 2014, http://ecos.fws.gov/docs/recovery_plan/ Pallid%20Sturgeon%20Recovery%20Plan%20First%20Revision%20signed%20version%2001912914_3.pdf (accessed February 12, 2016)

FIGURE 4.4

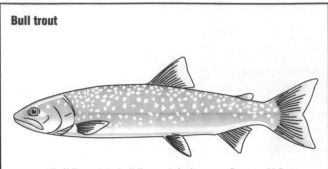

Bull trout

SOURCE: "Bull Trout," in *Bull Trout: Salvelinus confluentus*, U.S. Department of the Interior, U.S. Fish and Wildlife Service, January 2003, http://digitalmedia.fws.gov/cdm/singleitem/collection/document/id/1237/rec/1 (accessed February 12, 2016)

USFWS provides details of the plans in "Listed FWS/Joint FWS and NMFS Species and Populations with Recovery Plans" (April 2016, http://ecos.fws.gov/tess_public/pub/speciesRecovery.jsp?sort=1).

IMPERILED MARINE AND ANADROMOUS FISH

Marine fish inhabit the salty waters of seas and oceans. In reality, some species of fish thrive in both fresh- and marine waters. For example, anadromous fish migrate between freshwater and the sea for mating purposes. As of February 2016, there were 17 marine and anadromous fish species listed under the ESA in U.S. waters. (See Table 4.5.) They are under the jurisdiction of the National Marine Fisheries Service (NMFS).

FIGURE 4.5

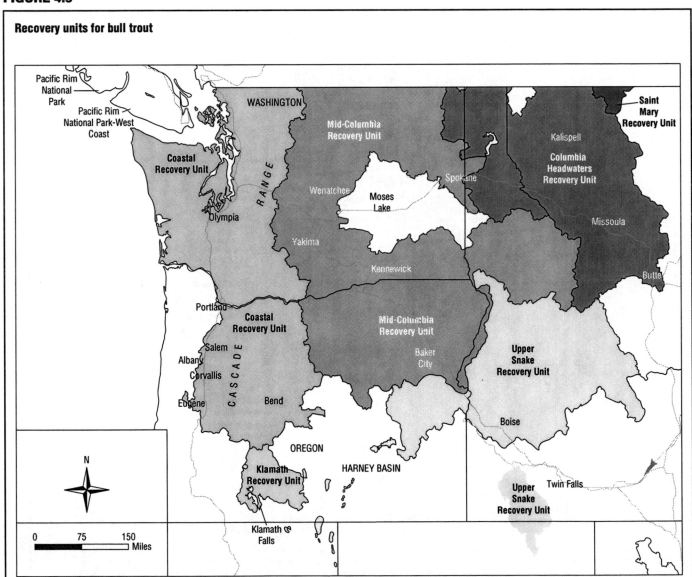

Recovery units for bull trout

SOURCE: Adapted from "Figure 4. Locations of the Six Bull Trout Recovery Units in the Coterminous United States," in *Recovery Plan for the Coterminous United States Population of Bull Trout (Salvelinus confluentus)*, U.S. Department of the Interior, U.S. Fish and Wildlife Service, September 2015, http://ecos.fws.gov/docs/recovery_plan/Final_Bull_Trout_Recovery_Plan_092915-corrected.pdf (accessed February 12, 2016)

TABLE 4.5

Endangered and threatened marine and anadromous fish species, February 2016

Species	Federal listing status*	Critical habitat	Recovery plan
Atlantic salmon (*Salmo salar*) 1 listed DPS			
• Gulf of Maine	E	Final	Final
Atlantic sturgeon (*Acipenser oxyrinchus oxyrinchus*) 5 listed DPSs			
• Gulf of Maine	T	No	No
• New York Bight	E	No	No
• Chesapeake Bay	E	No	No
• Carolina	E	No	No
• South Atlantic	E	No	No
Bocaccio (*Sebastes paucispinis*) 1 listed DPS			
• Puget Sound/Georgia Basin	E	Final	No
Canary rockfish (*Sebastes pinniger*) 1 listed DPS			
• Puget Sound/Georgia Basin	T	Final	No
Chinook salmon (*Oncorhynchus tshawytscha*) 9 listed DPS and 1 EXPN			
• California coastal	T	Final	Draft
• Central Valley spring-run	T	Final	Final
• Central Valley spring-run in the San Joaquin River, CA	EXPN	N/A	—
• Lower Columbia River	T	Final	Final
• Upper Columbia River spring-run	E	Final	Final
• Puget Sound	T	Final	Final
• Sacramento River winter-run	E	Final	Final
• Snake River fall-run	T	Final	Draft
• Snake River spring/summer-run	T	Final	In process
• Upper Willamette River	T	Final	Final
Chum salmon (*Oncorhynchus keta*) 2 listed ESUs			
• Columbia River	T	Final	Final
• Hood Canal summer-run	T	Final	Final
Coho salmon (*Oncorhynchus kisutch*) 4 listed ESUs			
• Central California coast	E	Final	Final
• Lower Columbia River	T	Proposed	Final
• Oregon coast	T	Final	Draft
• Southern Oregon & Northern California coasts	T	Final	Final
Eulachon, Pacific/smelt (*Thaleichthys pacificus*) 1 listed DPS			
• Southern DPS	T	Final	No
Green sturgeon (*Acipenser medirostris*) 1 listed DPS			
• Southern DPS	T	Final	In process
Gulf sturgeon (*Acipenser oxyrinchus desotoi*)	T	Final	Final
Largetooth sawfish (*Pristis pristis*)	E	No	No
Scalloped hammerhead shark (*Sphyrna lewini*) 3 listed DPSs in US waters			
• Central & Southwest Atlantic	T	No	No
• Eastern Pacific	E	No	No
• Indo-West Pacific	T	No	No
Shortnose sturgeon (*Acipenser brevirostrum*)	E	N/A	Final
Smalltooth sawfish (*Pristis pectinata*) 1 listed DPS in U.S. waters			
• U.S. portion of range	E	Final	Final
Sockeye salmon (*Oncorhynchus nerka*) 2 listed ESUs			
• Ozette Lake	T	Final	Final
• Snake River	E	Final	Final
Steelhead trout (*Oncorhynchus mykiss*) 11 listed DPSs & 1 EXPN			
• Puget Sound	T	Proposed	No
• Central California coast	T	Final	Draft
• Snake River Basin	T	Final	In process
• Upper Columbia River	T	Final	Final
• Southern California	E	Final	Final
• Middle Columbia River	T	Final	Final
• Middle Columbia River	EXPN	N/A	—
• Lower Columbia River	T	Final	Final
• Upper Willamette River	T	Final	Final
• Northern California	T	Final	Draft
• South-Central California coast	T	Final	Final
• California Central Valley	T	Final	Final
Yelloweye rockfish (*Sebastes ruberrimus*) 1 listed DPS			
• Puget Sound/Georgia Basin	T	Final	No

TABLE 4.5

Endangered and threatened marine and anadromous fish species, February 2016 [CONTINUED]

*E = Endangered. T = Threatened. EXPN = Experimental population, non-essential.
DPS = Distinct Population Segment. ESU = Evolutionarily Significant Unit. N/A = Not applicable.

SOURCE: Adapted from "Fish (Marine & Anadromous)," in *Endangered and Threatened Marine Species under NMFS' Jurisdiction*, U.S. Department of Commerce, National Oceanic and Atmospheric Administration, National Marine Fisheries Service, January 19, 2016, http://www.nmfs.noaa.gov/pr/species/esa/listed.htm (accessed February 19, 2016)

TABLE 4.6

The 10 listed marine and anadromous fish species with the highest expenditures under the Endangered Species Act, fiscal year 2014

Ranking	Species	Population	Expenditure
1	Steelhead (Oncorhynchus (=Salmo) mykiss)	Snake River Basin DPS	$52,178,312
2	Salmon, chinook (Oncorhynchus (=Salmo) tshawytscha)	Snake River spring/summer-run ESU	$49,199,036
3	Steelhead (Oncorhynchus (=Salmo) mykiss)	Middle Columbia River DPS	$48,512,887
4	Salmon, chinook (Oncorhynchus (=Salmo) tshawytscha)	Lower Columbia River ESU	$42,525,708
5	Salmon, chinook (Oncorhynchus (=Salmo) tshawytscha)	Snake River fall-run ESU	$35,442,077
6	Salmon, chinook (Oncorhynchus (=Salmo) tshawytscha)	Upper Columbia spring-run ESU	$33,836,557
7	Steelhead (Oncorhynchus (=Salmo) mykiss)	Upper Columbia River DPS	$31,683,743
8	Salmon, sockeye (Oncorhynchus (=Salmo) nerka)	Snake River ESU	$22,780,787
9	Salmon, chinook (Oncorhynchus (=Salmo) tshawytscha)	Puget Sound ESU	$21,124,534
10	Salmon, chinook (Oncorhynchus (=Salmo) tshawytscha)	Upper Willamette River ESU	$17,631,540

Notes: DPS = Distinct Population Segment; ESU = Evolutionarily Significant Unit.

SOURCE: Adapted from "Table 2. Species Ranked in Descending Order of Total FY 2014 Reported Expenditures, Not Including Land Acquisition Costs," in *Federal and State Endangered and Threatened Species Expenditures: Fiscal Year 2014*, U.S. Department of the Interior, U.S. Fish and Wildlife Service, March 2, 2016, http://www.fws.gov/endangered/esa-library/pdf/20160302_final_FY14_ExpRpt.pdf (accessed March 9, 2016)

Table 4.6 shows the 10 populations of listed marine and anadromous fish species with the highest expenses under the ESA during FY 2014. All of the listed species were steelhead and salmon populations found in the western United States, mostly in northern waters. Figure 4.6 shows the regional domains in which these fish are found. Pacific salmon and steelhead belong to the genus *Oncorhynchus*.

Pacific Salmonids

There are five species of Pacific salmon: chinook, chum, coho, pink, and sockeye. As of February 2016, all but the pink salmon were listed under the ESA as endangered or threatened. (See Table 4.5.) A detailed discussion about Pacific salmonids is provided by the USFWS in "Pacific Salmon (*Oncorhynchus spp.*)" (2016, http://www.fws.gov/species/species_accounts/bio_salm.html).

Chinook salmon are the largest of the Pacific salmonids, averaging about 24 pounds (11 kg) in adulthood. (See Figure 4.7.) They spend two to seven years in the ocean and travel up to 2,500 miles (4,000 km) from their home streams. Chum, coho, and sockeye salmon adults average approximately 10 to 12 pounds (4.5 to 5.4 kg).

PERILS OF MIGRATION. Pacific salmon pose unique protection challenges because they are anadromous. Throughout their lifetime they spend time in both freshwater and the ocean. (See Figure 4.8.) Salmon eggs (or roe) are laid in the bottom gravel of cold freshwater streams,

where they incubate for five to 10 weeks. Each egg ranges in size from 0.3 to 0.5 of an inch (0.8 to 1.3 cm) in size, depending on the species. The eggs hatch to release baby fish (or alevin) that are called fry as they mature. Once a fry reaches about 3 inches (7.6 cm) in length, it is called a fingerling. This typically takes less than a year.

At some point during their first two years the young salmon (now called smolts) migrate downstream to the ocean, where they spend several months or years of their adulthood. When they reach sexual maturity, males and females journey back to the streams where they were born to mate and deposit eggs. This is called spawning. Pacific salmon make the round-trip only once. They expend all their energy swimming back upstream and die soon after the eggs are laid and fertilized. Their upstream habitats can be hundreds and even thousands of miles away from their ocean habitats. It is a long and dangerous journey both ways.

Predator fish and birds eat salmon fry, fingerlings, and smolts as they make their way to the ocean. Bears, birds, marine mammals, and humans prey on the adult fish as they migrate upstream. Waterfalls, rapids, dams, and other water diversions pose tremendous obstacles to Pacific salmon as they try to travel across long distances.

PROTECTED SALMON STOCKS. Salmon heading to the same general location travel upstream in groups called stocks (or runs). Stocks migrate at different times of the year,

FIGURE 4.6

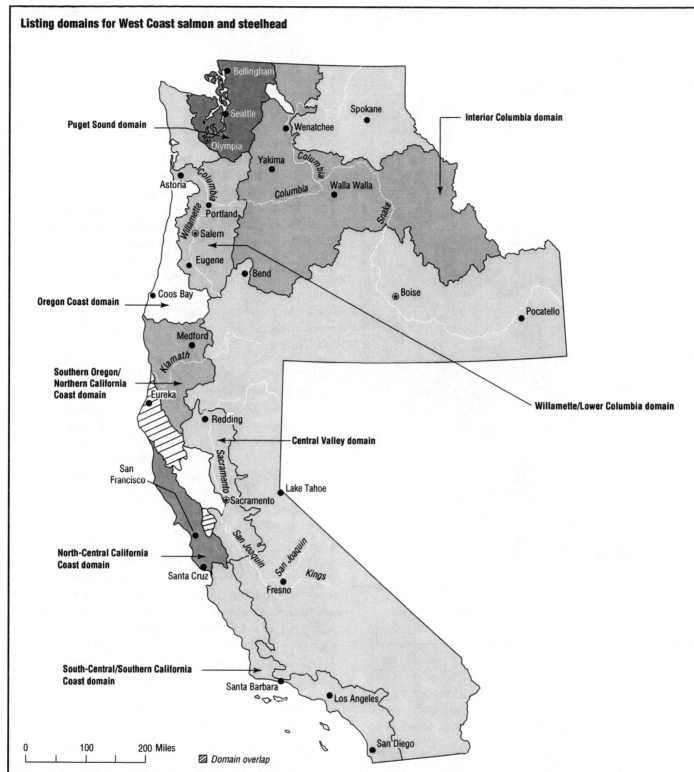

Listing domains for West Coast salmon and steelhead

SOURCE: Adapted from "Status of ESA Listings and Critical Habitat Designations for West Coast Salmon and Steelhead," in *West Coast Salmon & Steelhead Listings*, U.S. Department of Commerce, National Oceanic and Atmospheric Administration, National Marine Fisheries Service, October 31, 2012, http://www.westcoast.fisheries.noaa.gov/publications/protected_species/salmon_steelhead/status_of_esa_salmon_listings_and_ch_designations_map .pdf (accessed February 15, 2016)

depending on geographical and genetic factors. Endangered and threatened salmon are often identified by their water of origin (e.g., Snake River) and, in most cases, by their upstream migration season (e.g., spring). In 1990 the win-

ter-run stock of chinook salmon from the Sacramento River was designated as threatened under the ESA and was the first Pacific salmon to be listed. It was reclassified as endangered four years later. During the 1990s and the first decade of the

FIGURE 4.7

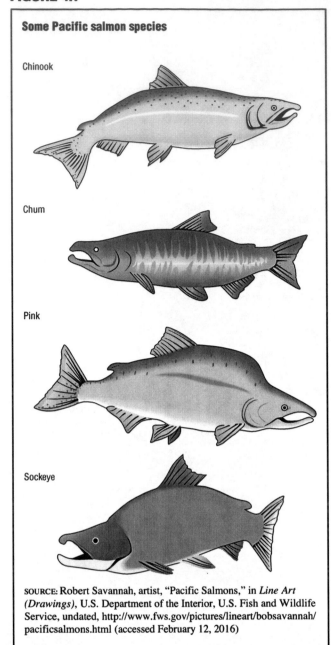

Some Pacific salmon species

Chinook

Chum

Pink

Sockeye

SOURCE: Robert Savannah, artist, "Pacific Salmons," in *Line Art (Drawings)*, U.S. Department of the Interior, U.S. Fish and Wildlife Service, undated, http://www.fws.gov/pictures/lineart/bobsavannah/pacificsalmons.html (accessed February 12, 2016)

21st century the NMFS identified dozens of distinct population segments (DPSs) and evolutionarily significant units of Pacific salmonids. As described in Chapter 2, these terms refer to particular stocks.

The protected stock descriptions for Pacific salmonids are complicated; some listings cover only "naturally spawned" fish while others include hatchery fish. Salmon raised in hatcheries that use specific government-approved genetic methods are covered under the ESA similarly to the wild populations. However, many other hatcheries propagate and release salmon species throughout the Pacific Northwest. According to the Washington Department of Fish and Wildlife (WDFW), in "Hatcheries: Salmon Recovery Relies on Support for Mass-Marking"

(2016, http://wdfw.wa.gov/hatcheries/mass_marking.html), the vast majority of hatchery-grown salmon are marked so they can be distinguished from wild populations. A small knob called the adipose fin that protrudes from a salmon's back near the tail is removed before the fish are released from the hatcheries.

The mass-marking program, as it is called, was begun during the 1990s and is largely credited with allowing salmon fishing (a major commercial and recreational activity in the Pacific Northwest) to continue. The WDFW explains that "prior to mass-marking, restrictions imposed by new ESA listings threatened to close—or greatly curtail—historic salmon fisheries throughout the region. In addition to the recreational and cultural values involved, the potential loss of fishing opportunities presented a severe economic threat to fishing families and entire communities, especially in rural areas of the Northwest." Rather than closing all fishing along a particular waterway during a salmon run, fisheries managers can impose rules that allow anglers to keep only marked (hatchery-raised) salmon. Wild (unmarked) salmon must be returned to the water.

DECLINING POPULATIONS. Daniel L. Bottom et al. estimate in *Salmon at River's End: The Role of the Estuary in the Decline and Recovery of Columbia River Salmon* (August 2005, http://www.nwfsc.noaa.gov/assets/25/6294_09302005_153156_SARETM68Final.pdf) that between 11 million and 16 million salmon per year migrated upstream in waters of the northwestern United States before the arrival of European settlers. Extensive fishing and canning operations quickly decimated the salmon population. As early as 1893 federal officials warned that the future of salmon fisheries had a "disastrous outlook." During the 1890s hatcheries began operating and stocking rivers and streams with farm-raised salmon. Throughout the next century salmon populations were further stressed as natural river flows were dramatically altered with dams, navigational structures, and irrigation systems. By 2016 dozens of salmon hatcheries and hundreds of dams had been constructed in the Columbia River basin of the Pacific Northwest.

THREATS TO SURVIVAL. Biologists blame four main threats for the imperiled state of Pacific salmonids:

- Habitat degradation—channelization, dredging, water withdrawals for irrigation, wetland losses, and diking have changed river, stream, and estuary environments.

- Harvesting levels—overfishing for more than a century decimated salmon populations.

- Hatcheries—biologists fear that hatchery releases overburden estuaries with too many competing fish at the same time.

- Hydropower—impassable dams have rendered some historical habitats unreachable by salmon. Most modern

FIGURE 4.8

Life cycle of Pacific salmon

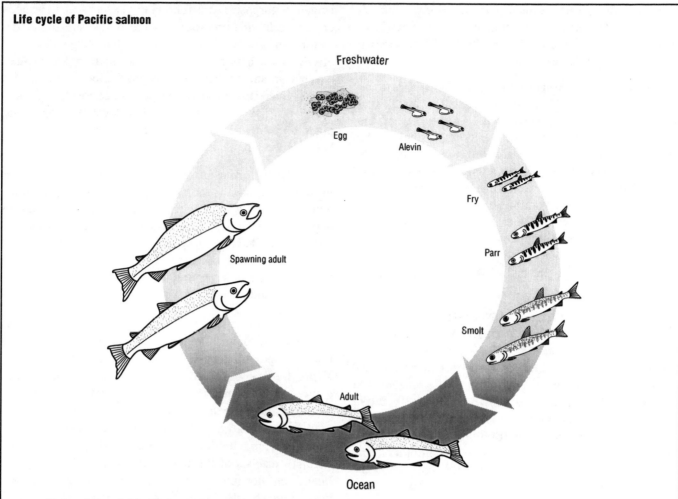

SOURCE: "Salmon Lifecycle," in *Handouts*, U.S. Department of Commerce, National Oceanic and Atmospheric Administration, National Marine Fisheries Service, Northwest Fisheries Science Center, undated, http://www.nwfsc.noaa.gov/education/documents/salmon%20life%20cycle%20handout.pdf (accessed February 12, 2016)

dams have fish ladders. However, all dams affect water temperature, flow, and quality.

Besides these threats, scientists believe climate change and the presence of nonnative aquatic species have depleted salmon populations.

SEA LION PREDATION. In recent years wildlife officials have grown increasingly concerned about predation on imperiled Pacific salmon by sea lions in the lower Columbia River. The problem is particularly severe on the downstream side of the Bonneville Dam. The dam spans the lower Columbia River between Oregon and Washington and is located approximately 145 miles (233 km) upstream of the river's mouth at the Pacific Ocean. In "Columbia River Sea Lion Management" (2016, http://wdfw.wa.gov/conservation/sealions/questions.html), the WDFW notes that sea lions have consumed thousands of fish, some of which are listed under the ESA. The fish congregate below the dam during their migration upstream; the dam is equipped with fish ladders that provide the fish passage

to upstream habitat. Each spring since 2002 trained observers at the dam have counted the number of sea lions preying on the fish and the number of fish eaten by the sea lions. The predators include California sea lions and Steller sea lions. The California sea lion is a thriving species that is not listed under the ESA, but is protected under the Marine Mammal Protection Act. The Steller sea lion (the eastern population) was a threatened species under the ESA, but was delisted in 2013 because of recovery.

According to the WDFW, hazing (the use of boats, underwater firecrackers, and rubber buckshot) is regularly conducted in an attempt to scare the sea lions away, but it interrupts the feeding only temporarily. In 2008 Idaho, Oregon, and Washington first received permission from the NMFS to remove or kill identifiable California sea lions that habitually prey on salmon at the dam. (The Steller sea lions were not targeted because of their ESA status.) The kill decision was challenged in court by the Humane Society of the United States, which argued that the California sea lions were being used as scapegoats by authorities who do not want to reduce fishing limits. A long legal battle ensued; however, state authorities have repeatedly received approval from the NMFS to remove or kill the California sea lions.

Ben Goldfarb explains in "Sea Lions Feast on Columbia Salmon" (HCN.org, August 17, 2015) that state authorities are allowed to kill up to 92 of the California sea lions each year. A record number of the animals were spotted in the Columbia River in 2015. Biologists believe that food shortages in ocean waters off the California coast are driving hungry sea lions to the river. Estimates vary on the percentage of the salmon runs that are being consumed by the sea lions. However, the hazing and killing practices were expected to continue in an effort to protect the multimillion-dollar investment by taxpayers in protecting the imperiled salmon under the ESA.

THE KLAMATH RIVER BASIN CONTROVERSY. The Klamath River originates in southern Oregon and flows southwest for more than 200 miles (320 km) across the southern part of Oregon and the northern part of California. (See Figure 4.9.) According to the NMFS, in *Klamath River Basin: 2009 Report to Congress* (June 30, 2009, http://www.nmfs.noaa.gov/pr/pdfs/klamath2009.pdf), the basin covers more than 10 million acres (4 million ha) and was once the third-largest producer of salmon on the West Coast. Over the past 100 years the salmon populations have been reduced to a fraction of what they once were. Demand for water in the basin has grown dramatically and has sparked bitter battles among fishing, agricultural, timber, mining, and environmental interests. These battles are complicated by the many stakeholders involved. The NMFS notes that approximately 6 million acres (2.4 million ha) in the basin are public lands. These include national wildlife refuges, national forests, national parks and monuments, and wild and scenic river designations—all managed by a variety of federal agencies and programs. In addition, approximately 96,000 acres (39,000 ha) are trust lands of six Native American tribes. The remaining 4 million acres (1.6 million ha) are in private hands. The basin is home to several anadromous species including stocks of chinook and coho salmon and steelhead, some of which are listed under the ESA.

Since the 1990s federal, tribal, state, and local authorities and other stakeholders have been trying to craft a plan acceptable to all parties for managing water supplies and fisheries in the basin. Freshwater resource management in the West is largely handled by the Bureau of Reclamation (BOR) under the U.S. Department of the Interior (DOI). Until 2001 the BOR managed to balance competing water demands from users in the basin and maintain river and stream flows for fish. In 2001 the region was struck by a drought, and the BOR allowed large water diversions for irrigation purposes. The following year tens of thousands of dead salmon were found in the basin, apparently the victims of low water flow. The BOR responded with drastic water cuts to farmers. This led to a full-fledged water war among Native American tribes, commercial fishing interests, conservation groups, farmers, and local water districts. Ever since, BOR-developed operating plans for water flows in the Klamath River basin have been continually challenged in court.

In 2008 dozens of stakeholders (federal, state, and local government agencies; irrigation districts; property owners; Native American tribes; and private conservation organizations) crafted the Klamath Basin Restoration Agreement (KBRA; http://www.edsheets.com/Klamath docs.html). The KBRA seeks to restore thriving fish populations in the river and satisfy local needs for irrigation water and power generation.

Meanwhile, a separate legal battle raged over efforts by PacifiCorp, an Oregon-based utility company, to renew a federal license for four dams it owns on the Klamath River. According to the NMFS, the license expired in 2006, but PacifiCorp can continue to operate the dams under the terms and conditions of its old license until it obtains a new license. One of the dams is called Iron Gate, and it blocks upstream fish passage to the northern reaches of the basin. (See Figure 4.9.) The old license did not require the company to provide fish ladders. However, the Federal Energy Regulatory Commission, which oversees power companies, has included fish passage requirements as a condition of relicensing the dam. The NMFS notes that the fish passages could open up more than 350 miles (560 km) of historical habitat for salmon and other migrating fish species. Since 2009 PacifiCorp has been negotiating with multiple stakeholders over possible removal of the dams.

According to the Klamath Basin Coordinating Council (http://www.klamathcouncil.org/), the KBRA terminated at year-end 2015 "because the federal authorizing legislation was not enacted." In other words, the agreement required congressional approval to continue forward, but failed to get that approval. In "Klamath Basin: Water Pact Crumbles in Congress after Years of Work" (OregonLive.com, December 19, 2015), Jeff Mapes explains how politics doomed the KBRA. He notes, "Among western Republicans, the idea of removing the dams has been viewed with great suspicion." According to Mapes, these critics feared "that it could create a precedent for fulfilling environmentalist fantasies for widespread dam removal in the West." However, in April 2016 numerous stakeholders (including the governors of Oregon and California) signed two new Klamath River basin agreements. The DOI explains in the press

FIGURE 4.9

Klamath River basin

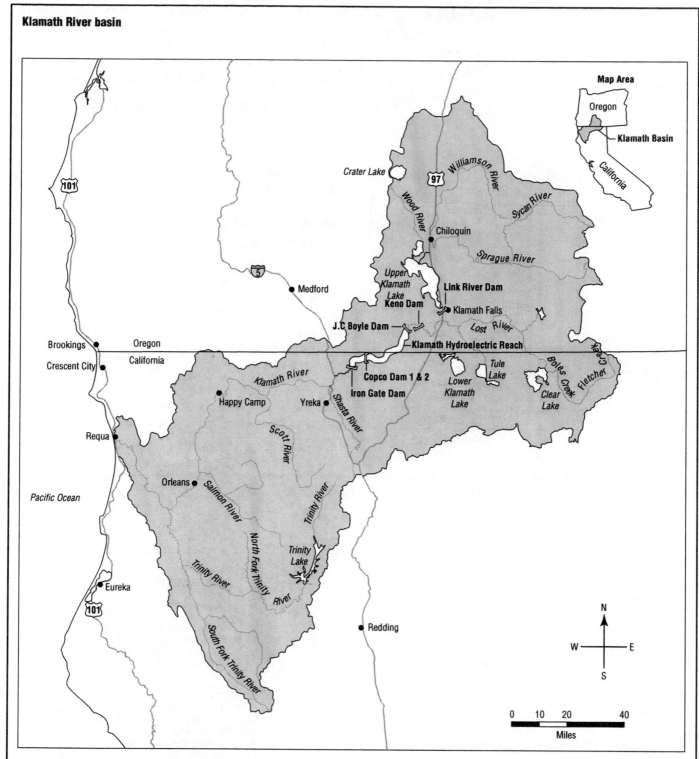

SOURCE: "Figure ES-1. The Klamath Basin," in *Klamath Facilities Removal Final Environmental Impact Statement/Environmental Impact Report*, vol. 1, U.S. Department of the Interior and California Department of Fish and Game, December 2012, http://klamathrestoration.gov/sites/klamathrestoration.gov/files/Additonal%20Files%20/1/4/Volume%20I_FEIS.pdf (accessed February 15, 2016)

release "Two New Klamath Basin Agreements Carve Out Path for Dam Removal and Provide Key Benefits to Irrigators" (April 6, 2016, https://www.doi.gov/press releases/two-new-klamath-basin-agreements-carve-out-path -dam-removal-and-provide-key-benefits) that the new agreements establish a process through which the four PacifiCorp dams will be removed by 2020. The DOI also notes that many of the tasks covered in the agreements will require congressional actions before they can be implemented.

Steelhead

Steelhead are members of the *Oncorhynchus* genus and have the scientific name *Oncorhynchus mykiss*. (See Figure 4.10.) Freshwater steelhead are called rainbow trout. Anadromous steelhead are also trout, but they are associated with salmon because of similarities in habitat and behavior. Steelhead are found in the Pacific Northwest and are anadromous like salmon but have two major differences: steelhead migrate individually, rather than in groups, and can spawn many times, not just once.

As of February 2016, there were 11 DPSs and one nonessential experimental population of steelhead listed under the ESA. (See Table 4.5.) Steelhead face the same threats as Pacific salmon: habitat loss and alteration, overharvesting, dams and other water obstacles, and competition with hatchery fish.

Imperiled Fish around the World

The International Union for Conservation of Nature (IUCN) indicates in *Red List of Threatened Species Version 2015.4* (http://www.iucnredlist.org/about/summary-statistics) that 2,271 out of 14,462 species of evaluated fish were threatened in November 2015. The IUCN notes that there are 33,200 known fish species, so it is expected that many more fish species will be listed in the future as more evaluations are completed.

As of February 2016, the USFWS listed 23 foreign species of fish as endangered or threatened. This includes the 18 species shown in Table 4.7. They are found in

FIGURE 4.10

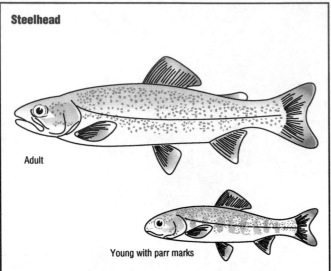

Steelhead

Adult

Young with parr marks

SOURCE: Adapted from "Steelhead Trout (and Rainbow Trout)," in *Fish of the Columbia River*, U.S. Department of Energy, Pacific Northwest National Laboratory, undated, http://ecology.pnnl.gov/rivers/colrvrfish/sh.htm (accessed February 15, 2016)

TABLE 4.7

Foreign endangered and threatened fish species (excluding sawfish), February 2016

Common name	Scientific name	Federal listing status*	Current distribution or historic range
Adriatic sturgeon	*Acipenser naccarii*	E	Adriatic Sea
Ala balik (trout)	*Salmo platycephalus*	E	Turkey
Asian bonytongue	*Scleropages formosus*	E	Thailand, Malaysia, Indonesia
Ayumodoki (loach)	*Hymenophysa curta*	E	Japan
Beluga sturgeon	*Huso huso*	T	Azerbaijan, Bosnia and Herzegovina, Bulgaria, Croatia, Czech Republic, Georgia, Hungary, Islamic Republic of Iran, Italy, Kazakhstan, Republic of Moldova, Romania, Russian Federation, Serbia and Montenegro, Turkey, Turkmenistan, Ukraine
Catfish	*Pangasius sanitwongsei*	E	Thailand
Chinese sturgeon	*Acipenser sinensis*	E	Northwest Pacific Ocean in China, Japan, South Korea, and North Korea
Cicek (minnow)	*Acanthorutilus handlirschi*	E	Turkey
European sturgeon	*Acipenser sturio*	E	North Sea, the English Channel, and most European coasts of the Atlantic Ocean, the Mediterranean Sea, and the Black Sea
Ikan temoleh (minnow)	*Probarbus jullieni*	E	Vietnam, Thailand, Malaysia, Laos, Cambodia
Kaluga sturgeon	*Huso dauricus*	E	Amur River basin, Sea of Okhotsk and the Sea of Japan
Mexican blindcat (catfish)	*Prietella phreatophila*	E	Mexico
Miyako tango (=Toyko bitterling)	*Tanakia tanago*	E	Japan
Nekogigi (catfish)	*Coreobagrus ichikawai*	E	Japan
Sakhalin sturgeon	*Acipenser mikadoi*	E	Northwest Pacific Ocean in Japan and Russia
Scalloped hammerhead shark	*Sphyrna lewini*	E; T	Eastern Atlantic Ocean, including Mediterranean Sea
Thailand giant catfish	*Pangasianodon gigas*	E	Thailand
Totoaba (seatrout or weakfish)	*Cynoscion macdonaldi*	E	Mexico (Gulf of California)

*E = Endangered. T = Threatened.

SOURCE: Adapted from "Generate Species List," in *Environmental Conservation Online System Species Reports*, U.S. Department of the Interior, U.S. Fish and Wildlife Service, February 2016, http://ecos.fws.gov/tess_public/pub/adHocSpeciesForm.jsp (accessed February 18, 2016), and "Untitled," in "Endangered and Threatened Wildlife and Plants; Adding Five Species of Sawfish to the List of Endangered and Threatened Wildlife," *Federal Register*, vol. 80, no. 16, January 26, 2015, https://www.gpo.gov/fdsys/pkg/FR-2015-01-26/pdf/2015-01348.pdf (accessed February 18, 2016)

TABLE 4.8

Sawfish listings under the Endangered Species Act

| Species | | | Vertebrate population where endangered | |
Common name	Scientific name	Historic range	or threatened	Status
Fishes				
Sawfish, dwarf	*Pristis davata*	Indo-Pacific, Western Pacific, and eastern Indian Oceans	Entire	E
Sawfish, green	*Pristis zijsron*	Indo-Pacific Ocean, Persian Gulf, Red sea	Entire	E
Sawfish, largetooth	*Pristis pristis (formerly Pristis perotteti, Pristis pristis, and Pristis microdon)*	Indian, Indo-Pacific, Eastern Pacific, and Atlantic Oceans, Gulf of Mexico	Entire	E
Sawfish, narrow	*Anoxypristis cuspidata*	Indian and Western Pacific Oceans, Red sea	Entire	E
Sawfish, smalltooth (Non-U.S. DPS)	*Pristis pectinata*	Atlantic Oceans, Caribbean Sea, Gulf of Mexico	Smalltooth sawfish originating from non-U.S. waters	E
Sawfish, smalltooth (U.S. DPS)	*Pristis pectinata*	North Atlantic Ocean (Mediterranean U.S. Atlantic, and Gulf of Mexico) and the Southwest Atlantic Ocean	Smalltooth sawfish originating from U.S. waters	E

SOURCE: Adapted from "Untitled," in "Endangered and Threatened Wildlife and Plants; Adding Five Species of Sawfish to the List of Endangered and Threatened Wildlife," *Federal Register*, vol. 80, no. 16, January 26, 2015, https://www.gpo.gov/fdsys/pkg/FR-2015-01-26/pdf/2015-01348.pdf (accessed February 18, 2016)

FIGURE 4.11

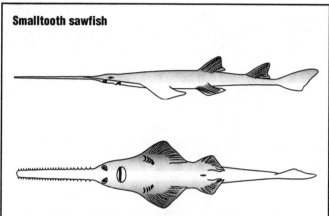

Smalltooth sawfish

SOURCE: "Smalltooth Sawfish," in *Frequently Asked Questions*, U.S. Department of Commerce, National Oceanic and Atmospheric Administration, Northeast Fisheries Science Center, June 16, 2011, http://www.nefsc.noaa.gov/faq/fishfaq1.html (accessed February 18, 2016)

waters around the world, but primarily in Asia. In January 2015 four foreign sawfish populations were listed as endangered under the ESA. (See Table 4.8 for a description of their historic ranges.) They joined a domestic DPS of the smalltooth sawfish that was already listed. (See Figure 4.11.)

CHAPTER 5
CLAMS, SNAILS, CRUSTACEANS, AND CORALS

CLAMS, SNAILS, AND CRUSTACEANS

Clams, snails, and crustaceans are small aquatic creatures. They are invertebrates, meaning they lack an internal skeleton made of bone or cartilage. Clams and snails are in the phylum Mollusca. Mollusks have soft bodies that are usually enclosed in a thin hard shell made of calcium. The U.S. Fish and Wildlife Service (USFWS) uses the generic term *clam* to refer to clams and mussels, but there are physical and reproductive differences between the two creatures. In general, mussels are larger than clams and have an oblong lopsided shell, as opposed to the round symmetrical shell of the clam.

Crustaceans are a large class of creatures with a hard exoskeleton (external skeleton), appendages, and antennae. This class includes lobsters, shrimps, and crabs. Corals are marine creatures of the phylum Cnidaria, along with jellyfish and anemones.

As of February 2016, there were 188 U.S. and foreign species of clams (including mussels), snails, crustaceans, and corals listed under the Endangered Species Act (ESA) as endangered or threatened. (See Table 1.3 in Chapter 1.) As shown in Table 1.2 in Chapter 1, one species—Sampson's pearlymussel (1984)—has been delisted because of extinction. The mussel once inhabited southeastern rivers and was likely decimated decades ago by dam building and other habitat disturbances. In 2013 the USFWS delisted the Magazine Mountain shagreen (a snail found in the Ozark Mountains in Arkansas) because of recovery. (See Table 2.7 in Chapter 2.) It was the first invertebrate to achieve that distinction under the ESA. According to the USFWS (May 15, 2013, http://www.gpo .gov/fdsys/pkg/FR-2013-05-15/html/2013-11541.htm), the snail was originally listed, in part, because of potential threats from planned military and state uses of Magazine Mountain. The U.S. Army (2013, http://www.asaie.army .mil/Public/ESOH/REEO/Central/docs/Central_Review _June_2013.pdf) notes that it abandoned its plans to use

the area after the snail was listed under the ESA in 1989. Other potential threats were minimized to protect the species and help realize its recovery.

Table 5.1 shows the 10 listed clam, snail, crustacean, and coral species with the highest expenditures under the ESA during fiscal year (FY) 2014. More than $13.4 million was spent on activities to conserve these 10 species.

CLAMS AND MUSSELS

There were 88 U.S. species of clams and mussels listed under the ESA as of February 2016. (See Table 5.2.) Most had an endangered listing, and nearly all had recovery plans in place. The vast majority of imperiled clams and mussels in the United States are freshwater species that inhabit inland rivers, primarily in the Southeast. Conservation efforts for freshwater mussels include the captive breeding and reintroduction of some species, as well as measures to restore damaged habitats.

Mussels are bivalved (two-shelled) creatures encased in hard hinged shells made of calcium. The freshwater species can grow to be up to 6 inches (15.2 cm) in length. The United States, with nearly 300 species, has the greatest diversity of freshwater mussels in the world. According to the U.S. Geological Survey (USGS), in "Conservation of Southeastern Mussels" (December 14, 2012, http:// fl.biology.usgs.gov/Southeastern_Aquatic_Fauna/Fresh water_Mussels/freshwater_mussels.html), approximately 90% of these creatures live in southeastern states. Most of them are found burrowed into the sand and gravel beds of rivers and streams making up the Mississippi River system. Mussels have a footlike appendage that acts like an anchor to hold them in place. They can use this appendage to move themselves slowly over small distances. Mussels tend to congregate in large groups called colonies.

Mussels are filter-feeders. They have a siphoning system that sucks in food and oxygen from the water. Their

TABLE 5.1

The 10 listed clam, snail, crustacean, and coral species with the highest expenditures under the Endangered Species Act, fiscal year 2014

Ranking	Species	Population	Expenditure
1	Fairy shrimp, vernal pool (*Branchinecta lynchi*)	Entire	$3,585,385
2	Tadpole shrimp, vernal pool (*Lepidurus packardi*)	Entire	$1,878,739
3	Abalone, black (*Haliotis cracherodii*)	Entire	$1,666,933
4	Coral, elkhorn (*Acropora palmata*)	Entire	$1,388,887
5	Coral, staghorn (*Acropora cervicornis*)	Entire	$1,357,008
6	Mussel, snuffbox (*Epioblasma triquetra*)	Entire	$1,002,972
7	Abalone, white (*Haliotis sorenseni*)	North America (West Coast from Point Conception, CA, U.S.A., to Punta Abreojos, Baja California, Mexico)	$749,899
8	Higgins eye (pearlymussel) (*Lampsilis higginsii*)	Entire	$628,537
9	Snails, Oahu tree (*Achatinella spp.*)	Entire	$626,181
10	Mucket, pink (pearlymussel) (*Lampsilis abrupta*)	Entire	$560,996

SOURCE: Adapted from "Table 2. Species Ranked in Descending Order of Total FY 2014 Reported Expenditures, Not Including Land Acquisition Costs," in *Federal and State Endangered and Threatened Species Expenditures: Fiscal Year 2014*, U.S. Department of the Interior, U.S. Fish and Wildlife Service, March 2, 2016, http://www.fws.gov/endangered/esa-library/pdf/20160302_final_FY14_ExpRpt.pdf (accessed March 9, 2016)

gills can filter impurities out of the water. Thus, mussels are tiny natural water purifiers. They are also an indicator species in that their level of health and well-being is highly indicative of the overall condition of the freshwater systems in which they live.

Most mussel species have a unique way of spreading their offspring. A female mussel can produce several thousand eggs in a year. After the eggs are fertilized, they develop into larvae and are released. The larvae latch onto the fins or gills of passing fish and stay there until they have grown into baby clams. At that point they turn loose of the fish and drop to the river bottom. The larvae are called glochidia. It is believed that glochidia are harmless to the fish on which they hitchhike. This parasitic relationship allows mussels to spread and distribute beyond their usual range.

Mussel Declines

The decline of freshwater mussels began during the 1800s. Many of the creatures have an interior shell surface with a pearl-like sheen. These pearlymussels were in great demand as a source of buttons for clothing until the invention of plastic. Collectors also killed many mussels by prying them open looking for pearls. Until the 1990s mussel shells were ground up and used in the oyster pearl industry. Another cause for decline has been habitat disturbance, especially water pollution and the modification of aquatic habitats by dams. In addition, erosion due to strip mining and agriculture causes siltation that can actually bury and suffocate mussels. The invasive zebra mussel and quagga mussel have also harmed native freshwater mussel species, such as the Higgins eye pearlymussel, by competing with them for food and other resources.

Higgins Eye Pearlymussel

The Higgins eye pearlymussel is a freshwater species native to the United States and found in the waters of Illinois, Iowa, Minnesota, Missouri, Nebraska, and Wisconsin.

According to the USFWS, in "Higgins Eye Pearlymussel *Lampsilis higginsii*" (April 14, 2015, http://www.fws.gov/midwest/endangered/clams/higginseye/higgins_fs.html), "Higgins eye are prey for wildlife like muskrats, otters, and raccoons; they filter water which improves water quality; and mussel beds create microhabitats on river bottoms that provide food and cover for other aquatic life." The species was named after its discoverer, Frank Higgins, who found some of the mussels in the Mississippi River near Muscatine, Iowa, during the mid-1800s. Over the next few decades Muscatine developed a thriving pearl-button industry that lasted into the 1940s. Higgins eye were also harvested for the commercial pearl industry.

In 1976 the Higgins eye pearlymussel was listed as an endangered species under the ESA. More than a century of scavenging by humans had severely depleted the species. Dams, navigational structures, and water quality problems in the upper Mississippi River system were contributing factors to its decline. In 1983 the USFWS published its first recovery plan for the Higgins eye. The plan identified areas that were deemed essential habitat for the species and called for limits on construction and harvesting in those areas.

In May 2004 the USFWS published *Higgins Eye Pearlymussel (*Lampsilis higginsii*) Recovery Plan: First Revision* (http://ecos.fws.gov/docs/recovery_plans/2004/040714.pdf). The plan examines more recent threats to the pearlymussel's survival, primarily the pervasive spread of zebra mussels, an invasive species. It acknowledges that there is no feasible way to eliminate zebra mussels to the extent needed to benefit the Higgins eye. Instead, the plan focuses on developing methods to prevent new zebra mussel infestations and working to lessen the impacts of already infested populations.

The USFWS indicates in "Saving the Higgins Eye Pearlymussel" (April 14, 2015, http://www.fws.gov/midwest/Endangered/clams/higginseye/propagation_fs.html) that

TABLE 5.2

Endangered and threatened clam and mussel species, February 2016

Common name	Scientific name	Federal listing status[a]	U.S. or U.S./foreign listed	Recovery plan date	Recovery plan stage[b]
Alabama (=inflated) heelsplitter	Potamilus inflatus	T	US	04/13/93	F
Alabama lampmussel	Lampsilis virescens	E; EXPN	US	07/02/85	F
Alabama moccasinshell	Medionidus acutissimus	T	US	11/17/00	F
Alabama pearlshell	Margaritifera marrianae	E	US	None	—
Altamaha spinymussel	Elliptio spinosa	E	US	None	—
Appalachian elktoe	Alasmidonta raveneliana	E	US	08/26/96	F
Appalachian monkeyface (pearlymussel)	Quadrula sparsa	E; EXPN	US	07/09/84	F
Arkansas fatmucket	Lampsilis powellii	T	US	02/10/92	F
Birdwing pearlymussel	Lemiox rimosus	E; EXPN	US	07/09/84	F
Black clubshell	Pleurobema curtum	E	US	11/14/89	F
Carolina heelsplitter	Lasmigona decorata	E	US	01/17/97	F
Chipola slabshell	Elliptio chipolaensis	T	US	09/19/03	F
Choctaw bean	Villosa choctawensis	E	US	None	—
Clubshell	Pleurobema clava	E; EXPN	US	09/21/94	F
Coosa moccasinshell	Medionidus parvulus	E	US	11/17/00	F
Cracking pearlymussel	Hemistena lata	E; EXPN	US	07/11/91	F
Cumberland bean (pearlymussel)	Villosa trabalis	E; EXPN	US	08/22/84	F
Cumberland elktoe	Alasmidonta atropurpurea	E	US	05/24/04	F
Cumberland monkeyface (pearlymussel)	Quadrula intermedia	E; EXPN	US	07/09/84	F
Cumberland pigtoe	Pleurobema gibberum	E	US	08/13/92	F
Cumberlandian combshell	Epioblasma brevidens	E; EXPN	US	05/24/04	F
Curtis pearlymussel	Epioblasma florentina curtisii	E	US	02/04/86	F
Dark pigtoe	Pleurobema furvum	E	US	11/17/00	F
Dromedary pearlymussel	Dromus dromas	E; EXPN	US	07/09/84	F
Dwarf wedgemussel	Alasmidonta heterodon	E	US/foreign	02/08/93	F
Fanshell	Cyprogenia stegaria	E; EXPN	US	07/09/91	F
Fat pocketbook	Potamilus capax	E	US	11/14/89	F
Fat threeridge (mussel)	Amblema neislerii	E	US	09/19/03	F
Finelined pocketbook	Lampsilis altilis	T	US	11/17/00	F
Finerayed pigtoe	Fusconaia cuneolus	E; EXPN	US	09/19/84	F
Flat pigtoe	Pleurobema marshalli	E	US	11/14/89	F
Fluted kidneyshell	Ptychobranchus subtentum	E	US	None	—
Fuzzy pigtoe	Pleurobema strodeanum	T	US	None	—
Georgia pigtoe	Pleurobema hanleyianum	E	US	11/06/14	F
Green blossom (pearlymussel)	Epioblasma torulosa gubernaculum	E	US	07/09/84	F
Gulf moccasinshell	Medionidus penicillatus	E	US	09/19/03	F
Heavy pigtoe	Pleurobema taitianum	E	US	11/14/89	F
Higgins eye (pearlymussel)	Lampsilis higginsii	E	US	07/14/04	RF(1)
James spinymussel	Pleurobema collina	E	US	09/24/90	F
Littlewing pearlymussel	Pegias fabula	E	US	09/22/89	F
Louisiana pearlshell	Margaritifera hembeli	T	US	12/03/90	F
Narrow pigtoe	Fusconaia escambia	T	US	None	—
Neosho mucket	Lampsilis rafinesqueana	E	US	None	—
Northern riffleshell	Epioblasma torulosa rangiana	E	US	09/21/94	F
Ochlockonee moccasinshell	Medionidus simpsonianus	E	US	09/19/03	F
Orangefoot pimpleback (pearlymussel)	Plethobasus cooperianus	E; EXPN	US	09/30/84	F
Orangenacre mucket	Lampsilis perovalis	T	US	11/17/00	F
Ouachita rock pocketbook	Arkansia wheeleri	E	US	06/02/04	F
Oval pigtoe	Pleurobema pyriforme	E	US	09/19/03	F
Ovate clubshell	Pleurobema perovatum	E	US	11/17/00	F
Oyster mussel	Epioblasma capsaeformis	E; EXPN	US	05/24/04	F
Pale lilliput (pearlymussel)	Toxolasma cylindrellus	E	US	08/22/84	F
Pink mucket (pearlymussel)	Lampsilis abrupta	E	US	01/24/85	F
Purple bankclimber (mussel)	Elliptoideus sloatianus	T	US	09/19/03	F
Purple bean	Villosa perpurpurea	E	US	05/24/04	F
Purple cat's paw (=Purple cat's paw pearlymussel)	Epioblasma obliquata obliquata	E; EXPN	US	03/10/92	F
Rabbitsfoot	Quadrula cylindrica cylindrica	T	US	None	—
Rayed bean	Villosa fabalis	E	US/foreign	None	—
Ring pink (mussel)	Obovaria retusa	E; EXPN	US	03/25/91	F
Rough pigtoe	Pleurobema plenum	E; EXPN	US	08/06/84	F
Rough rabbitsfoot	Quadrula cylindrica strigillata	E	US	05/24/04	F
Round ebonyshell	Fusconaia rotulata	E	US	None	—
Scaleshell mussel	Leptodea leptodon	E	US	04/07/10	F
Sheepnose mussel	Plethobasus cyphyus	E	US	None	—
Shiny pigtoe	Fusconaia cor	E; EXPN	US	07/09/84	F
Shinyrayed pocketbook	Lampsilis subangulata	E	US	09/19/03	F
Slabside pearlymussel	Pleuronaia dolabelloides	E	US	None	—
Snuffbox mussel	Epioblasma triquetra	E	US/foreign	None	—
Southern acornshell	Epioblasma othcaloogensis	E	US	11/17/00	F

the Genoa National Fish Hatchery in Genoa, Wisconsin, specializes in capturing female Higgins eye pearlymussels that have not yet released their glochidia. The glochidia are removed via a syringe and placed in tanks or buckets that

TABLE 5.2

Endangered and threatened clam and mussel species, February 2016 [CONTINUED]

Common name	Scientific name	Federal listing status[a]	U.S. or U.S./foreign listed	Recovery plan date	Recovery plan stage[b]
Southern clubshell	Pleurobema decisum	E	US	11/17/00	F
Southern combshell	Epioblasma penita	E	US	11/14/89	F
Southern kidneyshell	Ptychobranchus jonesi	E	US	None	—
Southern pigtoe	Pleurobema georgianum	E	US	11/17/00	F
Southern sandshell	Hamiota australis	T	US	None	—
Speckled pocketbook	Lampsilis streckeri	E	US	01/02/92	F
Spectaclecase (mussel)	Cumberlandia monodonta	E	US	None	—
Stirrupshell	Quadrula stapes	E	US	11/14/89	F
Tan riffleshell	Epioblasma florentina walkeri (= E. walkeri)	E	US	10/22/84	F
Tapered pigtoe	Fusconaia burkei	T	US	None	—
Tar River spinymussel	Elliptio steinstansana	E	US	05/05/92	RF(1)
Triangular kidneyshell	Ptychobranchus greenii	E	US	11/17/00	F
Tubercled blossom (pearlymussel)	Epioblasma torulosa torulosa	E; EXPN	US	01/25/85	F
Turgid blossom (pearlymussel)	Epioblasma turgidula	E; EXPN	US	01/25/85	F
Upland combshell	Epioblasma metastriata	E	US	11/17/00	F
White catspaw (pearlymussel)	Epioblasma obliquata perobliqua	E	US	01/25/90	F
White wartyback (pearlymussel)	Plethobasus cicatricosus	E; EXPN	US	09/19/84	F
Winged mapleleaf	Quadrula fragosa	E; EXPN	US	06/25/97	F
Yellow blossom (pearlymussel)	Epioblasma florentina florentina	E; EXPN	US	01/25/85	F

[a]E = Endangered. T = Threatened. EXPN = Experimental Population, Non-essential.
[b]F = Final. RF = Final Revision.

SOURCE: Adapted from "Generate Species List," in *Environmental Conservation Online System Species Reports*, U.S. Department of the Interior, U.S. Fish and Wildlife Service, February 2016, http://ecos.fws.gov/tess_public/pub/adHocSpeciesForm.jsp (accessed February 12, 2016), and "Listed FWS/Joint FWS and NMFS Species and Populations with Recovery Plans (Sorted by Listed Entity)," in *Recovery Plans Search*, U.S. Department of the Interior, U.S. Fish and Wildlife Service, February 2016, http://ecos.fws.gov/tess_public/pub/speciesRecovery.jsp?sort=1 (accessed February 12, 2016)

contain suitable host fish. The fish are either released into the environment or maintained at the hatchery until the glochidia are mature enough to live on their own. These juvenile mussels are then released into natural waters that are free from invasive mussel species.

In July 2014 the USFWS (https://www.gpo.gov/fdsys/pkg/FR-2014-07-08/pdf/2014-15867.pdf) initiated a five-year review for several species, including the Higgins eye pearlymussel. As explained in Chapter 2, the ESA requires all listed species to be reviewed at least every five years to determine whether they still require ESA protection. As of April 2016, the results of the review had not been issued.

ZEBRA AND QUAGGA MUSSELS: AN INFESTATION. In 1988 an unwelcome visitor was discovered in the waters of Lake St. Clair, Michigan: a zebra mussel (*Dreissena polymorpha*). The zebra mussel is native to eastern Europe. It is smaller than the freshwater mussels found in the United States and has a different method for spreading its young. The larvae of zebra mussels do not require a fish host to develop into babies. They can attach to any hard surface under the water. This allows zebra mussels to spread much easier and quicker than their American counterparts.

It is believed that the first zebra mussels migrated to the United States in the ballast water of ships. This is water held in large tanks below deck to improve the stability and control of ships. Ballast water is pumped in and out as needed during a journey. Zebra mussels

have also been found clinging to the hulls of small fishing boats and recreational craft. These boats are hauled overland on trailers, and this allows the creatures to travel great distances between inland water bodies.

Another foreign invader of concern is the quagga mussel (*Dreissena bugensis*), a native of Ukraine in eastern Europe. In 1989 the mussel was first sighted in the United States in Lake Erie. By the mid-1990s it had spread to other lakes in the upper Midwest. In 2007 the mussel was discovered in lakes in Arizona, Nevada, and Southern California. This finding is particularly troubling to scientists because of the large concentration of imperiled aquatic species in southwestern water bodies.

Figure 5.1 and Figure 5.2 show USGS maps of the distribution of zebra and quagga mussels, respectively, throughout the country as of December 2015. These invasive species have spread from the Great Lakes south to the Gulf of Mexico and east to New England and are beginning to show up in western waters. They have been found on boat hulls as far west as California. Throughout waterways in the Midwest, colonies of zebra mussels have clogged pipes and other structures that are used for municipal and industrial water supply. In addition, the pests have significantly degraded native mussel colonies by competing for available food, space, and resources.

The Invasive Mussel Collaborative is a partnership between the Great Lakes Commission, the USGS, the National Oceanic and Atmospheric Administration

FIGURE 5.1

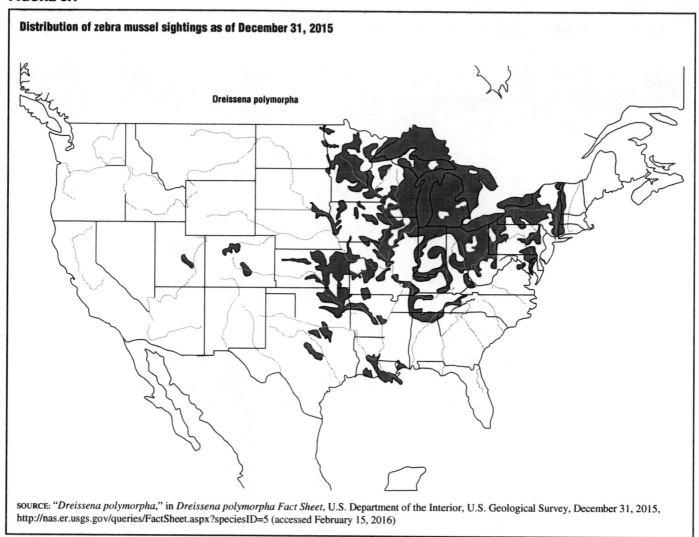

Distribution of zebra mussel sightings as of December 31, 2015

Dreissena polymorpha

SOURCE: "*Dreissena polymorpha*," in *Dreissena polymorpha Fact Sheet*, U.S. Department of the Interior, U.S. Geological Survey, December 31, 2015, http://nas.er.usgs.gov/queries/FactSheet.aspx?speciesID=5 (accessed February 15, 2016)

(NOAA), and the Great Lakes Fishery Commission. In "Invasive Mussel Collaborative" (April 8, 2015, http://64.9.200.103/imc/files/Invasive-Mussel-Collaborative-Prospectus_rev-4-8-2015.pdf), the Invasive Mussel Collaborative notes that biopesticides are being developed and tested for their ability to kill invasive mussels without harming native mussels. One example is the commercial product Zequanox, which is made from "a common soil bacterium." In January 2016 the Invasive Mussel Collaborative (http://invasivemusselcollaborative.net/events/webinar-case-studies-in-zebra-and-quagga-mussel-control-for-inland-waterbodies/) conducted a webinar in which case studies were presented on the use of biopesticides and other killing methods in relatively small inland waters around the United States. The results indicate that the eradication efforts were largely effective, but further research is still needed.

Snails

Snails belong to the class Gastropoda of mollusks. They typically have an external spiral-shaped shell and a distinct head that includes sensory organs. Snails inhabit terrestrial (land), marine (ocean), and freshwater environments. Most land snails prefer moist, heavily vegetated locations and survive on a diet of vegetation and algae. However, there are a few carnivorous (meat-eating) snail species. Snails are found throughout the United States. Most imperiled species are located in the West (including Hawaii) and the Southeast (primarily Alabama). Land snails are imperiled by a variety of factors including the destruction of habitat, being preyed on by rats and invasive carnivorous snails, and the spread of nonnative vegetation. Some marine snails have historically been prized by humans as a food source. Scientists say that snails play a valuable role in their ecosystems by recycling nutrients, such as nitrogen, that they ingest from food sources and then excrete back to the environment.

As of February 2016, there were 50 U.S. and foreign species of snails listed under the ESA. (See Table 5.3.) Most had an endangered listing and nearly all had recovery plans in place. As shown in Table 5.1, more than $2.4 million was spent under the ESA during FY 2014 to

FIGURE 5.2

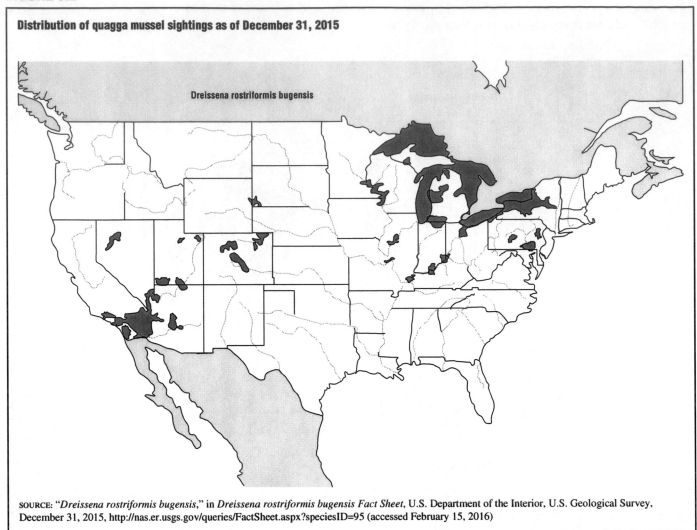

Distribution of quagga mussel sightings as of December 31, 2015

Dreissena rostriformis bugensis

SOURCE: "*Dreissena rostriformis bugensis*," in *Dreissena rostriformis bugensis Fact Sheet*, U.S. Department of the Interior, U.S. Geological Survey, December 31, 2015, http://nas.er.usgs.gov/queries/FactSheet.aspx?speciesID=95 (accessed February 15, 2016)

conserve the white abalone and black abalone. As marine species, they are under the jurisdiction of the National Marine Fisheries Service (NMFS), an agency within NOAA.

Abalone

Abalone are marine snails in the Haliotidae family. According to the NMFS, in *Status Review Report for Black Abalone* (January 2009, http://www.nmfs.noaa .gov/pr/pdfs/statusreviews/blackabalone.pdf), abalone were once abundant along the West Coast, primarily from Southern California to northern Mexico. Intense harvesting of the animals in the decades after World War II (1939–1945) severely depleted their populations.

As of January 2016, the NMFS (http://www.nmfs .noaa.gov/pr/species/invertebrates/) was monitoring five of the species. The green, pink, and pinto abalone were species of concern (or candidates for listing under the ESA). The white abalone was listed as endangered in 2001 and was the first marine invertebrate ever to be listed under the ESA. In the listing rule, the NMFS

(May 29, 2001, http://www.gpo.gov/fdsys/pkg/FR-2001-05-29/pdf/01-13430.pdf#page=1) indicated that it did not intend to designate critical habitat for the species because of fears about poaching (illegal hunting). The black abalone was listed as endangered in 2009. In October 2011 the NMFS (https://www.federalregister.gov/articles/2011/10/ 27/2011-27376/endangered-and-threatened-wildlife-and-plants-final-rulemaking-to-designate-critical-habitat-for) designated 139 square miles (360 sq km) of rocky California coastline as critical habitat for it. According to the NMFS, black abalone are much less desirable for human consumption than white abalone.

As of April 2016, a recovery plan had not been published for the black abalone, and the most recent recovery plan for the white abalone was published in October 2008. The NMFS indicates in *Final White Abalone Recovery Plan (Haliotis sorenseni)* (http:// ecos.fws.gov/docs/recovery_plan/whiteabalone.pdf) that recovery will be extremely difficult because of the low population size. In fact, the NMFS describes the population size in 2008 as "near zero." As such, no potential

TABLE 5.3

Endangered and threatened snail species, February 2016

Common name	Scientific name	Federal listing status[a]	U.S. or U.S./foreign listed	Recovery plan date	Recovery plan stage[b]
Alamosa springsnail	Tryonia alamosae	E	US	08/31/94	F
Anthony's riversnail	Athearnia anthonyi	E; EXPN	US	08/13/97	F
Armored snail	Pyrgulopsis (=Marstonia) pachyta	E	US	07/01/94	D
Banbury Springs limpet	Lanx sp.	E	US	11/26/95	F
Black abalone	Haliotis cracherodii	E	US	None	—
Bliss Rapids snail	Taylorconcha serpenticola	T	US	11/26/95	F
Bruneau hot springsnail	Pyrgulopsis bruneauensis	E	US	09/30/02	F
Chittenango ovate amber snail	Succinea chittenangoensis	T	US	08/21/06	RF(1)
Chupadera springsnail	Pyrgulopsis chupaderae	E	US	None	—
Cylindrical lioplax (snail)	Lioplax cyclostomaformis	E	US	12/02/05	F
Diamond tryonia	Pseudotryonia adamantina	E	US	None	—
Flat pebblesnail	Lepyrium showalteri	E	US	12/02/05	F
Flat-spired three-toothed snail	Triodopsis platysayoides	T	US	05/09/83	F
Fragile tree snail	Samoana fragilis	E	US	None	—
Gonzales tryonia	Tryonia circumstriata (=stocktonensis)	E	US	None	—
Guam tree snail	Partula radiolata	E	US	None	—
Humped tree snail	Partula gibba	E	US	None	—
Interrupted (=Georgia) rocksnail	Leptoxis foremani	E	US	None	—
Iowa Pleistocene snail	Discus macclintocki	E	US	03/22/84	F
Kanab ambersnail	Oxyloma haydeni kanabensis	E	US	10/12/95	F
Koster's springsnail	Juturnia kosteri	E	US	None	—
Lacy elimia (snail)	Elimia crenatella	T	US	12/02/05	F
Lanai tree snail	Partulina semicarinata	E	US	None	—
Lanai tree snail	Partulina variabilis	E	US	None	—
Langford's tree snail	Partula langfordi	E	US	None	—
Morro shoulderband (=Banded dune) snail	Helminthoglypta walkeriana	E	US	09/28/98	F
Newcomb's snail	Erinna newcombi	T	US	09/18/06	F
Newcomb's tree snail	Newcombia cumingi	E	US	None	—
Noonday globe	Patera clarki nantahala	T	US	09/07/84	F
Oahu tree snails	Achatinella spp.	E	US	06/30/92	F
Painted rocksnail	Leptoxis taeniata	T	US	12/02/05	F
Painted snake coiled forest snail	Anguispira picta	T	US	10/14/82	F
Pecos assiminea snail	Assiminea pecos	E	US/foreign	None	—
Phantom springsnail	Pyrgulopsis texana	E	US	None	—
Phantom tryonia	Tryonia cheatumi	E	US	None	—
Plicate rocksnail	Leptoxis plicata	E	US	12/02/05	F
Roswell springsnail	Pyrgulopsis roswellensis	E	US	None	—
Rough hornsnail	Pleurocera foremani	E	US	11/06/14	F
Round rocksnail	Leptoxis ampla	T	US	12/02/05	F
Royal marstonia (snail)	Pyrgulopsis ogmorhaphe	E	US	08/11/95	F
San Bernardino springsnail	Pyrgulopsis bernardina	T	US	None	—
Slender campeloma	Campeloma decampi	E	US	None	—
Snake River physa snail	Physa natricina	E	US	11/26/95	F
Socorro springsnail	Pyrgulopsis neomexicana	E	US	08/31/94	F
Stock Island tree snail	Orthalicus reses (not incl. nesodryas)	T	US	05/18/99	F
Three Forks springsnail	Pyrgulopsis trivialis	E	US	None	—
Tulotoma snail	Tulotoma magnifica	T	US	11/17/00	F
Tumbling Creek cavesnail	Antrobia culveri	E	US	09/22/03	F
Virginia fringed mountain snail	Polygyriscus virginianus	E	US	05/09/83	F
White abalone	Haliotis sorenseni	E	US/foreign	01/12/09	F

[a]E = Endangered. T = Threatened. EXPN = Experimental Population, Non-essential.
[b]F = Final. RF = Final Revision. D = Draft.

SOURCE: Adapted from "Generate Species List," in *Environmental Conservation Online System Species Reports*, U.S. Department of the Interior, U.S. Fish and Wildlife Service, February 2016, http://ecos.fws.gov/tess_public/pub/adHocSpeciesForm.jsp (accessed February 12, 2016), and "Listed FWS/Joint FWS and NMFS Species and Populations with Recovery Plans (Sorted by Listed Entity)," in *Recovery Plans Search*, U.S. Department of the Interior, U.S. Fish and Wildlife Service, February 2016, http://ecos.fws.gov/tess_public/pub/speciesRecovery.jsp?sort=1 (accessed February 12, 2016)

recovery date is given; however, the agency estimates that recovery will likely take "several decades and cost $20 million at a minimum."

In "White Abalone, What Turns You On?" (August 10, 2015, http://www.fisheries.noaa.gov/podcasts/2015/08/white_abalone.html), the NMFS describes a captive breeding program for white abalone at the Bodega Marine Laboratory at the University of California, Davis. White abalone have proven very difficult to propagate in captivity. However, the NMFS indicates that the program has successfully reared thousands of the snails and is working to find environmental cues that prompt the species to propagate.

Crustaceans

Crustaceans are a large class of mandibulate (jawed) creatures in the phylum Arthropoda. They are mostly aquatic and inhabit marine and freshwaters. The University of California Museum of Paleontology notes in "Introduction to the Crustaceamorpha" (2016, http://www.ucmp.berkeley.edu/arthropoda/crustacea/crustaceamorpha.html) that crustaceans are a highly varied species group and that "many serve as the main source of food for many fish and whales."

As of February 2016, there were 25 U.S. species listed as endangered or threatened under the ESA. (See Table 5.4.) Most had endangered listings and nearly all had recovery plans in place. Although imperiled crustacean species are found throughout the United States, they are mostly located in California. Nearly $3.6 million was spent under the ESA during FY 2014 on one California crustacean: the vernal pool fairy shrimp. (See Table 5.1.)

VERNAL POOL FAIRY SHRIMP. The vernal pool fairy shrimp (*Branchinecta lynchi*) was listed under the ESA as threatened in 1994. It is found in California and Oregon. The term *vernal* is from the Latin word for "spring." This species inhabits temporary small ponds and pools of water that appear during the rainy season (winter or springtime) and dry up during the dry season. Vernal pools are unique habitats, small temporary wetlands that harbor and nurture a rich variety of animals and plants. In "Vernal Pools Hold Waters of Life"

(UTSanDiego.com, March 16, 2010), Mike Lee notes, "Researchers and wildlife advocates describe vernal ecosystems as biological gold mines. One of their most important functions is providing protein, in the form of tiny invertebrates, for amphibians and migrating birds."

The vernal pool fairy shrimp lay their eggs in vernal pools when they contain water. The eggs go dormant in the dirt when the pools become dry. Baby shrimp hatch only when exposed to water that is approximately 50 degrees Fahrenheit (10 degrees C). Adults typically reach 0.4 to 1 inch (1 to 2.5 cm) in length. The shrimp have a life span of two to five months.

In 2003 critical habitat was designated for the vernal pool fairy shrimp along with several other species of vernal pool shrimp. In 2006 the USFWS published "Recovery Plan for Vernal Pool Ecosystems of California and Southern Oregon" (http://www.fws.gov/ecos/ajax/docs/recovery_plan/060614.pdf), a recovery plan that covers dozens of imperiled plant and animal species that inhabit vernal pool ecosystems in California and southern Oregon. The USFWS notes that vernal pool life-forms are threatened by urban and agricultural development and by invasion of nonnative species. The recovery of vernal pool species will require an ecosystem-wide

TABLE 5.4

Endangered and threatened crustacean species, February 2016

Common name	Scientific name	Federal listing status[a]	U.S. or U.S./foreign listed	Recovery plan date	Recovery plan stage[b]
Alabama cave shrimp	*Palaemonias alabamae*	E	US	09/04/97	F
Anchialine pool shrimp	*Vetericaris chaceorum*	E	US	None	—
California freshwater shrimp	*Syncaris pacifica*	E	US	07/31/98	F
Cave crayfish	*Cambarus aculabrum*	E	US	10/30/96	F
Cave crayfish	*Cambarus zophonastes*	E	US	09/26/88	F
Conservancy fairy shrimp	*Branchinecta conservatio*	E	US	03/07/06	F
Diminutive amphipod	*Gammarus hyalleloides*	E	US	None	—
Hay's Spring amphipod	*Stygobromus hayi*	E	US	None	—
Illinois cave amphipod	*Gammarus acherondytes*	E	US	09/20/02	F
Kauai cave amphipod	*Spelaeorchestia koloana*	E	US	07/19/06	F
Kentucky cave shrimp	*Palaemonias ganteri*	E	US	10/07/88	F
Lee County cave isopod	*Lirceus usdagalun*	E	US	09/30/97	F
Longhorn fairy shrimp	*Branchinecta longiantenna*	E	US	03/07/06	F
Madison Cave isopod	*Antrolana lira*	T	US	09/30/96	F
Nashville crayfish	*Orconectes shoupi*	E	US	02/08/89	RF(1)
Noel's amphipod	*Gammarus desperatus*	E	US	None	—
Peck's cave amphipod	*Stygobromus (=Stygonectes) pecki*	E	US	02/14/96	RF(1)
Pecos amphipod	*Gammarus pecos*	E	US	None	—
Riverside fairy shrimp	*Streptocephalus woottoni*	E	US	09/03/98	F
San Diego fairy shrimp	*Branchinecta sandiegonensis*	E	US	09/03/98	F
Shasta crayfish	*Pacifastacus fortis*	E	US	08/28/98	F
Socorro isopod	*Thermosphaeroma thermophilus*	E	US	02/16/82	F
Squirrel chimney cave shrimp	*Palaemonetes cummingi*	T	US	None	—
Vernal pool fairy shrimp	*Branchinecta lynchi*	T	US	03/07/06	F
Vernal pool tadpole shrimp	*Lepidurus packardi*	E	US	03/07/06	F

[a]E = Endangered. T = Threatened.
[b]F = Final. RF = Final Revision.

SOURCE: Adapted from "Generate Species List," in *Environmental Conservation Online System Species Reports*, U.S. Department of the Interior, U.S. Fish and Wildlife Service, February 2016, http://ecos.fws.gov/tess_public/pub/adHocSpeciesForm.jsp (accessed February 12, 2016), and "Listed FWS/Joint FWS and NMFS Species and Populations with Recovery Plans (Sorted by Listed Entity)," in *Recovery Plans Search*, U.S. Department of the Interior, U.S. Fish and Wildlife Service, February 2016, http://ecos.fws.gov/tess_public/pub/speciesRecovery.jsp?sort=1 (accessed February 12, 2016)

approach. The USFWS proposes establishing conservation areas and reserves to protect primary vernal pool habitat.

In May 2011 the USFWS (http://www.gpo.gov/fdsys/pkg/FR-2011-05-25/pdf/2011-12861.pdf) announced the initiation of a five-year review of the species. As of April 2016, the results of that review had not been published.

Imperiled Mollusks and Crustaceans around the World

According to the International Union for Conservation of Nature (IUCN), in *Red List of Threatened Species Version 2015.4* (November 2015, http://www.iucnredlist.org/about/summary-statistics), 1,950 species of mollusks and 728 species of crustaceans were threatened in 2015. For mollusks, this number accounted for 27% of the 7,216 species evaluated. The IUCN reports that approximately 85,000 mollusk species are known. Only 3,168 crustacean species were evaluated for the 2015 report. Threatened species accounted for 23% of this total. The IUCN notes that there are approximately 47,000 known species of crustaceans.

As shown in Table 5.5, only three foreign clam and snail species were listed under the ESA as of February 2016. All had endangered listings. They are found in Mexico and Papua New Guinea. No foreign crustacean species were listed under the ESA at that time.

CORALS

Corals are one of the most unusual members of the animal kingdom. Many people are familiar with coral reefs—vast and colorful undersea structures that are popular with scuba divers and snorkelers. (See Figure 5.3.) Most coral reefs are composed of many hundreds or thousands of individual coral organisms called polyps. Figure 5.4 shows a coral polyp with its common parts labeled. The polyp has an opening (or mouth) surrounded by tentacles that capture sea creatures for food. Following digestion in the polyp's stomach, waste materials are expelled out through the mouth.

Coral colonies provide key underwater habitats for numerous marine species, including fish and other aquatic creatures. Most reef-building coral polyps have a symbiotic (mutually beneficial) relationship with algae (tiny plant cells) called zooxanthellae. The algae perform photosynthesis, which creates oxygen and provides nutrients to the coral polyps, allowing them to grow and spread. Reef-building corals secrete calcium carbonate, a hard mineral compound that forms the reef skeleton. Zooxanthellae are also responsible for the bright and varied colors found in coral reefs. Without the algae, coral polyps are naturally translucent. Scientists believe zooxanthellae serve as sort of a "sunscreen" for warm-water corals, protecting them from the harsh ultraviolet rays of the sun.

Coral reefs are the largest living structures on the earth. They are primarily found in coastal, tropical waters. These reefs are located in relatively shallow waters, making them more susceptible to human activities. The U.S. Commission on Ocean Policy explains in *An Ocean Blueprint for the 21st Century: Final Report* (2004, http://govinfo.library.unt.edu/oceancommission/documents/full_color_rpt/000_ocean_full_report.pdf) that only 1% to 2% of warm-water corals are found in U.S. waters. Most warm-water corals are located in the waters of the South Pacific and around Indonesia. In addition, there are many cold-water reefs around the world that scientists are just beginning to study. These reefs are found in cold deep waters from depths of 100 feet (30.5 m) to more than 3 miles (4.8 km).

General Threats to Corals

In *An Ocean Blueprint for the 21st Century*, the Commission on Ocean Policy explains that coral reefs are imperiled by diseases and coastal development that spur the growth of unfriendly algae. Coastal development also increases the danger of the reefs being damaged by divers and boat anchors. Other serious threats to coral reef ecosystems include marine pollution, overfishing of species found around the corals, and destructive fishing methods used around the corals. The latter include explosives or chemicals, such as cyanide, that are used to stun coral inhabitants so they are easier to capture. Such methods are illegal and are known to be practiced in areas of Southeast Asia. The collection of tropical reef

TABLE 5.5

Foreign endangered and threatened clam, snail, and crustacean species, February 2016

Common name	Scientific name	Species group	Federal listing status*	Current distribution
Manus Island tree snail	*Papustyla pulcherrima*	Snails	E	Papua New Guinea
Nicklin's pearlymussel	*Megalonaias nicklineana*	Clams	E	Mexico
Tampico pearlymussel	*Cyrtonaias tampicoensis tecomatensis*	Clams	E	Mexico

*E = Endangered.

SOURCE: Adapted from "Generate Species List," in *Environmental Conservation Online System Species Reports*, U.S. Department of the Interior, U.S. Fish and Wildlife Service, February 2016, http://ecos.fws.gov/tess_public/pub/adHocSpeciesForm.jsp (accessed February 12, 2016)

FIGURE 5.3

Coral reefs are among the most diverse ecosystems in the world. They are also immediately threatened by global warming, which has caused unprecedented episodes of coral bleaching since the 1980s. ©*Dennis Sabo/Shutterstock.com.*

specimens for the aquarium trade has also damaged a number of species.

Perhaps the greatest immediate threat to coral reefs is rising water temperature due to global climate change. Overly warm water causes zooxanthellae to leave or be expelled from coral polyps. The resulting loss of color is known as coral bleaching. Bleached coral suffers from a lack of nutrients, becoming weak and lackluster and more susceptible to disease and other environmental stressors. Long-term zooxanthellae deficiencies can cause the coral to die. In "Susceptibility of Central Red Sea Corals during a Major Bleaching Event" (*Coral Reefs*, vol. 32, no. 2, June 2013), Kathryn A. Furby, Jessica Bouwmeester, and Michael L. Berumen state, "Alarmingly, the frequency of bleaching events and mortalities has increased dramatically since 1979."

As described in Chapter 1, global climate change is believed to be triggered by excessive anthropogenic (human-caused) emissions of carbon dioxide into the atmosphere. NOAA explains in "Ocean Acidification: The Other Carbon Dioxide Problem" (2016, http://www

.pmel.noaa.gov/co2/story/Ocean+Acidification) that the increasing uptake of atmospheric carbon dioxide by the earth's oceans is lowering the pH (potential hydrogen; the level of acidity, a lower value indicates more acid) of the water and reducing the availability of carbonate ions to marine organisms that need them. The phenomenon is known as ocean acidification, and scientists fear that it poses a serious threat to the health of coral systems.

Imperiled U.S. Corals

NOAA periodically publishes a comprehensive report that describes the condition of shallow-water coral reef ecosystems in the United States. As of April 2016, the most recent report was published in 2008. In *The State of Coral Reef Ecosystems of the United States and Pacific Freely Associated States: 2008* (April 2008, https://coastalscience.noaa.gov/research/docs/CoralReport 2008.pdf), NOAA's Coral Reef Conservation Program (CRCP) discusses the results of monitoring activities that were conducted by government, private, and academic entities engaged in assessing the condition of the nation's shallow-water coral reef ecosystems. According to the

FIGURE 5.4

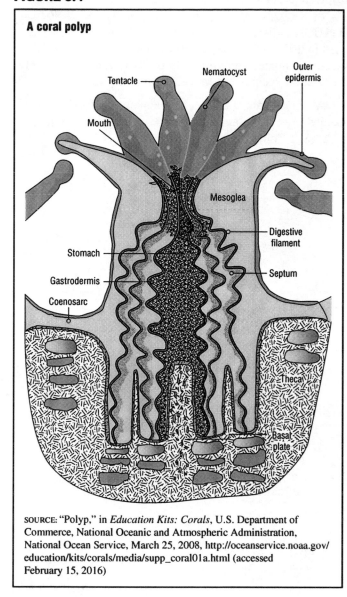

A coral polyp

SOURCE: "Polyp," in *Education Kits: Corals*, U.S. Department of Commerce, National Oceanic and Atmospheric Administration, National Ocean Service, March 25, 2008, http://oceanservice.noaa.gov/education/kits/corals/media/supp_coral01a.html (accessed February 15, 2016)

TABLE 5.6

Endangered and threatened coral species, February 2016

Species	Year listed	Status	Critical habitat	Recovery plan
Corals				
coral, [no common name] (*Acropora globiceps*)	2014	T	No	No
coral, [no common name] (*Acropora jacquelineae*)	2014	T	No	No
coral, [no common name] (*Acropora lokani*)	2014	T (F)	N/A	No
coral, [no common name] (*Acropora pharaonis*)	2014	T (F)	N/A	No
coral, [no common name] (*Acropora retusa*)	2014	T	No	No
coral, [no common name] (*Acropora rudis*)	2014	T (F)	N/A	No
coral, [no common name] (*Acropora speciosa*)	2014	T	No	No
coral, [no common name] (*Acropora tenella*)	2014	T (F)	N/A	No
coral, [no common name] (*Acropora spinosa*)	2014	T (F)	N/A	No
coral, [no common name] (*Cantharellus noumeae*)	2015	E (F)	N/A	No
coral, [no common name] (*Euphyllia paradivisa*)	2014	T	No	No
coral, [no common name] (*Isopora crateriformis*)	2014	T	No	No
coral, [no common name] (*Montipora australiensis*)	2014	T (F)	N/A	No
coral, [no common name] (*Pavona diffluens*)	2014	T (F)	No	No
coral, [no common name] (*Porites napopora*)	2014	T (F)	N/A	No
coral, [no common name] (*Seriatopora aculeata*)	2014	T	No	No
coral, [no common name] (*Siderastrea glynni*)	2015	E (F)	N/A	No
coral, [no common name] (*Tubastraea floreana*)	2015	E (F)	N/A	No
coral, boulder star (*Orbicella franksi*)	2014	T	No	No
coral, elkhorn (*Acropora palmata*)	2006	T	Final	Final
coral, lobed star (*Orbicella annularis*)	2014	T	No	No
coral, mountainous star (*Orbicella faveolata*)	2014	T	No	No
coral, pillar (*Dendrogyra cylindrus*)	2014	T	No	No
coral, rough cactus (*Mycetophyllia ferox*)	2014	T	No	No
coral, staghorn (*Acropora cervicornis*)	2006	T	Final	Final

Note: E = Endangered. T = Threatened. F = Foreign.

SOURCE: Adapted from "Marine Invertebrates (27 Listed "Species")," in *Endangered and Threatened Marine Species under NMFS' Jurisdiction*, U.S. Department of Commerce, National Oceanic and Atmospheric Administration, National Marine Fisheries Service, January 19, 2016, http://www.nmfs.noaa.gov/pr/species/esa/listed.htm (accessed February 19, 2016)

CRCP, approximately half the ecosystems were found to be in "poor" or "fair" condition.

As of February 2016, there were 14 U.S. species of coral listed under the ESA. (See Table 5.6.) All had threatened listings. As marine creatures, corals are under the jurisdiction of the NMFS. The first corals to be listed were elkhorn coral (*Acropora palmata*) and staghorn coral (*Acropora cervicornis*) in 2006. Both species are branching corals found in the Caribbean, including the coastal waters of Florida, Puerto Rico, and the U.S. Virgin Islands. Their range extends to many tropical countries of Central and South America. Another dozen U.S. coral species were listed under the ESA in 2014 and 2015.

In the original listing rule (December 14, 2007, http://www.nmfs.noaa.gov/pr/pdfs/fr/fr72-71102.pdf) for the elkhorn and staghorn corals, the NMFS noted that

the corals are primarily threatened by disease, hurricanes, and elevated sea surface temperatures. The agency called these threats "severe, unpredictable, [and] likely to increase in the foreseeable future." However, the corals are widely distributed. In addition, they reproduce asexually through a process called fragmentation in which branches break off and become reattached to the reef. This mechanism helps them recover from damaging events, such as hurricanes. As a result, the corals were not believed to be at risk of extinction throughout all or a significant part of their range. Thus, they were afforded a threatened, rather than an endangered, ranking. In November 2008 the NMFS (https://www.gpo.gov/fdsys/pkg/FR-2008-11-26/pdf/E8-27748.pdf#page=2) established critical habitat for the two species covering 2,959 square miles (7,664 square km) of habitat around Florida, Puerto Rico, and the U.S. Virgin Islands.

Imperiled Corals around the World

In *Red List of Threatened Species Version 2015.4,* the IUCN indicates that 237 species of corals were threatened in 2015. This number accounted for 27% of the 862 species evaluated. According to the IUCN, approximately 2,175 coral species are known to scientists.

As of February 2016, 11 exclusively foreign coral species were listed as endangered or threatened under the ESA. (See Table 5.6.)

CHAPTER 6
AMPHIBIANS AND REPTILES

Amphibians and reptiles are collectively known by biologists as herpetofauna. In *Red List of Threatened Species Version 2015.4* (November 2015, http://www.iucnredlist.org/about/summary-statistics), the International Union for Conservation of Nature (IUCN) notes that there are 7,448 described amphibian species and 10,272 described reptile species. New species in both of these groups are being discovered every year, particularly in remote tropical regions that are only now being explored.

Most of the herpetofauna native to the United States are found in wetlands and riparian habitat (the banks and immediate areas around water bodies, such as rivers and streams). Biologists indicate that amphibians and reptiles play a crucial role in these ecosystems by controlling insects, processing dead organic matter into a form that is edible by smaller creatures, and providing an important link in the food chain.

Many herpetofauna species are under threat, primarily due to declines and degradation in their habitats in recent decades.

AMPHIBIANS

Amphibians are vertebrate animals in the taxonomic class Amphibia. They represent the most ancient group of terrestrial vertebrates. The earliest amphibians lived during the early Devonian era, some 400 million years ago. The three groups of amphibians that have survived to the present day are salamanders, frogs and toads, and caecilians.

Salamanders belong to the order Caudata (also called Urodela). They have moist smooth skin, slender bodies, four short legs, and long tails. This category includes the amphibians commonly known as newts (land-dwelling salamanders) and sirens (salamanders that have both lungs and gills).

Frogs and toads are in the order Anura. These amphibians do not have tails as adults. They have small bodies with two short front legs and two long back legs. (See Figure 6.1.) Their feet are webbed, and they are good jumpers and hoppers. True frogs belong to the family Ranidae, whereas true toads belong to the family Bufonidae. There are many other families in this order whose members are commonly described as frogs or toads. Many of the species go through a swimming tadpole stage before metamorphosing into an adult. However, in some species eggs hatch directly as juvenile froglets, which are miniature versions of the adults. Tadpoles are most often herbivorous (plant-eating), although there are some carnivorous (meat-eating) tadpoles, including cannibalistic species. Adults are carnivorous and catch prey with their sticky tongue.

Caecilians belong to the order Gymnophiona (also called Apoda) and share a common ancestor with the other amphibians, but look much different. They are often mistaken for worms or snakes. They have long slender bodies with no limbs and are found primarily in the tropics.

Amphi means "both," and amphibians get their name from the fact that many species occupy both aquatic and terrestrial habitats. In particular, many amphibian species undergo a dramatic change called metamorphosis, in which individuals move from an aquatic larval stage to a terrestrial adult stage. For example, in many frog species aquatic swimming tadpoles metamorphose into terrestrial jumping frogs. In the process, they lose their muscular swimming tails and acquire forelimbs and hind limbs. Many amphibian species occupy terrestrial habitats through most of the year, but migrate to ponds to breed. However, there are also species that are either entirely aquatic or entirely terrestrial. Whatever their habitat, amphibians generally require some moisture to survive. This is because amphibians pass some oxygen

FIGURE 6.1

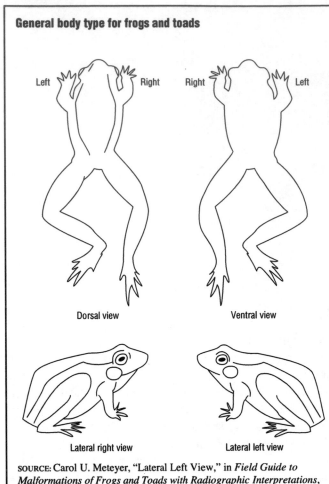

General body type for frogs and toads

Left Right Right Left

Dorsal view   Ventral view

Lateral right view   Lateral left view

SOURCE: Carol U. Meteyer, "Lateral Left View," in *Field Guide to Malformations of Frogs and Toads with Radiographic Interpretations*, U.S. Department of the Interior, U.S. Geological Survey, 2000, http://www.nwhc.usgs.gov/publications/fact_sheets/pdfs/frog.pdf (accessed February 15, 2016)

and other chemicals in and out of their body directly through their skin, using processes that require water to function.

Many amphibian species are in serious decline because of factors such as habitat loss, pollution, and climate change. Amphibians are particularly vulnerable to pollution because their skin readily absorbs water and other substances from the environment. For this reason, amphibians are frequently considered biological indicator species, meaning that their presence, condition, and numbers are monitored as a gauge of the overall well-being of their habitat.

The U.S. Geological Survey (USGS) operates the Amphibian Research and Monitoring Initiative (http://armi.usgs.gov/) to study amphibian trends and causes of decline. In the press release "USGS Study Confirms U.S. Amphibian Populations Declining at Precipitous Rates" (May 22, 2013, http://www.usgs.gov/newsroom/article .asp?ID=3597), the agency summarizes the results of a study performed on nearly 50 amphibian species between 2002 and 2011 at dozens of sites around the United States. The USGS notes that "on average, populations of all amphibians examined vanished from habitats at a rate of 3.7 percent each year. If the rate observed is representative and remains unchanged, these species would disappear from half of the habitats they currently occupy in about 20 years." One troubling aspect of the study was that the declines were measured even on lands such as national parks and national wildlife refuges that are specifically managed for conservation purposes.

In April 2009 the Public Broadcasting Service (PBS) began televising the documentary *Frogs: The Thin Green Line* (http://www.pbs.org/wnet/nature/episodes/frogs-the-thin-green-line/video-full-episode/4882/), which focuses on the worldwide decline of frog species and the resulting effects on ecosystems and humans. Frogs are particularly important from an ecological standpoint because they lie at the "middle" of the food chain. Tadpoles eat algae, a process that helps maintain clean water quality. Adult frogs eat insects, including insects such as mosquitoes and flies that can spread diseases to animals and humans. Frog eggs provide food for wasps and spiders. Fish and other aquatic creatures eat tadpoles, while birds and reptiles feed on adult frogs. Furthermore, PBS notes that scientists have discovered hundreds of chemicals in the skins of frogs, particularly tropical species. These chemicals hold promise in the development of anesthetics, painkillers, and other medicines that could greatly benefit humans.

THREATENED AND ENDANGERED SPECIES OF AMPHIBIANS

As of February 2016, there were 32 amphibian species listed as threatened or endangered under the Endangered Species Act (ESA). (See Table 6.1.) The list contains only salamander, frogs, and toads; no caecilian species were listed. Most of the listed species were endangered and nearly all had recovery plans in place. As shown in Table 1.2 in Chapter 1 and Table 2.7 in Chapter 2, no amphibian species have been delisted under the ESA because of extinction or recovery.

Table 6.2 shows the 10 listed amphibian species with the highest expenditures under the ESA during fiscal year (FY) 2014. More than $21.1 million was spent in an effort to conserve these species.

Imperiled Salamanders in the United States

Eighteen salamanders were listed under the ESA as of February 2016. (See Table 6.1; note that the Ozark hellbender is a salamander species.)

Some endangered salamanders, including many cave species, have highly restricted habitats. For example, the Barton Springs salamander is found only in and around

TABLE 6.1

Endangered and threatened amphibian species, February 2016

Common name	Scientific name	Federal listing status[a]	U.S. or U.S./foreign listed	Recovery plan date	Recovery plan stage[b]
Arroyo (=arroyo southwestern) toad	Anaxyrus californicus	E	US/foreign	07/24/99	F
Austin blind salamander	Eurycea waterlooensis	E	US	07/07/15	F
Barton Springs salamander	Eurycea sosorum	E	US	07/07/15	F
California red-legged frog	Rana draytonii	T	US/foreign	09/12/02	F
California tiger salamander	Ambystoma californiense	E; T	US	04/24/15	D
Cheat Mountain salamander	Plethodon nettingi	T	US	07/25/91	F
Chiricahua leopard frog	Rana chiricahuensis	T	US/foreign	06/04/07	F
Desert slender salamander	Batrachoseps aridus	E	US	08/12/82	F
Dusky gopher frog	Rana sevosa	E	US	09/09/15	F
Frosted Flatwoods salamander	Ambystoma cingulatum	T	US	None	—
Georgetown salamander	Eurycea naufragia	T	US	None	—
Golden coqui	Eleutherodactylus jasperi	T	US	04/19/84	F
Guajon	Eleutherodactylus cooki	T	US	09/24/04	F
Houston toad	Bufo houstonensis	E	US	09/17/84	F
Jemez Mountains salamander	Plethodon neomexicanus	E	US	None	—
Jollyville Plateau salamander	Eurycea tonkawae	T	US	None	—
Llanero coqui	Eleutherodactylus juanariveroi	E	US	None	—
Mountain yellow-legged frog	Rana muscosa	E; T	US	None	—
Oregon spotted frog	Rana pretiosa	T	US	None	—
Ozark hellbender	Cryptobranchus alleganiensis bishopi	E	US	None	—
Puerto Rican crested toad	Peltophryne lemur	T	US/foreign	08/07/92	F
Red Hills salamander	Phaeognathus hubrichti	T	US	11/23/83	F
Reticulated flatwoods salamander	Ambystoma bishopi	E	US	None	—
Salado salamander	Eurycea chisholmensis	T	US	None	—
San Marcos salamander	Eurycea nana	T	US	02/14/96	RF(1)
Santa Cruz long-toed salamander	Ambystoma macrodactylum croceum	E	US	07/02/99	RD(2)
Shenandoah salamander	Plethodon shenandoah	E	US	09/29/94	F
Sierra Nevada yellow-legged frog	Rana sierrae	E	US	None	—
Sonora tiger salamander	Ambystoma tigrinum stebbinsi	E	US/foreign	09/24/02	F
Texas blind salamander	Typhlomolge rathbuni	E	US	02/14/96	RF(1)
Wyoming toad	Bufo hemiophrys baxteri	E	US	07/16/15	RF(1)
Yosemite toad	Anaxyrus canorus	T	US	None	—

[a]E = Endangered. T = Threatened.
[b]F = Final. RF = Final Revision. D = Draft.

SOURCE: Adapted from "Generate Species List," in *Environmental Conservation Online System Species Reports*, U.S. Department of the Interior, U.S. Fish and Wildlife Service, February 2016, http://ecos.fws.gov/tess_public/pub/adHocSpeciesForm.jsp (accessed February 15, 2016), and "Listed FWS/Joint FWS and NMFS Species and Populations with Recovery Plans (Sorted by Listed Entity)," in *Recovery Plans Search*, U.S. Department of the Interior, U.S. Fish and Wildlife Service, February 2016, http://ecos.fws.gov/tess_public/pub/speciesRecovery.jsp?sort=1 (accessed February 15, 2016)

TABLE 6.2

The 10 listed amphibian species with the highest expenditures under the Endangered Species Act, fiscal year 2014

Ranking	Species	Population	Expenditure
1	Frog, California red-legged (*Rana draytonii*)	Entire	$8,087,462
2	Salamander, California tiger (*Ambystoma californiense*)	Sonoma County, CA	$5,135,895
3	Frog, Chiricahua leopard (*Rana chiricahuensis*)	Entire	$1,702,694
4	Toad, arroyo (=arroyo southwestern) (*Anaxyrus californicus*)	Entire	$1,034,476
5	Skink, sand (*Neoseps reynoldsi*)	Entire	$1,027,238
6	Salamander, California tiger (*Ambystoma californiense*)	Central CA DPS	$1,023,858
7	Toad, Wyoming (*Anaxyrus baxteri*)	Entire	$981,229
8	Lizard, blunt-nosed leopard (*Gambelia silus*)	Entire	$809,255
9	Frog, Oregon spotted (*Rana pretiosa*)	Entire	$676,681
10	Salamander, frosted flatwoods (*Ambystoma cingulatum*)	Entire	$634,681

Note: DPS = Distinct Population Segment.

SOURCE: Adapted from "Table 2. Species Ranked in Descending Order of Total FY 2014 Reported Expenditures, Not Including Land Acquisition Costs," in *Federal and State Endangered and Threatened Species Expenditures: Fiscal Year 2014*, U.S. Department of the Interior, U.S. Fish and Wildlife Service, March 2, 2016, http://www.fws.gov/endangered/esa-library/pdf/20160302_final_FY14_ExpRpt.pdf (accessed March 9, 2016)

spring-fed pools in Zilker Park in Austin, Texas. The species was first listed as endangered in 1997. Urban development has contributed to degradation of the local groundwater that feeds the spring. In addition, flows from the spring have decreased because of increasing human use of groundwater from the aquifer. Finally, the Barton

Springs salamander has been the subject of contentious debate between conservationists and those who wish to expand development around the area of the pools.

CALIFORNIA TIGER SALAMANDER. As shown in Table 6.2, nearly $6.2 million was spent under the ESA during FY 2014 on two populations of the California tiger salamander. (See Figure 6.2.) According to the U.S. Fish and Wildlife Service (USFWS), in "California Tiger Salamander (*Ambystoma californiense*)" (2016, http://ecos.fws.gov/tess_public/profile/speciesProfile?spcode=D01T), the salamander lives in terrestrial habitats and is relatively large, reaching a maximum length of about 8 inches (20.3 cm).

The ESA-listed populations are as follows:

- Sonoma County, California, population—endangered; the core habitat for this population is mainly in the Santa Rosa plain, which is depicted in Figure 6.3

- Santa Barbara County, California, population—endangered

- Central California distinct population segment (DPS), excluding the Sonoma County and Santa Barbara County populations—threatened

Overall, the salamander is listed across a long swath of coastal California, an area characterized by residential and commercial development close to the coast and ranching and farming activities inland.

As of April 2016, critical habitat had been designated for all three listed populations and draft recovery plans had been published:

- *Draft Recovery Plan for the Santa Rosa Plain* (2014, https://www.fws.gov/sacramento/outreach/2014/12-11/docs/Draft_Recovery_Plan-Santa_Rosa_Plain-12-4-14.pdf)

FIGURE 6.2

California tiger salamander. ©*U.S. Fish and Wildlife Service.*

FIGURE 6.3

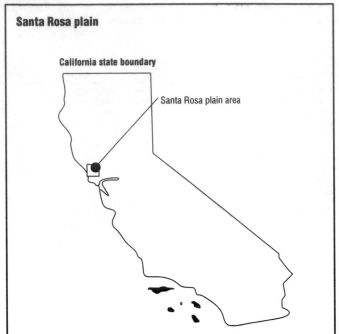

Santa Rosa plain

SOURCE: Adapted from "Figure 1. Santa Rosa Plain Portion of Recovery Planning Area," in *Draft Recovery Plan for the Santa Rosa Plain*, U.S. Department of the Interior, U.S. Fish and Wildlife Service, December 2014, http://ecos.fws.gov/docs/recovery_plan/Draft%20Recovery%20Plan%20for%20Santa%20Rosa%20Plain%20for%20publication%201-6-2015.pdf (accessed February 18, 2016)

- *Draft Recovery Plan for the Central California Distinct Population Segment of the California Tiger Salamander* (Ambystoma californiense) (2015, http://www.fws.gov/sacramento/outreach/2016/3-11/docs/DRAFT_RP_CTS-20160113.pdf)

- *Draft Recovery Plan for the Santa Barbara County Distinct Population Segment of the California Tiger Salamander* (Ambystoma californiense) (2015, https://www.indybay.org/uploads/2015/04/24/draft_recovery_plan_for_the_santa_barbara_dps_of_california_tiger_salamander.pdf)

In *Draft Recovery Plan for the Central California Distinct Population Segment of the California Tiger Salamander* (Ambystoma californiense), the USFWS indicates that the California tiger salamander lives mostly underground, but migrates to ponds and water pools to breed. Historically, the preferred breeding sites were vernal water bodies. (The term *vernal* is from the Latin word for "spring." Vernal ponds appear during the rainy season and dry up during the dry season.) The agency notes that the salamander is now found more often in human-made or human-modified water bodies, such as livestock ponds. It is imperiled by numerous threats, including habitat loss and fragmentation, intrusion of nonnative species (some of which prey on the salamander), and genetic loss due to breeding with nonnative barred tiger salamanders.

Benjamin M. Fitzpatrick and H. Bradley Shaffer of the University of California, Davis, note in "Hybrid Vigor between Native and Introduced Salamanders Raises New Challenges for Conservation" (*PNAS*, vol. 104, no. 4, October 2, 2007) that the nonnative barred tiger salamanders were first introduced to California from Texas sometime during the late 1940s to the late 1950s as larval fish bait. Subsequent interbreeding with the native species has produced a vigorous and fertile hybrid offspring that has been dubbed a "super salamander." In "Tracking California's 'Super Salamanders'" (SCPR.org, September 12, 2013), Sanden Totten notes the hybrid salamanders are bigger and much more aggressive hunters than their forebears. One researcher told Totten, "What we found was, basically, in ponds that had hybrids they ate nearly everything in the pond. Hardly any frogs were able to survive. Hardly any larval newts." The rise of the "super salamander" presents a troubling problem for wildlife managers who fear for the survival of the California tiger salamander as a species.

The recovery plans do include measures for dealing with the hybridization problem. For example, in *Draft Recovery Plan for the Central California Distinct Population Segment of the California Tiger Salamander* (Ambystoma californiense), the USFWS proposes to "conduct targeted eradication of hybrid tiger salamander populations when determined to be beneficial to the DPS as a whole." Once hybrids are removed from an area, native salamanders would be reintroduced to it. In addition, breeding habitats can be created in such a way that favors the native salamanders over the hybrids. The agency also intends to educate the public about the dangers of using nonnative barred tiger salamanders as bait, a practice that is illegal in California.

Imperiled Frogs and Toads in the United States

As shown in Table 6.1, there were 14 species of imperiled frogs and toads (including the golden coqui, guajon, and llanero coqui) in the United States as of February 2016. They are geographically diverse with habitats located in the West, Southeast, and Puerto Rico.

CALIFORNIA RED-LEGGED FROGS. The California red-legged frog is the largest native frog in the western United States. The frog was made famous by Mark Twain's (1835–1910) short story "The Celebrated Jumping Frog of Calaveras County" (1865). The species experienced a significant decline during the mid-20th century because of loss and degradation of habitat. In 1996 it was listed as threatened under the ESA. As noted in Table 6.2, nearly $8.1 million was spent under the ESA during FY 2014 on conserving the species.

California red-legged frogs require riverside habitats that are covered by vegetation and are close to deepwater pools. They are extremely sensitive to habitat disturbance and water pollution—tadpoles are particularly sensitive to varying oxygen levels and siltation (mud and other natural impurities) during metamorphosis. The frogs require three to four years to reach maturity and have a normal life span of eight to 10 years.

Water reservoir construction and agricultural and residential development are the primary factors in the decline of this species. Biologists find that California red-legged frogs generally disappear from habitats within five years of a reservoir or water diversion project. The removal of vegetation associated with flood control and the use of herbicides and restructuring of landscapes further degrade remaining habitat. Finally, nonnative species have also attacked red-legged frog populations. These include alien fish predators as well as competing species such as bullfrogs.

As of April 2016, the most recently published recovery plan for the species was dated May 2002. In *Recovery Plan for the California Red-Legged Frog* (Rana aurora draytonii) (http://ecos.fws.gov/docs/recovery_plans/2002/020528.pdf), the USFWS calls for eliminating threats in current habitats, restoring damaged habitats, and reintroducing populations into the historic range of the species. Critical habitat for the species was first set by the agency in 2001 and revised in 2006. In 2007 the Center for Biological Diversity filed a legal challenge arguing that the critical habitat designation was not sufficient. As a result, in March 2010 the USFWS (http://www.gpo.gov/fdsys/pkg/FR-2010-03-17/pdf/2010-4656.pdf#page=1) substantially increased the critical habitat from 450,000 acres (182,000 ha) to 1.6 million acres (660,000 ha).

In May 2011 the USFWS (http://www.gpo.gov/fdsys/pkg/FR-2011-05-25/pdf/2011-12861.pdf) initiated a five-year review for dozens of western species, including the California red-legged frog. As of April 2016, the results of the review had not been published.

Amphibian Deformities

Amphibian deformities first hit the spotlight during the mid-1990s, when reports about frogs with missing, extra, or misshapen limbs or other physical abnormalities began surfacing around the country. In *Field Guide to Malformations of Frogs and Toads* (April 2001, http://www.nwhc.usgs.gov/publications/fact_sheets/pdfs/frog.pdf), Carol U. Meteyer of the USGS indicates that as of 2000, frog malformations had been reported in more than 50 species of frogs and toads in 44 states.

The high incidence of amphibian deformities in some U.S. species in some areas appears to have multiple causes, as no single hypothesis accounts for all the different types of deformities seen. Probable causes include chemical contaminants, nutrient deficiencies, injuries (e.g., from predators), UV-B radiation, and parasites.

One of the difficulties associated with quantifying the scope of the problem is the lack of comprehensive data across populations. In 2013 the USFWS released the results of a study its scientists conducted on national wildlife refuges around the country. In the press release "Landmark Study Reveals Low National Rate of Frog Abnormalities on Wildlife Refuges" (November 19, 2013, http://www.fws.gov/mountain-prairie/pressrel/2013/11192013_amphibianStudy.php), the agency notes that the National Abnormal Amphibian Program sampled more than 68,000 frogs and toads on 152 national wildlife refuges, assembling "one of the world's largest databases on amphibian abnormalities." The researchers found on average that 2% of the frogs and toads sampled had skeletal or eye abnormalities (the most commonly studied types of deformities in amphibians). This value was within the expected naturally occurring range of 0% to 2% for such abnormalities. Only 0.025% of the sampled frogs had extra limbs. Nevertheless, there were some geographical "hot spots" around the country in which the abnormality rate was much greater, as high as 40% in a few cases. The hot spots were found in the Mississippi River valley, the Central Valley of California, and parts of Alaska. The researchers did not investigate the possible causes of the deformities.

The study included frogs from more than 30 species. However, only one species—the Oregon spotted frog—was listed on the ESA as of February 2016. (See Table 6.1.) It was listed as threatened in August 2014. In the listing document, the USFWS (https://www.gpo.gov/fdsys/pkg/FR-2014-08-29/pdf/2014-20059.pdf) notes that it is aware of some reports of malformations in Oregon spotted frogs in limited areas. However, the agency states, "At present, the extent of population-level impacts from malformations among Oregon spotted frogs is unknown." In "Conserving Amphibians: What the Amphibians Are Telling Us and Why We Should Listen" (May 28, 2015, http://www.fws.gov/endangered/news/amphibians.html), the USFWS discusses stressors on particular species of frogs and salamanders including both listed and candidate species. The agency does not mention deformities as a subject of concern for these particular species.

Imperiled Foreign Amphibians

The IUCN reports in *Red List of Threatened Species Version 2015.4* that 1,994 amphibian species were threatened in 2015. This represented 31% of the 6,460 amphibian species evaluated, the highest percentage for any group of animals evaluated.

As of February 2016, there were nine foreign amphibian species listed as threatened or endangered under the ESA. (See Table 6.3.) This list included seven frog and toad species and two salamander species.

REPTILES

Reptiles belong to the class Reptilia. Although they may appear similar, reptiles differ from amphibians in that reptile skin is cornified (made of dead cells). All reptiles obtain oxygen from the air using lungs. Most reptiles lay shelled eggs, although some species, particularly lizards and snakes, give birth to live young. According to the IUCN, in *Red List of Threatened Species Version 2015.4*, 10,272 species of reptiles were described as of November 2015.

Reptiles include crocodilians, lizards, snakes, and turtles. Birds are also technically reptiles (birds and crocodiles are actually close relatives), but have historically been treated separately.

Lizards and snakes represent the largest group of reptiles. Many reptiles are in serious decline. Several species are endangered because of habitat loss or degradation. In addition, humans hunt reptiles for their skins,

TABLE 6.3

Foreign endangered and threatened amphibian species, February 2016

Common name	Scientific name	Federal listing status*	Current distribution
African viviparous toads	*Nectophrynoides spp.*	E	Tanzania, Liberia, Ivory Coast, Guinea, Ethiopia, Cameroon
Cameroon toad	*Bufo superciliaris*	E	Equatorial Africa
Chinese giant salamander	*Andrias davidianus (= davidianus d.)*	E	Western China
Goliath frog	*Conraua goliath*	T	Gabon, Equatorial Guinea, Cameroon
Israel painted frog	*Discoglossus nigriventer*	E	Israel
Japanese giant salamander	*Andrias japonicus (= davidianus j.)*	E	Japan
Monte Verde golden toad	*Bufo periglenes*	E	Costa Rica
Panamanian golden frog	*Atelopus varius zeteki*	E	Panama
Stephen Island frog	*Leiopelma hamiltoni*	E	New Zealand

*T = Threatened. E = Endangered.

SOURCE: Adapted from "Generate Species List," in *Environmental Conservation Online System Species Reports*, U.S. Department of the Interior, U.S. Fish and Wildlife Service, February 2016, http://ecos.fws.gov/tess_public/pub/adHocSpeciesForm.jsp (accessed February 15, 2016)

shells, or meat. Global climate change has affected some reptile species, particularly turtles, in ominous ways—this is because in some reptiles ambient temperatures determine whether males or females are produced. Even a small increase in temperature can result in few or no males being born.

Natural disasters, such as hurricanes, can also negatively affect reptiles. For example, Christine Lagorio describes in "Katrina Displaces Sea Turtles" (CBSNews.com, August 29, 2005) the effects on nesting sea turtles by Hurricane Katrina, which struck the U.S. Gulf Coast in August 2005. Observers reported that newly hatched loggerhead sea turtles (an endangered species under the ESA) had difficulty making their way from their south Florida beach nests into the ocean because of the strong tides and waves produced by the storm. Lagorio notes that local residents, vacationers, and scientists from government agencies worked together to help temporarily rescue the struggling baby turtles until they could be released to the sea.

THREATENED AND ENDANGERED SPECIES OF REPTILES

As of February 2016, there were 38 U.S. reptile species listed as threatened or endangered under the ESA. (See Table 6.4.) Some species have dual status because they have separate populations in the United States. In addition, a few reptiles are listed as threatened because of similarity of appearance (SAT). This listing is applied to animals, such as the American alligator, that closely resemble imperiled species—in this case the American crocodile.

TABLE 6.4

Endangered and threatened reptile species, February 2016

Common name	Scientific name	Federal listing status[a]	U.S. or U.S./foreign listed	Recovery plan date	Recovery plan stage[b]
Alabama red-belly turtle	Pseudemys alabamensis	E	US	01/08/90	F
Alameda whipsnake (=striped racer)	Masticophis lateralis euryxanthus	T	US	04/07/03	D
American alligator	Alligator mississippiensis	SAT	US	None	—
American crocodile	Crocodylus acutus	T	US/foreign	05/18/99	F
Atlantic salt marsh snake	Nerodia clarkii taeniata	T	US	12/15/93	F
Black pine snake	Pituophis melanoleucus lodingi	T	US	None	—
Bluetail mole skink	Eumeces egregius lividus	T	US	05/18/99	F
Blunt-nosed leopard lizard	Gambelia silus	E	US	09/30/98	F
Bog (=Muhlenberg) turtle	Clemmys muhlenbergii	T; SAT	US	05/15/01	F
Coachella Valley fringe-toed lizard	Uma inornata	T	US	09/11/85	F
Copperbelly water snake	Nerodia erythrogaster neglecta	T	US	12/23/08	F
Culebra Island giant anole	Anolis roosevelti	E	US	01/28/83	F
Desert tortoise	Gopherus agassizii	T; SAT	US/foreign	05/06/11	RF(1)
Eastern indigo snake	Drymarchon corais couperi	T	US	04/22/82	F
Flattened musk turtle	Sternotherus depressus	T	US	02/26/90	F
Giant garter snake	Thamnophis gigas	T	US	12/22/15	D
Gopher tortoise	Gopherus polyphemus	T	US	12/26/90	F
Green sea turtle	Chelonia mydas	E; T	US/foreign	01/12/98	RF(1)
Hawksbill sea turtle	Eretmochelys imbricata	E	US/foreign	01/12/98	RF(1)
Kemp's ridley sea turtle	Lepidochelys kempii	E	US/foreign	09/22/11	RF(2)
Leatherback sea turtle	Dermochelys coriacea	E	US/foreign	01/12/98	RF(1)
Loggerhead sea turtle	Caretta caretta	E; T	US/foreign	01/16/09	RF(2)
Mona boa	Epicrates monensis monensis	T	US	04/19/84	F
Mona ground iguana	Cyclura stejnegeri	T	US	04/19/84	F
Monito gecko	Sphaerodactylus micropithecus	E	US	03/27/86	F
Narrow-headed gartersnake	Thamnophis rufipunctatus	T	US/foreign	None	—
New Mexican ridge-nosed rattlesnake	Crotalus willardi obscurus	T	US/foreign	03/22/85	F
Northern Mexican gartersnake	Thamnophis eques megalops	T	US/foreign	None	—
Olive ridley sea turtle	Lepidochelys olivacea	T	US/foreign	01/12/98	RF(1)
Plymouth redbelly turtle	Pseudemys rubriventris bangsi	E	US	05/06/94	RF(2)
Puerto Rican boa	Epicrates inornatus	E	US	03/27/86	F
Ringed map turtle	Graptemys oculifera	T	US	04/08/88	F
San Francisco garter snake	Thamnophis sirtalis tetrataenia	E	US	09/11/85	F
Sand skink	Neoseps reynoldsi	T	US	05/18/99	F
Slevin's skink	Emoia slevini	E	US	None	—
St. Croix ground lizard	Ameiva polops	E	US	03/29/84	F
Virgin Islands tree boa	Epicrates monensis granti	E	US/foreign	03/27/86	F
Yellow-blotched map turtle	Graptemys flavimaculata	T	US	03/15/93	F

[a] E = Endangered. T = Threatened. SAT = Similarity in Appearance to a Threatened Taxon.
[b] F = Final. RF = Final Revision. D = Draft.

SOURCE: Adapted from "Generate Species List," in *Environmental Conservation Online System Species Reports*, U.S. Department of the Interior, U.S. Fish and Wildlife Service, February 2016, http://ecos.fws.gov/tess_public/pub/adHocSpeciesForm.jsp (accessed February 15, 2016), and "Listed FWS/Joint FWS and NMFS Species and Populations with Recovery Plans (Sorted by Listed Entity)," in *Recovery Plans Search*, U.S. Department of the Interior, U.S. Fish and Wildlife Service, February 2016, http://ecos.fws.gov/tess_public/pub/speciesRecovery.jsp?sort=1 (accessed February 15, 2016)

Except for sea turtles, most of the imperiled U.S. reptiles are geographically clustered in either the Southeast, California, or Puerto Rico and the Virgin Islands. Sea turtles spend most of their life at sea and come onto land only to nest and lay eggs. Because there are many potential nesting sites along the U.S. coasts, sea turtles are listed in many states.

As shown in Table 2.7 in Chapter 2, three U.S. reptile species—the Concho water snake (2011), the Lake Erie water snake (2011), and the island night lizard (2014)—have been delisted because of recovery. Each species is found in a relatively small habitat area. For example, the Lake Erie water snake inhabits several small islands in Lake Erie. (See Figure 6.4.) No reptile species have been delisted because of extinction. (See Table 1.2 in Chapter 1.)

The 10 listed reptile species with the highest expenditures under the ESA during FY 2014 are shown in Table 6.5. The list is dominated by tortoise and sea turtle species.

Imperiled Tortoises in the United States

Terrestrial (land-dwelling) turtles inhabit inland areas and waterways; some species are generically called tortoises.

DESERT TORTOISES. The desert tortoise is a species native to the Sonoran and Mojave Deserts in the southwestern United States and into Mexico. (See Figure 6.5.) The tortoise has evolved to survive for long periods on little water and to eat scrubby desert plants. Because of the extreme temperatures in its environment the tortoise spends much of its time in underground burrows that it makes. These burrows also provide habitat for numerous other desert animals. Rachelle Meyer of the U.S. Forest Service notes in "*Gopherus agassizii*" (2008, http://www.fs.fed.us/database/feis/animals/reptile/goag/all.html) that "desert tortoises share burrows with other desert tortoises and with several other animals including mammal, reptile, bird, and invertebrate species." The species include squirrels, woodrats, owls, snakes, Gila monsters, spiders, and scorpions. As such, the desert tortoise is considered a

FIGURE 6.4

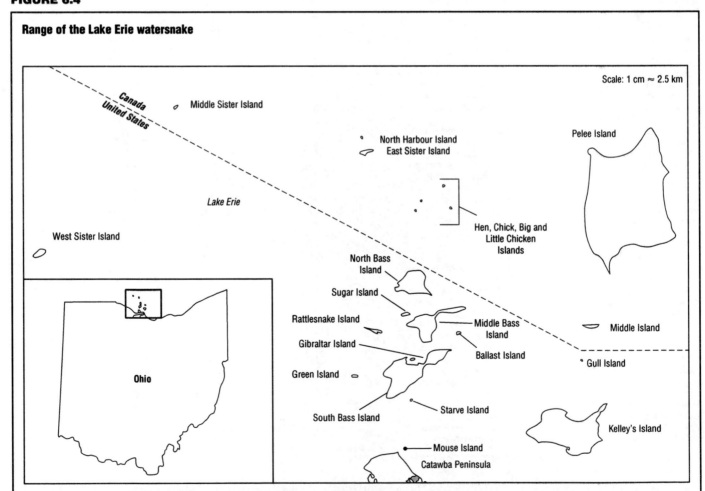

Range of the Lake Erie watersnake

SOURCE: Megan M. Seymour and Richard B. King, "Figure 1. Historic Range of the Lake Erie Watersnake on the Western Basin Lake Erie Islands," in *Lake Erie Watersnake (Nerodia sipedon insularum) Recovery Plan*, U.S. Department of the Interior, U. S. Fish and Wildlife Service, September 2003, http://ecos.fws.gov/docs/recovery_plan/030925b.pdf (accessed February 19, 2016)

TABLE 6.5

The 10 listed reptile species with the highest expenditures under the Endangered Species Act, fiscal year 2014

Ranking	Species	Population	Expenditure
1	Tortoise, desert (*Gopherus agassizii*)	Entire, except in Sonoran Desert	$33,677,623
2	Sea turtle, loggerhead (*Caretta caretta*)	Northwest Atlantic Ocean DPS	$8,660,093
3	Sea turtle, leatherback (*Dermochelys coriacea*)	Entire	$8,059,747
4	Sea turtle, green (*Chelonia mydas*)	Entire, except where endangered	$7,593,653
5	Sea turtle, hawksbill (*Eretmochelys imbricata*)	Entire	$6,763,446
6	Tortoise, gopher (*Gopherus polyphemus*)	West of Mobile and Tombigbee Rivers	$6,229,344
7	Sea turtle, Kemp's ridley (*Lepidochelys kempii*)	Entire	$5,636,214
8	Sea turtle, green (*Chelonia mydas*)	FL, Mexico nesting populations	$2,792,508
9	Snake, giant garter (*Thamnophis gigas*)	Entire	$2,390,199
10	Sea turtle, loggerhead (*Caretta caretta*)	North Pacific Ocean DPS	$2,358,970

Note: DPS = Distinct Population Segment.

SOURCE: Adapted from "Table 2. Species Ranked in Descending Order of Total FY 2014 Reported Expenditures, Not Including Land Acquisition Costs," in *Federal and State Endangered and Threatened Species Expenditures: Fiscal Year 2014*, U.S. Department of the Interior, U.S. Fish and Wildlife Service, March 2, 2016, http://www.fws.gov/endangered/esa-library/pdf/20160302_final_FY14_ExpRpt.pdf (accessed March 9, 2016)

FIGURE 6.5

The desert tortoise is threatened because of habitat destruction, livestock grazing, invasion of nonnative plant species, collection, and predation by ravens. ©*Ross Haley/U.S. Fish and Wildlife Service.*

keystone species because it provides a major benefit to fellow species in its ecosystem who would greatly suffer from its demise.

The desert tortoise has dual listings under the ESA. The population in Arizona, California, Nevada, and Utah was listed in 1980 as threatened except for those tortoises in Arizona south and east of the Colorado River. The latter were listed in 1990 as SAT. It was originally thought that *Gopherus agassizii* included two populations, known as the Mojave Desert population and the Sonoran Desert population. In "Genetic Analysis Splits Desert Tortoise into Two Species" (June 28, 2011, http://www.usgs.gov/newsroom/article.asp?ID=2842#.Vuf-v5wr LIU), the USGS reports that in 2011 researchers determined that the two populations are actually two different species. The so-called Sonoran Desert population has been officially named the Morafka's desert tortoise (*Gopherus morafkai*). In October 2015 the USFWS (https://www.gpo.gov/fdsys/ pkg/FR-2015-10-06/pdf/2015-25286.pdf) decided not to list the newly designated species under the ESA.

The decline of the desert tortoise has resulted from collection by humans, predation of young turtles by ravens, off-road vehicles, invasive plant species, and habitat destruction due to development for agriculture, mining, and livestock grazing.

Desert tortoise populations are constrained by the fact that females do not reproduce until they are 15 to 20 years of age (individuals can live 80 to 100 years) and by small clutch sizes (i.e., small numbers of eggs per laying). Juvenile mortality is also extremely high, in large part because of predation by ravens, whose populations in the desert tortoise's habitat have risen with increasing urbanization of desert areas—human garbage provides food for ravens and power lines provide perches.

Nearly $33.7 million was spent under the ESA during FY 2014 on conservation measures for the Mojave Desert population of the desert tortoise. (See Table 6.5.) In May 2011 the agency published *Revised Recovery Plan for the Mojave Population of the Desert Tortoise* (*Gopherus agassizii*) (http://ecos.fws.gov/docs/recovery_plan/RRP% 20for%20the%20Mojave%20Desert%20Tortoise%20-%20 May%202011_1.pdf). It estimates that the species can be recovered by 2025 at a cost of approximately $159 million.

GOPHER TORTOISES. In 1987 the western population of the gopher tortoise was listed as threatened under the ESA. (See Figure 6.6.) This population is found west of the Tombigbee and Mobile Rivers in Alabama and across Mississippi and into Louisiana. (See Figure 6.7.) Gopher tortoises are land-dwelling turtles that prefer habitat in longleaf pine ecosystems with sandy soils. The tortoises spend much of their time in sandy burrows that often provide shelter for other animals, such as snakes and frogs. Thus, gopher tortoises are a keystone species in their ecosystems. A recovery plan for the gopher tortoise

FIGURE 6.6

Gopher tortoise

SOURCE: Robert Savannah, artist, "Gopher Tortoise," in *Tortoises*, U.S. Department of the Interior, U.S. Fish and Wildlife Service, undated, http://www.fws.gov/pictures/lineart/bobsavannah/TIFFS/tortoise3.tif (accessed February 15, 2016)

FIGURE 6.7

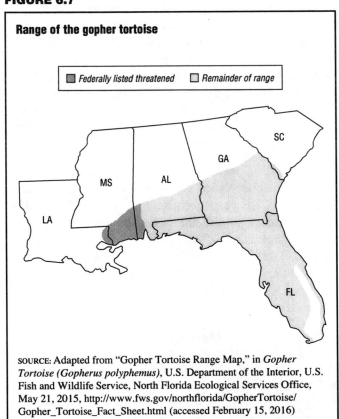

Range of the gopher tortoise

■ *Federally listed threatened*   □ *Remainder of range*

SOURCE: Adapted from "Gopher Tortoise Range Map," in *Gopher Tortoise (Gopherus polyphemus)*, U.S. Department of the Interior, U.S. Fish and Wildlife Service, North Florida Ecological Services Office, May 21, 2015, http://www.fws.gov/northflorida/GopherTortoise/Gopher_Tortoise_Fact_Sheet.html (accessed February 15, 2016)

Coastal longleaf pine forests in the Southeast have been highly degraded by centuries of land development. As this habitat has become more fragmented, isolated pockets of the species have resulted in poor reproduction rates. Scientists fear that genetic drift and interbreeding are already occurring within the population. During the Great Depression (1929–1939) gopher tortoises were a highly prized meat source. Since that time their numbers have been further reduced by road strikes and collection for the pet trade. Natural predators include raccoons, foxes, snakes, and fire ants that prey on eggs or hatchlings.

In *Gopher Tortoise (*Gopherus polyphemus*) Recovery Plan* (December 26, 1990, http://ecos.fws.gov/docs/recovery_plan/901226.pdf), the USFWS notes that better management of government-owned forests in the region could help the survival status of the gopher tortoise. However, most lands with suitable habitat are privately owned and have already undergone, or are likely to undergo, development for agricultural, residential, or commercial purposes.

In 2001 the USFWS, in conjunction with the Mobile Area Water and Sewer System and the conservation organizations Environmental Defense Fund and Southeastern Natural Resources, created a 222-acre (89.8-ha) gopher tortoise conservation bank near Big Creek Lake in Mobile, Alabama. Property owners can relocate gopher tortoises from their land to the conservation bank, which will remain undeveloped. As of 2016, the Mobile Area Water and Sewer System (http://www.mawss.com/faq.html) charged $3,500 per gopher tortoise admitted to the bank. This money is used to manage the habitat. Each bank tortoise is also equipped with a radio collar so that the USFWS can monitor its movement.

As shown in Table 6.5, more than $6.2 million was spent under the ESA during FY 2014 on the western population of the gopher tortoise. In April 2010 the USFWS (http://www.gpo.gov/fdsys/pkg/FR-2010-04-09/pdf/2010-8103.pdf#page=1) published notice of its intention to conduct a five-year review for 10 southeastern species, including the gopher tortoise. As of April 2016, the results of that review had not been published.

In 2006 the USFWS (September 9, 2009, http://www.gpo.gov/fdsys/pkg/FR-2009-09-09/pdf/E9-21481.pdf#page=1) received a petition submitted by two conservation groups—Save Our Big Scrub Inc. and Wild South—requesting that the eastern population of gopher tortoises be listed as threatened under the ESA. As shown in Figure 6.7, this population is found in Alabama (east of the Tombigbee and Mobile Rivers), Florida, Georgia, and into South Carolina. The species was designated as a candidate for listing. It retained this designation in the Candidate Notice of Review published in December 2015. (See Table 2.3 in Chapter 2.) Thus, it is not certain when a listing decision will be made.

was completed in 1990. At that time the primary threats to the species were habitat degradation and illegal taking (hunting, killing, capturing, and harassing).

Imperiled Sea Turtles in the United States

Sea (or marine) turtles are excellent swimmers and spend nearly their entire life in water. They feed on a wide array of food items, including mollusks, vegetation, and crustaceans. Some sea turtles are migratory, swimming thousands of miles between feeding and nesting areas. The latter are on beaches on which the turtles lay their eggs under the sand. Individuals are exposed to a variety of both natural and human threats. As a result, only an estimated one out of 10,000 sea turtles survives to adulthood.

There are seven species of sea turtles that exist worldwide. One species, the flatback turtle, occurs near Australia. Most of the other six species—green sea turtle, hawksbill sea turtle, Kemp's ridley sea turtle, leatherback sea turtle, loggerhead sea turtle, and olive ridley sea turtle—are found in marine waters around the world, especially near the equator. For example, Figure 6.8 shows the range of the green sea turtle. The same six sea turtle species are found in U.S. territorial waters, and as of February 2016 were listed under the ESA. (See

Table 6.4.) All had recovery plans in place. ESA-listed sea turtles fall under the jurisdiction of the USFWS while they are on U.S. land and under the jurisdiction of the National Marine Fisheries Service (NMFS) while they are at sea.

The green sea turtle, hawksbill sea turtle, Kemp's ridley sea turtle, leatherback sea turtle, and loggerhead sea turtle are shown in Figure 6.9.

PROTECTING SEA TURTLES. Sea turtles are at risk of human interference in their aquatic habitats (i.e., ocean waters) and at their nesting locations on sandy beaches.

Shrimp trawling is recognized as one of the most deadly human activities for sea turtles in the Gulf of Mexico and the Caribbean. During the late 1970s the NMFS began developing turtle excluder devices (TEDs), which allow sea turtles to escape from shrimp nets. (See Figure 6.10.)

Rusty Middleton notes in "Saving Sea Turtles" (TPWMagazine.com, June 2012) that a mandatory TED program was instituted by the NMFS in 1987, but it

FIGURE 6.8

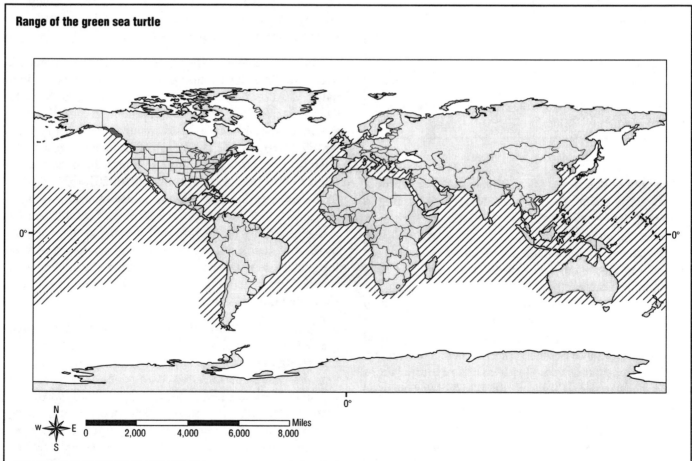

Range of the green sea turtle

Note: Map represents approximate range of species.

SOURCE: "Green Sea Turtle Range," in *Green Turtle (Chelonia mydas)*, U.S. Department of Commerce, National Oceanic and Atmospheric Administration, National Marine Fisheries Service, March 2009, http://www.nmfs.noaa.gov/pr/pdfs/rangemaps/green_turtle.pdf (accessed February 15, 2016)

FIGURE 6.9

Sea turtles that nest on U.S. coasts

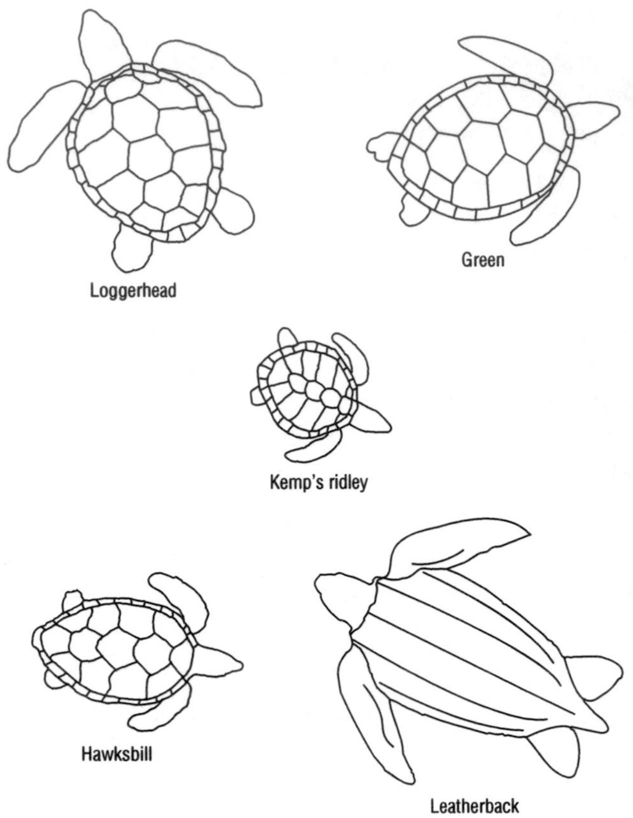

Loggerhead

Green

Kemp's ridley

Hawksbill

Leatherback

SOURCE: Adapted from "Untitled," in *You Can Help Protect Sea Turtles*, U.S. Department of the Interior, U.S. Fish and Wildlife Service, North Florida Ecological Services Office, July 2009, http://www.fws.gov/northflorida/SeaTurtles/20090700_You_Can_Help_ST.pdf (accessed February 15, 2016)

FIGURE 6.10

A bycatch reduction device designed to protect sea turtles

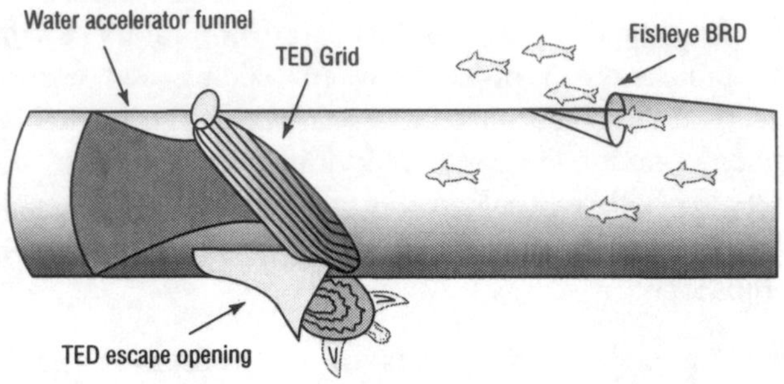

Water accelerator funnel

TED Grid

Fisheye BRD

TED escape opening

Notes: TED = Turtle excluder device. BRD = Bycatch reduction device.

SOURCE: Richard K. Wallace and Kristen M. Fletcher, "Figure 9," in *Understanding Fisheries Management: A Manual for Understanding the Federal Fisheries Management Process, Including Analysis of the 1996 Sustainable Fisheries Act*, 2nd ed., U.S. Department of Commerce, National Oceanic and Atmospheric Administration, National Sea Grant Office, Mississippi Alabama Sea Grant Consortium, 2001, http://nsgl.gso.uri.edu/masgc/masgch00001.pdf (accessed February 15, 2016)

applies only to deepwater shrimp boats. Smaller skimmer trawlers are not required to use the devices. According to Middleton, the smaller boats are forbidden to shrimp in Texas waters, but make up about two-thirds of the shrimp fleet in Louisiana. Although the skimmer trawlers are supposed to limit their underwater trawling time, this requirement is difficult to enforce. In 2011 conservation groups filed a lawsuit against the NMFS after more than 900 dead turtles washed up on Gulf Coast beaches and necropsies (animal autopsies) revealed that most had died from drowning. In 2012 the agency reached an agreement with the groups and proposed issuance of new regulations on skimmer trawlers. However, the NMFS later changed its mind and did not issue the regulations.

In "National Fisheries Services Holds Off on New Turtle Excluder Device Rules" (NOLA.com, November 27, 2012), Benjamin Alexander-Bloch quotes an NMFS spokesperson defending the decision, who said, "Information we now have suggests the conservation benefit does not justify the burden this rule would place on the industry. We need more research looking at different options." Conservation groups accused the agency of bowing to political pressure from Louisiana officials wanting to protect the state's shrimpers.

In 2015 the conservation group Oceana sued the NMFS over sea turtle deaths linked to the Gulf Coast shrimp industry. According to Barbara Liston, in "U.S. Sued to Curb Deaths of Sea Turtles by Shrimping Industry" (Reuters.com, April 15, 2015), the lawsuit seeks to compel the NMFS to require TEDs for all shrimp trawlers and to establish a sea turtle catch limit. In March 2016 the agency (https://www.federalregister.gov/articles/2016/03/15/2016-05769/notice-of-intent-to-prepare-an-environmental-impact-statement-for-sea-turtle-conservation-and) published a notice indicating its intention to investigate the potential impacts of new regulations on the shrimping industry in the southeastern United States. Various alternatives will be considered, including expanded TED requirements and shrimping time and area closures.

Under Public Law 101-162, Section 609, the United States bans the import of shrimp from countries that use harvesting methods deemed harmful to sea turtles. Each year the U.S. Department of State issues a list of nations that have been certified to import shrimp into the United States. Certification means that the shrimp were obtained using TEDs or in some other manner that does not endanger sea turtles. Shrimp imports are allowed from noncertified countries on a shipment-by-shipment basis if the respective governments can show that the shrimp were harvested in a manner not harmful to sea turtles.

Bottom longlines used for fishing pose another threat to sea turtles. In "Bottom Longlines: Fishing Gear and Risks to Protected Species" (January 30, 2014, http://www.nmfs.noaa.gov/pr/interactions/gear/bottomlongline.htm), the NMFS explains that a bottom longline can stretch for more than a mile and is anchored on the seafloor at both ends. (See Figure 6.11.) A longline can include as many as a thousand baited hooks. Sea turtles and marine mammals can become hooked and drown. According to the NMFS, it implemented regulations in 2005 that limit the number of hooks per fishing vessel, set time and area closures for certain fishing areas, and require vessels to carry instructions for safely releasing any sea turtles or smalltooth sawfish that become hooked. (As noted in Chapter 4, smalltooth sawfish are listed as an endangered species under the ESA.)

Sea turtles bury their eggs in nests on sandy beaches and then return to the sea. The hatchlings emerge approximately 60 days later and must make a treacherous march to the water. During the short trip they are highly prone to predation by birds and other animals.

The building of beachfront resorts and homes has destroyed a large proportion of nesting habitat over the decades. New development projects must comply with the ESA and applicable state and local laws. For example, the Florida Fish and Wildlife Conservation Commission explains in "Marine Turtle Protection" (2016, http://myfwc.com/wildlifehabitats/managed/sea-turtles/protection/) that it works with the Florida Department of Environmental Protection to review permits for coastal construction to ensure that sea turtles and their habitats will not be harmed. Florida's Marine Turtle Protection Act (379.2431, Florida Statutes; http://www.leg.state.fl.us/) also governs projects that transfer sand from the sea bottom to the beach, a practice known as renourishment that is widely used to replace beach sand that erodes away. Renourishment can be detrimental to sea turtles (and other species) if the newly sourced sand is too dense or compacted.

On beach areas where turtle nesting is known to take place, authorities typically erect barriers (such as fences) and post signs warning beachgoers not to interfere with the nests. Artificial lighting associated with coastal development also poses a problem—lights discourage females from nesting and cause hatchlings to become disoriented and wander inland instead of out to sea. As a result, some jurisdictions have regulations that govern beach lighting. For example, the Florida Fish and Wildlife Conservation Commission has developed a model local ordinance that serves as a guide for local governments that wish to regulate beach lighting. As of 2016, dozens of cities and counties within the state had adopted such ordinances.

Nesting sea turtles and hatchlings also benefit from the activities of numerous private conservation organizations and citizen volunteers that collaborate with government agencies. In "Dr. Shaver and the Division of Sea Turtle Science and Recovery" (2016, http://www.nps.gov/pais/learn/nature/stsr.htm), the National Park Service notes that it patrols beaches in the Padre Island National Park to detect and monitor nesting sea turtles and their nests and to rescue stranded sea turtles. It is helped in these efforts by the USFWS and the NMFS and by private and academic groups such as Animal Rehabilitation Keep and the University of Texas.

Imperiled Snakes and Lizards

As of February 2016, there were 13 snakes (including whipsnakes and boas) and nine lizards (including skinks, anoles, iguanas, and geckos) listed as endangered or threatened under the ESA. (See Table 6.4.) The following sections discuss three of the species: giant garter snake, eastern indigo snake, and Monito gecko.

GIANT GARTER SNAKES. As shown in Table 6.5, nearly $2.4 million was spent under the ESA during FY 2014 on the giant garter snake. This species is found only in California. It prefers agricultural wetlands (such as rice fields), canals, ponds, streams, and other small water bodies. Extensive land development in the Central Valley of the state has severely depleted the snake's habitat. Other threats to its survival include invasive predatory fish, water pollution, and flood control activities. The giant garter snake was listed as threatened under the ESA in 1993.

Aaron Cotter describes in "Building a Bank Takes More Than Just Snakes" (September 22, 2015, http://www.fws

FIGURE 6.11

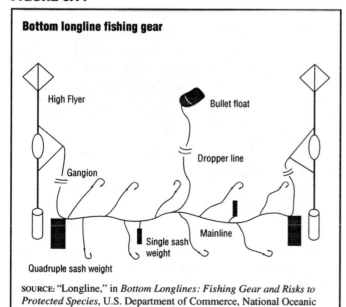

Bottom longline fishing gear

High Flyer

Bullet float

Dropper line

Gangion

Single sash weight

Mainline

Quadruple sash weight

SOURCE: "Longline," in *Bottom Longlines: Fishing Gear and Risks to Protected Species*, U.S. Department of Commerce, National Oceanic and Atmospheric Administration, National Marine Fisheries Service, January 30, 2014, http://www.nmfs.noaa.gov/pr/interactions/gear/bottomlongline.htm (accessed February 15, 2016)

.gov/sacramento/outreach/featured-stories/BuildingBanks-Snakes/outreach_featured-stories_BuildingBanksSnakes.htm) the Sutter Basin Conservation Bank in California. Established in 2008, the 429-acre (174-ha) bank provides marshy habitat for giant garter snakes and offers banking credits for fees that are used to operate the bank.

In 2015 the USFWS published *Revised Draft Recovery Plan for Giant Garter Snake* (Thamnophis gigas) (http://ecos.fws.gov/docs/recovery_plan/20151211_GGS%20Revised%20Draft%20Recovery%20Plan.pdf). The agency outlines conservation strategies for the species and notes that delisting due to recovery could occur by 2045. The USFWS does not include a recovery cost estimate, but expects to publish such an estimate in another revised version of the plan. As of April 2016, the revision had not been released.

EASTERN INDIGO SNAKES. The eastern indigo snake is a large thick-bodied black snake found only in Florida and the southern parts of Alabama and Georgia. (See Figure 6.12.) In 1978 it was listed as threatened under the ESA. Its recovery plan was finalized in 1982. In May 2008 the USFWS published *Eastern Indigo Snake* (Drymarchon couperi): *5-Year Review—Summary and Evaluation* (http://ecos.fws.gov/docs/five_year_review/doc1910.pdf). The agency decided to maintain the snake's threatened listing because of continued threats to its habitat. These include loss, degradation, and fragmentation of "wild land," particularly longleaf pine forests.

MONITO GECKOS. The endangered Monito gecko is a small lizard less than 2 inches (5 cm) long. (See Figure 6.13.) This species exists only on the 38-acre (15.4-ha) Monito Island off the Puerto Rican coast. Endangerment of the Monito gecko has resulted from human activity and habitat destruction. After World War II (1939–1945) the U.S. military used Monito Island as a site for bombing exercises, causing large-scale habitat destruction. In 1982 the USFWS observed only 24 Monito

FIGURE 6.12

Eastern indigo snake. ©*fivespots/Shutterstock.com.*

FIGURE 6.13

Monito gecko

SOURCE: "Monito Gecko," in *Endangered Species Coloring Book: Save Our Species*, U.S. Environmental Protection Agency, May 2008, http://www.epa.gov/sites/production/files/2013-08/documents/cbook.pdf (accessed February 15, 2016)

geckos on the island. In 1985 Monito Island was designated as critical habitat for the species. The Commonwealth of Puerto Rico is now managing the island for the gecko and as a refuge for seabirds; unauthorized human visitation is prohibited. In 2007 the USFWS initiated a five-year review of 18 Caribbean wildlife and plant species, including the Monito gecko. As of April 2016, the results of that review had not been published.

Imperiled Crocodilians

Crocodilians play a crucial role in their habitat. They control fish populations and dig water holes, which are important to many species in times of drought. The disappearance of alligators and crocodiles has a profound effect on the biological communities these animals occupy. There are two crocodilian species in the United States: the American alligator and the American crocodile. (See Figure 6.14.) They are similar in appearance with only slight differences. The crocodile has a narrower, more pointed snout and an indentation in its upper jaw that allows a tooth to be seen when its mouth is closed.

The American alligator has a unique history under the ESA. It was on the first list of endangered species published in 1967. (See Table 2.1 in Chapter 2.) During the 1970s and 1980s populations of the species in many states rebounded in abundance and could have been delisted. Instead, it was reclassified as threatened. This measure was taken, in part, because federal officials acknowledged

FIGURE 6.14

American crocodile. ©*U.S. Fish and Wildlife Service.*

a certain amount of "public hostility" toward the creatures and were concerned that delisting would open the population to excessive hunting. Also, it was feared that the American alligator was so similar in appearance to the highly endangered American crocodile that delisting the alligator might lead to accidental taking of the crocodile species. By 1987 the alligator was considered fully recovered in the United States. As of February 2016, the alligator was listed as SAT. (See Table 6.4.)

The American crocodile is considered a success story of the ESA. When the species was originally listed as endangered in 1975, less than 300 individuals existed. Over the next three decades the species thrived and expanded its nesting range to new locations on the east and west coasts of Florida. In 2005 the USFWS initiated a five-year status review of the species. In 2007 the western

DPS of the species in Florida was downlisted from endangered to threatened. At that time an estimated 2,000 American crocodiles lived in the state, not including hatchlings. Figure 6.15 shows a map of the critical habitat for the American crocodile and areas for which the USFWS provides consultation services regarding the species.

Threatened and Endangered Foreign Reptile Species

The IUCN reports in *Red List of Threatened Species Version 2015.4* that 944 reptile species were threatened in 2015. A total of 4,669 reptile species were evaluated out of the 10,272 known species.

As of February 2016, there were 84 totally foreign reptile species listed under the ESA. (See Table 6.6.) Most are found in the tropical regions of Africa, Mexico, South America, and Southeast Asia.

FIGURE 6.15

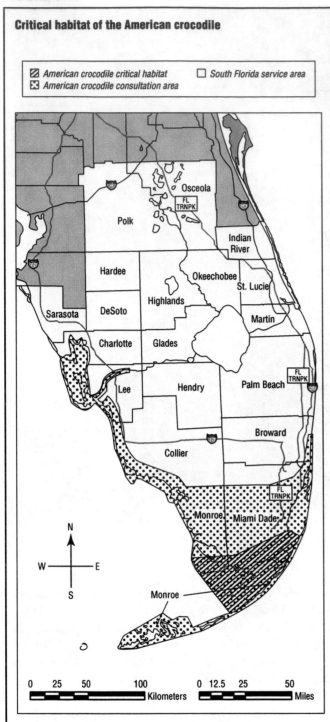

Critical habitat of the American crocodile

| ▨ American crocodile critical habitat | ☐ South Florida service area |
| ⊠ American crocodile consultation area | |

SOURCE: Adapted from "American Crocodile: Consultation Area Map," in *American Crocodile: Consultation Area*, U.S. Department of the Interior, U.S. Fish and Wildlife Service, South Florida Ecological Services Office, September 19, 2003, http://www.fws.gov/verobeach/ReptilesPDFs/AmericanCrocodileConsultationArea.pdf (accessed February 15, 2016)

TABLE 6.6

Foreign endangered and threatened reptile species, February 2016

Common name	Scientific name	Federal listing status*	Current distribution
Acklins ground iguana	*Cyclura rileyi nuchalis*	T	West Indies-Bahamas
African dwarf crocodile	*Osteolaemus tetraspis tetraspis*	E	West Africa
African slender-snouted crocodile	*Crocodylus cataphractus*	E	Western and Central Africa
Allen's Cay iguana	*Cyclura cychlura inornata*	T	West Indies-Bahamas
American crocodile	*Crocodylus acutus*	E	U.S.A. (FL), Mexico, Caribbean, Central and South America
Andros Island ground iguana	*Cyclura cychlura cychlura*	T	West Indies-Bahamas
Anegada ground iguana	*Cyclura pinguis*	E	British Virgin Islands (Anegada Islands)
Angulated tortoise	*Geochelone yniphora*	E	Malagasy Republic (Madagascar)
Apaporis River caiman	*Caiman crocodilus apaporiensis*	E	Colombia
Aquatic box turtle	*Terrapene coahuila*	E	Mexico
Aruba Island rattlesnake	*Crotalus unicolor*	T	Aruba Island (Netherland Antilles)
Barrington land iguana	*Conolophus pallidus*	E	Ecuador (Galapagos Islands)
Black caiman	*Melanosuchus niger*	E	Amazon Basin
Black softshell turtle	*Trionyx nigricans*	E	Bangladesh
Bolson tortoise	*Gopherus flavomarginatus*	E	Mexico
Brazilian sideneck turtle	*Phrynops hogei*	E	Brazil
Broad-snouted caiman	*Caiman latirostris*	E; T	Brazil, Argentina, Paraguay, Uruguay
Brother's Island tuatara	*Sphenodon guntheri*	E	New Zealand (Brothers Island)
Brown caiman	*Caiman crocodilus fuscus (includes Caiman crocodilus chiapasius)*	SAT	Venezuela, Peru, Mexico, Ecuador, Central America, Colombia
Burmese peacock turtle	*Morenia ocellata*	E	Burma (Myanmar)
Cat Island turtle	*Trachemys terrapen*	E	Cat Island in the Bahamas; West Indies-Jamaica, Bahamas
Cayman Brac ground iguana	*Cyclura nubila caymanensis*	T	West Indies-Cayman Islands
Central American river turtle	*Dermatemys mawii*	E	Mexico, Guatemala, Belize
Ceylon mugger crocodile	*Crocodylus palustris kimbula*	E	Sri Lanka
Chinese alligator	*Alligator sinensis*	E	China
Common caiman	*Caiman crocodilus crocodilus*	SAT	Venezuela, Suriname, Peru, Guyana, French Guiana, Ecuador, Colombia, Brazil, Bolivia
Congo dwarf crocodile	*Osteolaemus tetraspis osborni*	E	Congo River drainage
Cuatro Cienegas softshell turtle	*Trionyx ater*	E	Mexico
Cuban crocodile	*Crocodylus rhombifer*	E	Cuba
Cuban ground iguana	*Cyclura nubila nubila*	T	Cuba
Day gecko	*Phelsuma edwardnewtoni*	E	Indian Ocean-Mauritius
Desert monitor	*Varanus griseus*	E	North Africa to Aral Sea, through Central Asia to Pakistan, Northwest India
Dusky sea snake	*Aipysurus fuscus*	E	New Guinea, Australia
Exuma Island iguana	*Cyclura cychlura figginsi*	T	West Indies-Bahamas
Fiji banded iguana	*Brachylophus fasciatus*	E	Pacific-Tonga, Fiji
Fiji crested iguana	*Brachylophus vitiensis*	E	Pacific-Fiji
Galapagos tortoise	*Geochelone nigra (=elephantopus)*	E	Ecuador (Galapagos Islands)
Gavial	*Gavialis gangeticus*	E	Pakistan, Nepal, India, Burma, Bangladesh
Geometric turtle	*Psammobates geometricus*	E	South Africa
Grand Cayman ground iguana	*Cyclura nubila lewisi*	E	West Indies-Cayman Islands
Hierro giant lizard	*Gallotia simonyi simonyi*	E	Spain (Canary Islands)
Ibiza wall lizard	*Podarcis pityusensis*	T	Spain (Balearic Islands)
Inagua Island turtle	*Trachemys stejnegeri malonei*	E	Bahamas (Great Inagua Island)
Indian (=Bengal) monitor	*Varanus bengalensis*	E	Vietnam, Thailand, Sri Lanka, Myanmar (Burma), Malaysia, Iraq, Iran, India, Afghanistan
Indian python	*Python molurus molurus*	E	Sri Lanka and India
Indian sawback turtle	*Kachuga tecta tecta*	E	India
Indian softshell turtle	*Trionyx gangeticus*	E	Pakistan, India
Jamaican boa	*Epicrates subflavus*	E	Jamaica
Jamaican iguana	*Cyclura collei*	E	West Indies-Jamaica
Komodo Island monitor	*Varanus komodoensis*	E	Indonesia (Komodo, Rintja, Padar, and western Flores Island)
Lar Valley viper	*Vipera latifii*	E	Iran
Loggerhead sea turtle	*Caretta caretta*	E; T	Mediterranean Sea Basin; Northeast Atlantic Ocean Basin; North Indian Ocean Basin; South Atlantic Ocean Basin; Southeast Indian Ocean Basin; South Pacific Ocean Basin as far east as 141 degrees E. Long; South Pacific Ocean Basin; Southwest Indian Ocean Basin
Madagascar radiated tortoise	*Geochelone radiata*	E	Malagasy Republic (Madagascar)
Maria Island ground lizard	*Cnemidophorus vanzoi*	E	St Lucia (Maria Islands); West Indies-St Lucia (Maria Islands)
Maria Island snake	*Liophus ornatus*	E	St Lucia (Maria Islands)
Mayaguana iguana	*Cyclura carinata bartschi*	I	West Indies-Bahamas
Mugger crocodile	*Crocodylus palustris palustris*	E	Pakistan, Iran, India, Bangladesh
Nile crocodile	*Crocodylus niloticus*	T	Middle East, Africa
Olive ridley sea turtle	*Lepidochelys olivacea*	E	Mexico (Pacific Coast breeding pop only); Mexico (Pacific Coast breeding population only).
Orinoco crocodile	*Crocodylus intermedius*	E	South America-Orinoco River Basin
Peacock softshell turtle	*Trionyx hurum*	E	India, Bangladesh

TABLE 6.6

Foreign endangered and threatened reptile species, February 2016 [CONTINUED]

Common name	Scientific name	Federal listing status*	Current distribution
Philippine crocodile	*Crocodylus novaeguineae mindorensis*	E	Philippine Islands
River terrapin	*Batagur baska*	E	Malaysia, Indonesia, India, Burma, Bangladesh
Round Island bolyeria boa	*Bolyeria multocarinata*	E	Indian Ocean-Mauritius
Round Island casarea boa	*Casarea dussumieri*	E	Indian Ocean-Mauritius
Round Island day gecko	*Phelsuma guentheri*	E	Indian Ocean-Mauritius
Round Island skink	*Leiolopisma telfairi*	T	Indian Ocean-Mauritius
Saltwater crocodile	*Crocodylus porosus*	E; T	Southeast Asia, Austrailia, Papua New Guinea, Islands of the West Pacific Ocean
San Esteban Island chuckwalla	*Sauromalus varius*	E	Mexico
Serpent Island gecko	*Cyrtodactylus serpensinsula*	T	Indian Ocean-Mauritius
Short-necked or western swamp turtle	*Pseudemydura umbrina*	E	Australia
Siamese crocodile	*Crocodylus siamensis*	E	Southeast Asia, Malay Peninsula
South American red-lined turtle	*Trachemys scripta callirostris*	E	Venezuela, Colombia
Spotted pond turtle	*Geoclemys hamiltonii*	E	North India, Pakistan
Tartaruga	*Podocnemis expansa*	E	South America-Orinoco River and Amazon River Basins
Three-keeled Asian turtle	*Melanochelys tricarinata*	E	Central India; Central India to Bangladesh and Burma (Myanmar)
Tomistoma	*Tomistoma schlegelii*	E	Malaysia, Indonesia
Tracaja	*Podocnemis unifilis*	E	South America-Orinoco River and Amazon River Basins
Tuatara	*Sphenodon punctatus*	E	New Zealand
Turks and Caicos iguana	*Cyclura carinata carinata*	T	West Indies-Turks and Caicos Islands
Watling Island ground iguana	*Cyclura rileyi rileyi*	E	West Indies-Bahamas
White Cay ground iguana	*Cyclura rileyi cristata*	T	West Indies-Bahamas
Yacare caiman	*Caiman yacare*	T	Paraguay, Brazil, Bolivia, Argentina
Yellow monitor	*Varanus flavescens*	E	West Pakistan through India to Bangladesh

*E = Endangered. T = Threatened. SAT = Similarity in Appearance to a Threatened Taxon.

SOURCE: Adapted from "Generate Species List," in *Environmental Conservation Online System Species Reports*, U.S. Department of the Interior, U.S. Fish and Wildlife Service, February 2016, http://ecos.fws.gov/tess_public/pub/adHocSpeciesForm.jsp (accessed February 15, 2016)

CHAPTER 7
TERRESTRIAL MAMMALS

Terrestrial animals are animals that inhabit the land. Mammals are warm-blooded, breathe air, have hair at some point during their life, give birth to live young (as opposed to laying eggs), and nourish their young by secreting milk.

The biggest cause of terrestrial mammalian decline and extinction is habitat loss and degradation. As humans convert forests, grasslands, rivers, and wetlands for various uses, they relegate many species to precarious existences in small, fragmented habitat patches. In addition, some terrestrial mammals have been purposely eliminated by humans. For example, bison (buffalo), elk, and beaver stocks were severely depleted in the United States following colonization by European settlers. All three species were nearly hunted to extinction by the end of the 1800s. The disappearance of native large game had consequences on other species. Wolves and other predators began preying on livestock and became the target of massive kill-offs by humans.

Some terrestrial mammal species have been imperiled, in part because they are considered dangerous to human life. This has been the case for many bears, wolves, and mountain lions. Changing attitudes have led to interest in preserving all species, and conservation measures have allowed several terrestrial mammals to recover.

ENDANGERED AND THREATENED U.S. SPECIES

As of February 2016, there were 76 species of terrestrial mammals in the United States listed under the Endangered Species Act (ESA) as endangered or threatened. (See Table 7.1.) Nearly all had an endangered listing, meaning that they are at risk of extinction, and most had recovery plans in place.

The imperiled species fall into nine broad categories:

- Bats

- Bears

- Canines—foxes and wolves

- Deer, caribou, pronghorns, bighorn sheep, and bison

- Felines—jaguars, jaguarundis, lynx, margay, ocelots, panthers, and pumas

- Ferrets

- Rabbits

- Rodents—beavers, gophers, mice, prairie dogs, rats, squirrels, and voles

- Shrews

Table 7.2 shows the 10 terrestrial mammal species with the highest expenditures under the ESA during fiscal year (FY) 2014. The Indiana bat was the most expensive ($15.2 million), followed by the grizzly bear ($8 million) and the black-footed ferret ($5.5 million).

Bats

Bats belong to the taxonomic order Chiroptera, which means "hand-wing." They are the only true flying mammals. They typically weigh less than 2 ounces (57 g) and have wingspans of less than 20 inches (51 cm). Most are insectivores, meaning that insects are their primary food source. As such, bats are valued by humans for keeping in check populations of insects that are agricultural pests or carry diseases (such as mosquitoes). Bats prefer to sleep during the day and feed after dusk. Biologists believe that bats are vastly underappreciated for their role in controlling nighttime insect populations.

As of February 2016, 12 bat species were listed by the U.S. Fish and Wildlife Service (USFWS) as endangered or threatened under the ESA (see Table 7.1):

- Florida bonneted bat

- Gray bat

- Hawaiian hoary bat

- Indiana bat

TABLE 7.1

Endangered and threatened terrestrial mammal species, February 2016

Common name	Scientific name	Federal listing status[a]	U.S. or U.S./foreign listed	Recovery plan date	Recovery plan stage[b]
Alabama beach mouse	*Peromyscus polionotus ammobates*	E	US	08/12/87	F
Amargosa vole	*Microtus californicus scirpensis*	E	US	09/15/97	F
American black bear	*Ursus americanus*	SAT	US	None	—
Anastasia Island beach mouse	*Peromyscus polionotus phasma*	E	US	09/23/93	F
Black-footed ferret	*Mustela nigripes*	E; EXPN	US/foreign	12/23/13	RF(2)
Buena Vista Lake ornate shrew	*Sorex ornatus relictus*	E	US	09/30/98	F
Canada lynx	*Lynx canadensis*	T	US	09/14/05	O
Carolina northern flying squirrel	*Glaucomys sabrinus coloratus*	E	US	09/24/90	F
Choctawhatchee beach mouse	*Peromyscus polionotus allophrys*	E	US	08/12/87	F
Columbia Basin pygmy rabbit	*Brachylagus idahoensis*	E	US	01/23/13	F
Columbian white-tailed deer	*Odocoileus virginianus leucurus*	E	US	06/14/83	RF(1)
Eastern puma (=cougar)	*Puma (= Felis) concolor couguar*	E	US/foreign	08/02/82	F
Florida bonneted bat	*Eumops floridanus*	E	US	None	—
Florida panther	*Puma (= Felis) concolor coryi*	E	US	12/18/08	RF(3)
Florida salt marsh vole	*Microtus pennsylvanicus dukecampbelli*	E	US	09/30/97	F
Fresno kangaroo rat	*Dipodomys nitratoides exilis*	E	US	09/30/98	F
Giant kangaroo rat	*Dipodomys ingens*	E	US	09/30/98	F
Gray bat	*Myotis grisescens*	E	US	07/08/82	F
Gray wolf	*Canis lupus*	E; T; EXPN	US	01/31/92	RF(1)
Grizzly bear	*Ursus arctos horribilis*	T; EXPN	US	05/03/13	RF(1)
Gulf Coast jaguarundi	*Herpailurus (= Felis) yagouaroundi cacomitli*	E	US/foreign	12/20/13	F
Hawaiian hoary bat	*Lasiurus cinereus semotus*	E	US	05/11/98	F
Hualapai Mexican vole	*Microtus mexicanus hualpaiensis*	E	US	08/19/91	F
Indiana bat	*Myotis sodalis*	E	US	04/16/07	RD(1)
Jaguar	*Panthera onca*	E	US/foreign	04/20/12	O
Key deer	*Odocoileus virginianus clavium*	E	US	05/18/99	F
Key Largo cotton mouse	*Peromyscus gossypinus allapaticola*	E	US	05/18/99	F
Key Largo woodrat	*Neotoma floridana smalli*	E	US	05/18/99	F
Lesser long-nosed bat	*Leptonycteris curasoae yerbabuenae*	E	US/foreign	03/04/97	F
Little Mariana fruit bat	*Pteropus tokudae*	E	US	11/02/90	F
Louisiana black bear	*Ursus americanus luteolus*	T	US	09/27/95	F
Lower Keys marsh rabbit	*Sylvilagus palustris hefneri*	E	US	05/18/99	F
Margay	*Leopardus (= Felis) wiedii*	E	US/foreign	None	—
Mariana fruit bat (=Mariana flying fox)	*Pteropus mariannus mariannus*	T	US	03/30/10	RD(1)
Mexican long-nosed bat	*Leptonycteris nivalis*	E	US/foreign	09/08/94	F
Mexican wolf	*Canis lupus baileyi*	E; EXPN	US/foreign	09/15/82	F
Morro Bay kangaroo rat	*Dipodomys heermanni morroensis*	E	US	01/25/00	RD(1)
Mount Graham red squirrel	*Tamiasciurus hudsonicus grahamensis*	E	US	05/27/11	RD(1)
New Mexico meadow jumping mouse	*Zapus hudsonius luteus*	E	US	06/09/14	O
Northern Idaho ground squirrel	*Urocitellus brunneus*	T	US	09/16/03	F
Northern long-eared bat	*Myotis septentrionalis*	T	US/foreign	None	—
Ocelot	*Leopardus (= Felis) pardalis*	E	US/foreign	08/26/10	RD(1)
Olympia pocket gopher	*Thomomys mazama pugetensis*	T	US	None	—
Ozark big-eared bat	*Corynorhinus (= Plecotus) townsendii ingens*	E	US	03/28/95	RF(1)
Pacific pocket mouse	*Perognathus longimembris pacificus*	E	US	09/28/98	F
Pacific sheath-tailed bat	*Emballonura semicaudata rotensis*	E	US/foreign	None	—
Peninsular bighorn sheep	*Ovis canadensis nelsoni*	E	US/foreign	10/25/00	F
Perdido Key beach mouse	*Peromyscus polionotus trissyllepsis*	E	US	08/12/87	F
Point Arena mountain beaver	*Aplodontia rufa nigra*	E	US	06/02/98	F
Preble's meadow jumping mouse	*Zapus hudsonius preblei*	T	US	None	—
Puma (=mountain lion)	*Puma (= Felis) concolor (all subsp. except coryi)*	SAT	US	None	—
Red wolf	*Canis rufus*	E; EXPN	US	10/26/90	RF(2)
Rice rat	*Oryzomys palustris natator*	E	US	05/18/99	F
Riparian brush rabbit	*Sylvilagus bachmani riparius*	E	US	09/30/98	F
Riparian woodrat (=San Joaquin Valley)	*Neotoma fuscipes riparia*	E	US	09/30/98	F
Roy Prairie pocket gopher	*Thomomys mazama glacialis*	T	US	None	—
Salt marsh harvest mouse	*Reithrodontomys raviventris*	E	US	02/26/14	F
San Bernardino Merriam's kangaroo rat	*Dipodomys merriami parvus*	E	US	None	—
San Joaquin kit fox	*Vulpes macrotis mutica*	E	US	09/30/98	F
San Miguel Island fox	*Urocyon littoralis littoralis*	E	US	03/09/15	F
Santa Catalina Island fox	*Urocyon littoralis catalinae*	E	US	03/09/15	F
Santa Cruz Island fox	*Urocyon littoralis santacruzae*	E	US	03/09/15	F
Santa Rosa Island fox	*Urocyon littoralis santarosae*	E	US	03/09/15	F
Sierra Nevada bighorn sheep	*Ovis canadensis sierrae*	E	US	02/13/08	F
Sinaloan jaguarundi	*Herpailurus (= Felis) yagouaroundi tolteca*	E	US/foreign	None	—
Sonoran pronghorn	*Antilocapra americana sonoriensis*	E; EXPN	US/foreign	06/30/15	D
Southeastern beach mouse	*Peromyscus polionotus niveiventris*	T	US	09/23/93	F
St. Andrew beach mouse	*Peromyscus polionotus peninsularis*	E	US	12/28/10	F
Stephens' kangaroo rat	*Dipodomys stephensi (incl. D. cascus)*	E	US	06/23/97	D

TABLE 7.1

Endangered and threatened terrestrial mammal species, February 2016 [CONTINUED]

Common name	Scientific name	Federal listing status[a]	U.S. or U.S./foreign listed	Recovery plan date	Recovery plan stage[b]
Tenino pocket gopher	*Thomomys mazama tumuli*	T	US	None	—
Tipton kangaroo rat	*Dipodomys nitratoides nitratoides*	E	US	09/30/98	F
Utah prairie dog	*Cynomys parvidens*	T	US	04/26/12	RF(1)
Virginia big-eared bat	*Corynorhinus (=Plecotus) townsendii virginianus*	E	US	05/08/84	F
Wood bison	*Bison bison athabascae*	T	US/foreign	None	—
Woodland caribou	*Rangifer tarandus caribou*	E	US/foreign	03/04/94	RF(1)
Yelm pocket gopher	*Thomomys mazama yelmensis*	T	US	None	—

[a]E = Endangered; T = Threatened; EXPN = Experimental population, non-essential; SAT = Similarity in appearance to a threatened taxon.
[b]F = Final; RD = Draft revision; RF = Final revision; O = other.

SOURCE: Adapted from "Generate Species List," in *Environmental Conservation Online System Species Reports*, U.S. Department of the Interior, U.S. Fish and Wildlife Service, February 2016, http://ecos.fws.gov/tess_public/pub/adHocSpeciesForm.jsp (accessed February 15, 2016), and "Listed FWS/Joint FWS and NMFS Species and Populations with Recovery Plans (Sorted by Listed Entity)," in *Recovery Plans Search*, U.S. Department of the Interior, U.S. Fish and Wildlife Service, February 2016, http://ecos.fws.gov/tess_public/pub/speciesRecovery.jsp?sort=1 (accessed February 15, 2016)

TABLE 7.2

The 10 listed terrestrial mammal species with the highest expenditures under the Endangered Species Act, fiscal year 2014

Ranking	Species	Population	Expenditure
1	Bat, Indiana (*Myotis sodalis*)	Entire	$15,192,756
2	Bear, grizzly (*Ursus arctos horribilis*)	Lower 48 states, except where listed as an experimental population or delisted	$8,036,953
3	Ferret, black-footed (*Mustela nigripes*)	WY, and specific portions of AZ, CO, MT, SD, and UT	$5,462,546
4	Lynx, Canada (*Lynx canadensis*)	Contiguous U.S. DPS	
5	Fox, San Joaquin kit (*Vulpes macrotis mutica*)	Wherever found	$5,263,502
6	Wolf, gray (*Canis lupus*)	All of AL, AR, CA, CO, CT, DE, FL, GA, IA, IN, IL, KS, KY, LA, MA, MD, ME, MI, MO, MS, NC, ND, NE, NH, NJ, NV, NY, OH, OK, PA, RI, SC, SD, TN, TX, VA, VT, WI, and WV; and portions of AZ, NM, OR, UT, and WA. Mexico.	$4,276,236 $4,103,313
7	Panther, Florida (*Puma (=Felis) concolor coryi*)	Entire	
8	Wolf, gray (*Canis lupus*)-Mexican gray wolf	EXPN	$3,773,509
9	Bat, gray (*Myotis grisescens*)	Entire	$2,470,481
10	Squirrel, Delmarva Peninsula fox (*Sciurus niger cinereus*)	Entire, except where experimental	$1,973,625 $1,616,739

Note: DPS = Distinct Population Segment. EXPN = Experimental Population, Non-essential.

SOURCE: Adapted from "Table 2. Species Ranked in Descending Order of Total FY 2014 Reported Expenditures, Not Including Land Acquisition Costs," in *Federal and State Endangered and Threatened Species Expenditures: Fiscal Year 2014*, U.S. Department of the Interior, U.S. Fish and Wildlife Service, March 2, 2016, http://www.fws.gov/endangered/esa-library/pdf/20160302_final_FY14_ExpRpt.pdf (accessed March 9, 2016)

- Lesser long-nosed bat
- Little Mariana fruit bat
- Mariana fruit bat
- Mexican long-nosed bat
- Northern long-eared bat
- Ozark big-eared bat
- Pacific sheath-tailed bat
- Virginia big-eared bat

Bats are imperiled for a variety of reasons, including habitat degradation, disturbance of hibernating and maternity colonies, direct extermination by humans, and the indirect effects of pesticide use on insects. During the first decade of the 21st century, a new threat to bat survival emerged called white-nose syndrome (WNS). The USFWS reports in "White-Nose Syndrome (WNS)" (March 2016, https://www.whitenosesyndrome.org/sites/default/files/resource/white-nose_fact_sheet_3-2016.pdf) that the disease was first documented in the winter of 2006–07 and is evidenced by the appearance of a white fungus on the muzzle and other parts of afflicted bats. Researchers believe WNS is caused by the fungus *Pseudogeomyces destructans*. The USFWS notes, "WNS is estimated to have killed more than 5.5 million bats in the Northeast and Canada. In some sites, 90 to 100 percent of bats have died."

In May 2011 the USFWS published *A National Plan for Assisting States, Federal Agencies, and Tribes in Managing*

White-Nose Syndrome in Bats (http://www.whitenose syndrome.org/sites/default/files/white-nose_syndrome _national_plan_may_2011.pdf), which provides information about WNS and outlines a national plan for collaboration between federal, state, tribal, and local agencies for managing bats that are imperiled by WNS. The USFWS indicates that cave bats (species that hibernate in caves or mines during the winter months) are the most susceptible to WNS.

The USFWS along with academic and industry group partners hosts a website (https://www.whitenosesyndrome .org/) devoted to WNS issues. It provides data and news about the disease and its effects on bat populations.

INDIANA BATS. The Indiana bat is a medium-sized, brown-colored bat found throughout a region encompassing the mid-Atlantic states and part of the Midwest. The bats spend their winters in hibernation spots (or hibernacula) consisting primarily of large caves and abandoned mines. For decades the USFWS has led winter hibernacula surveys during which it estimates the species population size. As of April 2016, the most recent results were from 2015. The USFWS (http://www.fws.gov/midwest/Endangered/ mammals/inba/pdf/2015IBatPopEstimate25Aug2015v2.pdf) estimates that hibernacula surveyed during January and February 2015 contained 523,636 Indiana bats. This number is down from 1981 when the population size was 677,327 bats. Figure 7.1 shows the breakdown by state of the hibernacula surveyed in 2015. Most of the bats were found in Indiana and Missouri. The USFWS estimates that 99% of the Indiana bat population in 2015 was hibernating in sites known or suspected to be infected with WNS.

Bats are extremely sensitive to any disturbances during hibernation. In "Indiana Bat" (2016, http://www.dec .ny.gov/animals/6972.html), the New York State Department of Environmental Conservation indicates that awakened bats become agitated and waste precious energy flying around frantically. This can leave them too weak and malnourished to survive the remainder of the winter. During the springtime adult females move to wooded areas and form maternity colonies. The loss of suitable habitat due to deforestation has disrupted this natural process. In addition, the bats have a low reproductive rate, producing only one baby per year. This makes it difficult for their populations to grow.

The Indiana bat was on the first list of endangered species, which was issued in 1967. (See Table 2.1 in Chapter 2.) In April 2007 the USFWS published *Indiana Bat (*Myotis sodalis*) Draft Recovery Plan: First Revision* (http://ecos.fws.gov/docs/recovery_plan/070416.pdf). The agency was optimistic that the species would be fully recovered by the 2020s; however, this was before WNS emerged. As of April 2016, a revised recovery plan had not been issued for the species.

FIGURE 7.1

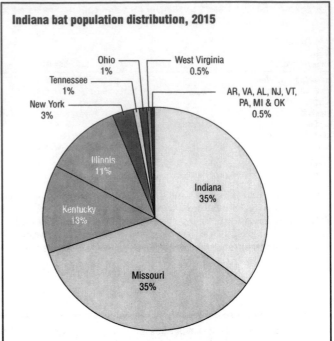

Indiana bat population distribution, 2015

SOURCE: "Figure 1. Percentage of the 2015 Indiana Bat Range-Wide Population (Approx. 523,636 bats) Hibernating within Each State," in *2015 Rangewide Population*, U.S. Department of the Interior, U.S. Fish and Wildlife Service, August 25, 2015, http://www.fws.gov/midwest/ Endangered/mammals/inba/pdf/2015IBatPopEstimate25Aug2015v2 .pdf (accessed February 17, 2016)

Bears

Bears belong to the Ursidae family. Their furry bodies are large and heavy, with powerful arms and legs and short tails. For the most part, they feed on fruits and insects, but they also eat meat.

As of February 2016, there were three bear species listed under the ESA as endangered or threatened in the United States: the American black bear, the Louisiana black bear, and the grizzly bear. (See Table 7.1; note that the polar bear is not included in this table because it is considered a marine mammal and is discussed in Chapter 3.) The American black bear is listed as threatened because of similarity of appearance. American black bears look similar to threatened Louisiana black bears. The listing is designed to prevent harmful actions by humans who might mistake Louisiana black bears for American black bears. Both species are found in Louisiana, Mississippi, and Texas. Grizzly bears inhabit Alaska and the northwestern states, primarily Idaho, Montana, Washington, and Wyoming.

In general, bears are endangered because of habitat loss. Some bears have been hunted because they are considered predatory or threatening, whereas others have been hunted for sport.

GRIZZLY BEARS. Grizzly bears are large animals, standing 4 feet (1.2 m) high at the shoulder when on four paws and as tall as 7 feet (2.1 m) when upright. Males weigh 500 pounds (230 kg) on average but are sometimes as large as 900 pounds (410 kg). Females weigh 350 pounds (160 kg) on average. Grizzlies have a distinctive shoulder hump, which actually represents a massive digging muscle. Their claws are 2 inches to 4 inches (5.1 cm to 10.2 cm) long.

The grizzly bear was originally found throughout the continental United States but was eventually eliminated from all but Alaska and a handful of western habitats. It was first listed as endangered in 1967. (See Table 2.1 in Chapter 2.) As of April 2016, the grizzly bear population in Alaska was thriving and not listed under the ESA. Two populations in the lower 48 states were listed:

- Portions of Idaho and Montana—experimental population, nonessential (as explained in Chapter 2, this listing means that the survival of this population is not believed essential to the survival of the species as a whole; thus, the population receives less protection under the ESA)

- Remainder of the lower 48 states—threatened

The USFWS indicates in "Grizzly Bear (*Ursus arctos horribilis*)" (2016, http://ecos.fws.gov/speciesProfile/ profile/speciesProfile.action?spcode=A001) that over the decades it has published numerous recovery plans and supplements for specific populations of grizzly bears. Figure 7.2 shows the recovery zones that have been designated for the species. Recovery efforts are coordinated

FIGURE 7.2

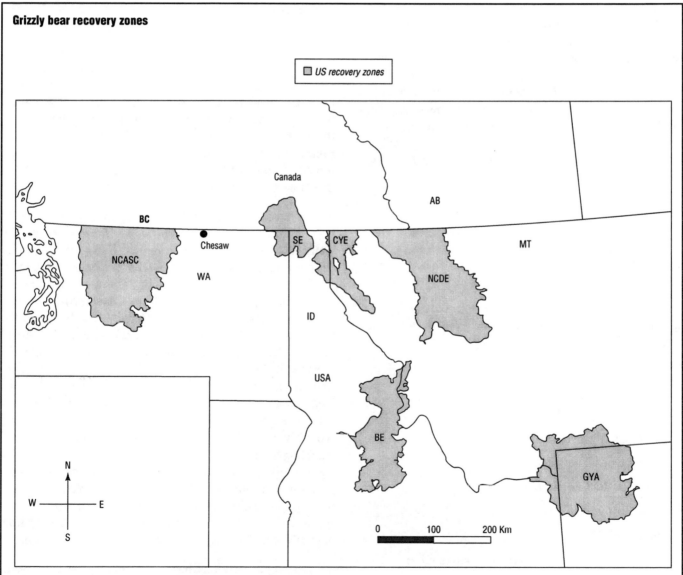

Grizzly bear recovery zones

NCASC = North Cascades ecosystem. SE = Selkirk ecosystem. CYE = Cabinet-Yaak ecosystem.
NCDE = North Continental Divide ecosystem. BE = Bitterroot ecosystem. GYA = Greater Yellowstone Area ecosystem.

SOURCE: Adapted from "Figure 1. Current Grizzly Bear Recovery Ecosystems," in *Grizzly Bear (Ursus arctos horribilis) 5-Year Review: Summary and Evaluation*, U.S. Department of the Interior, U.S. Fish and Wildlife Service, Grizzly Bear Recovery Office, August 2011, http://ecos.fws.gov/docs/five_ year_review/doc3847.review_August%202011.pdf (accessed February 17, 2016)

by the Interagency Grizzly Bear Committee (2016, http://igbconline.org/about-us), which was created in 1983. The committee is made up of representatives from the USFWS, the Bureau of Land Management, the Canadian Wildlife Service, the National Park Service, the U.S. Forest Service, the U.S. Geological Survey, and the wildlife agencies of Idaho, Montana, Washington, and Wyoming.

The grizzly bear has a long and complicated legal history under the ESA. As of April 2016, the USFWS had received nearly two dozen petitions since 1985 requesting listing status changes for individual grizzly bear populations. For example, in 2015 Lincoln County, Montana, petitioned for the Cabinet-Yaak ecosystem population to be delisted due to recovery. A year prior, the conservation group Alliance for the Wild Rockies had petitioned for that same population to be uplisted from threatened to endangered status. In January 2016 the USFWS (https://www.gpo.gov/fdsys/pkg/FR-2016-01-12/pdf/2016-00157.pdf) found that neither petition presented substantial information supporting its claims. In March 2015 the agency (http://ecos.fws.gov/docs/species/uplisting/doc4748.pdf) indicated that it was considering an uplisting for the North Cascades ecosystem population. The status change was given a warranted-but-precluded finding, meaning that the agency believes the uplisting is warranted but has a lower priority than other pressing matters.

Canines

Canine is the common term used to describe a member of the Canidae family of carnivorous (meat-eating) animals. This family includes coyotes, foxes, jackals, wolves, and domestic dogs.

As of February 2016, there were three wolf species and five fox species listed under the ESA in the United States (see Table 7.1):

- Gray wolf
- Mexican wolf
- Red wolf
- San Joaquin kit fox
- San Miguel Island fox
- Santa Catalina Island fox
- Santa Cruz Island fox
- Santa Rosa Island fox

All the species were listed as endangered except for specific wolf population segments.

WOLVES. Wolves were once among the most widely distributed mammals on the earth. Before European settlement, wolves ranged over most of North America, from central Mexico to the Arctic Ocean. Their decline

FIGURE 7.3

The red wolf is found in the eastern United States. ©*U.S. Fish and Wildlife Service.*

was mostly due to hunting. In 1914 Congress authorized funding for the removal of all large predators, including wolves, from federal lands. By the 1940s wolves had been eliminated from most of the contiguous United States. In 1967 the gray wolf (which was then called the timber wolf) and the red wolf (which is shown in Figure 7.3) were on the first list of endangered species issued by the USFWS. (See Table 2.1 in Chapter 2.) By that time both species had all but disappeared.

In April 1994 the USFWS noted in *The Reintroduction of Gray Wolves to Yellowstone National Park and Central Idaho: Final Environmental Impact Statement* (http://www.fws.gov/mountain-prairie/species/mammals/wolf/eis_1994.pdf) the following: "Currently, as a result of natural dispersal of wolves from Canada over the past 15 years, about five wolf packs (65 wolves) live in northwest Montana. While lone wolves are occasionally seen or killed in the Yellowstone or central Idaho areas, wolf packs still do not exist in these areas." The agency outlined its decision to capture and release wolves in Yellowstone National Park and central Idaho. The USFWS acknowledged that reestablishing wolf packs in those areas would have some negative economic impacts due to less spending by hunters (because of lower big game availability) and losses of livestock. However, the annual economic losses were estimated at less than $1 million. By contrast, the agency estimated that reintroduced wolves would result in an economic benefit of at least $23 million annually due to increased tourism and related spending.

The reintroductions began in 1995. Over a two-year period 66 gray wolves from southwestern Canada were introduced to Yellowstone National Park and central Idaho. Wolf reintroductions were not greeted with universal enthusiasm. Ranchers in particular were concerned that wolves would attack livestock. They were also worried that their land would be open to government restrictions as a result of the wolves' presence. Several measures were adopted to address the ranchers' concerns. The most significant was that ranchers would be reimbursed for livestock losses from a compensation fund. Until 2010 the fund was maintained by the Defenders of Wildlife, a private conservation group, and financed by private donors. Since 2010 the USFWS has included compensation payments in grants to state wildlife agencies and Native American tribes. In "U.S. Fish and Wildlife Service Announces $900,000 in Wolf Livestock Demonstration Project Grants" (September 24, 2015, http://www.fws.gov/news/ShowNews.cfm?ref=u.s.-fish-and-wildlife-service-announces-$900000---in-wolf-livestock-&_ID=35240), the agency indicates that $900,000 was allocated to the program in 2015. The USFWS states, "The grants assist livestock producers in undertaking proactive, non-lethal activities to reduce the risk of livestock loss from predation by wolves, and compensate producers for livestock losses caused by wolves."

Wolf introductions were legally challenged in 1997, when the American Farm Bureau Federation initiated a lawsuit calling for the removal of wolves from Yellowstone. The farm coalition scored an initial victory, but in 2000 the 10th Circuit Court of Appeals in Denver, Colorado, overturned the decision on appeal by the U.S. Department of the Interior, the World Wildlife Fund (WWF), and other conservation groups.

The listing status of the gray wolf is complicated because the USFWS recognizes multiple populations of the species. In addition, efforts to delist gray wolf populations have been repeatedly challenged in court. For example, a population in Minnesota was delisted in 2007 because of recovery and then relisted in September 2009 following a court order. It was again delisted in 2011 but relisted as threatened in 2014 following a court decision regarding the Western Great Lakes distinct population segment (DPS). (See Figure 7.4.) The USFWS (http://www.gpo.gov/fdsys/pkg/FR-2011-12-28/pdf/2011-32825.pdf) designated the latter DPS in December 2011 and at the same time removed it from the ESA, noting that the DPS "does not meet the definitions of threatened or endangered under the Act." The Humane Society of the United States and other parties challenged the decision in court and won. The USFWS (https://www.gpo.gov/fdsys/pkg/FR-2015-02-20/pdf/2015-03503.pdf) indicates that the result of the 2014 decision was that gray wolves in all of Minnesota were again classified as threatened, and gray wolves formerly considered part of the Western Great Lakes DPS were relisted as endangered.

The northern Rocky Mountain DPS once consisted of wolves in eastern Washington and Oregon, a small part of north-central Utah, and all of Idaho, Montana, and Wyoming (excluding a nonessential experimental population). The DPS was the subject of intense litigation and

political controversy. It was delisted in 2008, but that listing was vacated after 12 parties sued and prevailed in court. In April 2009 the USFWS again attempted to delist the DPS because of recovery, but the delisting was overturned in court. In April 2011 Congress passed a spending bill that included an amendment that essentially delisted the DPS. Actually, Congress (http://www.gpo.gov/fdsys/pkg/PLAW-112publ10/html/PLAW-112publ10.htm) ordered the agency to reissue the April 2009 delisting rule and forbade any further "judicial review" of the decision. The latter condition triggered multiple lawsuits by conservation and wildlife groups alleging that the prohibition against judicial review of a congressional decision is unconstitutional. The congressional action, however, was upheld in court.

In 2011 the USFWS officially delisted the northern Rocky Mountain DPS (excluding the Wyoming population). The following year the agency (http://www.gpo.gov/fdsys/pkg/FR-2012-09-10/pdf/2012-21988.pdf) delisted the Wyoming population. Nevertheless, Defenders of Wildlife and the Humane Society challenged the decision in court and won. As a result, in 2015 the USFWS (https://www.gpo.gov/fdsys/pkg/FR-2015-02-20/pdf/2015-03503.pdf) reclassified Wyoming wolves as a nonessential experimental population.

In June 2013 the USFWS (http://www.fws.gov/southwest/es/mexicanwolf/pdf/NR_wolf_press_release.pdf) proposed delisting the remaining gray wolves in the United States. At the same time, the agency (http://www.gpo.gov/fdsys/pkg/FR-2013-06-13/pdf/2013-13982.pdf) proposed listing the Mexican wolf (a subspecies of the gray wolf with the scientific name of *Canis lupus baileyi*) as endangered under the ESA. In January 2015 the USFWS (https://www.gpo.gov/fdsys/pkg/FR-2015-01-16/pdf/2015-00441.pdf) finalized the listing of the Mexican wolf. As of April 2016, a final decision had not been made on delisting the remaining listed populations of gray wolves in the United States.

Deer, Caribou, Pronghorns, Bighorn Sheep, and Bison

Deer and caribou are members of the Cervidae family, along with elk and moose. Pronghorn are the last surviving members of the Antilocapridae family and are often confused with antelopes. Bighorn sheep and bison belong to the large Bovidae family, which also contains antelopes, gazelles, and domesticated sheep, cattle, and goats. Although these species are diverse in taxonomy, the wild populations share a common threat: they are popular big game animals for hunters.

As shown in Table 7.1, seven species of big game were listed under the ESA as of February 2016:

• Columbian white-tailed deer

• Key deer

FIGURE 7.4

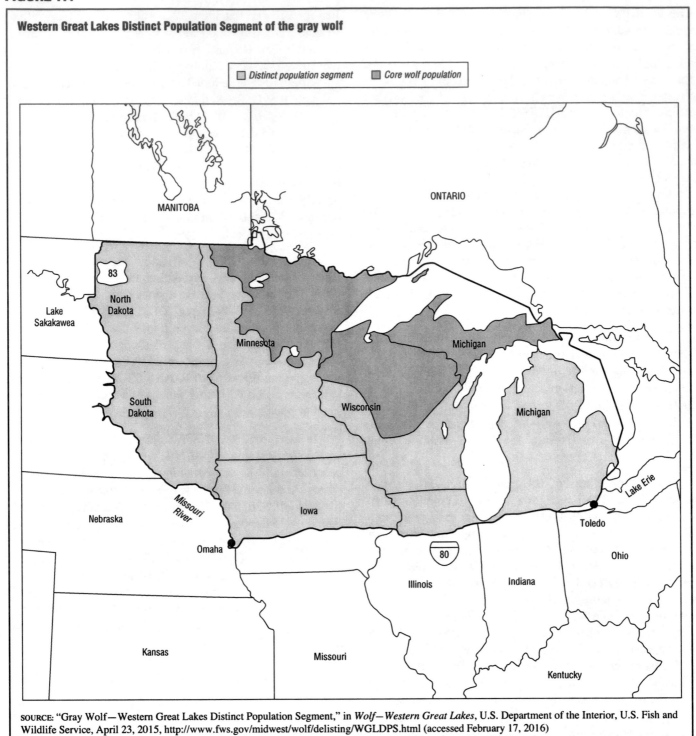

Western Great Lakes Distinct Population Segment of the gray wolf

☐ Distinct population segment   ☐ Core wolf population

SOURCE: "Gray Wolf—Western Great Lakes Distinct Population Segment," in *Wolf—Western Great Lakes*, U.S. Department of the Interior, U.S. Fish and Wildlife Service, April 23, 2015, http://www.fws.gov/midwest/wolf/delisting/WGLDPS.html (accessed February 17, 2016)

• Peninsular bighorn sheep

• Sierra Nevada bighorn sheep

• Sonoran pronghorn

• Wood bison

• Woodland caribou

Most of these species had endangered listings, and all but the wood bison had recovery plans in place.

COLUMBIAN WHITE-TAILED DEER. According to the USFWS in "Columbian White-Tailed Deer: *Odocoileus virginianus leucurus*" (2016, http://www.fws.gov/oregonfwo/species/data/columbianwhitetaileddeer/), white-tailed deer occur throughout the United States. The Columbian white-tailed deer is the westernmost subspecies with historical range in Washington and Oregon. Once quite populous, the subspecies was severely depleted by habitat disruption and loss. In 1968, when it was first listed as endangered under a precursor law to the ESA, only one "small" population was known to exist along the Columbia River, which forms most of the border between the two states. The USFWS notes that during the 1970s a second "small" population was found near Roseburg in Douglas County in southwestern Oregon. As shown in Table 2.7 in Chapter 2, the latter population was delisted because of recovery in 2003. In November 2013 the USFWS published *Columbia River Distinct Population Segment of the Columbian White-Tailed Deer (*Odocoileus virginianus leucurus*): 5-Year Review—Summary and Evaluation* (http://ecos.fws.gov/docs/five _year _review/doc4319.pdf), which recommended that the DPS be downlisted to threatened status because of continued population stability. In October 2015 the agency (https://www.gpo.gov/fdsys/pkg/FR-2015-10-08/pdf/2015-25260 .pdf) officially proposed the downlisting action. As of April 2016, the proposal had not been finalized.

Felines

Feline is the common term used for a member of the Felidae family. This diverse family includes bobcats, cheetahs, cougars, jaguars, jaguarundis, leopards, lions, lynx, panthers, pumas, tigers, and domesticated cats. All the wild species are under threat as land development has left them with less natural habitat in which to live.

As of February 2016 (see Table 7.1), there were eight wild feline species listed as endangered or threatened under the ESA in the United States:

- Canada lynx
- Eastern puma (= cougar)
- Florida panther (See Figure 7.5.)
- Gulf Coast jaguarundi
- Jaguar
- Ocelot
- Puma (= mountain lion)
- Sinaloan jaguarundi

Almost all these species had endangered listings. The exceptions were the Canada lynx, which was threatened, and the puma (= mountain lion), which in Florida was threatened because of similarity of appearance to the Florida panther.

CANADA LYNX. The Canada lynx is a medium-sized feline. Adults average 30 inches to 35 inches (76 cm to 89 cm) in length and weigh about 20 pounds (9 kg). The animal has tufted ears, a short tail, long legs, and large flat paws that allow it to walk on top of the snow. The Canada lynx inhabits cold, moist northern forests that are dominated by coniferous trees. Its primary food source is the snowshoe hare. Habitat modification, chiefly forest fragmentation due to timber harvesting,

FIGURE 7.5

Florida panther

SOURCE: Robert Savannah, artist, "Florida Panthers," in *Line Art (Drawings)*, U.S. Department of the Interior, U.S. Fish and Wildlife Service, undated, http://www.fws.gov/pictures/lineart/bobsavannah/ floridapanthers.html (accessed February 17, 2016)

forest fire suppression, and human development, is blamed for imperiling both the snowshoe hare and the Canada lynx. In FY 2014 nearly $5.3 million was spent under the ESA to conserve the Canada lynx. (See Table 7.2.)

In 1982 the USFWS designated the Canada lynx as a candidate species for listing. However, no action was taken on listing until 1994, when the agency proposed to list the species as threatened. The decision was challenged in court by a group of conservation organizations led by the Defenders of Wildlife. This began a protracted legal battle over the listing status and critical habitat designation for the species. In December 2009 the USFWS (http://frwebgate.access .gpo.gov/cgi-bin/getdoc.cgi?dbname=2009_register&docid =fr17de09-15) published a 12-month finding on a petition it had received in 2007 from seven conservation groups requesting that the DPS be expanded to include the mountains of north-central New Mexico. The agency concluded that the DPS change was warranted but was "precluded by higher priority actions" (the DPS was deemed a candidate species). The decision was challenged in court and overturned.

TABLE 7.3

Critical habitat of the Canada lynx

[Area estimates reflect all land within designated critical habitat unit boundaries]

	Federal	State	Private	Other	Total
Idaho	45 (117)	0.04 (0.1)	0 (0)	0 (0)	45 (117)
Maine	0 (0)	819 (2,122)	9,281 (24,039)	22 (57)	10,123 (26,218)
Minnesota	3,863 (10,005)	2,947 (7,633)	1,259 (3,206)	0 (0)	8,069 (20,899)
Montana	10,978 (28,433)	168 (437)	979 (2,535)	0.5 (1.3)	12,126 (31,405)
Washington	1,829 (4,737)	0 (0)	5 (14)	0 (0)	1,834 (4,751)
Wyoming	6,688 (17,321)	10 (26)	60 (155)	0 (0)	6,758 (17,502)
Total	**23,402 (60,612)**	**3,945 (10,217)**	**11,584 (30,003)**	**23 (59)**	**38,954 (100,891)**

Note: Area sizes may not sum due to rounding. Areas in square miles; square kilometers in parentheses.

SOURCE: "Table 2. Designated Critical Habitat for Canada Lynx by State and Ownership," in "Endangered and Threatened Wildlife and Plants; Revised Designation of Critical Habitat for the Contiguous United States Distinct Population Segment of the Canada Lynx and Revised Distinct Population Segment Boundary," *Federal Register*, vol. 79, no. 177, September 12, 2014, https://www.gpo.gov/fdsys/pkg/FR-2014-09-12/pdf/2014-21013.pdf (accessed February 17, 2016)

As of April 2016, the USFWS (http://ecos.fws.gov/speciesProfile/profile/speciesProfile.action?spcode=A073) indicated that the threatened listing applied to the so-called contiguous United States DPS of Canada lynx, including the populations in California, Colorado, Idaho, Maine, Michigan, Minnesota, Montana, New Mexico, Oregon, Utah, Washington, Wisconsin, and Wyoming. Table 7.3 shows the designated critical habitat for the species which covers 38,954 square miles (100,891 sq km).

The most recent recovery document for the Canada lynx was published in 2005. In *Recovery Outline: Contiguous United States Distinct Population Segment of the Canada Lynx* (September 14, 2005, http://ecos.fws.gov/docs/recovery_plan/final%20draft%20Lynx%20Recovery%20Outline%209-05.pdf), the USFWS states that the document sets out an "interim strategy" for recovery until a draft recovery plan can be issued. The agency acknowledges that global warming poses a serious threat to the species' survival, noting, "continued warming trends may eventually have a profound effect on the winter conditions that create the habitats for which lynx are highly adapted, and could result in a substantial reduction or even elimination of lynx habitats from the contiguous United States."

Ferrets

The ferret is a member of the Mustelidae family, along with badgers, mink, muskrats, otters, skunks, and weasels. Ferrets are small, furry creatures with long, skinny bodies typically less than 2 feet (0.6 m) long. They have short legs and elongated necks with small heads. Ferrets are carnivores; in the wild they feed on rodents, rabbits, reptiles, and insects.

As shown in Table 7.1, as of February 2016 there was one U.S. species of ferret listed under the ESA: the black-footed ferret, which is depicted in Figure 7.6. The species was listed as endangered, except in nonessential experimental populations in portions of Arizona, Colorado, Montana, South Dakota, Utah, and Wyoming.

FIGURE 7.6

Black-footed ferret. ©*Laura Romin & Larry Dalton/Alamy.*

BLACK-FOOTED FERRETS. The black-footed ferret is a small, furrow-digging mammal. It is a nocturnal creature and helps control populations of snakes and rodents, including its primary prey: black-tailed prairie dogs. The black-footed ferret once ranged over 11 Rocky Mountain states and parts of Canada. Its population has declined because of the large-scale conversion of prairie habitats to farmland and because its main prey, the prairie dog, has been nearly exterminated by humans. Prairie dogs are considered pests because they dig holes and tunnels just beneath the ground surface. These holes can cause serious injury to horses or other large animals that step into them. Poisons that are used to kill prairie dogs may also kill some ferrets.

Black-footed ferret populations declined so drastically that the species was included on the first list of endangered species published in 1967. (See Table 2.1 in Chapter 2.) However, prairie dog poisonings continued, and by 1979 it was believed that the black-footed ferret was extinct. During the 1980s a small colony was discovered in Wyoming. These individuals were captured and entered into a captive breeding program. The Black-Footed Ferret Recovery Implementation Team was created in 1996 to integrate the efforts of dozens of agencies and nonprofit organizations working to save the species.

In November 2013 the USFWS published *Black-Footed Ferret Recovery Plan* (http://ecos.fws.gov/docs/recovery_plan/20131108%20BFF%202nd%20Rev.%20Final%20Recovery%20Plan.pdf). The agency cites the recovery criteria for the black-footed ferret as requiring 10 separate "successful" populations containing 1,500 breeding adults. As of 2013, only about 400 breeding adults were believed to exist in the wild. Another 300 animals were being managed in captive breeding facilities. The agency notes, "We believe that downlisting [from endangered to threatened status] of the black-footed ferret could be accomplished in approximately 10 years if conservation actions continue at existing reintroduction sites and if additional reintroduction sites are established."

Rabbits

Rabbits are members of the Leporidae family, along with hares. Rabbits are generally smaller than hares and have somewhat shorter ears. Both species have tall slender ears and short bodies with long limbs and thick soft fur. Domesticated rabbits are all descended from European species.

As of February 2016, there were three rabbit species listed as endangered under the ESA in the United States. (See Table 7.1.) The species and their primary locations are:

- Columbia basin pygmy rabbit—Washington
- Lower Keys marsh rabbit—Florida
- Riparian brush rabbit—California

All the species had recovery plans in place. As of April 2016, the most recently published recovery plan was for the Columbia basin pygmy rabbit. In *Recovery Plan for the*

Columbia Basin Distinct Population Segment of the Pygmy Rabbit (Brachylagus idahoensis) (2012, http://ecos.fws.gov/docs/recovery_plan/Columbia%20Basin%20Pygmy%20Rabbit%20Final%20RP.pdf), the USFWS notes that pygmy rabbits inhabit semiarid shrubby habitat in the western United States. This particular DPS is isolated in the Columbia basin, a lowland area bordering the Columbia River in central Washington. The USFWS does not estimate recovery costs or a recovery date for the DPS because of its small population size noting, "few, if any, Columbia basin pygmy rabbits currently survive in the wild as established populations. Only about 100 intercrossed individuals have been recently reintroduced to habitats historically occupied by the species within the Columbia basin, and the success of future translocation, field-breeding, and reintroduction efforts cannot yet be accurately predicted."

Rodents

Rodents are members of the order Rodentia, the single largest group of mammals. This order includes beavers, chipmunks, gophers, mice, prairie dogs, rats, squirrels, voles, and many other species. Rodents are characterized by their distinctive teeth, particularly a pair of chisel-shaped incisors in each jaw. Although most rodents are plant eaters, some species include insects in their diet.

As shown in Table 2.7 in Chapter 2, two rodents have been delisted due to recovery—the Delmarva Peninsula fox squirrel (2015; see Figure 7.7) and the Virginia northern flying squirrel (2013).

FIGURE 7.7

Delmarva fox squirrel

SOURCE: "Untitled," in *Delmarva Fox Squirrel (Sciurus niger cinereus) Recovery Plan, Second Revision*, U.S. Department of the Interior, U.S. Fish and Wildlife Service, Northeast Region, June 8, 1993, http://ecos.fws.gov/docs/recovery_plan/930608.pdf (accessed February 19, 2016)

As of February 2016, there were 32 rodent species listed under the ESA as endangered or threatened (see Table 7.1):

- Kangaroo rat—six species

- Mountain beaver—one species

- Mouse—11 species

- Pocket gopher—four species

- Prairie dog—one species

- Rat—three species

- Squirrel—three species

- Vole—three species

One imperiled rodent species of particular interest is the Utah prairie dog. The USFWS reports in *Federal and State Endangered and Threatened Species Expenditures: Fiscal Year 2014* (March 2016, http://www.fws.gov/endangered/esa-library/pdf/20160302_final_FY14_ExpRpt.pdf) that in FY 2014 nearly $1.1 million was spent on this controversial species under the ESA.

UTAH PRAIRIE DOGS. Prairie dogs are members of the Sciuridae family, along with chipmunks and squirrels. (See Figure 7.8.) They are endemic (limited) to the United States and inhabit mostly arid grasslands. They are found from Montana and North Dakota south to Texas. The 19th-century explorers Meriwether Lewis (1774–1809) and William Clark (1770–1838) allegedly named the animals prairie dogs because of their barklike calls.

Before settlers moved into the West, it is believed that millions of prairie dogs inhabited the area. Prairie dogs are burrowing creatures and live in colonies. They produce holes, tunnels, and dirt mounds that can be damaging to land that is used for agriculture. The holes also pose a tripping hazard to horses and cattle. As a result, ranchers of the late 1800s and early 1900s tried to eradicate the prairie dog by using poison on a large scale. They were assisted in their efforts by the federal government.

According to the USFWS, in *Utah Prairie Dog (Cynomys parvidens) Draft Revised Recovery Plan* (August 2010, http://ecos.fws.gov/docs/recovery_plan/100917.pdf), by the mid-1970s the Utah population had been reduced to about 3,300 individuals. Massive poisoning by humans, disease (a form of plague), and loss of suitable habitat are blamed for the population decline. In 1973 the USFWS listed the species as endangered under the ESA. Over the next decade conservation efforts led to an increase in its population, and angry farmers began reporting massive crop damage caused by the creatures. The state of Utah petitioned the USFWS to downlist the species from endangered to threatened, and in May 1984 the USFWS (http://ecos.fws.gov/docs/federal_register/fr838.pdf) did so. In addition, the agency established a section 4(d) rule under the ESA allowing the Utah Division

FIGURE 7.8

Prairie dog

SOURCE: Robert Savannah, artist, "Prairie Dogs," in *Line Art (Drawings)*, U.S. Department of the Interior, U.S. Fish and Wildlife Service, undated, http://www.fws.gov/pictures/lineart/bobsavannah/prairiedogs.html (accessed February 17, 2016)

of Wildlife Resources to issue permits to private landowners who wished to kill Utah prairie dogs on their property. Also, the USFWS began relocating Utah prairie dogs from private lands to federal-controlled lands. The USFWS (June 2, 2011, http://www.gpo.gov/fdsys/pkg/FR-2011-06-02/pdf/2011-13684.pdf) notes that its issuance of the 4(d) rule sparked years of litigation against the agency by conservation groups.

In May 2012 the agency published *Utah Prairie Dog (Cynomys parvidens): 5-Year Review—Summary and Evaluation* (http://www.fws.gov/mountain-prairie/species/mammals/utprairiedog/5-yearReview_UPD_May2012_FINAL_signed_(withRPappendix).pdf). The USFWS recommends that the species retain its threatened listing because of continuing problems with habitat loss and disease, noting, "Although recent Utah prairie dog population trends appear to be relatively stable, the species remains vulnerable to serious threats."

Shrews

Shrews belong to the order Soricomorpha, along with moles and their relatives. They are small furry animals about the size of mice. Shrews are primarily insectivores (insect eaters) with long snouts and small eyes.

As of February 2016, only one shrew, the Buena Vista Lake ornate shrew, was listed under the ESA. (See Table 7.1.) It was designated as endangered. According to the USFWS, in "Buena Vista Lake Ornate Shrew (*Sorex ornatus relictus*)" (February 26, 2014, http://ecos.fws.gov/tess_public/profile/speciesProfile?spcode=A0DV), the species is found in California and is about 4 inches (10 cm) long when fully grown, including a 1.5-inch (3.8-cm) tail. In *Buena Vista Lake Ornate Shrew (*Sorex ornatus relictus*): 5-Year Review—Summary and Evaluation* (September 2011, http://ecos.fws.gov/docs/five_year_review/doc3889.pdf), the agency noted that the species has lost more than 95% of its historic wetland habitat due to channelization and agricultural and urban uses of water resources. The USFWS recommended maintaining an endangered listing for the shrew.

IMPERILED TERRESTRIAL MAMMALS AROUND THE WORLD

The International Union for Conservation of Nature (IUCN) indicates in *Red List of Threatened Species Version 2015.4* (http://www.iucnredlist.org/about/summary-statistics) that 1,197 mammal species were threatened as of November 2015. The IUCN does not break down the number by marine and terrestrial species. However, as noted in Chapter 3, the IUCN has designated as threatened approximately three dozen marine mammal species. Thus, more than 1,100 terrestrial mammal species were considered threatened by the IUCN in 2015.

As of February 2016, the USFWS listed 257 totally foreign species of terrestrial mammals as endangered or threatened under the ESA. (See Table 7.4.) Many of the species are from groups that are also imperiled in the United States, such as bats, bears, big game, canines, felines, rabbits, and rodents. In addition, there are exotic animals not native to this country, particularly elephants, pandas, primates, and rhinoceros.

Big Cats

The IUCN (2016, http://www.iucnredlist.org/details/15955/0) recognizes six subspecies of tigers that are believed to be extant (still in existence) in the wild:

- Amur tiger (or Siberian tiger, see Figure 7.9)—eastern Russia and northeastern China

- Bengal tiger—Indian subcontinent

- Northern Indochinese tiger—Indochina north of Malaya

- Malayan tiger—Malaya Peninsula

- South China tiger—China

- Sumatran tiger—Sumatra

Wild tigers are found exclusively in Asia, from India to Siberia. Although the world tiger population surpassed 100,000 during the 19th century, experts fear that fewer than 10,000 remained by the turn of the 21st century. Besides habitat loss, countless tigers fall victim to the illegal wildlife trade every year. Many tiger body parts are used as ingredients in traditional Chinese medicine, and the big cats are also prized in the exotic pet industry. In addition, ecologists warn that tigers, which hunt deer, wild pigs, cattle, antelope, and other large mammals, are seriously threatened by the loss of prey, much of which consists of nonprotected species that are being eliminated by hunters. Many tiger populations have also been weakened by inbreeding, which increases the possibility of reproductive problems and birth defects.

A census of tigers conducted in 2014 suggested that efforts to end a century of decline in the tiger population were beginning to show positive results. In "For the First Time in 100 Years, Tiger Numbers Are Growing" (April 10, 2016, https://www.worldwildlife.org/stories/for-the-first-time-in-100-years-tiger-numbers-are-growing), the WWF announced that for the first time in more than a century, the number of tigers counted in the wild increased. The WWF reports that in 2014, 3,890 tigers were counted in the wild, an increase of 22% from an estimated 3,200 in 2010. Reporting on the survey results in "Tiger Numbers Rise for First Time in a Century" (NationalGeographic.com, April 10, 2016), Brian Clark Howard notes that the tiger count in India increased to 2,226 in 2014, up from 1,706 in 2010, and in Russia the count increased to 443 from 360 in 2010. Other notable tiger populations in 2014 included Indonesia (371), Malaysia (250), Nepal (198), Thailand (189), Bangladesh (106), and Bhutan (103). Countries with small numbers of tigers in the 2014 survey included China (7), Vietnam (5), and Laos (2).

Elephants

Elephants are the largest land animals on the earth. They are frequently described as the "architects" of the savanna habitats in which they live. Elephants dig water holes, keep forest growth in check, and open up grasslands that support other species, including the livestock of African herders. Elephants are highly intelligent, emotional animals and form socially complex herds. There are two species of elephants: African elephants and Asian elephants, both of which are highly endangered. The African elephant, which can weigh as much as 6 tons (5.4 t), is the larger species. (See Figure 7.10.)

Elephants have huge protruding teeth (tusks) made of ivory. Ivory is valued by humans for several reasons, particularly for use in making jewelry and figurines. Piano keys were also once made almost exclusively of ivory; however, this practice has ceased. The market for ivory

TABLE 7.4

Foreign endangered and threatened terrestrial mammal species, February 2016

Common name	Scientific name	Federal listing status*	Current distribution (if available)
Addax	*Addax nasomaculatus*	E	North Africa
African elephant	*Loxodonta africana*	T	
African wild ass	*Equus africanus*	E	
African wild dog	*Lycaon pictus*	E	
Andean cat	*Felis jacobita*	E	
Apennine chamois	*Rupicapra rupicapra ornata*	E	
Arabian gazelle	*Gazella gazella*	E	Arabian Peninsula, Palestine, Sinai
Arabian oryx	*Oryx leucoryx*	E	Arabian Peninsula
Arabian tahr	*Hemitragus jayakari*	E	Oman
Argali	*Ovis ammon*	E; T	
Asian elephant	*Elephas maximus*	E	
Asian golden (=Temmnick's) cat	*Catopuma (=Felis) temminckii*	E	Nepal, China, Southeast Asia, Indonesia (Sumatra)
Asian tapir	*Tapirus indicus*	E	Burma, Laos, Cambodia, Vietnam, Malaysia, Indonesia, Thailand
Asian wild ass	*Equus hemionus*	E	
Australian native mouse	*Notomys aquilo*	E	Australia
Australian native mouse	*Zyzomys pedunculatus*	E	Australia
Avahi	*Avahi laniger (entire genus)*	E	
Aye-aye	*Daubentonia madagascariensis*	E	
Babirusa	*Babyrousa babyrussa*	E	
Bactrian camel	*Camelus bactrianus*	E	
Bactrian deer	*Cervus elaphus bactrianus*	E	Former U.S.S.R., Afghanistan
Baluchistan bear	*Ursus thibetanus gedrosianus*	E	
Banded hare wallaby	*Lagostrophus fasciatus*	E	Australia
Banteng	*Bos javanicus*	E	
Barbary deer	*Cervus elaphus barbarus*	E	
Barbary hyena	*Hyaena hyaena barbara*	E	Morocco, Algeria, Tunisia
Barbary serval	*Leptailurus (=Felis) serval constantina*	E	Algeria
Barbary stag	*Cervus elaphus barbarus*	E	
Barred bandicoot	*Perameles bougainville*	E	
Beaver (Mongolian)	*Castor fiber birulai*	E	
Black colobus monkey	*Colobus satanas*	E	Equatorial Guinea, People's Republic of Congo, Cameroon, Gabon
Black howler monkey	*Alouatta pigra*	T	Mexico, Guatemala, Belize
Black rhinoceros	*Diceros bicornis*	E	Sub-Saharan Africa
Black-faced impala	*Aepyceros melampus petersi*	E	Namibia, Angola
Black-footed cat	*Felis nigripes*	E	
Bontebok	*Damaliscus pygarus (=dorcas) dorcas*	E	
Brazilian three-toed sloth	*Bradypus torquatus*	E	Brazil
Brindled nail-tailed wallaby	*Onychogalea fraenata*	E	Australia
Brown bear	*Ursus arctos arctos*	E	Italy
Brown bear	*Ursus arctos pruinosus*	E	China (Tibet)
Brown hyena	*Parahyaena (=Hyaena) brunnea*	E	Southern Africa
Brush-tailed rat-kangaroo	*Bettongia penicillata*	E	Australia
Buff-headed marmoset	*Callithrix flaviceps*	E	
Bulmer's fruit bat (=flying fox)	*Aproteles bulmerae*	E	
Bumblebee bat	*Craseonycteris thonglongyai*	E	
Cabrera's hutia	*Capromys angelcabrerai*	E	Cuba
Calamianes (=Philippine) deer	*Axis porcinus calamianensis*	E	Philippines (Calamian Islands)
Capped langur	*Trachypithecus (=Presbytis) pileatus*	E	India, Burma, Bangladesh
Cedros Island mule deer	*Odocoileus hemionus cerrosensis*	E	Mexico (Cedros Island)
Central American tapir	*Tapirus bairdii*	E	Southern Mexico to Colombia and Ecuador
Cheetah	*Acinonyx jubatus*	E	Africa to India
Chiltan (=wild goat) markhor	*Capra falconeri (=aegragrus) chiltanensis*	E	Chiltan Range of west-central Pakistan
Chimpanzee	*Pan troglodytes*	E	Wherever found in captivity
Chinchilla	*Chinchilla brevicaudata boliviana*	E	
Clark's gazelle	*Ammodorcas clarkei*	E	
Clouded leopard	*Neofelis nebulosa*	E	Southeast and south-central Asia, Taiwan
Corsican red deer	*Cervus elaphus corsicanus*	E	France (Corsica), Italy (Sardinia); France, Italy
Costa Rican puma	*Puma (=Felis) concolor costaricensis*	E	Panama, Nicaragua, Costa Rica
Cotton-top tamarin	*Saguinus oedipus*	E	Costa Rica to Colombia
Crescent nail-tailed wallaby	*Onychogalea lunata*	E	Australia
Cuban solenodon	*Solenodon cubanus*	E	Cuba
Dama gazelle	*Gazella dama*	E	
Desert (=plain) rat-kangaroo	*Caloprymnus campestris*	E	Australia
Desert bandicoot	*Perameles eremiana*	E	
Dhole	*Cuon alpinus*	E	Former U.S.S.R., North Korea, South Korea, China, India, Southeast Asia
Diana monkey	*Cercopithecus diana*	E	Coastal West Africa
Dibbler	*Antechinus apicalis*	E	Australia

has had tragic consequences for African elephants. In "Africa's Environment in Crisis" (November 2002, http://diglib1.amnh.org/articles/Africa/Africa_environment.pdf), Gordy Slack of the American Museum of Natural

TABLE 7.4

Common name	Scientific name	Federal listing status*	Current distribution (If available)
Douc langur	*Pygathrix nemaeus*	E	Vietnam, Laos, Cambodia
Drill	*Mandrillus (= Papio) leucophaeus*	E	
Dwarf hutia	*Capromys nana*	E	Cuba
Eastern jerboa marsupial	*Antechinomys laniger*	E	
Eastern native-cat	*Dasyurus viverrinus*	E	Australia
Eld's brow-antlered deer	*Cervus eldi*	E	India; India to Southeast Asia
False water rat	*Xeromys myoides*	E	Australia
Fea's muntjac	*Muntiacus feae*	E	Northern Thailand, Myanmar
Field's mouse	*Pseudomys fieldi*	E	Australia
Flat-headed cat	*Prionailurus (= Felis) planiceps*	E	
Formosan rock macaque	*Macaca cyclopis*	T	
Formosan sika deer	*Cervus nippon taiouanus*	E	
Formosan yellow-throated marten	*Martes flavigula chrysospila*	E	
Francois' langur	*Trachypithecus (= Presbytis) francoisi*	E	China (Kwangsi), Indochina
Gaimard's rat-kangaroo	*Bettongia gaimardi*	E	Australia
Gelada baboon	*Theropithecus gelada*	T	
Giant armadillo	*Priodontes maximus*	E	Venezuela and Guyana to Argentina
Giant panda	*Ailuropoda melanoleuca*	E	China
Giant sable antelope	*Hippotragus niger variani*	E	
Gibbons	*Hylobates spp. (including Nomascus)*	E	China, India, Southeast Asia
Goeldi's marmoset	*Callimico goeldii*	E	
Golden langur	*Trachypithecus (= Presbytis) geei*	E	India (Assam), Bhutan
Golden-rumped tamarin	*Leontopithecus spp.*	E	Brazil
Goral	*Naemorhedus goral*	E	East Asia
Gorilla	*Gorilla gorilla*	E	Central and western Africa
Gould's mouse	*Pseudomys gouldii*	E	Australia
Gray (=entellus) langur	*Semnopithecus (= Presbytis) entellus*	E	Bangladesh, China (Tibet), India, Kashmir, Pakistan, Sikkim, Sri Lanka
Great Indian rhinoceros	*Rhinoceros unicornis*	E	Nepal, India
Grevy's zebra	*Equus grevyi*	T	Somalia, Kenya, Ethiopia
Guatemalan jaguarundi	*Herpailurus (= Felis) yagouaroundi fossata*	E	Mexico, Nicaragua
Guizhou snub-nosed monkey	*Rhinopithecus brelichi*	E	China
Haitian solenodon	*Solenodon paradoxus*	E	Haiti, Dominican Republic
Hartmann's mountain zebra	*Equus zebra hartmannae*	T	Namibia, Angola
Hispid hare	*Caprolagus hispidus*	E	India, Nepal, Bhutan
Indochina hog deer	*Axis porcinus annamiticus*	E	Thailand, Indochina
Indri lemur	*Indri indri*	E	Malagasy Republic (=Madagascar)
Iriomote cat	*Prionailurus (= Felis) bengalensis iriomotensis*	E	Japan (Iriomote Island, Ryukyu Islands)
Japanese macaque	*Macaca fuscata*	T	Japan (Shikoku, Kyushu and Honshu Islands)
Javan rhinoceros	*Rhinoceros sondaicus*	E	Bangladesh, Myanmar, Indochina, Indonesia, Malaysia, India (Sikkim), Thailand
Jentink's duiker	*Cephalophus jentinki*	E	
Kashmir stag	*Cervus elaphus hanglu*	E	Kashmir
Koala	*Phascolarctos cinereus*	T	Australia
Kouprey	*Bos sauveli*	E	Vietnam, Thailand, Laos, Cambodia
Kuhl's (=Bawean) deer	*Axis porcinus kuhli*	E	Indonesia
Large desert marsupial-mouse	*Sminthopsis psammophila*	E	
Large-eared hutia	*Capromys auritus*	E	Cuba
Leadbeater's possum	*Gymnobelideus leadbeateri*	E	Australia
Lemurs	*Lemuridae (incl. genera Lemur, Phaner, Hapalemur, Lepilemur, Microcebus, Allocebus, Cheirogaleus, Varecia)*	E	Malagasy Republic (Madagascar)
Leopard	*Panthera pardus*	E; T	Africa, Asia
Leopard cat	*Prionailurus (= Felis) bengalensis bengalensis*	E	India, Southeast Asia
Lesser rabbit bandicoot	*Macrotis leucura*	E	
Lesser slow loris	*Nycticebus pygmaeus*	T	
Lesueur's rat-kangaroo	*Bettongia lesueur*	E	Australia
L'hoest's monkey	*Cercopithecus lhoesti*	E	Upper Eastern Congo Basin, Cameroon
Lion	*Panthera leo ssp. leo*	E	Southern African continent
Lion	*Panthera leo ssp. melanochaita*	T	
Lion-tailed macaque	*Macaca silenus*	E	India
Little earth hutia	*Capromys sanfelipensis*	E	Cuba
Little planigale	*Planigale ingrami subtilissima*	E	Australia
Long-tailed langur	*Presbytis potenziani*	T	Indonesia
Long-tailed marsupial-mouse	*Sminthopsis longicaudata*	E	
Lowland anoa	*Bubalus depressicornis*	E	
Malabar large-spotted civet	*Viverra civettina (=megaspila c.)*	E	
Mandrill	*Mandrillus (= Papio) sphinx*	E	Equatorial West Africa
Maned wolf	*Chrysocyon brachyurus*	E	Uruguay, Paraguay, Brazil, Bolivia, Argentina
Mantled howler monkey	*Alouatta palliata*	E	Mexico to South America

History states that their numbers dropped from between 5 million and 10 million individuals in 1930 to only 600,000 in 1989. As a result of this decline, the Convention on International Trade in Endangered Species of Wild Fauna and Flora (CITES) banned worldwide commerce in ivory and other elephant products in 1990. However, like rhinoceros

Common name	Scientific name	Federal listing status*	Current distribution (if available)
Marbled cat	Pardofelis (= Felis) marmorata	E	Nepal, Southeast Asia, Indonesia
Marsh deer	Blastocerus dichotomus	E	Argentina, Bolivia, Brazil, Paraguay, Uruguay
McNeill's deer	Cervus elaphus macneilii	E	China; China (Sinkiang, Tibet)
Mexican bobcat	Lynx (= Felis) rufus escuinapae	E	Central Mexico
Mexican grizzly bear	Ursus arctos	E	Mexico
Mexican prairie dog	Cynomys mexicanus	E	Mexico
Mhorr gazelle	Gazella dama mhorr	E	
Mongolian saiga (antelope)	Saiga tatarica mongolica	E	Mongolia
Moroccan gazelle	Gazella dorcas massaesyla	E	
Mountain (=Cuvier's) gazelle	Gazella cuvieri	E	
Mountain anoa	Bubalus quarlesi	E	
Mountain pygmy possum	Burramys parvus	E	Australia
Mountain tapir	Tapirus pinchaque	E	Colombia, Ecuador and possibly Peru and Venezuela
Mountain zebra	Equus zebra zebra	E	South Africa
Musk deer	Moschus spp. (all species)	E	Central and East Afghanistan, Asia, Bhutan, Myanmar, China (Tibet, Yunnan), India, Nepal, Pakistan, India (Sikkim)
New Holland mouse	Pseudomys novaehollandiae	E	Australia
North Andean huemul	Hippocamelus antisensis	E	Ecuador, Peru, Chile, Bolivia, Argentina
North China sika deer	Cervus nippon mandarinus	E	China (Shantung and Chihli Provinces)
Northern swift fox	Vulpes velox hebes	E	Canada
Northern white rhinoceros	Ceratotherium simum cottoni	E	Zaire, Uganda, Sudan, Central African Republic
Numbat	Myrmecobius fasciatus	E	Australia
Orangutan	Pongo pygmaeus	E	Borneo, Sumatra
Pagi Island langur	Nasalis concolor	E	Indonesia
Pakistan sand cat	Felis margarita scheffeli	E	
Pampas deer	Ozotoceros bezoarticus	E	Uruguay, Paraguay, Brazil, Bolivia, Argentina
Panamanian jaguarundi	Herpailurus (= Felis) yagouaroundi panamensis	E	Panama, Nicaragua, Costa Rica
Parma wallaby	Macropus parma	E	Australia
Pelzeln's gazelle	Gazella dorcas pelzelni	E	
Peninsular pronghorn	Antilocapra americana peninsularis	E	Mexico (Baja California)
Persian fallow deer	Dama mesopotamica (= dama m.)	E	Iraq, Iran
Philippine tarsier	Tarsius syrichta	T	Philippines
Pied tamarin	Saguinus bicolor	E	Northern Brazil
Pig-footed bandicoot	Chaeropus ecaudatus	E	
Pink fairy armadillo	Chlamyphorus truncatus	E	
Preuss' red colobus monkey	Procolobus (= Colobus) preussi (= badius p.)	E	Cameroon
Proboscis monkey	Nasalis larvatus	E	Borneo
Przewalski's horse	Equus przewalskii	E	Mongolia, China
Pudu	Pudu pudu	E	Southern South America
Purple-faced langur	Presbytis senex	T	Sri Lanka
Pygmy chimpanzee	Pan paniscus	E	
Pygmy hog	Sus salvanius	E	Nepal, Bhutan, India, Sikkim
Pyrenean ibex	Capra pyrenaica pyrenaica	E	Spain
Queensland hairy-nosed wombat (incl. Barnard's)	Lasiorhinus krefftii (formerly L. barnardi and L. gillespiei)	E	Australia
Queensland rat-kangaroo	Bettongia tropica	E	Australia
Quokka	Setonix brachyurus	E	Australia
Rabbit bandicoot	Macrotis lagotis	E	
Red lechwe	Kobus leche	T	Southern Africa
Red-backed squirrel monkey	Saimiri oerstedii	E	Panama, Costa Rica
Red-bellied monkey	Cercopithecus erythrogaster	E	Western Nigeria
Red-eared nose-spotted monkey	Cercopithecus erythrotis	E	Nigeria, Fernando Po, Cameroon; Western Nigeria
Rio de Oro Dama gazelle	Gazella dama lozanoi	E	
Rodrigues fruit bat (=flying fox)	Pteropus rodricensis	E	Mauritius (Rodrigues Island)
Ryukyu rabbit	Pentalagus furnessi	E	Japan (Ryukyu Islands)
Ryukyu sika deer	Cervus nippon keramae	E	Japan (Ryukyu Islands)
Sand gazelle	Gazella subgutturosa marica	E	Jordan, Arabian Peninsula
Saudi Arabian gazelle	Gazella dorcas saudiya	E	Israel, Iraq, Jordan, Syria, Arabian Peninsula
Scaly-tailed possum	Wyulda squamicaudata	E	Australia
Scimitar-horned oryx	Oryx dammah	E	North Africa
Seledang	Bos gaurus	E	Bangladesh, Southeast Asia, India
Serow	Naemorhedus (= Capricornis) sumatraensis	E	East Asia, Sumatra
Shansi sika deer	Cervus nippon grassianus	E	China (Shansi Province)
Shapo	Ovis vignei vignei	E	Kashmir
Shark Bay mouse	Pseudomys praeconis	E	Australia
Shortridge's mouse	Pseudomys shortridgei	E	Australia
Shou	Cervus elaphus wallichi	E	China (Tibet), Bhutan
Siamang	Symphalangus syndactylus	E	Malaysia, Indonesia
Sichuan snub-nosed monkey	Rhinopithecus roxellana	E	China

horns, elephant tusks continue to be illegally traded. Thousands of African elephants are believed killed every year for their ivory.

Pandas

Few creatures have engendered more human affection than the giant panda, with its roly-poly character,

TABLE 7.4

Common name	Scientific name	Federal listing status*	Current distribution (if available)
Sifakas	*Propithecus spp.*	E	Malagasy Republic (=Madagascar)
Simien fox	*Canis simensis*	E	
Singapore roundleaf horseshoe bat	*Hipposideros ridleyi*	E	
Slender-horned gazelle	*Gazella leptoceros*	E	Sudan, Egypt, Algeria, Libya
Smoky mouse	*Pseudomys fumeus*	E	Australia
Snow leopard	*Uncia (=Panthera) uncia*	E	Central Asia
South American (=Brazilian) tapir	*Tapirus terrestris*	E	Colombia and Venezuela south to Paraguay and Argentina
South Andean huemul	*Hippocamelus bisulcus*	E	Chile, Argentina
South China sika deer	*Cervus nippon kopschi*	E	Southern China
Southern bearded saki	*Chiropotes satanas satanas*	E	Brazil
Southern planigale	*Planigale tenuirostris*	E	Australia
Southern white rhinoceros	*Ceratotherium simum ssp. simum*	SAT	
Spanish lynx	*Felis pardina*	E	Spain, Portugal
Spider monkey	*Ateles geoffroyi frontatus*	E	Nicaragua, Costa Rica
Spider monkey	*Ateles geoffroyi panamensis*	E	Panama, Costa Rica
Spotted linsang	*Prionodon pardicolor*	E	India (Assam), Myanmar, Cambodia, Laos, Nepal, Vietnam
Stick-nest rat	*Leporillus conditor*	E	Australia
Straight-horned markhor	*Capra falconeri megaceros*	T	Pakistan, Afghanistan
Stump-tailed macaque	*Macaca arctoides*	T	India (Assam) to southern China
Sumatran rhinoceros	*Dicerorhinus sumatrensis*	E	Bangladesh to Vietnam to Indonesia (Borneo)
Swamp deer	*Cervus duvauceli*	E	Nepal, India
Swayne's hartebeest	*Alcelaphus buselaphus swaynei*	E	Ethiopia, Somalia
Tamaraw	*Bubalus mindorensis*	E	Philippines
Tana River mangabey	*Cercocebus galeritus galeritus*	E	
Tana River red colobus monkey	*Procolobus (=Colobus) rufomitratus (=badius r.)*	E	Kenya
Tasmanian forester kangaroo	*Macropus giganteus tasmaniensis*	E	Australia (Tasmania)
Tasmanian tiger	*Thylacinus cynocephalus*	E	Australia
Temnick's ground pangolin	*Manis temminckii*	E	Africa
Thin-spined porcupine	*Chaetomys subspinosus*	E	Brazil
Tibetan antelope	*Panthalops hodgsonii*	E	
Tiger	*Panthera tigris*	E	Temperate and tropical Asia
Tiger cat	*Leopardus (=Felis) tigrinus*	E	Costa Rica to northern Argentina
Tonkin snub-nosed monkey	*Rhinopithecus avunculus*	E	Vietnam
Toque macaque	*Macaca sinica*	T	Sri Lanka
Tora hartebeest	*Alcelaphus buselaphus tora*	E	Ethiopia, Sudan, Egypt
Uakari (all species)	*Cacajao spp.*	E	Peru, Brazil, Ecuador, Colombia, Venezuela
Urial	*Ovis musimon ophion*	E	Cyprus
Vancouver Island marmot	*Marmota vancouverensis*	E	Canada (Vancouver Island)
Vicuna	*Vicugna vicugna*	E; T	Ecuador (DPS)
Visayan deer	*Cervus alfredi*	E	Philippines
Volcano rabbit	*Romerolagus diazi*	E	Mexico
Walia ibex	*Capra walie*	E	Ethiopia
Western giant eland	*Taurotragus derbianus derbianus*	E	Senegal to Ivory Coast
Western hare wallaby	*Lagorchestes hirsutus*	E	Australia
Western mouse	*Pseudomys occidentalis*	E	Australia
White-collared mangabey	*Cercocebus torquatus*	E	Senegal to Ghana; Nigeria to Gabon
White-eared (=buffy tufted-ear) marmoset	*Callithrix aurita (=jacchus a.)*	E	
White-footed tamarin	*Saguinus leucopus*	T	Colombia
White-nosed saki	*Chiropotes albinasus*	E	Brazil
Wild yak	*Bos mutus (=grunniens m.)*	E	China (Tibet), India
Woolly spider monkey	*Brachyteles arachnoides*	E	Brazil
Yarkand deer	*Cervus elaphus yarkandensis*	E	China (Sinkiang)
Yellow-footed rock wallaby	*Petrogale xanthopus*	E	Australia
Yellow-tailed woolly monkey	*Lagothrix flavicauda*	E	Andes of northern Peru
Yunnan snub-nosed monkey	*Rhinopithecus bieti*	E	China
Zanzibar red colobus monkey	*Procolobus (=Colobus) pennantii (=kirki) kirki*	E	Tanzania
Zanzibar suni	*Neotragus moschatus moschatus*	E	Tanzania (Zanzibar and adjacent islands)

*E = Endangered; T = Threatened; SAT = Similarity in Appearance to a Threatened Taxon.

SOURCE: Adapted from "Generate Species List," in *Environmental Conservation Online System Species Reports*, U.S. Department of the Interior, U.S. Fish and Wildlife Service, February 2016, http://ecos.fws.gov/tess_public/pub/adHocSpeciesForm.jsp (accessed February 15, 2016)

small ears, and black eye patches on a snow-white face. Giant pandas are highly endangered. According to the IUCN (http://www.iucnredlist.org/details/712/0), there were fewer than 2,500 adult giant pandas in the wild in 2015. Pandas are endemic to portions of southwestern China, where they inhabit a few fragmentary areas of high-altitude bamboo forest. Unlike other bear species, to which they are closely related, pandas have a vegetarian diet that consists entirely of bamboo.

Pandas have become star attractions at many zoos, where they draw scores of visitors. Zoos typically pay

FIGURE 7.9

The Siberian tiger is one of the most endangered species in the world. It now occupies forest habitats in the Amur-Ussuri region of Siberia. ©*Henner Damke/Shutterstock.com.*

FIGURE 7.10

Elephants are highly intelligent and social animals. Once on the verge of extinction, elephants have recovered somewhat after a worldwide ban on the ivory trade. ©*Four Oaks/Shutterstock.com.*

China millions of dollars for the loan of adult pandas. These funds are used to support panda conservation efforts in China, including the purchase of land for refuges as well as the development of habitat corridors to link protected areas.

Big Game

Most big game species are members of the Artiodactyla order. This order contains a variety of ungulates (hoofed animals), including antelopes, bison, buffalo, camels, deer, gazelles, goats, hartebeests, hippopotamuses, impalas, and sheep. Many of the wild species have been overhunted for their meat, bones, or horns.

Horns are used in traditional Chinese medicine and are popular trophies for big game hunters. Big game species also face threats from domesticated livestock because of competition for habitat and food resources.

Primates

The endangerment of primate species is mostly due to loss of habitat and overhunting. Primates are dependent on large expanses of tropical forests, a habitat that is under siege worldwide. Countries with large numbers of primate species include Brazil, the Democratic Republic of the Congo, Indonesia, and Madagascar. Many of the most endangered primate species are found in Madagascar, which has a diverse and unique primate fauna. Most of Madagascar's primate species are endemic.

Habitat loss, especially the fragmentation and conversion of tropical forests for road building and agriculture, contributes to the decline of nearly all imperiled primates. For example, in Indonesia and Borneo, which are home to most of the world's orangutans, deforestation has dramatically shrunk orangutan habitat. (See Figure 7.11.) Logging and extensive burning have caused many orangutans to flee the forests for villages, where they have been killed or captured by humans.

Some threatened primates face pressures from excessive hunting and poaching. They are also used in medical research because of their close biological relationship with humans. As of 2013, almost all countries had either banned or strictly regulated the trade of primates, but these laws were often hard to enforce.

Rhinoceros

Rhinoceros are among the largest land mammals. They weigh up to 4 tons (3.6 t) and are herbivorous (plant-eating) grazers. The name *rhinoceros* consists of two Greek words meaning "nose" and "horn," and rhinos are the only animals on the earth that have a horn on their nose. Rhinoceros are found in the wild only in Africa and Asia. Figure 7.12 shows an African white rhinoceros with two horns. The female may be identified by her longer, more slender primary horn.

Rhinoceros have roamed the earth for more than 40 million years, but in less than a century humans have reduced their populations to dangerously low levels. Hunting has been the primary cause of rhinoceros decline. Rhinoceros horn is highly prized as an aphrodisiac (although its potency has never been proven), as well as an ingredient in traditional Chinese medicine. Rhinoceros were first listed by CITES in 1976. This listing banned international trade in the species and its products. In 1992 CITES also started requiring the destruction of horn caches that were confiscated from poachers. Nonetheless, people continue to buy and consume rhinoceros horn, and many poachers are willing to risk death to acquire it.

FIGURE 7.11

The orangutan is highly endangered, along with the majority of the world's primate species. ©*Eric Gevaert/Shutterstock.com.*

FIGURE 7.12

The white rhinoceros is native to Africa and can weigh up to 8,000 pounds. ©*U.S. Fish and Wildlife Service.*

CHAPTER 8

BIRDS

Birds belong to the class Aves, which contains dozens of orders. Birds are warm-blooded vertebrates with wings, feathers, and light hollow bones. The vast majority of birds are capable of flight. In *Red List of Threatened Species Version 2015.4* (November 2015, http://www.iucnredlist.org/about/summary-statistics), the International Union for Conservation of Nature (IUCN) states that 10,424 species of birds have been identified around the world. An estimated 600 to 900 of these species spend all or part of their life in the United States.

Besides taxonomy, birds are broadly classified by their physical characteristics (such as feet or beak structure), eating habits, primary habitats, or migratory habits. For example, raptors (birds of prey) have curved beaks and talons that are well suited for catching prey. This category includes buzzards, eagles, hawks, owls, and vultures. Perching birds have a unique foot structure with three toes in front and one large flexible toe to the rear. Ducks and geese are known as open-water or swimming birds and have webbed feet. Habitat categories include seabirds, shore birds, and arboreal (tree-dwelling) birds. Some birds migrate over long distances, whereas others, such as turkeys and quail, do not migrate at all.

Birds include a particularly diverse group of species. As such they play a variety of different roles in their ecosystems. In "Ecosystem Services Provided by Birds" (*Annals of the New York Academy of Sciences*, vol. 1134, June 2008), Christopher J. Whelan, Daniel G. Wenny, and Robert J. Marquis note that birds benefit ecosystems by serving as "predators, pollinators, scavengers, seed dispersers, seed predators, and ecosystem engineers." These services also directly or indirectly benefit human society. Many bird species prey on insects that pose a threat to agricultural crops or carry disease. For example, the southwestern willow flycatcher (as its name implies) is a voracious consumer of insects, including mosquitoes.

ENDANGERED AND THREATENED U.S. SPECIES

As of February 2016, there were 94 bird species listed under the Endangered Species Act (ESA) as endangered or threatened in the United States. (See Table 8.1.) As shown in Table 1.2 in Chapter 2, four bird species—dusky seaside sparrow (1990), Guam broadbill (2004), Mariana mallard (2004), and Santa Barbara song sparrow (1983)—have been delisted under the ESA because of extinction.

The vast majority of the listed species shown in Table 8.1 had an endangered listing as of February 2016, meaning that they are at risk of extinction. Nearly all had a recovery plan in place.

The imperiled birds come from many different genera (plural of genus) and represent a variety of habitats. Most are perching birds, seabirds, or shore birds. There are also a handful of other bird types, including woodpeckers and raptors, such as the northern spotted owl and the Puerto Rican broad-winged hawk.

Table 8.2 shows the 10 bird species with the highest expenditures under the ESA during fiscal year (FY) 2014. The three most expensive species were the red-cockaded woodpecker ($28.1 million), southwestern willow flycatcher ($23.2 million), and northern spotted owl ($13.4 million).

The following sections describe the categories of birds that are found on the list of endangered and threatened species.

Woodpeckers

Woodpeckers belong to the order Piciformes and the family Picidae. They are characterized by their physiology. They have hard chisel-like beaks and a unique foot structure with two toes pointing forward and two toes pointing backward. This allows them to take a firm grip on tree trunks and extend horizontally from vertical surfaces.

TABLE 8.1

Endangered and threatened bird species, February 2016

Common name	Scientific name	Federal listing status[a]	U.S. or U.S./foreign listed	Recovery plan date	Recovery plan stage[b]
`O`u (honeycreeper)	Psittirostra psittacea	E	US	09/22/06	RF(1)
Akekee	Loxops caeruleirostris	E	US	06/17/10	O
Akiapola`au (honeycreeper)	Hemignathus munroi	E	US	09/22/06	RF(1)
Akikiki	Oreomystis bairdi	E	US	09/22/06	RF(1)
Attwater's greater prairie-chicken	Tympanuchus cupido attwateri	E	US	04/26/10	RF(2)
Audubon's crested caracara	Polyborus plancus audubonii	T	US	05/18/99	F
Bachman's warbler (=wood)	Vermivora bachmanii	E	US/foreign	None	—
Black-capped vireo	Vireo atricapilla	E	US/foreign	09/30/91	F
Bridled white-eye	Zosterops conspicillatus conspicillatus	E	US	09/28/90	F
California clapper rail	Rallus longirostris obsoletus	E	US	02/26/14	F
California condor	Gymnogyps californianus	E; EXPN	US/foreign	04/25/96	RF(3)
California least tern	Sterna antillarum browni	E	US/foreign	09/27/85	RF(1)
Cape Sable seaside sparrow	Ammodramus maritimus mirabilis	E	US	05/18/99	F
Coastal California gnatcatcher	Polioptila californica californica	T	US/foreign	None	—
Crested honeycreeper	Palmeria dolei	E	US	09/22/06	RF(1)
Eskimo curlew	Numenius borealis	E	US/foreign	None	—
Everglade snail kite	Rostrhamus sociabilis plumbeus	E	US/foreign	05/18/99	F
Florida grasshopper sparrow	Ammodramus savannarum floridanus	E	US	05/18/99	F
Florida scrub-jay	Aphelocoma coerulescens	T	US	05/09/90	F
Golden-cheeked warbler (=wood)	Dendroica chrysoparia	E	US/foreign	09/30/92	F
Guam kingfisher	Todiramphus cinnamominus	E	US	11/14/08	RF(1)
Guam rail	Rallus owstoni	E; EXPN	US	09/28/90	F
Gunnison sage-grouse	Centrocercus minimus	T	US	None	—
Hawaii akepa (honeycreeper)	Loxops coccineus coccineus	E	US	09/22/06	RF(1)
Hawaii creeper	Oreomystis mana	E	US	09/22/06	RF(1)
Hawaiian (='alala) crow	Corvus hawaiiensis	E	US	04/17/09	RF(1)
Hawaiian (=koloa) duck	Anas wyvilliana	E	US	01/19/12	RF(2)
Hawaiian (='lo) hawk	Buteo solitarius	E	US	05/09/84	F
Hawaiian common gallinule	Gallinula chloropus sandvicensis	E	US	01/19/12	RF(2)
Hawaiian coot	Fulica americana alai	E	US	01/19/12	RF(2)
Hawaiian goose	Branta (=Nesochen) sandvicensis	E	US	09/24/04	RD(1)
Hawaiian petrel	Pterodroma sandwichensis	E	US	04/25/83	F
Hawaiian stilt	Himantopus mexicanus knudseni	E	US	01/19/12	RF(2)
Inyo California towhee	Pipilo crissalis eremophilus	T	US	04/10/98	F
Ivory-billed woodpecker	Campephilus principalis	E	US/foreign	07/19/10	F
Kauai `o`o (honeyeater)	Moho braccatus	E	US	09/22/06	RF(1)
Kauai akialoa (honeycreeper)	Hemignathus procerus	E	US	09/22/06	RF(1)
Kirtland's warbler	Setophaga kirtlandii (= Dendroica kirtlandii)	E	US/foreign	09/30/85	RF(1)
Large Kauai (=kamao) thrush	Myadestes myadestinus	E	US	09/22/06	RF(1)
Laysan duck	Anas laysanensis	E	US	09/22/09	RF(1)
Laysan finch (honeycreeper)	Telespyza cantans	E	US	10/04/84	F
Least Bell's vireo	Vireo bellii pusillus	E	US/foreign	05/06/98	D
Least tern	Sterna antillarum	E	US	09/19/90	F
Lesser prairie-chicken	Tympanuchus pallidicinctus	T	US	None	—
Light-footed clapper rail	Rallus longirostris levipes	E	US/foreign	06/24/85	RF(1)
Marbled murrelet	Brachyramphus marmoratus	T	US	09/24/97	F
Mariana (=aga) crow	Corvus kubaryi	E	US	01/11/06	RD(1)
Mariana common moorhen	Gallinula chloropus guami	E	US	09/30/91	F
Mariana gray swiftlet	Aerodramus vanikorensis bartschi	E	US	09/30/91	F
Masked bobwhite (quail)	Colinus virginianus ridgwayi	E	US/foreign	04/21/95	RF(2)
Maui akepa (honeycreeper)	Loxops coccineus ochraceus	E	US	09/22/06	RF(1)
Maui parrotbill (honeycreeper)	Pseudonestor xanthophrys	E	US	09/22/06	RF(1)
Mexican spotted owl	Strix occidentalis lucida	T	US/foreign	12/18/12	RF(1)
Micronesian megapode	Megapodius laperouse	E	US/foreign	04/10/98	F
Mississippi sandhill crane	Grus canadensis pulla	E	US	09/06/91	RF(3)
Molokai creeper	Paroreomyza flammea	E	US	09/22/06	RF(1)
Molokai thrush	Myadestes lanaiensis rutha	E	US	09/22/06	RF(1)
Newell's Townsend's shearwater	Puffinus auricularis newelli	T	US	04/25/83	F
Nightingale reed warbler (old world warbler)	Acrocephalus luscinia	E	US	04/10/98	F
Nihoa finch (honeycreeper)	Telespyza ultima	E	US	10/04/84	F
Nihoa millerbird (old world warbler)	Acrocephalus familiaris kingi	E	US	10/04/84	F
Northern aplomado falcon	Falco femoralis septentrionalis	E; EXPN	US/foreign	06/08/90	F
Northern spotted owl	Strix occidentalis caurina	T	US/foreign	07/01/11	RF(1)
Nukupu`u (honeycreeper)	Hemignathus lucidus	E	US	09/22/06	RF(1)
Oahu creeper	Paroreomyza maculata	E	US	09/22/06	RF(1)
Oahu elepaio	Chasiempis sandwichensis ibidis	E	US	09/22/06	RF(1)
Palila (honeycreeper)	Loxioides bailleui	E	US	09/22/06	RF(1)
Piping plover	Charadrius melodus	E; T	US/foreign	05/02/96	RF(1)
Po`ouli (honeycreeper)	Melamprosops phaeosoma	E	US	09/22/06	RF(1)
Puerto Rican broad-winged hawk	Buteo platypterus brunnescens	E	US	09/08/97	F

Woodpeckers prefer arboreal habitats, primarily dead trees in old-growth forests. The birds hammer at the bark on the trees to dig out insects living there. They often form deep cavities in the tree to use as roosting and nesting holes.

TABLE 8.1

Endangered and threatened bird species, February 2016 [CONTINUED]

Common name	Scientific name	Federal listing status[a]	U.S. or U.S./foreign listed	Recovery plan date	Recovery plan stage[b]
Puerto Rican nightjar	*Caprimulgus noctitherus*	E	US	04/19/84	F
Puerto Rican parrot	*Amazona vittata*	E	US	06/17/09	RF(1)
Puerto Rican plain pigeon	*Columba inornata wetmorei*	E	US	10/14/82	F
Puerto Rican sharp-shinned hawk	*Accipiter striatus venator*	E	US	09/08/97	F
Red knot	*Calidris canutus rufa*	T	US/foreign	None	—
Red-cockaded woodpecker	*Picoides borealis*	E	US	03/20/03	RF(2)
Roseate tern	*Sterna dougallii dougallii*	E; T	US/foreign	09/24/93	F
Rota bridled white-eye	*Zosterops rotensis*	E	US	10/19/07	F
San Clemente loggerhead shrike	*Lanius ludovicianus mearnsi*	E	US	01/26/84	F
San Clemente sage sparrow	*Amphispiza belli clementeae*	T	US	01/26/84	F
Short-tailed albatross	*Phoebastria (=Diomedea) albatrus*	E	US/foreign	05/20/09	F
Small Kauai (=puaiohi) thrush	*Myadestes palmeri*	E	US	09/22/06	RF(1)
Southwestern willow flycatcher	*Empidonax traillii extimus*	E	US/foreign	08/30/02	F
Spectacled eider	*Somateria fischeri*	T	US/foreign	08/12/08	F
Steller's eider	*Polysticta stelleri*	T	US	08/13/08	F
Streaked Horned lark	*Eremophila alpestris strigata*	T	US	None	—
Thick-billed parrot	*Rhynchopsitta pachyrhyncha*	E	US/foreign	06/20/09	D
Western snowy plover	*Charadrius alexandrinus nivosus*	T	US/foreign	09/24/07	F
White-necked crow	*Corvus leucognaphalus*	E	US	None	—
Whooping crane	*Grus americana*	E; EXPN	US/foreign	05/29/07	RF(3)
Wood stork	*Mycteria americana*	T	US	01/27/97	RF(1)
Yellow-billed cuckoo	*Coccyzus americanus*	T	US/foreign	None	—
Yellow-shouldered blackbird	*Agelaius xanthomus*	E	US	11/12/96	RF(1)
Yuma clapper rail	*Rallus longirostris yumanensis*	E	US/foreign	02/10/10	RD(1)

[a]E = Endangered. T = Threatened. EXPN = Experimental population, non-essential. [b]F = Final. RD = Draft revision. RF = Final revision. O = Other.

SOURCE: Adapted from "Generate Species List," in *Environmental Conservation Online System Species Reports*, U.S. Department of the Interior, U.S. Fish and Wildlife Service, February 2016, http://ecos.fws.gov/tess_public/pub/adHocSpeciesForm.jsp (accessed February 17, 2016), and "Listed FWS/Joint FWS and NMFS Species and Populations with Recovery Plans (Sorted by Listed Entity)," in *Recovery Plans Search*, U.S. Department of the Interior, U.S. Fish and Wildlife Service, February 2016, http://ecos.fws.gov/tess_public/pub/speciesRecovery.jsp?sort=1 (accessed February 17, 2016)

TABLE 8.2

The 10 listed bird species with the highest expenditures under the Endangered Species Act, fiscal year 2014

Ranking	Species	Population	Expenditure
1	Woodpecker, red-cockaded (*Picoides borealis*)	Entire	$28,091,150
2	Flycatcher, southwestern willow (*Empidonax traillii extimus*)	Entire	$23,157,345
3	Owl, northern spotted (*Strix occidentalis caurina*)	Entire	$13,396,766
4	Plover, piping (*Charadrius melodus*)	Entire, except Great Lakes watershed	$11,685,179
5	Tern, least (*Sterna antillarum*)	Interior population	$9,334,565
6	Owl, Mexican spotted (*Strix occidentalis lucida*)	Entire	$5,863,127
7	Scrub-jay, Florida (*Aphelocoma coerulescens*)	Entire	$5,011,138
8	Murrelet, marbled (*Brachyramphus marmoratus*)	California, Oregon, and Washington	$4,908,883
9	Plover, western snowy (*Charadrius alexandrinus nivosus*)	Pacific coastal population	$4,226,021
10	Prairie chicken, lesser (*Tympanuchus pallidicinctus*)	Entire	$4,009,488

SOURCE: Adapted from "Table 2. Species Ranked in Descending Order of Total FY 2014 Reported Expenditures, Not Including Land Acquisition Costs," in *Federal and State Endangered and Threatened Species Expenditures: Fiscal Year 2014*, U.S. Department of the Interior, U.S. Fish and Wildlife Service, March 2, 2016, http://www.fws.gov/endangered/esa-library/pdf/20160302_final_FY14_ExpRpt.pdf (accessed March 9, 2016)

RED-COCKADED WOODPECKERS. The red-cockaded woodpecker is named for the red patches, or cockades, of feathers on the head of the male. (See Figure 8.1.) This species is found in old pine forests in the southeastern United States, where family groups (consisting of a breeding male and female as well as several helpers) nest within self-dug cavities in pine trees. Tree cavities serve as nesting sites and provide protection from predators. Because red-cockaded woodpeckers rarely nest in trees less than 80 years old, heavy logging has destroyed much of their former habitat.

The red-cockaded woodpecker is considered a keystone species, which as explained in Chapter 1, means that other species are highly dependent on it, and its loss would have severe negative impacts on them. In "The Red-Cockaded Woodpecker's Role in the Southern Pine Ecosystem, Population Trends and Relationships with Southern Pine Beetles (August 1997, http://www.treesearch.fs.fed.us/pubs/535), Richard N. Conner et al. of Texas A&M University note that dozens of other species use the bird's cavities and conclude, "Because of the dependence of many other cavity nesters on

FIGURE 8.1

Red-cockaded woodpecker

SOURCE: Robert Savannah, artist, "Red Cockaded Woodpeckers," in *Line Art (Drawings)*, U.S. Department of the Interior, U.S. Fish and Wildlife Service, undated, http://www.fws.gov/pictures/lineart/bobsavannah/redcockadedwoodpeckers.html (accessed February 17, 2016)

Red-cockaded Woodpecker cavities, forest biodiversity would suffer substantially in the absence of this endangered woodpecker in southern pine ecosystems."

The red-cockaded woodpecker was first listed under the ESA in 1970. It is found in fragmented populations in the southeastern seaboard westward into Texas. As of April 2016, its most recent recovery plan was published in 2003.

In *Red-Cockaded Woodpecker (*Picoides borealis*): Five-Year Review—Summary and Evaluation* (October 2006, http://ecos.fws.gov/docs/five_year_review/doc787.pdf), the U.S. Fish and Wildlife Service (USFWS) reports that over 6,000 active clusters (occupied territories) of the bird have been documented, up from about 4,700 active clusters reported during the early 1990s. However, the USFWS believes the bird still faces significant threats from the loss, degradation, and fragmentation of nesting and foraging habitat.

The USFWS indicates in "Red-Cockaded Woodpecker (*Picoides borealis*)" (2016, http://ecos.fws.gov/tess_public/profile/speciesProfile?spcode=B04F) that critical habitat has not been designated for the red-cockaded woodpecker. However, eight states (Alabama, Florida, Georgia, Louisiana, North Carolina, South Carolina, Texas,

and Virginia) have established statewide Safe Harbor Agreements with the USFWS. These are voluntary agreements in which nonfederal landowners agree to conserve and manage listed species on their property. In exchange, the federal government provides assurances that it will not impose certain restrictions on the conservation activities. For example, if a landowner improves or expands red-cockaded woodpecker habitat and more of the birds move into the habitat, the landowner will not face increased regulatory requirements.

Passerines

Just over half of all bird species belong to the order Passeriformes and are called passerines. They are informally known as perching birds or songbirds, although not all passerines are truly songbirds. This order includes many well-known species, such as blackbirds, cardinals, crows, finches, larks, mockingbirds, sparrows, starlings, swallows, and wrens. Over one-third of the U.S. species of endangered and threatened birds listed in Table 8.1 are passerine (perching) birds. The following sections describe some species of note.

SOUTHWESTERN WILLOW FLYCATCHERS. The southwestern willow flycatcher is a small bird that has a grayish-green back and wings with a pale yellow belly and a white-colored throat. It feeds on insects and prefers riparian areas (dense vegetation near rivers or streams) for its habitat. According to the Arizona Game and Fish Department, in "Wild Kids" (June 2002, http://www.azgfd.gov/i_e/ee/resources/wild_kids/endangered46.pdf), the bird's scientific name (*Empidonax traillii extimus*) means "mosquito king."

The species was first listed as endangered in 1995. In August 2002 the USFWS published *Final Recovery Plan: Southwestern Willow Flycatcher (*Empidonax traillii extimus*)* (http://ecos.fws.gov/docs/recovery_plans/2002/020830c.pdf). At that time the agency reported that approximately 900 to 1,100 pairs of the bird were believed to exist. The species migrates from the southwestern United States to Mexico and Central and South America for the winter. It is endangered primarily because of the loss of riparian vegetation. In ranching areas this vegetation is often stripped by grazing livestock. Another factor in its decline is harm from brood parasites (bird species that lay their eggs in the nests of other species). Brown-headed cowbirds are brood parasites that threaten southwestern willow flycatchers. They lay their eggs in the flycatchers' nests, and the unsuspecting flycatchers raise the cowbirds' young as their own.

Since 1997 the USFWS has repeatedly designated and revised critical habitat for the southwestern willow flycatcher in response to litigation. In January 2013 the agency (https://www.gpo.gov/fdsys/pkg/FR-2013-01-03/pdf/2012-30634.pdf) designated 1,227 stream miles

(1,975 stream km) in Arizona, California, Colorado, Nevada, New Mexico, and Utah as critical habitat.

In 2014 the USFWS (http://ecos.fws.gov/docs/five _year_review/doc4437.pdf) published a five-year review for the species. The agency indicates that six large recovery units were assessed for breeding sites/territories; however, the number was less than that required for either downlisting or delisting the bird. In addition, needed conservation and management plans had not been finalized. The USFWS concluded that the species should maintain its endangered listing. In 2015, however, the agency (http://ecos.fws.gov/docs/petitions/92210/676 .pdf) received a petition from the Pacific Legal Foundation representing various western business interests. They argue that the southwestern willow flycatcher should be delisted under the ESA because it is not a valid subspecies of willow flycatcher and its habitat area and population size are increasing. In March 2016 the USFWS (https:// www.gpo.gov/fdsys/pkg/FR-2016-03-16/pdf/2016-05699 .pdf) concluded that the petition presented substantial information supporting its claims. The agency initiated a status review (a comprehensive investigation) to further research the claims. As of April 2016, that review had not been completed.

HAWAIIAN HONEYCREEPERS. Hawaiian honeycreepers are a group of songbirds endemic (limited) to Hawaii. The honeycreepers are named for the characteristic creeping behavior some species exhibit as they search for nectar. Hawaiian honeycreepers are extremely diverse in their diet; different species are insect, nectar, or seed eaters. (The nectar-consuming honeycreepers are particularly valued for their role in pollinating flowering plants.) Species also differ in the shapes of their beaks and in plumage coloration. The birds are found in forest habitats at high elevations.

As shown in Table 8.1, as of February 2016, more than a dozen Hawaiian honeycreepers were listed under the ESA.

Some honeycreeper species are among the most endangered animals on the earth, with only a few individuals left. One of the primary factors involved in honeycreeper endangerment is loss of habitat. In addition, the introduction of predators that hunt birds or eat their eggs, such as cats, mongooses, and rats, have contributed to the decline of many species. The introduction of bird diseases, particularly those spread by introduced mosquitoes, has decimated honeycreeper populations. Finally, competition with introduced bird species for food and habitat has also been a significant cause of decline.

In Revised Recovery Plan for Hawaiian Forest Birds (September 22, 2006, http://ecos.fws.gov/docs/recovery _plan/060922a.pdf), the USFWS covers 19 endangered Hawaiian forest birds. The agency reports that 10 of these

species have not been observed in at least a decade and may well be extinct. Most of these species are native to rain forests at elevations above 4,000 feet (1,200 m) on the islands of Hawaii (Big Island), Kauai, and Maui. Major threats to endangered forest species include habitat loss and modification, other human activity, disease, and predation. Of particular importance are nonnative plants, which have converted native plant communities to alien ecosystems that are unsuitable as habitat.

MIGRATORY SONGBIRDS. In the fact sheet "Neotropical Migratory Bird Basics" (January 1, 1999, http:// nationalzoo.si.edu/scbi/migratorybirds/fact_sheets/?id=9), Mary Deinlein of the Smithsonian Migratory Bird Center states that there are nearly 200 species of songbirds known as neotropical migrators. Every year these birds migrate between the United States and tropical areas in Mexico, the Caribbean, and Central and South America. Migratory songbirds play a vital role in many ecosystems. For example, during spring migration in the Ozarks, dozens of migratory bird species arrive and feed on the insects that inhabit oak trees, thereby helping control insect populations.

Migratory species are particularly vulnerable because they are dependent on suitable habitat in both their winter and spring ranges. In North America, land development has eliminated many forest habitats. Migratory songbird habitats are also jeopardized in Central and South America, where farmers and ranchers have been burning and clearing tropical forests to plant crops and graze livestock. Some countries, including Belize, Costa Rica, Guatemala, and Mexico, have set up preserves for songbirds, but improved forest management is needed to save them.

Raptors

The term raptor is derived from the Latin word raptores, which was once the order on the taxonomy table to which birds of prey were assigned. Eventually, scientists split the birds into three orders:

- Accipitriformes—buzzards, eagles, hawks, vultures
- Falconiformes—falcons
- Strigiformes—owls

As of February 2016, there were fewer than a dozen raptors listed as endangered or threatened in the United States. (See Table 8.1.) Species of note include the northern spotted owl and the California condor.

NORTHERN SPOTTED OWLS. The northern spotted owl occupies old-growth forests in the Pacific Northwest, where it nests in the cavities of trees 200 years old or older. (See Figure 8.2.) The bird is called an indicator species because its well-being is indicative of the overall well-being of the forests in which it lives. Its populations have declined primarily because of habitat loss. Most of

FIGURE 8.2

The northern spotted owl, which inhabits old-growth forests in the Pacific Northwest, was the subject of a lengthy battle pitting environmentalists against logging interests. ©*U.S. Fish and Wildlife Service.*

the private lands in its range have been heavily logged, leaving only public lands, such as national forests and national parks, for habitat. In 1990 the northern spotted owl was listed under the ESA. Court battles began over continued logging in national forest habitats.

In 1992 the USFWS set aside 7 million acres (2.8 million ha) as critical habitat for the species and published a recovery plan. Two years later the Northwest Forest Plan (http://www.fs.usda.gov/detail/r5/landmanagement/planning/?cid=STELPRD3830167) was established. It reduced logging in 13 national forests by about 85% to protect northern spotted owl habitats. However, populations of the northern spotted owl continued to decline, this despite the unanticipated discovery of 50 pairs of nesting adults in California's Marin County, just north of the Golden Gate Bridge.

The USFWS has repeatedly designated critical habitat for the species in response to litigation. In November 2012 the agency (http://www.fws.gov/oregonfwo/species/data/NorthernSpottedOwl/Documents/11-21-12_NSO_Press Release.pdf) designated 9.3 million acres (3.8 million ha) of federal lands and nearly 300,000 acres (121,406 ha) on state lands.

In June 2011 the USFWS issued *Revised Recovery Plan for the Northern Spotted Owl (*Strix occidentalis caurina*)* (http://ecos.fws.gov/docs/recovery_plan/Revised NSORecPlan2011_1.pdf). The agency indicates that competition from the barred owl is the most important threat facing the spotted owl. Other threats include ongoing habitat losses due to logging, wildfires, and other disturbances and lost habitat due to past actions. The USFWS estimates that at least $127.1 million will be required to fund recovery efforts over the next 30 years.

As of April 2016, the USFWS (http://ecos.fws.gov/tess_public/profile/speciesProfile?spcode=B08B) had conducted two five-year reviews for the northern spotted owl—the first in 2004 and the second in 2011. In the latter review (http://www.fws.gov/pacific/ecoservices/endangered/recovery/documents/NSO5-YrReview-R8 SignedCopy10-26-2011.pdf), the agency notes that data collected between 2006 and 2011 indicate the species population continued to decline at a rate of 2.7% per year. The decrease was blamed on habitat loss and the presence of barred owls which compete for habitat. In April 2015 the USFWS (https://www.gpo.gov/fdsys/pkg/FR-2015-04-10/pdf/2015-07837.pdf) published its findings on a petition submitted by the Environmental Protection Information Center requesting that the northern spotted owl be uplisted to endangered status. The agency concluded that the petition did present substantial information supporting its request and initiated a review for the species. As of April 2016, the results of the review had not been issued.

CALIFORNIA CONDORS. The California condor has a wingspan of more than 9 feet (2.7 m) and is among the continent's most impressive birds. Ten thousand years ago this species soared over most of North America. However, its range contracted at the end of the Ice Age, and eventually it was found only along the Pacific coast. Like other vulture species, the California condor is a carrion eater and feeds on the carcasses of deer, sheep, and smaller species such as rodents. Random shooting, egg collection, poisoning (particularly from lead in bullets used by hunters to kill game), and loss of habitat devastated the condor population. The species was listed as endangered in 1967. (See Table 2.1 in Chapter 2.) In "For Only the Second Time in 14 Years, Rare California Condor Chick Takes Flight in Southern California" (November 16, 2006, http://www.fws.gov/fieldnotes/regmap.cfm?arskey=20144), the USFWS states that by late 1984 only 15 condors remained in the wild. After seven of these birds died, the agency decided to capture the remaining population.

An intense captive breeding program for the California condor was initiated in 1987. The breeding program was successful enough that California condors were released into the wild beginning in 1992. The introduced birds in parts of Arizona, Nevada, and Utah were designated a nonessential experimental population. (Nonessential experimental populations are not believed essential to the survival of a species as whole. Thus, they receive less rigorous protections under the ESA.) According to the USFWS, in "California Condor Recovery Program" (http://www.fws.gov/cno/es/pdf%20 files/Ca-Condor-Recovery-Prog2015PopulationStatus.pdf), the population size as of December 31, 2015, was 435 birds with 268 of them living in the wild and 167 in captivity.

Waterbirds

Waterbirds live in and around bodies of water. Some prefer marine (ocean) habitats, and others are found only near freshwater. Many species inhabit swamps, marshes, and wetlands. These areas may be inland or intertidal (along the sea coast).

As of February 2016, there were more than two dozen waterbirds listed as endangered or threatened in the United States. (See Table 8.1.) They include a variety of species from many different taxonomic orders.

MIGRATORY SHORE BIRDS. Migratory shore birds are found most often in marshes, mudflats, estuaries, and other wetland areas where the sea meets freshwater. This category includes avocets, oystercatchers, plovers, sandpipers, shearwaters, snipes, and stilts. These birds vary greatly in size and color, but nearly all migrate over long distances. Most of them breed near the North Pole during the spring and spend their winters anywhere from the southern United States to South America. During their migrations the birds stop to rest and feed at specific locations, known as staging areas, in the United States. Major staging areas include Cheyenne Bottoms in Kansas, the Copper River delta in Alaska, Delaware Bay, the Great Salt Lake in Utah, and San Francisco Bay. The birds eat insect larvae (including mosquito larvae), leeches, worms, and aquatic invertebrates.

The piping plover is an imperiled migratory shorebird first listed under the ESA in 1985. The USFWS (http://ecos.fws.gov/tess_public/profile/speciesProfile?spcode=B079) recognizes three distinct populations of the species. As of April 2016, a population in the Great Lakes watershed was listed as endangered. Piping plovers in the rest of the United States, including a northern Great Plains population, were listed as threatened. The birds breed and raise their young in northern areas during the spring and summer and migrate to the south Atlantic coast, the Gulf coast, and the Caribbean and Mexican coasts for the winter.

In September 2009 the USFWS published *Piping Plover (Charadrius melodus): 5-Year Review—Summary and Evaluation* (http://ecos.fws.gov/docs/five_year _review/doc3009.pdf) and concluded that no changes were warranted to its listings under the ESA. The agency noted that the endangered Great Lakes population contained only 63 breeding pairs, which was well below the recovery goal of 150 breeding pairs. The USFWS also indicated that all three populations face continuing threats to their survival from development of coastal lands in their breeding and wintering habitats.

In March 2016 the USFWS published a two-volume recovery plan for the species. The first volume (http://ecos.fws.gov/docs/recovery_plan/Vol%20I%20NGP%20 Draft%20Revised%20Breeding%20Rec%20Plan%20(JR% 20Edits)%20(kk)%2020160224_1.pdf) covers the bird's breeding range, and the second volume (http://ecos.fws .gov/docs/recovery_plan/Vol%20II%20NGP%20Draft% 20Revised%20Winter%20Rec%20Plan%206_05_15_2 .pdf) covers the coastal migration and wintering portions of the range. The agency estimates that the piping plover can be recovered by 2035 at a cost of $797 million.

Another imperiled migratory shorebird is the least tern. (See Figure 8.3.) The least tern is the smallest member of the gull and tern family. According to the Texas Parks and Wildlife Department, in "Interior Least Tern (*Sterna antillarum athalassos*)" (2016, http://www .tpwd.state.tx.us/huntwild/wild/species/leasttern/), there are three North American populations of the least tern. An Atlantic coast population is not listed under the ESA. As of April 2016, the California least tern and what is known as the interior population were listed as endangered. The latter is distributed throughout the nation's midsection from Montana to Texas and as far east as Tennessee. In 2013 the USFWS (http://www.fws.gov/ southeast/5yearReviews/5yearreviews/interiorLeastTern5 yrReivew102413.pdf) published a five-year status review for the interior least tern. The agency notes that the population is "biologically recovered." However, before officially recommending the bird for delisting the USFWS plans to confirm its assessment using computer modeling, obtain conservation agreements with other stakeholders (such as the states), and prepare a rangewide monitoring strategy and plan. As of April 2016, the interior least tern had not been proposed for delisting.

SEABIRDS. Seabirds spend most of their time out at sea, but they nest on land. They are also known as pelagic birds because pelagic means oceanic (associated with the open seas). Seabird species include albatrosses, auks and auklets, cormorants, gulls, kittiwakes, murres and murrelets, petrels, penguins, and puffins.

FIGURE 8.3

Least tern

SOURCE: Laurel Ovitt, artist, "Untitled," in *Threatened and Endangered Species: Least Tern Sterna antillarum Fact Sheet*, U.S. Department of Agriculture Natural Resources Conservation Service, November 2005, http://efotg.nrcs.usda.gov/references/public/MT/LeastTern.pdf (accessed February 17, 2016)

FIGURE 8.4

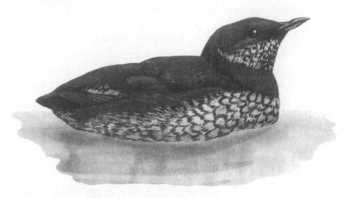

Marbled murrelet. ©*Universal Images Group North America LLC/Alamy.*

The marbled murrelet is one of a handful of seabirds listed under the ESA. The bird was first listed under the ESA in 1992; as of April 2016, it was designated as threatened in California, Oregon, and Washington. The marbled murrelet is about 9 inches (23 cm) long and has a distinctive two-tone pattern of light and dark markings. (See Figure 8.4.) The species nests in the trees of old-growth forests along the northwest Pacific coastline. Logging and other types of habitat degradation have resulted in population declines.

In June 2009 the USFWS published *Marbled Murrelet* (Brachyramphus marmoratus)*: 5-Year Review* (http://ecos.fws.gov/docs/five_year_review/doc2417.pdf). The agency concluded that the marbled murrelet should retain its listing as threatened. However, the USFWS noted deep concern about "the apparent substantial downward trend of the population and the species' continued vulnerability from a broad range of threats" and indicated that "a change in listing status to endangered may be warranted in the future."

The USFWS received a petition from various business interests requesting that the California/Oregon/Washington distinct population segment (a distinct population of a species that is capable of interbreeding and lives in a specific geographic area) be delisted. After finding the request to be warranted, the agency initiated a status review. In January 2010 the USFWS (http://www.gpo.gov/fdsys/pkg/FR-2010-01-21/pdf/2010-951.pdf#page=1) declined to delist the bird because it "continues to be subject to a broad range of threats, such as nesting habitat loss, habitat fragmentation, and predation." The agency noted that although some threats have been reduced since the species was first listed, new threats have arisen, such as becoming entangled in abandoned fishing gear and being harmed by algal blooms and declining quality of marine prey.

In August 2015 the USFWS (https://www.gpo.gov/fdsys/pkg/FR-2015-08-25/pdf/2015-20837.pdf) proposed designating critical habitat for the marbled murrelet covering nearly 3.7 million acres (1.5 million ha). As of April 2016, the proposal had not been finalized.

WADING BIRDS. Wading birds are unusual birds characterized by long skinny legs and extended necks and beaks. They wade in shallow waters of swamps, wetlands, and bays, where they feed on aquatic life-forms. Wading birds include species of crane, egret, ibis, and stork. As of April 2016, three wading birds of note were listed under the ESA: the wood stork, the whooping crane, and the Mississippi sandhill crane.

The wood stork weighs about 5 pounds (2.3 kg) and stands up to 3 feet (0.9 m) tall with a 5-foot (1.5-m) wingspan. At one time tens of thousands of the birds inhabited the southeastern coastline. In 1984 the species was listed under the ESA as endangered in Alabama, Florida, Georgia, and South Carolina. A recovery plan for the bird was published in 1999. At that time about 5,000 breeding pairs lived in the wild. Throughout the first decade of the 21st century populations declined in the Everglades in southern Florida but increased in coastal areas farther north. In September 2010 the USFWS (http://www.gpo.gov/fdsys/pkg/FR-2010-09-21/pdf/2010-23138.pdf#page=1) published a 90-day finding on a petition to reclassify the wood stork from endangered to threatened. The petition was submitted by the Pacific Legal Foundation on behalf of the Florida Homebuilders Association. In June 2014 the USFWS (https://www.gpo.gov/fdsys/pkg/FR-2014-06-30/pdf/2014-14761.pdf) officially downlisted the wood stork to threatened status.

Standing 5 feet (1.5 m) tall, the whooping crane is North America's tallest bird and among the best-known

FIGURE 8.5

The whooping crane is highly endangered. Each year whooping cranes migrate from breeding grounds in Canada to wintering grounds in south Texas. ©Al Mueller/Shutterstock.com.

endangered species in the United States. (See Figure 8.5.) Its name comes from its loud and distinctive call, which can be heard for miles. Historically, whooping cranes lived in the Great Plains and along the southeastern coast of the United States. The birds were once heavily hunted for their meat as well as for their beautiful, long white feathers. In addition, the heavy loss of wetland areas in the United States deprived whooping cranes of much of their original habitat. In 1937 it was discovered that fewer than 20 whooping cranes were left in the wild in two small populations: a migratory population that nested in Canada and wintered on the Texas coast and a non-migratory population that lived in Louisiana.

Every fall the migratory whooping cranes fly 2,500 miles (4,000 km) from nesting grounds in Wood Buffalo National Park in Canada to Aransas, Texas, for the winter before returning north during the spring to breed. Whooping cranes return to the same nesting site each year with the same mate. In 1937 the Aransas National Wildlife Refuge was established in southern Texas to protect the species' wintering habitat. Conservation efforts for the whooping crane are coordinated with the Canadian government, which manages the birds' breeding areas.

As of April 2016, the whooping crane was listed under the ESA as endangered in Kansas, Montana, Nebraska, North Dakota, Oklahoma, South Dakota, and Texas. Since 1993 nonessential experimental populations have been designated in dozens of states from Wyoming to Florida. In 2001 the first introduced cranes in Wisconsin were led to their Florida wintering grounds along the migration route by ultralight aircraft. Ever since, the birds have been successfully migrating between their nesting and wintering grounds.

The Mississippi sandhill crane is a gray-colored bird that is about 4 feet (1.2 m) tall when standing upright. It was first listed as endangered under the ESA in 1973. In September 1991 the USFWS (http://ecos.fws.gov/docs/recovery_plan/910906.pdf) published a recovery plan for the bird. At that time the species was in critical danger of becoming extinct with only one population existing in a small area of Jackson County, Mississippi. The bird was imperiled because of loss and degradation of its pine savanna habitat and reproductive isolation from other sandhill crane subspecies. The USFWS operates a captive breeding program at its Mississippi Sandhill Crane National Wildlife Refuge in Gautier, Mississippi. According to the agency (November 21, 2014, http://www.fws.gov/refuge/Mississippi_Sandhill_Crane/wildlife_and_habitat/mississippi_sandhill_crane.html), by late 2014 the refuge was home to about 100 of the birds, up from only 30 to 35 individuals reported during the 1970s.

OTHER BIRDS. Other types of birds listed under the ESA include nonmigratory shore birds, such as the California clapper rail and the Guam rail (a flightless bird); swimming birds, including coots, ducks, eiders, and geese; and ground-dwelling birds, such as the prairie chicken.

GENERAL THREATS TO IMPERILED U.S. BIRD SPECIES

The driving force behind current declines in most imperiled bird species in the United States is the destruction, degradation, and fragmentation of habitat due to increasing human population size and consumption of resources. For example, natural habitats are lost because of agriculture, urban sprawl and other development, logging, mining, and road building. Other general threats include chemical contaminants, such as pesticides and oil, that are released to the environment and invasive species that prey on imperiled birds or compete with them for food and resources.

Pesticides

During the latter half of the 20th century pesticides and other toxic chemicals were recognized as a major cause of avian mortality and a primary factor in the endangerment of several species, including the bald eagle and the peregrine falcon. Many harmful pesticides, such as dichlorodiphenyltrichloroethane (DDT) and toxaphene, have been banned. The U.S. Environmental Protection Agency (EPA) evaluates the potential risks of pesticides to listed species and any designated critical habitat through a process called an "effects determination." The EPA (http://www.epa.gov/oppfead1/endanger/litstatus/effects/) has published the results of dozens of effects determinations on hundreds of imperiled species.

Oil

Another threat to imperiled birds is oil. During the 1970s and 1980s oil spills from seagoing tanker ships were a major environmental problem for coastal birds and seabirds. Birds coming into contact with spilled oil often died immediately, either from losing the insulation of their feathers or by ingesting lethal amounts of oil when they tried to clean themselves. (See Figure 8.6.) According to the Exxon Valdez Oil Spill Trustee Council (2014, http://www.evostc.state.ak.us/facts/qanda.cfm), the worst oil tanker spill in U.S. waters occurred on March 24, 1989, when the *Exxon Valdez* tanker released approximately 257,000 barrels of crude oil into Alaska's Prince William Sound. Hundreds of thousands of seabirds are estimated to have died as a result of the accident. Ever since, large-volume oil tanker spills have become much less common because of strict international regulation of oil tankers.

In April 2010 the largest oil spill in U.S. history occurred when an explosion on the Deepwater Horizon, an offshore drilling platform in the Gulf of Mexico, released nearly 5 million barrels of oil. The drilling platform was leased by the BP (formerly British Petroleum) oil company and located approximately 41 miles (66 km) off the coast of Louisiana. The oil spill affected aquatic wildlife and water quality across a huge area of the Gulf of Mexico.

A much greater threat to bird species than oil spills is oil-field waste pits. These pits hold oil-containing water that is pumped out of the ground during oil extraction. In "Contaminant Issues—Oil Field Waste Pits" (2013, http://www.fws.gov/mountain-prairie/contaminants/contaminants1a.html), the USFWS notes that an estimated 500,000 to 1 million birds per year die in these pits and similar oil field wastewater facilities, such as lagoons. Birds mistake the pits and lagoons for freshwater and become oiled when they light on the water or dive into it after prey. The main avian victims are waterfowl. Nevertheless, songbirds and raptors, such as hawks and owls, are also killed. It is unknown how many endangered and threatened species might be among the victims.

FIGURE 8.6

An oil-contaminated guillemot is cleaned after a spill. ©*Corepics/Shutterstock.com.*

Invasive Species

Invasive species have damaged bird populations in some parts of the world, particularly those that occupy islands. Guam's unique bird fauna has been all but wiped out by the brown tree snake, an invasive species that probably arrived in ship cargo decades ago. According to the National Zoo, in the fact sheet "Where Have the Birds of Guam Gone?" (2016, http://nationalzoo.si.edu/Animals/Birds/Facts/fact-guambirds.cfm), as many as 14,000 snakes may live in a single square mile (2.6 sq km) in some Guam forest habitats. Nine out of 18 bird species have already gone extinct on Guam, including the Guam flycatcher, the Rufus fantail, the white-throated ground dove, and the cardinal honeyeater. Several other Guam bird species are close to extinction. Many of these birds are or were unique to Guam. Measures have been implemented to try to keep this destructive snake from invading other islands, including careful inspection of all cargo arriving from Guam. The removal of the brown tree snake in select habitat areas on Guam (which is a high-effort project, requiring the constant trapping of snakes) allowed the reintroduction of one bird, the flightless Guam rail, in 1998. The Guam rail had gone extinct in the wild, but a population is being maintained in captivity.

Other particularly destructive invasive species include several that are associated with humans, including cats, dogs, and rats, which often prey on birds and their eggs.

BACK FROM THE BRINK: SUCCESS STORIES

As shown in Table 2.7 and Table 2.8 in Chapter 2, 10 U.S. and foreign bird species under ESA protection have recovered (i.e., been delisted). Four of the species—the Palau fantail flycatcher, the Palau ground dove, the Palau owl, and the Tinian (old world flycatcher) monarch—inhabit the small islands of Palau and Tinian, respectively, in the Pacific Ocean. All four species were listed in 1970. The Palau species were delisted in 1985 and the Tinian species in 2004.

Bald Eagles

The bald eagle is a raptor with special emphasis in the United States. (See Figure 8.7.) A symbol of honor, courage, nobility, and independence (eagles do not fly in flocks), the bald eagle is found only in North America, and its image is engraved on the official seal of the United States of America.

Bald eagles came dangerously close to extinction during the 20th century, largely due to DDT, which was introduced in 1947. Two decades later the bird was listed as endangered in 1967. (See Table 2.1 in Chapter 2.) Populations started to recover with the banning of DDT in 1972. The species also benefited from habitat protection

FIGURE 8.7

The bald eagle was once endangered because of habitat destruction and pollution by pesticides, such as DDT. Its populations have recovered with protection and a ban on DDT. ©nialat/Shutterstock.com.

and attempts to clean up water pollution. In 1995 the bald eagle's status under the ESA was changed from endangered to threatened. In 1999 the species was proposed for delisting. A year later all delisting criteria contained in species recovery plans were achieved. However, the USFWS was slow to complete the delisting process. In June 2007 the bald eagle was finally delisted because of recovery. At that time the USFWS estimated there were 9,789 nesting pairs of the bird in the United States.

Peregrine Falcons

Many falcon species have declined with the spread of humans. Like other predatory species, falcons were often hunted, either for sport or because they were considered a threat to chickens or livestock. They also declined because of being exposed to DDT. In 1970 the American peregrine falcon (see Figure 8.8) and the arctic peregrine falcon were listed as endangered. Both subspecies ranged throughout the United States.

The recovery of the peregrine falcons was made possible by the banning of DDT and by the establishment of special captive breeding centers on several continents. The arctic peregrine falcon and the American peregrine falcon were delisted in 1994 and 1999, respectively.

Aleutian Canada Geese

Aleutian Canada geese inhabit the Aleutian Islands off the coast of Alaska and migrate back and forth to the Northern California and Oregon coasts. (See Figure 8.9.) The species was first listed as endangered in 1967. (See Table 2.1 in Chapter 2.) It was officially delisted in 2001. In the delisting notice (March 20, 2001, http://www.fws.gov/policy/library/66fr15643.html), the USFWS indicates that the population increased to about 37,000 individuals in 2000 from fewer than 1,000 individuals during the 1960s. The conservation efforts that led to recovery

FIGURE 8.8

FIGURE 8.9

Peregrine falcon. ©*Cheryl Ann Quigley/Shutterstock.com.*

Aleutian Canada goose. ©*U.S. Fish and Wildlife Service.*

included captive breeding, removal of foxes that preyed on the birds, and relocation and reintroduction of geese to unoccupied islands.

Brown Pelicans

The brown pelican is a coastal bird found in the United States along the Atlantic coast from Virginia southward, along the Gulf coast in Alabama, Louisiana, and Texas, and along the Pacific coast. (See Figure 8.10.) Its brownish-gray feathers were highly sought after for women's hats during the late 1800s and early 1900s. As a result, the species underwent a dramatic decline. Its numbers were further decimated following World War I (1914–1918), when fishermen killed thousands of the birds, claiming they were competing for food fish. The use of DDT over the following decades took a huge toll on the birds by causing severe weakening of the shells of their eggs.

In 1970 the brown pelican was listed as endangered throughout its range. By the mid-1980s DDT restrictions

and conservation efforts had allowed the Atlantic coast population of the species to rebound. In 1985 that population was delisted because of recovery. In 2009 the brown pelican throughout the remainder of the United States was also delisted.

FOREIGN SPECIES OF ENDANGERED AND THREATENED BIRDS

The IUCN indicates in *Red List of Threatened Species Version 2015.4* that in 2015 a total of 1,375 bird species were considered threatened out of 10,424 evaluated and known species.

As of February 2016, there were 238 totally foreign species of birds listed under the ESA. (See Table 8.3.) Categories include various species, such as cranes, eagles, owls, parakeets, parrots, pheasants, pigeons, and warblers.

FIGURE 8.10

Brown pelican

SOURCE: Robert Savannah, artist, "Brown Pelicans," in *Line Art (Drawings)*, U.S. Department of the Interior, U.S. Fish and Wildlife Service, undated, http://www.fws.gov/pictures/lineart/bobsavannah/brownpelicans.html (accessed February 17, 2016)

TABLE 8.3

Foreign endangered and threatened bird species, February 2016

Common name	Scientific name	Federal listing status*	Current distribution (if available)
Abbott's booby	Papasula (= Sula) abbotti	E	—
African penguin	Spheniscus demersus	E	Atlantic Ocean—South Africa, Namibia
Alaotra grebe	Tachybaptus rufolavatus	E	Madagascar
Aldabra warbler (old world warbler)	Nesillas aldabranus	E	Indian Ocean—Seychelles (Aldabra Island)
Algerian nuthatch	Sitta ledanti	E	Algeria
Amsterdam albatross	Diomedia amsterdamensis	E	Indian Ocean—Amsterdam Island
Andean condor	Vultur gryphus	E	Colombia to Chile and Argentina
Andean flamingo	Phoenicoparrus andinus	E	Argentina, Bolivia, Chile, Peru
Andrew's frigatebird	Fregata andrewsi	E	East Indian Ocean
Anjouan Island sparrowhawk	Accipiter francesii pusillus	E	Indian Ocean—Comoros Islands
Anjouan scops owl	Otus rutilus capnodes	E	Indian Ocean—Comoro Island
Arabian ostrich	Struthio camelus syriacus	E	Saudi Arabia, Jordan
Ash-breasted tit-tyrant	Anairetes alpinus	E	Bolivia, Peru
Atitlan grebe	Podilymbus gigas	E	Guatemala
Audouin's gull	Larus audouinii	E	Mediterranean Sea
Aukland Island rail	Rallus pectoralis muelleri	E	New Zealand
Azores wood pigeon	Columba palumbus azorica	E	Portugal (Azores)
Bahaman or Cuban parrot	Amazona leucocephala	E	West Indies—Cuba, Bahamas, Caymans
Banded cotinga	Cotinga maculata	E	Brazil
Banded wattle-eye	Platysteira laticincta	E	Cameroon
Bannerman's turaco	Tauraco bannermani	E	—
Barbados yellow warbler (=wood)	Dendroica petechia petechia	E	West Indies—Barbados
Bar-tailed pheasant	Syrmaticus humaie	E	Myanmar (Burma), China
Bermuda petrel	Pterodroma cahow	E	North Atlantic Ocean—Bermuda
Black hooded (black-headed) antwren	Formicivora erythronotos	E	Brazil
Black stilt	Himantopus novaezelandiae	E	New Zealand
black-breasted puffleg	Eriocnemis nigrivestis	E	South America, Ecuador
Black-fronted piping-guan	Pipile jacutinga	E	Argentina
Black-necked crane	Grus nigricollis	E	China (Tibet)
Blue-billed curassow	Crax alberti	E	—
Blue-throated (=ochre-marked) parakeet	Pyrrhura cruentata	E	Brazil
Blue-throated macaw	Ara glaucogularis	E	—
Blyth's tragopan pheasant	Tragopan blythii	E	Myanmar (Burma), India, China
Brazillian merganser	Mergus octosetaceus	E	Paraguay, Brazil, Argentina
Brown eared pheasant	Crossoptilon mantchuricum	E	China
Brown-banded antpitta	Grallaria milleri	E	—
Cabot's tragopan pheasant	Tragopan caboti	E	China
Caerulean Paradise flycatcher	Eutrichomyias rowleyi	E	Indonesia
Campbell Island flightless teal	Anas aucklandica nesiotis	E	New Zealand—Campbell Island
Canarian black oystercatcher	Haematopus meadewaldoi	E	Atlantic Ocean Spain (Canary Islands)
Cantabrian capercaillie	Tetrao urogallus cantabricus	E	—
Cauca guan	Penelope perspicax	E	—
Cebu black shama (thrush)	Copsychus niger cebuensis	E	Philippines
Chatham Island petrel	Pterodroma axillaris	E	Pacific Ocean—New Zealand (Chatham Islands)
Chatham Island pigeon	Hemiphaga novaeseelandiae chathamensis	E	New Zealand
Chatham Island robin	Petroica traversi	E	New Zealand
Cheer pheasant	Catreus wallichii	E	Pakistan, Nepal, India
Cherry-throated tanager	Nemosia rourei	E	—
Chilean woodstar	Eulidia yarrellii	E	Chile, Peru
Chinese egret	Egretta eulophotes	E	Korea, China
Chinese monal pheasant	Lophophorus lhuysii	E	China
Christmas Island goshawk	Accipiter fasciatus natalis	E	Indian Ocean—Christmas Island
Clarke's weaver	Ploceus golandi	E	Kenya
Cloven-feathered dove	Drepanoptila holosericea	E	Southwest Pacific Ocean—New Caledonia
Cuba hook-billed kite	Chondrohierax uncinatus wilsonii	E	West Indies—Cuba
Cuba sandhill crane	Grus canadensis nesiotes	E	West Indies—Cuba
Dappled mountain robin	Arcanator orostruthus	T	Tanzania, Mozambique
Djibouti francolin	Francolinus ochropectus	E	Djibouti
Edward's pheasant	Lophura edwardsi	E	Vietnam
Eiao Marquesas reed-warbler	Acrocephalus percernis aquilonis	E	French Polynesian Marquesas Archipelago (Eiao Island)
Elliot's pheasant	Syrmaticus ellioti	E	China
erect-crested penguin	Eudyptes sclateri	T	New Zealand, Bounty Islands and Antipodes Islands
Esmeraldas woodstar	Chaetocercus berlepschi	E	—
Euler's flycatcher	Empidonax euleri johnstonei	E	West Indies—Grenada
Eurasian peregrine falcon	Falco peregrinus peregrinus	E	Europe, Eurasia south to Africa and Mideast
Eyrean grasswren (flycatcher)	Amytornis goyderi	E	Australia
Fiji petrel	Pseudobulweria macgillivrayi	E	Pacific Ocean—Fiji (Gau Island)
fiordland crested penguin	Eudyptes pachyrhynchus	T	New Zealand, South Island and offshore Islands
Floreana tree-finch	Camarhynchus pauper	E	—
Forbes' parakeet	Cyanoramphus auriceps forbesi	E	New Zealand

TABLE 8.3

Foreign endangered and threatened bird species, February 2016 [CONTINUED]

Common name	Scientific name	Federal listing status*	Current distribution (if available)
Freira	*Pterodroma madeira*	E	Portugal (Madeira Island)
Fringe-backed fire-eye	*Pyriglena atra*	E	Brazil
Galapagos hawk	*Buteo galapagoensis*	E	Ecuador (Galapagos Islands)
Galapagos penguin	*Spheniscus mendiculus*	E	Ecuador (Galapagos Islands)
Galapagos petrel	*Pterodroma phaeopygia*	T	Pacific Ocean—Ecuador (Galapagos Islands)
Giant ibis	*Pseudibis gigantea*	E	Vietnam, Thailand, Cambodia, Lao PDR
Giant scops owl	*Mimizuku (=Otus) gurneyi*	E	Philippines: Marinduque and Mindanao Island
Glaucous macaw	*Anodorhynchus glaucus*	E	Uruguay, Paraguay, Brazil
Golden parakeet	*Aratinga guarouba*	E	Brazil
Golden-shouldered parakeet	*Psephotus chrysopterygius*	E	Australia
Gorgeted wood-quail	*Odontophorus strophium*	E	—
Great green macaw	*Ara ambiguus*	E	—
Great Indian bustard	*Ardeotis (=Choriotis) nigriceps*	E	Pakistan, India
Greater adjutant	*Leptoptilos dubius*	E	—
Greenland white-tailed eagle	*Haliaeetus albicilla groenlandicus*	E	Greenland and adjacent Atlantic Islands
Grenada gray-fronted dove	*Leptotila rufaxilla wellsi*	E	West Indies—Grenada
Grenada hook-billed kite	*Chondrohierax uncinatus mirus*	E	West Indies—Grenada
Grey-necked rockfowl	*Picathartes oreas*	E	Gabon, Cameroon
Ground parrot	*Pezoporus wallicus*	E	Australia
Guadeloupe house wren	*Troglodytes aedon guadeloupensis*	E	West Indies—Guadeloupe
Gurney's pitta	*Pitta gurneyi*	E	Thailand, Myanmar
Harpy eagle	*Harpia harpyja*	E	Mexico south to Argentina
Heinroth's shearwater	*Puffinus heinrothi*	T	Pacific Ocean—Papua New Guinea (Bougainville Island), Solomon Islands (Kolom—bangara and Rendova)
Helmeted honeyeater	*Lichenostomus melanops cassidix (=Meliphaga c.)*	E	Australia
Helmeted hornbill	*Buceros (=Rhinoplax) vigil*	E	Thailand, Malaysia
Honduran emerald hummingbird	*Amazilia luciae*	E	—
Hooded crane	*Grus monacha*	E	Japan, Russia; Japan, former U.S.S.R.
Hook-billed hermit (hummingbird)	*Ramphodon (=Glaucis) dohrnii*	E	Brazil
Horned guan	*Oreophasis derbianus*	E	Mexico, Guatemala
Humboldt penguin	*Spheniscus humboldti*	T	Eastern Pacific Ocean—Peru, Chile
Ibadan malimbe	*Malimbus ibadanensis*	E	Nigeria
Imperial parrot	*Amazona imperialis*	E	West Indies—Dominica
Imperial pheasant	*Lophura imperialis*	E	Vietnam
Imperial woodpecker	*Campephilus imperialis*	E	Mexico
Indigo macaw	*Anodorhynchus leari*	E	Brazil
Japanese crane	*Grus japonensis*	E	China, Japan, North Korea, South Korea, Russia
Japanese crested ibis	*Nipponia nippon*	E	China, Japan, former U.S.S.R., North Korea, South Korea
Jerdon's courser	*Rhinoptilus bitorquatus*	E	India
Junin grebe	*Podiceps taczanowskii*	E	Peru
Junin rail	*Laterallus tuerosi*	E	Peru
Kaempfer's tody-tyrant	*Hemitriccus kaempferi*	E	Brazil
Kagu	*Rhynochetos jubatus*	E	South Pacific Ocean—New Caledonia
Kakapo	*Strigops habroptilus*	E	New Zealand
Koch's pitta	*Pitta kochi*	E	Philippines
Kokako (wattlebird)	*Callaeas cinerea*	E	New Zealand
Lesser rhea (incl. Darwin's)	*Rhea (=Pterocnemia) pennata*	E	Uruguay, Peru, Bolivia, Argentina
Little blue macaw	*Cyanopsitta spixii*	E	Brazil
Long-legged warbler	*Trichocichla rufa*	E	—
Long-tailed ground roller	*Uratelornis chimaera*	E	Malagasy Republic (Madagascar)
Lord Howe wood rail	*Gallirallus (=Tricholimnas) sylvestris*	E	Australia (Lord Howe Island)
Madagascar pochard	*Aythya innotata*	E	Madagascar
Madagascar red owl	*Tyto soumagnei*	E	Madagascar
Madagascar sea eagle	*Haliaeetus vociferoides*	E	Madagascar
Madagascar serpent eagle	*Eutriorchis astur*	E	Madagascar
Magenta petrel	*Pterodroma magentae*	E	Pacific Ocean—New Zealand (Chatham Islands)
Maleo megapode	*Macrocephalon maleo*	E	Indonesia (Celebes)
Margaretta's hermit	*Phaethornis malaris margarettae*	E	Brazil
Marquesas pigeon	*Ducula galeata*	E	French Polynesia
Martinique trembler (thrasher)	*Cinclocerthia ruficauda gutturalis*	E	—
Marungu sunbird	*Nectarinia prigoginei*	E	—
Mascarene black petrel	*Pterodroma aterrima*	E	Indian Ocean—Mauritius (Reunion Island)
Mauritius cuckoo-shrike	*Coquus typicus*	E	Indian Ocean—Mauritius
Mauritius fody	*Foudia rubra*	E	Indian Ocean—Mauritius
Mauritius kestrel	*Falco punctatus*	E	Indian Ocean—Mauritius
Mauritius olivaceous bulbul	*Hypsipetes borbonicus olivaceus*	E	Indian Ocean—Mauritius
Mauritius parakeet	*Psittacula echo*	E	Indian Ocean—Mauritius
Merriam's Montezuma quail	*Cyrtonyx montezumae merriami*	E	Mexico (Vera Cruz)
Mikado pheasant	*Syrmaticus mikado*	E	Taiwan
Military macaw	*Ara militaris*	E	—
Mindoro imperial (=zone-tailed) pigeon	*Ducula mindorensis*	E	Philippines

Common name	Scientific name	Federal listing status*	Current distribution (if available)
Morden's owlet	*Otus ireneae*	E	Kenya
New Zealand bushwren	*Xenicus longipes*	E	New Zealand
New Zealand shore plover	*Thinornis novaeseelandiae*	E	New Zealand
New Zealand thrush (wattlebird)	*Turnagra capensis*	E	—
Night (=Australian) parrot	*Geopsittacus occidentalis*	E	Australia
Noisy scrub-bird	*Atrichornis clamosus*	E	Australia
Nordmann's greenshank	*Tringa guttifer*	E	Former U.S.S.R., Japan south to Malaya, Borneo
Norfolk Island parakeet	*Cyanoramphus cookii (= novaezelandiae c.)*	E	Australia (Norfolk Island)
Norfolk Island white-eye	*Zosterops albogularis*	E	Indian Ocean—Norfolk Island
Northern bald ibis	*Geronticus eremita*	E	Southern Europe, Southwestern Asia, Northern Africa
Orange-bellied parakeet	*Neophema chrysogaster*	E	Australia
Oriental white stork	*Ciconia boyciana (= ciconia b.)*	E	China, Japan, North Korea, South Korea, former U.S.S.R.
Palawan peacock pheasant	*Polyplectron emphanum*	E	Philippines
Paradise parakeet	*Psephotus pulcherrimus*	E	Australia
Peruvian plantcutter	*Phytotoma raimondii*	E	Peru
Philippine cockatoo	*Cacatua haematuropygia*	E	—
Philippine eagle	*Pithecophaga jefferyi*	E	Philippines
Pink pigeon	*Columba mayeri*	E	Indian Ocean—Mauritius
Pink-headed duck	*Rhodonessa caryophyllacea*	E	India
Plain wanderer (=collared-hemipode)	*Pedionomous torquatus*	E	Australia
Pollen's vanga	*Xenopirostris polleni*	T	Madagascar
Ponape greater white-eye	*Rukia longirostra*	E	FM; Caroline Islands (FSM), Western Pacific
Ponape mountain starling	*Aplonis pelzelni*	E	FM; Caroline Islands (FSM), Western Pacific
Queen Charlotte goshawk	*Accipiter gentilis laingi*	T	That portion of British Columbia that includes Vancouver Island and its surrounding islands, the mainland coast west of the crest of the Coast Range and adjacent islands, and the Queen Charlotte Islands
Raso lark	*Alauda razae*	E	Atlantic Ocean Cape Verde (Raso Island)
Razor-billed curassow	*Mitu mitu mitu*	E	Brazil (Eastern)
Red siskin	*Carduelis cucullata*	E	South America
Red-billed curassow	*Crax blumenbachii*	E	Brazil
Red-browed parrot	*Amazona rhodocorytha*	E	Brazil
Red-capped parrot	*Pionopsitta pileata*	E	Brazil
Red-faced malkoha (cuckoo)	*Phaenicophaeus pyrrhocephalus*	E	Sri Lanka
Red-necked parrot	*Amazona arausiaca*	E	West Indies—Dominica
Red-spectacled parrot	*Amazona pretrei pretrei*	E	Brazil, Argentina
Red-tailed parrot	*Amazona brasiliensis*	E	Brazil
Relict gull	*Larus relictus*	E	India, China
Resplendent quetzel	*Pharomachrus mocinno*	E	Mexico to Panama
Reunion cuckoo-shrike	*Coquus newtoni*	E	Indian Ocean—Reunion
Rodrigues fody	*Foudia flavicans*	E	Indian Ocean—Mauritius (Rodrigues Island)
Rodrigues warbler (old world warbler)	*Bebrornis rodericanus*	E	Mauritius (Rodrigues Islands)
Rothschild's starling (myna)	*Leucopsar rothschildi*	E	Indonesia (Bali)
Royal cinclodes	*Cinclodes aricomae*	E	Bolivia, Peru
Salmon-crested cockatoo	*Cacatua moluccensis*	T	Seram, Haruku, Saparua, and Ambon, Indonesia
Sao Miguel bullfinch (finch)	*Pyrrhula pyrrhula murina*	E	Eastern Atlantic Ocean (Azores), Portugal; Portugal (Azores)
Scarlet-breasted robin (flycatcher)	*Petroica multicolor multicolor*	E	Australia (Norfolk Island)
Scarlet-chested parakeet	*Neophema splendida*	E	Australia
Sclater's monal pheasant	*Lophophorus sclateri*	E	Myanmar (Burma), India, China
Semper's warbler (=wood)	*Leucopeza semperi*	E	West Indies—Saint Lucia
Seychelles fody (weaver-finch)	*Foudia sechellarum*	E	Indian Ocean—Seychelles
Seychelles kestrel	*Falco araea*	E	Indian Ocean—Seychelles Islands
Seychelles lesser vasa parrot	*Coracopsis nigra barklyi*	E	Indian Ocean—Seychelles (Praslin Island)
Seychelles magpie-robin (thrush)	*Copsychus sechellarum*	E	Indian Ocean—Seychelles Islands
Seychelles paradise flycatcher	*Terpsiphone corvina*	E	Indian Ocean—Seychelles
Seychelles scops owl	*Otus magicus (= insularis) insularis*	E	Indian Ocean—Seychelles Islands
Seychelles turtle dove	*Streptopelia picturata rostrata*	E	—
Seychelles warbler (old world warbler)	*Bebrornis sechellensis*	E	Indian Ocean—Seychelles Island
Seychelles white-eye	*Zosterops modesta*	E	Indian Ocean—Seychelles
Siberian white crane	*Grus leucogeranus*	E	Former U.S.S.R. (Siberia) to India, including Iran and China
Slender-billed curlew	*Numenius tenuirostris*	E	—
Slender-billed grackle	*Quisicalus palustris*	E	Mexico
Socorro mockingbird	*Mimus graysoni*	E	Mexico
Solitary tinamou	*Tinamus solitarius*	E	—
Southeastern rufous-vented ground cuckoo	*Neomorphus geoffroyi dulcis*	E	Brazil
Southern rockhopper penguin	*Eudyptes chrysocome*	T	New Zealand—Australia DPS, associated with the Campbell Plateau and Macquarie Island
Spanish imperial eagle	*Aquila heliaca adalberti*	E	Spain, Morocco, Algeria
St. Vincent parrot	*Amazona guildingii*	E	West Indies—St. Vincent
St. Lucia Forest thrush	*Cichlherminia iherminieri santaeluciae*	E	West Indies—St. Lucia
St. Lucia house wren	*Troglodytes aedon mesoleucus*	E	West Indies—Saint Lucia

TABLE 8.3

Foreign endangered and threatened bird species, February 2016 [CONTINUED]

Common name	Scientific name	Federal listing status*	Current distribution (if available)
St. Lucia parrot	*Amazona versicolor*	E	West Indies—St. Lucia
Swinhoe's pheasant	*Lophura swinhoii*	E	Taiwan
Tahiti flycatcher	*Pomarea nigra*	E	South Pacific Ocean—Tahiti
Taita thrush	*Turdus olivaceus helleri*	E	—
Thyolo alethe	*Alethe choloensis*	E	Mozambique, Malawi
Trinidad white-headed curassow	*Pipile pipile pipile*	E	West Indies—Trinidad
Tristam's woodpecker	*Dryocopus javensis richardsi*	E	Korea
Turquoise parakeet	*Neophema pulchella*	E	Australia
Ulugura bush-shrike	*Malaconotus alius*	T	Tanzania
Van Dam's vanga	*Xenopirostris damii*	T	Madagascar
Vinaceous-breasted parrot	*Amazona vinacea*	E	Brazil
West African ostrich	*Struthio camelus spatzi*	E	Spanish Sahara
Western bristlebird	*Dasyornis longirostris (= brachypterus l.)*	E	Australia
Western rufous bristlebird	*Dasyornis broadbenti littoralis*	E	Australia
Western tragopan pheasant	*Tragopan melanocephalus*	E	Pakistan, India
Western whipbird	*Psophodes nigrogularis*	E	Australia
White cockatoo	*Cacatua alba*	T	—
White eared pheasant	*Crossoptilon crossoptilon*	E	China (Tibet), India
White-breasted guineafowl	*Agelastes meleagrides*	T	West Africa
White-breasted thrasher	*Ramphocinclus brachyurus*	E	—
White-browed tit-spinetail	*Leptasthenura xenothorax*	E	Peru
White-flippered penguin	*Eudyptula albosignata*	T	New Zealand, South Island
White-naped crane	*Grus vipio*	E	Mongolia
White-necked rockfowl	*Picathartes gymnocephalus*	E	Africa: Togo to Sierra Leone
White-tailed laurel pigeon	*Columba junoniae*	T	Spain (Canary Islands)
White-winged cotinga	*Xipholena atropurpurea*	E	Brazil
White-winged guan	*Penelope albipennis*	E	Peru
White-winged wood duck	*Cairina scutulata*	E	Thailand, Malaysia, Indonesia, India
Yellow-billed parrot	*Amazona collaria*	T	—
Yellow-crested cockatoo	*Cacatua sulphurea*	E	—
Yellow-eyed penguin	*Megadyptes antipodes*	T	New Zealand, South Island and offshore Islands

*E = Endangered. T = Threatened.

SOURCE: Adapted from "Generate Species List," in *Environmental Conservation Online System Species Reports*, U.S. Department of the Interior, U.S. Fish and Wildlife Service, February 2016, http://ecos.fws.gov/tess_public/pub/adHocSpeciesForm.jsp (accessed February 17, 2016)

CHAPTER 9

INSECTS AND SPIDERS

Insects are members of the Animalia kingdom and belong to the phylum Arthropoda, along with crustaceans. There are many classes of arthropods, including insects and arachnids. Both are invertebrates, but insects have six legs, whereas arachnids have eight legs. The arachnids include spiders, mites, ticks, scorpions, and harvestmen.

Insects are the most diverse group in the animal kingdom. Scientists are not certain of the total number of insect species; estimates range as high as 30 million species. The International Union for Conservation of Nature (IUCN) indicates in *Red List of Threatened Species Version 2015.4* (November 2015, http://www.iucnredlist.org/about/summary-statistics) that 1 million of the species have been described. Insects have not been as thoroughly studied as the vertebrate groups, so there are likely to be many endangered insects whose state is unknown.

With the exception of butterflies, which are esteemed for their beauty, many insects and arachnids are not appreciated by humans. However, the creatures play important roles in nature, and their extinction would have negative impacts on many ecosystems and society in general. One of the most beneficial activities is pollination. Bees, wasps, flies, butterflies, moths, and beetles help plants reproduce. In "A Class of Distinction" (2007, http://www.cals.ncsu.edu/course/ent425/text01/impact1.html), John R. Meyer calls insects "allies" to humans, noting "we depend on them to keep the natural environment clean and productive." He goes on to state, "They have shaped human cultures and civilizations in countless ways, they supply unique natural products, they regulate the population densities of many potential pest species, they dispose of our wastes, bury the dead, and recycle organic nutrients. Indeed, we seldom stop to consider what life would be like without insects and how much we depend on them for our very survival."

Insects and arachnids, like many other species, suffer from diminished habitat as a result of encroaching development, industrialization, changing land use patterns, and invasive species.

THREATENED AND ENDANGERED INSECT SPECIES IN THE UNITED STATES

As of February 2016, 78 U.S. insect species were listed under the Endangered Species Act (ESA). (See Table 9.1.) The predominant species types include beetles, butterflies, and pomace flies. Other listed insects include damselflies, flies, moths, skippers, a dragonfly, a grasshopper, and a naucorid. (See Figure 9.1.) Most of the listed insects are endangered, and nearly all have recovery plans in place.

According to the U.S. Fish and Wildlife Service (USFWS), most of the imperiled insects are found exclusively in either California, Hawaii, or Texas.

Table 9.2 shows the 10 insect species with the highest expenditures under the ESA during fiscal year (FY) 2014. Nearly $9.9 million was spent on these species.

During the late 20th century, reports of mass deaths of honeybees began rising in the United States. North America has no native honeybee species. Honeybees were imported to the colonies from Europe during the 1600s and over the centuries have become "farmed" animals that live in human-made and monitored hives. Honeybees are extensively bred and sold as commercial products. As such, they do not qualify for protection under the ESA.

The U.S. Department of Agriculture explains in "Honey Bee Health and Colony Collapse Disorder" (November 5, 2015, http://www.ars.usda.gov/News/docs.htm?docid=15572) that the high death rate among honeybees is blamed on a variety of problems, including viruses and other pathogens, parasites, invasive pests, malnutrition, and pesticide exposure. It is concerning because honeybees are major pollinators of the nation's agricultural crops. Native wild bees also do some of this

TABLE 9.1

Endangered and threatened insect species, February 2016

Common name	Scientific name	Federal listing status[a]	U.S. or U.S./foreign listed	Recovery plan date	Recovery plan stage[b]
[no common name] beetle	*Rhadine exilis*	E	US	10/04/11	F
[no common name] beetle	*Rhadine infernalis*	E	US	10/04/11	F
[Unnamed] pomace fly	*Drosophila aglaia*	E	US	None	—
[Unnamed] pomace fly	*Drosophila differens*	E	US	None	—
[Unnamed] pomace fly	*Drosophila hemipeza*	E	US	None	—
[Unnamed] pomace fly	*Drosophila heteroneura*	E	US	None	—
[Unnamed] pomace fly	*Drosophila montgomeryi*	E	US	None	—
[Unnamed] pomace fly	*Drosophila mulli*	T	US	None	—
[Unnamed] pomace fly	*Drosophila musaphilia*	E	US	None	—
[Unnamed] pomace fly	*Drosophila neoclavisetae*	E	US	None	—
[Unnamed] pomace fly	*Drosophila obatai*	E	US	None	—
[Unnamed] pomace fly	*Drosophila ochrobasis*	E	US	None	—
[Unnamed] pomace fly	*Drosophila substenoptera*	E	US	None	—
[Unnamed] pomace fly	*Drosophila tarphytrichia*	E	US	None	—
American burying beetle	*Nicrophorus americanus*	E; EXPN	US/foreign	09/27/91	F
Ash Meadows naucorid	*Ambrysus amargosus*	T	US	09/28/90	F
Bartram's hairstreak butterfly	*Strymon acis bartrami*	E	US	None	—
Bay checkerspot butterfly	*Euphydryas editha bayensis*	T	US	09/30/98	F
Behren's silverspot butterfly	*Speyeria zerene behrensii*	E	US	01/20/04	D
Blackburn's sphinx moth	*Manduca blackburni*	E	US	09/28/05	F
Blackline Hawaiian damselfly	*Megalagrion nigrohamatum nigrolineatum*	E	US	None	—
Callippe silverspot butterfly	*Speyeria callippe callippe*	E	US	None	—
Carson wandering skipper	*Pseudocopaeodes eunus obscurus*	E	US	09/13/07	F
Casey's June beetle	*Dinacoma caseyi*	E	US	04/01/13	O
Cassius blue butterfly	*Leptotes cassius theonus*	SAT	US	None	—
Ceraunus blue butterfly	*Hemiargus ceraunus antibubastus*	SAT	US	None	—
Coffin Cave mold beetle	*Batrisodes texanus*	E	US	08/25/94	F
Comal Springs dryopid beetle	*Stygoparnus comalensis*	E	US	02/14/96	RF(1)
Comal Springs riffle beetle	*Heterelmis comalensis*	E	US	02/14/96	RF(1)
Crimson Hawaiian damselfly	*Megalagrion leptodemas*	E	US	None	—
Dakota skipper	*Hesperia dacotae*	T	US/foreign	None	—
Delhi Sands flower-loving fly	*Rhaphiomidas terminatus abdominalis*	E	US	09/14/97	F
Delta green ground beetle	*Elaphrus viridis*	T	US	03/07/06	F
El Segundo blue butterfly	*Euphilotes battoides allyni*	E	US	09/28/98	F
Fender's blue butterfly	*Icaricia icarioides fenderi*	E	US	06/29/10	F
Florida leafwing butterfly	*Anaea troglodyta floridalis*	E	US	None	—
Flying earwig Hawaiian damselfly	*Megalagrion nesiotes*	E	US	None	—
Hawaiian picture-wing fly	*Drosophila digressa*	E	US	None	—
Hawaiian picture-wing fly	*Drosophila sharpi*	E	US	None	—
Helotes mold beetle	*Batrisodes venyivi*	E	US	10/04/11	F
Hine's emerald dragonfly	*Somatochlora hineana*	E	US	09/27/01	F
Hungerford's crawling water beetle	*Brychius hungerfordi*	E	US/foreign	09/28/06	F
Karner blue butterfly	*Lycaeides melissa samuelis*	E	US/foreign	09/19/03	F
Kern primrose sphinx moth	*Euproserpinus euterpe*	T	US	02/08/84	F
Kretschmarr Cave mold beetle	*Texamaurops reddelli*	E	US	08/25/94	F
Laguna Mountains skipper	*Pyrgus ruralis lagunae*	E	US	01/26/16	D
Lange's metalmark butterfly	*Apodemia mormo langei*	E	US	04/25/84	RF(1)
Lotis blue butterfly	*Lycaeides argyrognomon lotis*	E	US	12/26/85	F
Mariana eight-spot butterfly	*Hypolimnas octocula mariannensis*	E	US	None	—
Mariana wandering butterfly	*Vagrans egistina*	E	US	None	—
Miami blue butterfly	*Cyclargus (= Hemiargus) thomasi bethunebakeri*	E	US	None	—
Mission blue butterfly	*Icaricia icarioides missionensis*	E	US	10/10/84	F
Mitchell's satyr butterfly	*Neonympha mitchellii mitchellii*	E	US	04/02/98	F
Mount Charleston blue butterfly	*Icaricia (Plebejus) shasta charlestonensis*	E	US	None	—
Mount Hermon June beetle	*Polyphylla barbata*	E	US	09/28/98	F
Myrtle's silverspot butterfly	*Speyeria zerene myrtleae*	E	US	09/29/98	F
Nickerbean blue butterfly	*Cyclargus ammon*	SAT	US	None	—
Northeastern beach tiger beetle	*Cicindela dorsalis dorsalis*	T	US	09/29/94	F
Oceanic Hawaiian damselfly	*Megalagrion oceanicum*	E	US	None	—
Ohlone tiger beetle	*Cicindela ohlone*	E	US	09/28/98	F
Oregon silverspot butterfly	*Speyeria zerene hippolyta*	T	US	08/22/01	RF(1)
Pacific Hawaiian damselfly	*Megalagrion pacificum*	E	US	None	—
Palos Verdes blue butterfly	*Glaucopsyche lygdamus palosverdesensis*	E	US	01/19/84	F
Pawnee montane skipper	*Hesperia leonardus montana*	T	US	09/21/98	F
Poweshiek skipperling	*Oarisma poweshiek*	E	US	None	—
Puritan tiger beetle	*Cicindela puritana*	T	US	09/29/93	F
Quino checkerspot butterfly	*Euphydryas editha quino (= E. e. wrighti)*	E	US/foreign	09/17/03	F
Rota blue damselfly	*Ischnura luta*	E	US	None	—
Saint Francis' satyr butterfly	*Neonympha mitchellii francisci*	E	US	04/23/96	F
Salt Creek tiger beetle	*Cicindela nevadica lincolniana*	E	US	07/16/15	D

important work. They include bumblebees, carpenter bees, mud bees, sweat bees, and thousands of other species.

There is growing worry about the health of wild bee populations. The Xerces Society is a conservation society

TABLE 9.1

Endangered and threatened insect species, February 2016 [CONTINUED]

Common name	Scientific name	Federal listing status[a]	U.S. or U.S./foreign listed	Recovery plan date	Recovery plan stage[b]
San Bruno elfin butterfly	*Callophrys mossii bayensis*	E	US	10/10/84	F
Schaus swallowtail butterfly	*Heraclides aristodemus ponceanus*	E	US	05/18/99	F
Smith's blue butterfly	*Euphilotes enoptes smithi*	E	US	11/09/84	F
Taylor's (=whulge) checkerspot	*Euphydryas editha taylori*	E	US	None	—
Tooth Cave ground beetle	*Rhadine persephone*	E	US	08/25/94	F
Uncompahgre fritillary butterfly	*Boloria acrocnema*	E	US	03/17/94	F
Valley elderberry longhorn beetle	*Desmocerus californicus dimorphus*	T	US	06/28/84	F
Zayante band-winged grasshopper	*Trimerotropis infantilis*	E	US	09/28/98	F

[a]E = Endangered. T = Threatened. EXPN = Experimental population, non-essential. SAT = Similarity in appearance to a threatened taxon.
[b]D = Draft. F = Final. RF = Final revision. O = Other.

SOURCE: Adapted from "Generate Species List," in *Environmental Conservation Online System Species Reports*, U.S. Department of the Interior, U.S. Fish and Wildlife Service, February 2016, http://ecos.fws.gov/tess_public/pub/adHocSpeciesForm.jsp (accessed February 17, 2016), and "Listed FWS/Joint FWS and NMFS Species and Populations with Recovery Plans (Sorted by Listed Entity)," in *Recovery Plans Search*, U.S. Department of the Interior, U.S. Fish and Wildlife Service, February 2016, http://ecos.fws.gov/tess_public/pub/speciesRecovery.jsp?sort=1 (accessed February 17, 2016)

FIGURE 9.1

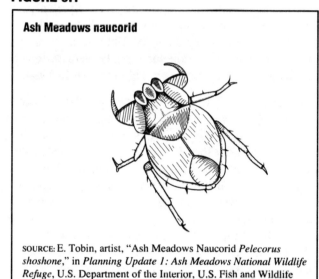

Ash Meadows naucorid

SOURCE: E. Tobin, artist, "Ash Meadows Naucorid *Pelecorus shoshone*," in *Planning Update 1: Ash Meadows National Wildlife Refuge*, U.S. Department of the Interior, U.S. Fish and Wildlife Service, January 1999, http://www.fws.gov/pacific/planning/am_pu1.pdf (accessed February 18, 2016)

devoted to invertebrates. The nonprofit organization (http://www.xerces.org/pollinator-redlist/) maintains a "red list" of what it says are dozens of wild bee species in decline. The vast majority are found in Hawaii. As of April 2016, no wild bees had been listed under the ESA.

Beetles

According to the San Diego Zoo (2016, http://animals.sandiegozoo.org/animals/beetle), beetles constitute the largest group within the animal kingdom, with about 350,000 known species. They vary widely in size and color, but all have antler-like antennae on their heads. Most live on land. Beetles are beneficial members of their ecosystems. The San Diego Zoo notes, "Beetles create usable soil for vegetation by eating animal waste, rotten wood, and animal carcasses. They pollinate flowers and keep other insect populations in balance through predation."

As shown in Table 9.1 there were more than a dozen beetle species listed under the ESA as of February 2016. Like many other imperiled animals, they face threats from habitat loss and alteration, particularly urban and agricultural development.

AMERICAN BURYING BEETLES. In *American Burying Beetle (*Nicrophorus americanus*) Recovery Plan* (1991, http://ecos.fws.gov/docs/recovery_plan/910927.pdf), the USFWS notes that the American burying beetle (ABB) grows to 1.4 inches (3.5 cm) in length. It is shiny black with orange-red markings. The species was once found throughout the warmer regions of eastern North America, but its population declined dramatically through much of the 20th century. The reasons for its decline are not known, but scientists suspect its fragmented habitat played a major role.

The ABB was listed under the ESA in 1989. According to the USFWS (http://ecos.fws.gov/tess_public/profile/speciesProfile?spcode=I028), as of April 2016 there were two listed populations. An endangered population inhabits scattered habitats in the eastern United States (namely Massachusetts and Rhode Island) and in the Midwest and Southwest (primarily Arkansas, Kansas, Nebraska, Ohio, Oklahoma, South Dakota, and Texas.) There is also a nonessential experimental population in two Missouri counties. No critical habitat has been designated for the species.

During 2014 more than $2.1 million was spent under the ESA on the ABB. (See Table 9.2.)

The ABB is a controversial species because of its presence in areas of Texas and other states with thriving oil and natural gas industries. In 2013 the USFWS (https://www.gpo.gov/fdsys/pkg/FR-2013-02-01/pdf/2013-02256.pdf) posted a

TABLE 9.2

The 10 listed insect species with the highest expenditures under the Endangered Species Act, fiscal year 2014

Ranking	Species	Population	Expenditure
1	Beetle, American burying (*Nicrophorus americanus*)	Entire	$2,140,182
2	Beetle, valley elderberry longhorn (*Desmocerus californicus dimorphus*)	Entire	$1,832,848
3	Butterfly, callippe silverspot (*Speyeria callippe callippe*)	Entire	$1,229,185
4	Butterfly, Fender's blue (*Icaricia icarioides fenderi*)	Entire	$985,098
5	Checkerspot, Taylor's (=whulge) (*Euphydryas editha taylori*)	Entire	$935,487
6	Tiger beetle, Puritan (*Cicindela puritana*)	Entire	$889,486
7	Butterfly, Karner blue (*Lycaeides melissa samuelis*)	Entire	$770,946
8	Butterfly, Oregon silverspot (*Speyeria zerene hippolyta*)	Entire	$437,915
9	Beetle, [no common name] (*Rhadine infernalis*)	Entire	$417,345
10	Butterfly, Saint Francis' satyr (*Neonympha mitchellii francisci*)	Entire	$220,413

SOURCE: Adapted from "Table 2. Species Ranked in Descending Order of Total FY 2014 Reported Expenditures, Not Including Land Acquisition Costs," in *Federal and State Endangered and Threatened Species Expenditures: Fiscal Year 2014*, U.S. Department of the Interior, U.S. Fish and Wildlife Service, March 2, 2016, http://www.fws.gov/endangered/esa-library/pdf/20160302_final_FY14_ExpRpt.pdf (accessed March 9, 2016)

public notification that it plans to prepare a draft Environmental Impact Statement (EIS) to evaluate the impacts associated with issuing a conservation plan allowing incidental take of the ABB. Incidental take is taking (hunting, killing, capturing, and harassing) that is incidental to, but not the purpose of, an otherwise lawful activity. In this case the EIS will examine incidental take related to the construction, maintenance, operation, and repair of oil and gas pipelines, and related well field activities. If the conservation plan is approved, then individual companies wishing to engage in these activities would apply for incidental take permits under the ESA and agree to implement the plan. As of April 2016, the EIS had not been published.

As explained in Chapter 2, Republican legislators in western states are generally hostile toward the ESA because they believe it unnecessarily burdens industry and economic development. In 2015 Representative Frank Lucas (1960–; R-OK) added an amendment to a national defense bill that would have forced the USFWS to delist the ABB; however, the amendment was later stripped from the bill. Also in 2015 the agency received a petition from a group of oil industry interests requesting that the ABB be delisted under the ESA. The petitioners argued that there are not sufficient threats against the beetle to justify its continued listing. In March 2016 the USFWS (https://www.gpo.gov/fdsys/pkg/FR-2016-03-16/pdf/2016-05699.pdf) found that the petition did present substantial information supporting delisting and initiated a 12-month status review for the species. As of April 2016, the status review was ongoing.

VALLEY ELDERBERRY LONGHORN BEETLES. Another insect with a contentious ESA history is the valley elderberry longhorn beetle (VELB). As shown in Table 9.2, in 2014 more than $1.8 million was devoted to this species found only in California. It is a stout-bodied beetle nearly 1 inch (2.5 cm) long when fully grown. The VELB overwhelmingly prefers only one type of host plant: elderberry

shrubs along creeks and rivers in California's Central Valley. This is an area that experienced extensive agricultural and urban development during the 20th century. Long-term destruction and fragmentation of riparian (river and stream) ecosystems imperiled the beetle population. It was first listed under the ESA in 1980 as a threatened species. Two areas in Sacramento County were designated critical habitat. A recovery plan was finalized in 1984.

In September 2006 the USFWS published *Valley Elderberry Longhorn Beetle (Desmocerus californicus dimorphus): 5-Year Review—Summary and Evaluation* (http://ecos.fws.gov/docs/five_year_review/doc779.pdf) and recommended that the species be delisted. However, the agency failed to do so in a timely manner and was sued by the Pacific Legal Foundation (PLF), a private organization that typically litigates against the ESA. In January 2011 (http://www.gpo.gov/fdsys/search/citation.result.FR.action?federalRegister.volume=2011&federalRegister.page=3069&publication=FR), the agency again published a finding that delisting was warranted but failed to finalize the delisting. The PLF sued again. In October 2012 the USFWS (https://www.federalregister.gov/articles/2012/10/02/2012-23843/endangered-and-threatened-wildlife-and-plants-removal-of-the-valley-elderberry-longhorn-beetle-from#h-14) officially proposed to delist the beetle because of recovery. However, in September 2014 the agency (https://www.gpo.gov/fdsys/pkg/FR-2014-09-17/pdf/2014-21585.pdf) withdrew its proposal, noting, "the proposed rule did not fully analyze the best information." As of April 2016, the VELB retained a threatened listing under the ESA.

Butterflies, Moths, and Skippers

Butterflies, moths, and skippers are flying insects that belong to the order Lepidoptera. Scientists believe there could be several hundred thousand species in this order. Skippers have stockier bodies than butterflies and are structurally different from moths. As such, they are considered to be an intermediate between butterflies and moths.

Like amphibians, many butterflies and moths are considered indicator species (meaning that their well-being gives scientists a good indication of the general health of their habitat) because they are particularly sensitive to environmental degradation. The decline of these species serves as a warning to humans about the condition of the environment. For example, certain moth species feed on lichen, a fungus-based organism that grows on trees, rocks, and other solid surfaces. Lichen are very susceptible to air pollutants. Reductions in the number of lichen-feeding moths can indicate the presence of harmful air pollution in an area. Part of the reason butterflies are sensitive to many aspects of the environment is that these species undergo a drastic metamorphosis, or change, from larva to adult as a natural part of their life cycle. Butterfly larvae are generally crawling, herbivorous (plant-eating) caterpillars, whereas butterfly adults fly and eat nectar. Butterflies can thrive only when intact habitats are available for both caterpillars and adults. Consequently, healthy butterfly populations tend to occur in areas with healthy ecosystems. Because many species are extremely sensitive to changing environmental conditions, butterflies and moths are carefully monitored by scientists and conservationists around the world.

As shown in Table 9.1 there were nearly three dozen butterflies, skippers, and moths listed under the ESA as of February 2016. Most had endangered listings and did have recovery plans in place.

The major threats to these species include:

- Habitat destruction

- Mowing of pastures, ditches, and highway rights-of-way

- Collisions with moving automobiles

- Insecticides

KARNER BLUE BUTTERFLIES. The Karner blue butterfly was listed under the ESA in 1992 as an endangered species. According to the USFWS (http://ecos.fws.gov/tess_public/profile/speciesProfile?spcode=I00F), it is a small butterfly measuring about one inch (2.5 cm) across. Historically, it occupied habitats in the eastern United States from Minnesota to Maine as well as in Ontario, Canada. It is now found only in portions of Indiana, Michigan, Minnesota, New Hampshire, New York, Ohio, and Wisconsin. Most of the populations are extremely small and in danger of extinction.

The caterpillars of the Karner blue butterfly feed only on a species of wild lupine. The butterflies are weak flyers and prefer to stay near their favorite lupine patches. In 2003 the USFWS published *Final Recovery Plan for the Karner Blue Butterfly* (Lycaeides melissa samuelis) (http://ecos.fws.gov/docs/recovery_plan/030919.pdf), which outlines the status of the species and the steps required to conserve it. In February 2011 the USFWS (http://www.fws.gov/midwest/endangered/insects/kbb/pdf/kbbRecPlanRevision2011.pdf) issued a memorandum making a minor update to the plan by adding a new potential recovery unit. Figure 9.2 shows the updated map of recovery units, or populations, of the species, sites for potential recovery units, and other sites where the species has historically been found.

Hawaiian Insects

As of February 2016, Hawaiian insects listed under the ESA included 12 subspecies of the pomace fly, five damselflies, two Hawaiian picture-wing flies, and the Blackburn's sphinx moth. (See Table 9.1.)

POMACE FLIES. Pomace flies (also known as Hawaiian picture-wing flies) belong to the genus *Drosophila*, a group commonly called fruit flies. (See Figure 9.3.) There are more than 100 species of *Drosophila*. They are relatively large flies with elaborate markings on their wings. The Hawaiian subspecies are renowned for their colorful wing patterns. They prefer mostly mesic (adequately moist) forest and wet forest habitats. Each fly is dependent on one or more specific host plants. This dependence is one of the factors that has imperiled the flies. All the host plants face threats to their survival because of competition with nonnative plants and trampling and ingestion by livestock and wild animals.

In 2006 all 12 Hawaiian subspecies were listed under the ESA. All but one were designated as endangered. (See Table 9.1.) *Drosophila mulli* was designated as threatened. As of April 2016, a recovery plan had not been issued for the Hawaiian pomace flies.

THREATENED AND ENDANGERED FOREIGN SPECIES OF INSECTS

In *Red List of Threatened Species Version 2015.4*, the IUCN indicates that in 2015, 1,046 species of insects were threatened. This number accounted for 19% of the 5,573 evaluated species and less than 0.1% of the 1 million described species.

As of February 2016, there were four foreign insects listed under the ESA. (See Table 9.3.) All four were butterfly species and were listed as endangered. They are found in portions of France and Italy and in Jamaica, the Philippines, and Papua New Guinea.

THREATENED AND ENDANGERED ARACHNID SPECIES IN THE UNITED STATES

Arachnids are invertebrates with eight legs. They include spiders, mites, ticks, scorpions, and harvestmen. As of February 2016, 12 U.S. species of arachnids were listed under the ESA. (See Table 9.4.) All the arachnids had endangered status, and all had

FIGURE 9.2

Recovery units for Karner blue butterfly

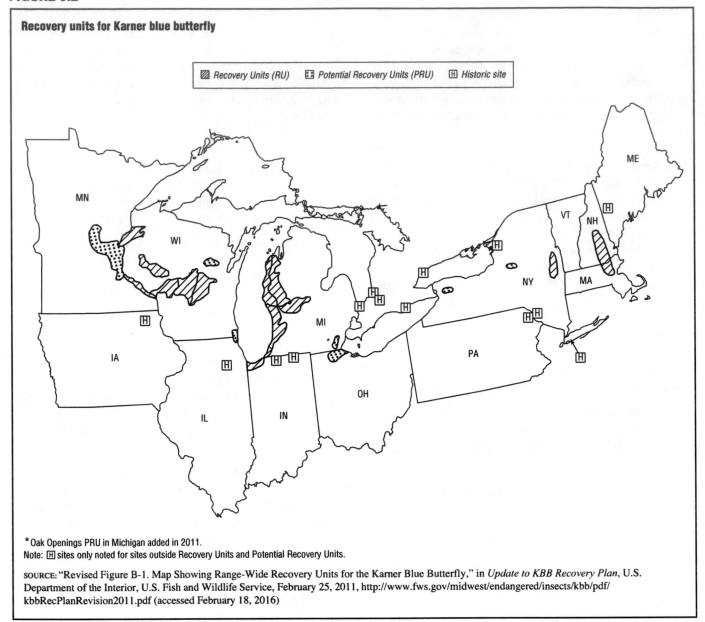

| Recovery Units (RU) | Potential Recovery Units (PRU) | H Historic site |

*Oak Openings PRU in Michigan added in 2011.

Note: ⊞ sites only noted for sites outside Recovery Units and Potential Recovery Units.

SOURCE: "Revised Figure B-1. Map Showing Range-Wide Recovery Units for the Karner Blue Butterfly," in *Update to KBB Recovery Plan*, U.S. Department of the Interior, U.S. Fish and Wildlife Service, February 25, 2011, http://www.fws.gov/midwest/endangered/insects/kbb/pdf/kbbRecPlanRevision2011.pdf (accessed February 18, 2016)

recovery plans in place. The imperiled arachnids fall into four species types:

- Harvestmen—three species
- Meshweaver—four species
- Pseudoscorpion—one species
- Spider—four species

Ten of the arachnids are cave-dwelling species found only in Texas. The only imperiled arachnids outside of Texas are the Kauai Cave wolf spider, which inhabits Hawaii, and the spruce-fir moss spider, which is found in North Carolina and Tennessee.

Table 9.5 shows the 10 listed arachnid species with the highest expenditures under the ESA during FY 2014. Nearly $1.3 million was spent conserving these species.

Texas Cave Arachnids

Ten of the listed arachnids are found only in underground karst caves in three counties in Texas. (See Figure 9.4.) Karst is a geological term referring to a type of underground terrain resulting when limestone bedrock is exposed to mildly acidic groundwater over a long period. Eventually, the bedrock becomes a honeycomb of cracks, fissures, holes, and other openings. There are dozens of these karst caves located in Bexar, Travis, and Williamson Counties in Texas. In recent decades scientists have discovered unusual invertebrate species living in these caves. The tiny cave dwellers are eyeless and have no pigment (color) to their bodies. Ten of the creatures have been added to the endangered species list. They include four meshweavers (tiny web-making arachnids), three harvestmen (commonly known as daddy longlegs or granddaddy longlegs), two true spiders, and one pseudoscorpion.

FIGURE 9.3

Fruit fly

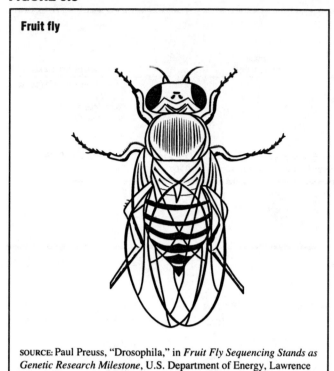

SOURCE: Paul Preuss, "Drosophila," in *Fruit Fly Sequencing Stands as Genetic Research Milestone*, U.S. Department of Energy, Lawrence Berkeley National Laboratory, March 23, 2000, http://www.lbl.gov/Science-Articles/Archive/drosophila-sequenced.html (accessed February 18, 2016)

The species were listed under the ESA after a collection of conservation groups petitioned the USFWS in 1992. The creatures were listed as endangered in 2000. In 2003 approximately 1,000 acres (405 ha) were designated as critical habitat for six of the arachnids. In addition, four of the species are included in the USFWS's *Recovery Plan for Endangered Karst Invertebrates in Travis and Williamson Counties, Texas* (August 1994, http://ecos.fws.gov/docs/recovery_plan/940825.pdf), which also covers other imperiled invertebrate species living in the caves. The other six arachnids are included in *Bexar County Karst Invertebrates Recovery Plan* (August 2011, http://ecos.fws.gov/docs/recovery_plan/Final%202001%20Bexar%20Co%20Invertebrates%20Rec%20Plan_1.pdf).

In December 2009 the USFWS published five-year reviews for four of the arachnids: Bee Creek Cave harvestman, Bone Cave harvestman, Tooth Cave pseudoscorpion, and Tooth Cave spider. The agency recommended maintaining the endangered listings for all of the species, noting that no significant steps had been taken toward protecting the caves in which the spiders occur.

THREATENED AND ENDANGERED FOREIGN SPECIES OF SPIDERS

The IUCN notes in *Red List of Threatened Species Version 2015.4* that 164 species of arachnids were threatened in 2015. This number accounted for 78% of the 210 evaluated species, but less than 0.2% of the more than 102,000 described arachnid species.

As of April 2016, there were no foreign spiders listed under the ESA.

TABLE 9.3

Foreign endangered and threatened insect species, February 2016

Common name	Scientific name	Federal listing status*	Current distribution
Corsican swallowtail butterfly	Papilio hospiton	E	France (Corsica), Italy (Sardinia)
Homerus swallowtail butterfly	Papilio homerus	E	Jamaica
Luzon peacock swallowtail butterfly	Papilio chikae	E	Philippines
Queen Alexandra's birdwing butterfly	Troides alexandrae	E	Papua New Guinea

*E = Endangered.

SOURCE: Adapted from "Generate Species List," in *Environmental Conservation Online System Species Reports*, U.S. Department of the Interior, U.S. Fish and Wildlife Service, February 2016, http://ecos.fws.gov/tess_public/pub/adHocSpeciesForm.jsp (accessed February 17, 2016)

TABLE 9.4

Endangered and threatened arachnid species, February 2016

Common name	Scientific name	Federal listing status[a]	U.S. or U.S./foreign listed	Recovery plan date	Recovery plan stage[b]
Bee Creek Cave harvestman	Texella reddelli	E	US	08/25/94	F
Bone Cave harvestman	Texella reyesi	E	US	08/25/94	F
Braken Bat Cave meshweaver	Cicurina venii	E	US	10/04/11	F
Cokendolpher Cave harvestman	Texella cokendolpheri	E	US	10/04/11	F
Government Canyon Bat Cave meshweaver	Cicurina vespera	E	US	10/04/11	F
Government Canyon Bat Cave spider	Neoleptoneta microps	E	US	10/04/11	F
Kauai cave wolf or pe'e pe'e maka 'ole spider	Adelocosa anops	E	US	07/19/06	F
Madla's Cave meshweaver	Cicurina madla	E	US	10/04/11	F
Robber Baron Cave meshweaver	Cicurina baronia	E	US	10/04/11	F
Spruce-fir moss spider	Microhexura montivaga	E	US	09/11/98	F
Tooth Cave pseudoscorpion	Tartarocreagris texana	E	US	08/25/94	F
Tooth Cave spider	Neoleptoneta myopica	E	US	08/25/94	F

[a]E = Endangered.
[b]F = Final.

SOURCE: Adapted from "Generate Species List," in *Environmental Conservation Online System Species Reports*, U.S. Department of the Interior, U.S. Fish and Wildlife Service, February 2016, http://ecos.fws.gov/tess_public/pub/adHocSpeciesForm.jsp (accessed February 17, 2016), and "Listed FWS/Joint FWS and NMFS Species and Populations with Recovery Plans (Sorted by Listed Entity)," in *Recovery Plans Search*, U.S. Department of the Interior, U.S. Fish and Wildlife Service, February 2016, http://ecos.fws.gov/tess_public/pub/speciesRecovery.jsp?sort=1 (accessed February 17, 2016)

TABLE 9.5

The 10 listed arachnid species with the highest expenditures under the Endangered Species Act, fiscal year 2014

Ranking	Species	Population	Expenditure
1	Meshweaver, Madla's Cave (Cicurina madla)	Entire	$342,545
2	Meshweaver, Braken Bat Cave (Cicurina venii)	Entire	$342,345
3	Harvestman, Bone Cave (Texella reyesi)	Entire	$152,336
4	Meshweaver, Government Canyon Bat Cave (Cicurina vespera)	Entire	$76,850
5	Spider, Government Canyon Bat Cave (Neoleptoneta microps)	Entire	$75,200
6	Harvestman, Cokendolpher Cave (Texella cokendolpheri)	Entire	$75,000
7	Meshweaver, Robber Baron Cave (Cicurina baronia)	Entire	$75,000
8	Pseudoscorpion, Tooth Cave (Tartarocreagris texana)	Entire	$50,000
9	Spider, Tooth Cave (Leptoneta myopica)	Entire	$50,000
10	Spider, spruce-fir moss (Microhexura montivaga)	Entire	$33,000

SOURCE: Adapted from "Table 2. Species Ranked in Descending Order of Total FY 2014 Reported Expenditures, Not Including Land Acquisition Costs," in *Federal and State Endangered and Threatened Species Expenditures: Fiscal Year 2014*, U.S. Department of the Interior, U.S. Fish and Wildlife Service, March 2, 2016, http://www.fws.gov/endangered/esa-library/pdf/20160302_final_FY14_ExpRpt.pdf (accessed March 9, 2016)

FIGURE 9.4

A karst cave provides habitat for endangered invertebrates

SOURCE: Lisa O'Donnell, William R. Elliott, and Ruth A. Stanford, "Front Cover," in *Recovery Plan for Endangered Karst Invertebrates in Travis and Williamson Counties, Texas*, U.S. Department of the Interior, U.S. Fish and Wildlife Service, 1994, http://ecos.fws.gov/docs/recovery_plans/1994/940825.pdf (accessed February 18, 2016)

CHAPTER 10
PLANTS

Plants belong to the Plantae kingdom. In general, there are two types of land-growing plants: vascular and nonvascular. Vascular plants have specially developed organs similar to veins that move liquids through their system. This category includes trees, shrubs, flowers, and grasses. Nonvascular plants are mosses, liverworts, and hornworts. The vast majority of plant species on the earth are vascular plants that reproduce through their flowers.

In science, plants are more often identified by their scientific name than are animals. Plant species are so abundant and diverse that many plants have multiple common names. However, there are plants that have no common names because they are rare or are geographically remote. To avoid confusion, this chapter will include the scientific name for any specific common name given.

Several factors contribute to the endangerment of plant species. Many species are the victims of habitat loss because of land and agricultural development. Others have declined because of pollution or habitat damage, or as a result of competition with invasive species. Still other imperiled plants have succumbed to introduced or unknown plant diseases. Finally, collectors or dealers often illegally seek rare, showy, or unusual plants and have depleted populations through overcollection.

The preservation of plant species is important for many reasons. Not only are plants of aesthetic value, but also they are crucial components of every ecosystem on the earth. Furthermore, plants serve several functions that are directly beneficial to humans. First, they provide genetic variation that is used in the breeding of new crop varieties (native plants provide genes that allow for adaptation to local environments and resistance to pests, disease, or drought). In addition, plants are the source of many human medicines.

AMERICAN CHESTNUT TREE: MAKING A COMEBACK?

During the 1800s the American chestnut (*Castanea dentata*) was the predominant tree of many forests in the eastern United States. Its range extended from Maine to Mississippi. (See Figure 10.1.) In *American Chestnut... an American Wood* (February 1973, http://www.fpl.fs.fed.us/documnts/usda/amwood/230chest.pdf), the U.S. Forest Service indicates that the heaviest concentrations were in the southern Appalachian Mountains, where the tree made up more than one-third of the overstory trees (the topmost layer of foliage in a forest). Mature trees reached 3 feet to 5 feet (0.9 m to 1.5 m) in diameter and rose to 90 feet (27 m) in height with a huge canopy. The species was fast growing and produced a light, durable wood that was extremely popular for firewood and for making furniture, shingles, caskets, telephone poles, railroad ties, and other products. The trees were also valued for their chestnuts and tannin content. Tannin is an extract used in the leather industry.

In 1904 observers in New York City reported that an unknown blight (disease) was killing American chestnut trees at the Bronx Zoo. By 1940 the blight had spread through the entire range of the species, leaving all the trees dead or dying. The tree structure was not damaged by the disease, so the harvesting of dead trees continued for several more decades. Although sprouts would grow from the stumps that were left behind, they eventually succumbed to the blight. By the 1970s the American chestnut had been virtually eliminated. Approximately 3 billion to 4 billion trees had been killed. The culprit was a fungus originally called *Endothia parasitica* but later renamed *Cryphonectria parasitica*. Scientists believe the disease came into the United States with ornamental chestnut trees that were imported from Japan or China. Oriental trees could carry the disease, but not succumb to it, because they had a natural immunity to it.

FIGURE 10.1

Historical distribution of the American chestnut

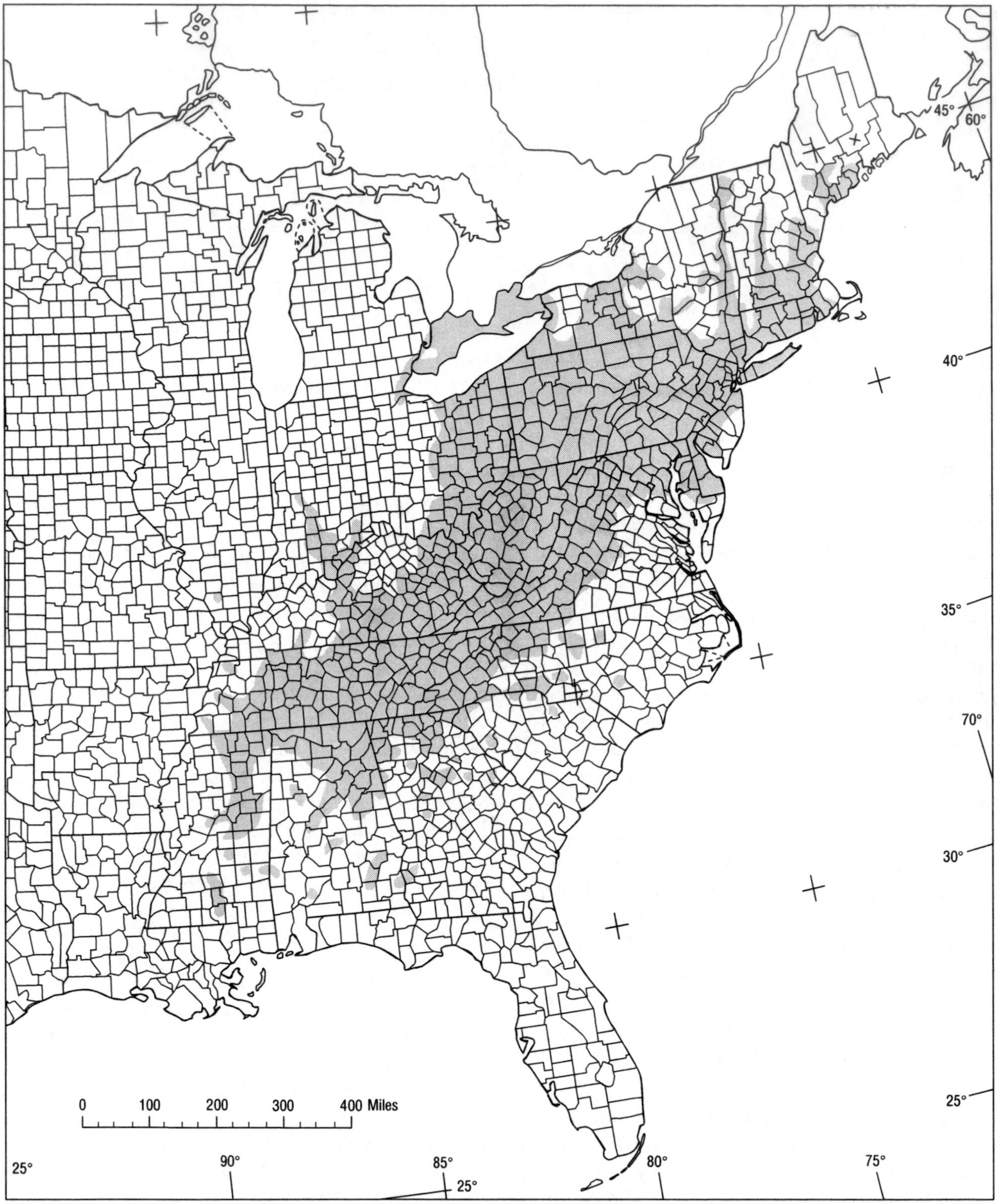

SOURCE: Joseph R. Saucier, "Figure 1. Natural Range of American Chestnut," in *American Chestnut (Castanea dentata). An American Wood*, U.S. Department of Agriculture, U.S. Forest Service, February 1973, http://www.fpl.fs.fed.us/documnts/usda/amwood/230chest.pdf (accessed February 19, 2016)

During the 1920s scientists began crossing the remaining American chestnut trees with the oriental species. Although the hybrid trees resulted with some resistance to the blight, they were inferior in quality to the original American species. Advances in genetic research and forestry techniques have gradually led to better hybrids. Three organizations have played a key role in the research: the American Chestnut Foundation, the American Chestnut Research and Restoration Center at the State University of New York, and the American Chestnut Cooperators' Foundation at Virginia Tech University. The American Chestnut Foundation and the American Chestnut Research and Restoration Center focus on crossing naturally blight-resistant Asiatic species with American species, whereas the American Chestnut Cooperators' Foundation produces crosses between American chestnut trees that are found to have some resistance to the blight in hopes of eventually producing offspring with higher resistance. All three organizations are confident that vigorous blight-resistant American chestnut trees can be developed.

The fate of the once-plentiful American chestnut shows the vulnerability of even hardy plant species to devastating events. As of 2016, forest owners and managers were continuing to fight numerous diseases and pests impacting tree species. Major examples include the emerald ash borer (an invasive Asian beetle that infests and eats ash trees) and Dutch elm disease, a fungus that attacks Dutch elm trees.

PROTECTION OF PLANTS UNDER THE ENDANGERED SPECIES ACT

The Endangered Species Act (ESA) of 1973 protects listed plants from deliberate destruction or vandalism. Plants also receive protection under the consultation requirements of the act; that is, all federal agencies must consult with the U.S. Fish and Wildlife Service (USFWS) to determine how best to conserve species and to ensure that no issued permits will jeopardize listed species or harm their habitat.

Regardless, many conservationists believe plants receive less protection than animals under the ESA. First, the ESA only protects plants that are found on federal lands. It imposes no restrictions on private landowners whose property is home to endangered plants. Critics also complain that the USFWS has been slow to list plant species and that damage to plant habitats is not addressed with the same seriousness as for animal species. However, the USFWS points out that the number of plants listed under the ESA has risen dramatically over the past three decades. As of February 2016, this number was at 900. (See Table 1.3 in Chapter 1). In fact, plants (and lichens) accounted for 40% of all species listed under the ESA at that time.

In 2000, in an effort to bolster conservation efforts for plants, the USFWS formed an agreement with the Center for Plant Conservation, a national association of botanical gardens and arboretums. The two organizations are cooperating in developing conservation measures to help save North American plant species, particularly those that are listed as threatened or endangered. Central to the effort is the creation of educational programs that are aimed at informing the public about the importance of plant species for aesthetic, economic, biological, and medical reasons. The Center for Plant Conservation also aids in developing recovery plans for listed plant species and collects listed species for preservation. As of April 2016, the center's (http://www.centerforplantconservation.org/) collection included more than 780 "of America's most imperiled native plants."

THREATENED AND ENDANGERED U.S. PLANT SPECIES

As of February 2016, 897 U.S. plant species were listed under the ESA. (See Table 10.1.) Nearly all the plants had recovery plans in place. Because several species of imperiled plants are often found in the same ecosystem, many recovery plans cover multiple plant species.

The status of most plant species has not been studied in detail. Thus, many more plants are probably in danger of extinction than are listed under the ESA.

The 10 listed plants with the highest expenditures under the ESA during fiscal year (FY) 2014 are listed in Table 10.2. Johnson's seagrass (*Halophila johnsonii*) dominated the list with nearly $3.1 million in spending. It is a plant that lives underwater in salty lagoons in southeastern Florida. (See Figure 10.2.) Almost $1.2 million was spent on the Contra Costa goldfields (*Lasthenia conjugans*), a flowering plant found in California.

As of February 2016, there were recovery plans for hundreds of listed plant species. (See Table 10.1.) Many of the plans cover multiple species, and some are administered jointly by the USFWS and the National Marine Fisheries Service (NMFS). Links to the plans and details about them are published in "Listed FWS/Joint FWS and NMFS Species and Populations with Recovery Plans" (2016, http://ecos.fws.gov/tess_public/pub/speciesRecovery.jsp?sort=1).

PLANT TAXONOMY AND CATEGORIZATION

The taxonomy of plant species can be quite complicated and is plagued by disagreements among scientists. Historically, plants were categorized by morphology (physical characteristics, such as shape or color of their leaves, fruit, and bark). During the 1960s a new classification scheme emerged that groups plants based on their evolutionary similarities, for example, their chemical

TABLE 10.1

Endangered and threatened plant species, February 2016

Common name	Scientific name	Species group	Federal listing status[a]	U.S. or U.S./foreign listed	Recovery plan date	Recovery plan stage[b]	Family	Current distribution
(=Na`ena`e) lo`ulu	*Pritchardia hardyi*	Flowering plants	E	US	06/17/10	O	Asteraceae	HI; U.S.A. (HI)
(=Native yellow hibiscus) ma`o hau hele	*Hibiscus brackenridgei*	Flowering plants	E	US	12/10/02	F	Malvaceae	HI; U.S.A. (HI)
`Ahinahina	*Argyroxiphium sandwicense ssp. macrocephalum*	Flowering plants	T	US	07/29/97	F	Asteraceae	HI; U.S.A. (HI)
`Ahinahina	*Argyroxiphium sandwicense ssp. sandwicense*	Flowering plants	E	US	09/30/93	F	Asteraceae	HI; U.S.A. (HI)
`Aiakeakua, popolo	*Solanum sandwicense*	Flowering plants	E	US	08/23/98	F	Solanaceae	HI; U.S.A. (HI)
`Aiea	*Nothocestrum breviflorum*	Flowering plants	E	US	05/11/98	F	Solanaceae	HI; U.S.A. (HI)
`Aiea	*Nothocestrum peltatum*	Flowering plants	E	US	09/20/95	F	Solanaceae	HI; U.S.A. (HI)
`Akoko	*Euphorbia celastroides var. kaenana*	Flowering plants	E	US	08/10/98	F	Euphorbiaceae	HI; U.S.A. (HI)
`Akoko	*Euphorbia deppeana*	Flowering plants	E	US	08/10/98	F	Euphorbiaceae	HI; U.S.A. (HI)
`Akoko	*Euphorbia eleanoriae*	Flowering plants	E	US	06/17/10	O	Euphorbiaceae	HI; U.S.A. (HI)
`Akoko	*Euphorbia haeleeleana*	Flowering plants	E	US	07/10/99	F	Euphorbiaceae	HI; U.S.A. (HI)
`Akoko	*Euphorbia herbstii*	Flowering plants	E	US	08/10/98	F	Euphorbiaceae	HI; U.S.A. (HI)
`Akoko	*Euphorbia kuwaleana*	Flowering plants	E	US	08/10/98	F	Euphorbiaceae	HI; U.S.A. (HI)
`Akoko	*Euphorbia remyi var. kauaiensis*	Flowering plants	E	US	06/17/10	O	Euphorbiaceae	HI; U.S.A. (HI)
`Akoko	*Euphorbia remyi var. remyi*	Flowering plants	E	US	06/17/10	O	Euphorbiaceae	HI; U.S.A. (HI)
`Akoko	*Euphorbia rockii*	Flowering plants	E	US	08/10/98	F	Euphorbiaceae	HI; U.S.A. (HI)
`Aku	*Cyanea tritomantha*	Flowering plants	E	US	None	—	Campanulaceae	HI;
`Aku`aku	*Cyanea platyphylla*	Flowering plants	E	US	09/26/96	F	Campanulaceae	HI; U.S.A. (HI)
`Ala `ala wai nui	*Peperomia subpetiolata*	Flowering plants	E	US	None	—	Piperaceae	HI;
`Anaunu	*Lepidium arbuscula*	Flowering plants	E	US	08/10/98	F	Brassicaceae	HI; U.S.A. (HI)
`Anunu	*Sicyos albus*	Flowering plants	E	US	05/11/98	F	Cucurbitaceae	HI; U.S.A. (HI)
`Awikiwiki	*Canavalia molokaiensis*	Flowering plants	E	US	08/28/13	F	Fabaceae	HI; U.S.A. (HI)
`Awikiwiki	*Canavalia napaliensis*	Flowering plants	E	US	06/17/10	O	Fabaceae	HI; U.S.A. (HI)
`Awikiwiki	*Canavalia pubescens*	Flowering plants	E	US	None	—	Fabaceae	HI;
`Oha wai	*Clermontia drepanomorpha*	Flowering plants	E	US	09/26/96	F	Campanulaceae	HI; U.S.A. (HI)
`Oha wai	*Clermontia lindseyana*	Flowering plants	E	US	09/26/96	F	Campanulaceae	HI; U.S.A. (HI)
`Oha wai	*Clermontia oblongifolia ssp. brevipes*	Flowering plants	E	US	05/20/98	F	Campanulaceae	HI; U.S.A. (HI)
`Oha wai	*Clermontia oblongifolia ssp. mauiensis*	Flowering plants	E	US	07/29/97	F	Campanulaceae	HI; U.S.A. (HI)
`Oha wai	*Clermontia peleana*	Flowering plants	E	US	09/26/96	F	Campanulaceae	HI; U.S.A. (HI)
`Oha wai	*Clermontia pyrularia*	Flowering plants	E	US	05/11/98	F	Campanulaceae	HI; U.S.A. (HI)
`Oha wai	*Clermontia samuelii*	Flowering plants	E	US	07/10/99	F	Campanulaceae	HI; U.S.A. (HI)
`Ohe`ohe	*Polyscias gymnocarpa*	Flowering plants	E	US	08/10/98	F	Araliaceae	HI; U.S.A. (HI)
A`e	*Zanthoxylum dipetalum var. tomentosum*	Flowering plants	E	US	09/26/96	F	Rutaceae	HI; Entire
A`e	*Zanthoxylum hawaiiense*	Flowering plants	E	US	05/11/98	F	Rutaceae	HI; U.S.A. (HI)
A`e	*Zanthoxylum oahuense*	Flowering plants	E	US	None	—	Rutaceae	FL;
Aboriginal prickly-apple	*Harrisia (=Cereus) aboriginum (=gracilis)*	Flowering plants	E	US/foreign	None	—	Cactaceae	FL;
Acuna cactus	*Echinomastus erectocentrus var. acunensis*	Flowering plants	E	US	None	—	Cactaceae	AZ;
`Akoko	*Euphorbia halemanui*	Flowering plants	E	US	08/23/98	F	Euphorbiaceae	HI; U.S.A. (AL)
Alabama canebrake pitcher-plant	*Sarracenia rubra ssp. alabamensis*	Flowering plants	E	US	10/08/92	F	Sarraceniaceae	AL; U.S.A. (AL)
Alabama leather flower	*Clematis socialis*	Flowering plants	E	US	12/27/89	F	Ranunculaceae	AL, GA; U.S.A. (AL)
Alabama streak-sorus fern	*Thelypteris pilosa var. alabamensis*	Ferns and allies	T	US	10/25/96	F	Thelypteridaceae	AL; U.S.A. (AL)
Alani	*Melicope adscendens*	Flowering plants	E	US	07/29/97	F	Rutaceae	HI; U.S.A. (HI)
Alani	*Melicope balloui*	Flowering plants	E	US	07/29/97	F	Rutaceae	HI; U.S.A. (HI)
Alani	*Melicope christophersenii*	Flowering plants	E	US	None	—	Rutaceae	HI; U.S.A. (HI)
Alani	*Melicope degeneri*	Flowering plants	E	US	06/17/10	O	Rutaceae	HI; U.S.A. (HI)
Alani	*Melicope haupuensis*	Flowering plants	E	US	09/20/95	F	Rutaceae	HI; U.S.A. (HI)
Alani	*Melicope hiiakae*	Flowering plants	E	US	None	—	Rutaceae	HI; U.S.A. (HI)
Alani	*Melicope knudsenii*	Flowering plants	E	US	09/20/95	F	Rutaceae	HI; U.S.A. (HI)
Alani	*Melicope lydgatei*	Flowering plants	E	US	08/10/98	F	Rutaceae	HI; U.S.A. (HI)
Alani	*Melicope makahae*	Flowering plants	E	US	None	—	Rutaceae	HI; U.S.A. (HI)
Alani	*Melicope mucronulata*	Flowering plants	E	US	07/29/97	F	Rutaceae	HI; U.S.A. (HI)

TABLE 10.1
Endangered and threatened plant species, February 2016 [CONTINUED]

Common name	Scientific name	Species group	Federal listing status[a]	U.S. or U.S./foreign listed	Recovery plan date	Recovery plan stage[b]	Family	Current distribution
Alani	Melicope munroi	Flowering plants	E	US	07/10/99	F	Rutaceae	HI; U.S.A. (HI)
Alani	Melicope ovalis	Flowering plants	E	US	07/29/97	F	Rutaceae	HI; U.S.A. (HI)
Alani	Melicope pallida	Flowering plants	E	US	09/20/95	F	Rutaceae	HI; U.S.A. (HI)
Alani	Melicope paniculata	Flowering plants	E	US	06/17/10	O	Rutaceae	HI; U.S.A. (HI)
Alani	Melicope puberula	Flowering plants	E	US	06/17/10	O	Rutaceae	HI; U.S.A. (HI)
Alani	Melicope quadrangularis	Flowering plants	E	US	08/23/98	F	Rutaceae	HI; U.S.A. (HI)
Alani	Melicope reflexa	Flowering plants	E	US	09/26/96	F	Rutaceae	HI; U.S.A. (HI)
Alani	Melicope saint-johnii	Flowering plants	E	US	08/10/98	F	Rutaceae	HI; U.S.A. (HI)
Alani	Melicope zahlbruckneri	Flowering plants	E	US	05/11/98	F	Rutaceae	HI; U.S.A. (HI)
Aleutian shield fern	Polystichum aleuticum	Ferns and allies	E	US	09/30/92	F	Dryopteridaceae	AK; upper slopes of Mount Reed on Adak Island, Alaska. Type specimen from Atka Island, but that population has not been relocated.; U.S.A. (AK)
Amargosa niterwort	Nitrophila mohavensis	Flowering plants	E	US	09/28/90	F	Chenopodiaceae	CA, NV; U.S.A. (NV, CA)
American chaffseed	Schwalbea americana	Flowering plants	E	US	09/29/95	F	Scrophulariaceae	AL, FL, GA, LA, NC, NJ, SC; U.S.A. (VA, TN, SC, NY, NJ, NC, MS, MI, MD, MA, LA, GA, FL, DE, CT, AL)
American hart's-tongue fern	Asplenium scolopendrium var. americanum	Ferns and allies	T	US/foreign	09/15/93	F	Aspleniaceae	AL, MI, NY, TN; Canada (Ont.); U.S.A. (TN, NY, MI, AL), Canada (Ont.)
Antioch Dunes evening-primrose	Oenothera deltoides ssp. howellii	Flowering plants	E	US	04/25/84	RF(1)	Onagraceae	CA; U.S.A. (CA)
Apalachicola rosemary	Conradina glabra	Flowering plants	E	US	09/27/94	F	Lamiaceae	FL; U.S.A. (FL)
Aplokating-palaoan	Psychotria malaspinae	Flowering plants	E	US	None	—	Rubiaceae	
Applegate's milk-vetch	Astragalus applegatei	Flowering plants	E	US	04/10/98	F	Fabaceae	CA, OR; The current range of the Applegate's milk-vetch is confined to Klamath County, Oregon from Klamath Falls to Worden, about 13 miles. The historic range was probably only slightly larger.; U.S.A. (OR)
Arizona cliffrose	Purshia (= Cowania) subintegra	Flowering plants	E	US	06/16/95	F	Rosaceae	AZ; U.S.A. (AZ)
Arizona hedgehog cactus	Echinocereus triglochidiatus var. arizonicus	Flowering plants	E	US	09/30/84	D	Cactaceae	AZ; U.S.A. (AZ)
Ash Meadows blazingstar	Mentzelia leucophylla	Flowering plants	T	US	09/28/90	F	Loasaceae	NV; U.S.A. (NV)
Ash Meadows gumplant	Grindelia fraxinipratensis	Flowering plants	T	US	09/28/90	F	Asteraceae	NV; U.S.A. (NV, CA)
Ash Meadows ivesia	Ivesia kingii var. eremica	Flowering plants	T	US	09/28/90	F	Rosaceae	NV; U.S.A. (NV)
Ash meadows milk-vetch	Astragalus phoenix	Flowering plants	T	US	09/28/90	F	Fabaceae	NV; U.S.A. (NV)
Ash Meadows sunray	Enceliopsis nudicaulis var. corrugata	Flowering plants	T	US	09/28/90	F	Asteraceae	NV; U.S.A. (NV)
Ash-grey paintbrush	Castilleja cinerea	Flowering plants	T	US	None	—	Scrophulariaceae	CA; U.S.A. (CA)
Ashy dogweed	Thymophylla tephroleuca	Flowering plants	E	US	07/29/88	F	Asteraceae	TX; U.S.A. (TX)
Asplenium-leaved diellia	Diellia erecta	Ferns and allies	E	US	12/10/02	F	Aspleniaceae	HI; U.S.A. (HI)
Aupaka	Isodendrion hosakae	Flowering plants	E	US	05/23/94	F	Violaceae	HI; U.S.A. (HI)
Aupaka	Isodendrion laurifolium	Flowering plants	E	US	12/10/02	F	Violaceae	HI; U.S.A. (HI)
Aupaka	Isodendrion longifolium	Flowering plants	T	US	12/10/02	F	Violaceae	HI; U.S.A. (HI)
Autumn buttercup	Ranunculus aestivalis (= acriformis)	Flowering plants	E	US	09/16/91	F	Ranunculaceae	UT; U.S.A. (UT)
Avon Park harebells	Crotalaria avonensis	Flowering plants	E	US	05/18/99	F	Fabaceae	FL; U.S.A. (FL)
Awiwi	Centaurium sebaeoides	Flowering plants	E	US	12/10/02	F	Gentianaceae	HI; U.S.A. (HI)
'Awiwi	Kadua cookiana	Flowering plants	E	US	08/23/98	F	Rubiaceae	HI; U.S.A. (HI)
Baker's larkspur	Delphinium bakeri	Flowering plants	E	US	08/03/15	F	Ranunculaceae	CA; U.S.A. (CA)
Bakersfield cactus	Opuntia treleasei	Flowering plants	E	US	09/30/98	F	Cactaceae	CA; U.S.A. (CA)
Bariaco	Trichilia triacantha	Flowering plants	E	US	08/20/91	F	Meliaceae	PR; Endemic to Puerto Rico; U.S.A. (PR)
Barneby reed-mustard	Schoenocrambe barnebyi	Flowering plants	E	US	09/14/94	F	Brassicaceae	UT; U.S.A. (UT)
Barneby ridge-cress	Lepidium barnebyanum	Flowering plants	E	US	07/23/93	F	Brassicaceae	UT; U.S.A. (UT)
Beach jacquemontia	Jacquemontia reclinata	Flowering plants	E	US	05/18/99	F	Convolvulaceae	FL; U.S.A. (FL)
Beach layia	Layia carnosa	Flowering plants	E	US	09/29/98	F	Asteraceae	CA; U.S.A. (CA)
Bear Valley sandwort	Arenaria ursina	Flowering plants	T	US	None	—	Caryophyllaceae	CA; U.S.A. (CA)
Beautiful goetzea	Goetzea elegans	Flowering plants	E	US	04/28/87	F	Solanaceae	PR; Endemic to Puerto Rico; U.S.A. (PR)
Beautiful pawpaw	Deeringothamnus pulchellus	Flowering plants	E	US	05/18/99	F	Annonaceae	FL; U.S.A. (FL)
Ben Lomond spineflower	Chorizanthe pungens var. hartwegiana	Flowering plants	E	US	09/28/98	F	Polygonaceae	CA; U.S.A. (CA)

TABLE 10.1

Endangered and threatened plant species, February 2016 [CONTINUED]

Common name	Scientific name	Species group	Federal listing status[a]	U.S. or U.S./foreign listed	Recovery plan date	Recovery plan stage[b]	Family	Current distribution
Ben Lomond wallflower	Erysimum teretifolium	Flowering plants	E	US	09/28/98	F	Brassicaceae	CA; U.S.A. (CA)
Berenghenas halomtano	Solanum guamense	Flowering plants	E	US	None	—	Solanaceae	
Big-leaved crownbeard	Verbesina dissita	Flowering plants	T	US/foreign	None	—	Asteraceae	CA; U.S.A. (CA), Mexico
Black lace cactus	Echinocereus reichenbachii var. albertii	Flowering plants	E	US	03/18/87	F	Cactaceae	TX; U.S.A. (TX)
Black spored quillwort	Isoetes melanospora	Ferns and allies	E	US	07/07/93	F	Isoetaceae	GA, SC; U.S.A. (SC, GA)
Blowout penstemon	Penstemon haydenii	Flowering Plants	E	US	07/17/92	F	Scrophulariaceae	NE, WY; U.S.A. (NE)
Blue Ridge goldenrod	Solidago spithamaea	Flowering plants	T	US	10/28/87	F	Asteraceae	NC, TN; U.S.A. (TN, NC)
Bradshaw's desert-parsley	Lomatium bradshawii	Flowering plants	E	US	06/29/10	F	Apiaceae	OR, WA; U.S.A. (WA, OR)
Brady pincushion cactus	Pediocactus bradyi	Flowering plants	E	US	03/28/85	F	Cactaceae	AZ; U.S.A. (AZ)
Braun's rock-cress	Arabis perstellata	Flowering plants	E	US	07/22/97	F	Brassicaceae	KY, TN; U.S.A. (TN, KY)
Braunton's milk-vetch	Astragalus brauntonii	Flowering plants	E	US	09/30/99	F	Fabaceae	CA; U.S.A. (CA)
Britton's beargrass	Nolina brittoniana	Flowering plants	E	US	06/20/96	RF(1)	Agavaceae	FL; U.S.A. (FL); Xeric, sandy ridges of central Florida
Brooksville bellflower	Campanula robinsiae	Flowering plants	E	US	06/20/94	F	Campanulaceae	FL; Known to occur along pond margins in Hernando and Hillsborough Counties in Florida.; U.S.A. (FL)
Bunched arrowhead	Sagittaria fasciculata	Flowering plants	E	US	09/08/83	F	Alismataceae	NC, SC; U.S.A. (SC, NC)
Bunched cory cactus	Coryphantha ramillosa	Flowering plants	T	US/foreign	04/13/90	F	Cactaceae	TX; Mexico-Coahuila; U.S.A. (TX), Mexico (Coahuila)
Burke's goldfields	Lasthenia burkei	Flowering plants	E	US	12/11/14	D	Asteraceae	CA; U.S.A. (CA)
Butte County meadowfoam	Limnanthes floccosa ssp. californica	Flowering plants	E	US	03/07/06	F	Limnanthaceae	CA; U.S.A. (CA)
California jewelflower	Caulanthus californicus	Flowering plants	E	US	09/30/98	F	Brassicaceae	CA; U.S.A. (CA)
California Orcutt grass	Orcuttia californica	Flowering plants	E	US	09/03/98	F	Poaceae	CA; U.S.A. (CA)
California seablite	Suaeda californica	Flowering plants	E	US	02/26/14	F	Chenopodiaceae	CA; U.S.A. (CA)
California taraxacum	Taraxacum californicum	Flowering plants	E	US	None	—	Asteraceae	CA; U.S.A. (CA)
Calistoga allocarya	Plagiobothrys strictus	Flowering plants	E	US	None	—	Boraginaceae	CA; U.S.A. (CA)
Canby's dropwort	Oxypolis canbyi	Flowering plants	E	US	04/10/90	F	Apiaceae	DE, GA, MD, NC, SC; U.S.A. (SC, NC, MD, GA, DE)
Canelo Hills ladies'-tresses	Spiranthes delitescens	Flowering plants	E	US	None	—	Orchidaceae	AZ; U.S.A. (AZ)
Capa rosa	Callicarpa ampla	Flowering plants	E	US	07/31/95	F	Verbenaceae	PR; El Yunque National Forest; U.S.A. (PR)
Cape Sable thoroughwort	Chromolaena frustrata	Flowering plants	E	US	None	—	Asteraceae	FL;
Carter's mustard	Warea carteri	Flowering plants	E	US	05/18/99	F	Brassicaceae	FL; U.S.A. (FL)
Carter's panicgrass	Panicum fauriei var. carteri	Flowering plants	E	US	12/09/93	D	Poaceae	HI; U.S.A. (HI)
Carter's small-flowered flax	Linum carteri carteri	Flowering plants	E	US	None	—	Linaceae	FL;
Catalina Island mountain-mahogany	Cercocarpus traskiae	Flowering plants	E	US	None	—	Rosaceae	CA; U.S.A. (CA)
Cebello halumtano	Bulbophyllum guamense	Flowering plants	T	US	None	—	Orchidaceae	CA; U.S.A. (CA)
Chapman rhododendron	Rhododendron chapmanii	Flowering plants	E	US	09/08/83	F	Ericaceae	FL; U.S.A. (FL)
Chinese Camp brodiaea	Brodiaea pallida	Flowering plants	T	US	None	—	Liliaceae	CA; U.S.A. (CA)
Chisos Mountain hedgehog cactus	Echinocereus chisoensis var. chisoensis	Flowering plants	T	US	12/08/93	F	Cactaceae	TX; U.S.A. (TX)
Chorro Creek bog thistle	Cirsium fontinale var. obispoense	Flowering plants	E	US	09/28/98	F	Asteraceae	CA; U.S.A. (CA)
Chupacallos	Pleodendron macranthum	Flowering plants	E	US/foreign	09/11/98	F	Canellaceae	PR; Endemic to Puerto Rico. Known from the Rio Abajo Commonwealth Forest and El Yunque National Forest; U.S.A. (PR)
Clara Hunt's milk-vetch	Astragalus clarianus	Flowering plants	E	US	None	—	Fabaceae	CA; U.S.A. (CA)
Clay phacelia	Phacelia argillacea	Flowering plants	E	US	04/12/82	F	Hydrophyllaceae	UT; U.S.A. (UT)
Clay reed-mustard	Schoenocrambe argillacea	Flowering plants	T	US	09/14/94	F	Brassicaceae	UT; U.S.A. (UT)
Clay-Loving wild buckwheat	Eriogonum pelinophilum	Flowering plants	E	US	11/10/88	F	Polygonaceae	CO; U.S.A. (CO)
Clay's hibiscus	Hibiscus clayi	Flowering plants	E	US	09/20/95	F	Malvaceae	HI; U.S.A. (HI)
Clover lupine	Lupinus tidestromii	Flowering plants	E	US	09/29/98	F	Fabaceae	CA; U.S.A. (CA)
Coachella Valley milk-vetch	Astragalus lentiginosus var. coachellae	Flowering plants	E	US	None	—	Fabaceae	CA; U.S.A. (CA)
Coastal dunes milk-vetch	Astragalus tener var. titi	Flowering plants	E	US	08/19/04	F	Fabaceae	CA; U.S.A. (CA)
Cobana negra	Stahlia monosperma	Flowering plants	T	US/foreign	11/01/96	F	Fabaceae	PR; Puerto Rico and Dominican Republic; U.S.A. (PR), Dominican Republic
Cochise pincushion cactus	Coryphantha robbinsiorum	Flowering plants	T	US/foreign	09/27/93	F	Cactaceae	AZ; Mexico-Sonora; U.S.A. (AZ), Mexico (Sonora)
Colorado Butterfly plant	Gaura neomexicana var. coloradensis	Flowering plants	T	US	05/25/10	O	Onagraceae	CO, NE, WY; U.S.A. (WY, NE, CO)
Colorado hookless cactus	Sclerocactus glaucus	Flowering plants	T	US	04/14/10	O	Cactaceae	CO; U.S.A. (CO)

TABLE 10.1

Endangered and threatened plant species, February 2016 [CONTINUED]

Common name	Scientific name	Species group	Federal listing status[a]	U.S. or U.S./foreign listed	Recovery plan date	Recovery plan stage[b]	Family	Current distribution
Colusa grass	*Neostapfia colusana*	Flowering plants	T	US	03/07/06	F	Poaceae	CA; U.S.A. (CA)
Conejo dudleya	*Dudleya abramsii ssp. parva*	Flowering plants	T	US	09/30/99	F	Crassulaceae	CA; U.S.A. (CA)
Contra Costa goldfields	*Lasthenia conjugens*	Flowering plants	E	US	03/07/06	F	Asteraceae	CA; U.S.A. (CA)
Contra Costa wallflower	*Erysimum capitatum var. angustatum*	Flowering plants	E	US	04/25/84	RF(1)	Brassicaceae	CA; U.S.A. (CA)
Cooke's kokiʻo	*Kokia cookei*	Flowering plants	E	US	05/27/98	F	Malvaceae	HI; U.S.A. (HI)
Cook's holly	*Ilex cookii*	Flowering plants	E	US	01/31/91	F	Aquifoliaceae	PR; Endemic to Puerto Rico. Known from Toro Negro Commonwealth Forest; U.S.A. (PR)
Cook's lomatium	*Lomatium cookii*	Flowering plants	E	US	03/22/13	F	Apiaceae	OR; U.S.A. (OR)
Cooley's meadowrue	*Thalictrum cooleyi*	Flowering plants	E	US	04/21/94	F	Ranunculaceae	FL, GA, NC; U.S.A. (NC, FL)
Cooley's water-willow	*Justicia cooleyi*	Flowering plants	E	US	06/20/94	F	Acanthaceae	FL; Known to occur in hardwood pine forests in Hernando and Sumter Counties in Florida.; U.S.A. (FL)
Coyote ceanothus	*Ceanothus ferrisae*	Flowering plants	E	US	09/30/98	F	Rhamnaceae	CA; U.S.A. (CA)
Crenulate lead-plant	*Amorpha crenulata*	Flowering plants	E	US	05/18/99	F	Fabaceae	FL; U.S.A. (FL)
Cumberland rosemary	*Conradina verticillata*	Flowering plants	T	US	07/12/96	F	Lamiaceae	KY, TN; U.S.A. (TN, KY)
Cumberland sandwort	*Arenaria cumberlandensis*	Flowering plants	E	US	06/20/96	F	Caryophyllaceae	KY, TN; U.S.A. (TN, KY)
Cushenbury buckwheat	*Eriogonum ovalifolium var. vineum*	Flowering plants	E	US	09/30/97	D	Polygonaceae	CA; U.S.A. (CA)
Cushenbury milk-vetch	*Astragalus albens*	Flowering plants	E	US	09/30/97	D	Fabaceae	CA; U.S.A. (CA)
Cushenbury oxytheca	*Oxytheca parishii var. goodmaniana*	Flowering plants	E	US	09/30/97	D	Polygonaceae	CA; U.S.A. (CA)
Davis' green pitaya	*Echinocereus viridiflorus var. davisii*	Flowering plants	E	US	09/20/84	F	Cactaceae	TX; U.S.A. (TX)
DeBeque phacelia	*Phacelia submutica*	Flowering plants	T	US	01/23/13	O	Hydrophyllaceae	CO; U.S.A. (CO)
Decurrent false aster	*Boltonia decurrens*	Flowering plants	T	US	09/28/90	O	Asteraceae	IL, MO; U.S.A. (MO, IL)
Del Mar manzanita	*Arctostaphylos glandulosa ssp. crassifolia*	Flowering plants	E	US/foreign	None	—	Ericaceae	CA; U.S.A. (CA), Mexico
Deltoid spurge	*Chamaesyce deltoidea ssp. deltoidea*	Flowering plants	E	US	05/18/99	F	Euphorbiaceae	FL; U.S.A. (FL)
Deseret milk-vetch	*Astragalus desereticus*	Flowering plants	T	US	None	—	Fabaceae	UT; U.S.A. (UT)
Desert yellowhead	*Yermo xanthocephalus*	Flowering plants	T	US	02/22/10	O	Asteraceae	WY; U.S.A. (WY)
Diamond Head schiedea	*Schiedea adamantis*	Flowering plants	E	US	02/02/94	F	Caryophyllaceae	HI; U.S.A. (HI)
Dudley Bluffs bladderpod	*Lesquerella congesta*	Flowering plants	T	US	08/13/93	F	Brassicaceae	CO; U.S.A. (CO)
Dudley Bluffs twinpod	*Physaria obcordata*	Flowering plants	T	US	08/13/93	F	Brassicaceae	CO; U.S.A. (CO)
Dwarf bear-poppy	*Arctomecon humilis*	Flowering plants	E	US	12/31/85	F	Papaveraceae	UT; U.S.A. (UT)
Dwarf iliau	*Wilkesia hobdyi*	Flowering plants	E	US	09/20/95	F	Asteraceae	HI; U.S.A. (HI)
Dwarf lake iris	*Iris lacustris*	Flowering plants	T	US/foreign	08/01/13	F	Iridaceae	MI, WI; Canada (Ont.); U.S.A. (WI, MI), Canada (Ont.)
Dwarf naupaka	*Scaevola coriacea*	Flowering plants	E	US	07/29/97	F	Goodeniaceae	HI; U.S.A. (HI)
Dwarf-flowered heartleaf	*Hexastylis naniflora*	Flowering plants	T	US	None	—	Aristolochiaceae	NC, SC; U.S.A. (SC, NC)
Eastern prairie fringed orchid	*Platanthera leucophaea*	Flowering plants	T	US/foreign	09/29/99	F	Orchidaceae	IA, IL, IN, ME, MI, MO, OH, VA, WI; Canada (N.B.Ont.); U.S.A. (WI,VA, PA, OK, OH, NY, NJ, NE, MO, MI, ME, IIN, IL, IA, AR), Canada (Ont., N.B.)
El Dorado bedstraw	*Galium californicum ssp. sierrae*	Flowering plants	E	US	08/30/02	F	Rubiaceae	CA; U.S.A. (CA)
Elfin tree fern	*Cyathea dryopteroides*	Ferns and allies	E	US	01/31/91	F	Cyatheaceae	PR; Endemic to Puerto Rico; U.S.A. (PR)
Encinitas baccharis	*Baccharis vanessae*	Flowering plants	T	US	None	—	Asteraceae	CA; U.S.A. (CA)
Erubia	*Solanum drymophilum*	Flowering plants	E	US	07/09/92	F	Solanaceae	PR; Endemic to Puerto Rico; U.S.A. (PR)
Etonia rosemary	*Conradina etonia*	Flowering plants	E	US	09/27/94	F	Lamiaceae	FL; Known to occur in sand pine scrub found at Etonia Creek State Forest and Dunns Creek State Park in Putnam County, Florida.; U.S.A. (FL)
Eureka Dune grass	*Swallenia alexandrae*	Flowering plants	E	US	12/13/82	F	Poaceae	CA; U.S.A. (CA)
Eureka Valley evening-primrose	*Oenothera avita ssp. eurekensis*	Flowering plants	E	US	12/13/82	F	Onagraceae	CA; U.S.A. (CA)
Ewa Plains 'akoko	*Euphorbia skottsbergii var. skottsbergii*	Flowering plants	E	US	10/05/93	D	Euphorbiaceae	HI; U.S.A. (HI)
Fadang	*Cycas micronesica*	Conifers and cycads	T	US	None	—	Cycadaceae	
Fassett's locoweed	*Oxytropis campestris var. chartacea*	Flowering plants	T	US	03/29/91	F	Fabaceae	WI; U.S.A. (WI)
Few-flowered navarretia	*Navarretia leucocephala ssp. pauciflora (= N.pauciflora)*	Flowering plants	E	US	03/07/06	F	Polemoniaceae	CA; U.S.A. (CA)
Fickeisen plains cactus	*Pediocactus peeblesianus fickeiseniae*	Flowering plants	E	US	None	—	Cactaceae	AZ;

TABLE 10.1

Endangered and threatened plant species, February 2016 [CONTINUED]

Common name	Scientific name	Species group	Federal listing status[a]	U.S. or U.S./foreign listed	Recovery plan date	Recovery plan stage[b]	Family	Current distribution
Fish Slough milk-vetch	Astragalus lentiginosus var. piscinensis	Flowering plants	T	US	09/30/98	F	Fabaceae	CA; U.S.A. (CA)
Fleshy owl's-clover	Castilleja campestris ssp. succulenta	Flowering plants	T	US	03/07/06	F	Scrophulariaceae	CA; U.S.A. (CA)
Fleshy-fruit gladecress	Leavenworthia crassa	Flowering plants	E	US	None	—	Brassicaceae	AL;
Florida bonamia	Bonamia grandiflora	Flowering plants	T	US	06/20/96	RF(1)	Convolvulaceae	FL; U.S.A. (FL); xeric uplands on central Florida sand ridges
Florida brickell-bush	Brickellia mosieri	Flowering plants	E	US	None	—	Asteraceae	FL;
Florida bristle fern	Trichomanes punctatum ssp. floridanum	Ferns and allies	E	US	None	—	Hymenophyllaceae	FL;
Florida golden aster	Chrysopsis floridana	Flowering plants	E	US	08/29/88	F	Asteraceae	FL; Known to occur in scrub habitat in Hardee, Hillsborough, Manatee, and Pinellas Counties in Florida. Most sites are on conservation lands with the exception of Hardee County where all the sites are on private lands.; U.S.A. (FL)
Florida perforate cladonia	Cladonia perforata	Lichens	E	US	05/18/99	F	Cladoniaceae	FL; U.S.A. (FL)
Florida semaphore cactus	Consolea corallicola	Flowering plants	E	US	None	—	Cactaceae	FL;
Florida skullcap	Scutellaria floridana	Flowering plants	T	US	06/22/94	F	Lamiaceae	FL; U.S.A. (FL)
Florida torreya	Torreya taxifolia	Conifers and cycads	E	US	09/09/86	F	Taxaceae	FL; GA; U.S.A. (GA, FL)
Florida ziziphus	Ziziphus celata	Flowering plants	E	US	05/18/99	F	Rhamnaceae	FL; U.S.A. (FL)
Fosberg's love grass	Eragrostis fosbergii	Flowering plants	E	US	08/10/98	F	Poaceae	HI; U.S.A. (HI)
Fountain thistle	Cirsium fontinale var. fontinale	Flowering plants	E	US	09/30/98	F	Asteraceae	CA; U.S.A. (CA)
Four-petal pawpaw	Asimina tetramera	Flowering plants	E	US	05/18/99	F	Annonaceae	FL; U.S.A. (FL)
Fragrant prickly-apple	Cereus eriophorus var. fragrans	Flowering plants	E	US	05/18/99	F	Cactaceae	FL; U.S.A. (FL)
Franciscan manzanita	Arctostaphylos franciscana	Flowering plants	E	US	02/13/13	O	Ericaceae	CA; U.S.A. (CA)
Fringed campion	Silene polypetala	Flowering plants	E	US	10/01/96	D	Caryophyllaceae	FL, GA; Majority of species abundance found in Piedmont Fall line ravines of Georgia and extending barely into Atlantic Coastal Plain in Georgia. Located in the Gulf Coastal Plain along the Florida/Georgia border on the Appalachicola River. In Piedmont, species found typically over Biotite Gneiss geology, over various limestones in the Coastal Plain.; U.S.A. (GA, FL)
Furbish lousewort	Pedicularis furbishiae	Flowering plants	E	US/foreign	07/02/91	RF(1)	Scrophulariaceae	ME; Canada (N.B.); The species is found in the St. John River in Aroostook County, Maine and in New Brunswick, Canada,; U.S.A. (ME), Canada (N.B.)
Gambel's watercress	Rorippa gambellii	Flowering plants	E	US	09/28/98	F	Brassicaceae	CA; U.S.A. (CA)
Garber's spurge	Chamaesyce garberi	Flowering plants	T	US	05/18/99	F	Euphorbiaceae	FL; U.S.A. (FL)
Garrett's mint	Dicerandra christmanii	Flowering plants	E	US	05/18/99	F	Lamiaceae	FL; Lake Wales Ridge; U.S.A. (FL)
Gaviota tarplant	Deinandra increscens ssp. villosa	Flowering plants	E	US	None	—	Asteraceae	CA; U.S.A. (CA)
Gentian pinkroot	Spigelia gentianoides	Flowering plants	E	US	03/26/12	F	Loganiaceae	AL, FL; U.S.A. (FL, AL)
Gentner's fritillary	Fritillaria gentneri	Flowering plants	E	US	08/28/03	F	Liliaceae	CA, OR; U.S.A. (OR)
Georgia rockcress	Arabis georgiana	Flowering plants	T	US	None	—	Brassicaceae	AL, GA;
Gierisch mallow	Sphaeralcea gierischii	Flowering plants	E	US	None	—	malvaceae	AZ, UT;
Godfrey's butterwort	Pinguicula ionantha	Flowering plants	T	US	06/22/94	F	Lentibulariaceae	FL; U.S.A. (FL)
Golden paintbrush	Castilleja levisecta	Flowering plants	T	US/foreign	08/23/00	F	Scrophulariaceae	OR, WA; Canada (B.C.); U.S.A. (WA, OR), Canada (B.C.)
Golden sedge	Carex lutea	Flowering plants	E	US	05/21/14	F	Cyperaceae	NC; U.S.A. (NC)
Gowen cypress	Cupressus goveniana ssp. goveniana	Conifers and cycads	T	US	08/19/04	F	Cupressaceae	CA; U.S.A. (CA)
Green pitcher-plant	Sarracenia oreophila	Flowering plants	E	US	12/12/94	RF(2)	Sarraceniaceae	AL, GA, NC; U.S.A. (TN, NC, GA, AL)
Greene's tuctoria	Tuctoria greenei	Flowering plants	E	US	03/07/06	F	Poaceae	CA, OR; U.S.A. (CA)
Guthrie's (=Pyne's) ground-plum	Astragalus bibullatus	Flowering plants	E	US	08/09/11	F	Fabaceae	TN; U.S.A. (TN)
Gypsum wild-buckwheat	Eriogonum gypsophilum	Flowering plants	T	US	03/30/84	F	Polygonaceae	NM; U.S.A. (NM)
Ha'iwale	Cyrtandra crenata	Flowering plants	E	US	08/10/98	F	Gesneriaceae	HI; U.S.A. (HI)
Ha'iwale	Cyrtandra dentata	Flowering plants	E	US	08/10/98	F	Gesneriaceae	HI; U.S.A. (HI)
Ha'iwale	Cyrtandra filipes	Flowering plants	E	US	None	—	Gesneriaceae	HI;
Ha'iwale	Cyrtandra giffardii	Flowering plants	E	US	09/26/96	F	Gesneriaceae	HI; U.S.A. (HI)
Ha'iwale	Cyrtandra kaulantha	Flowering plants	E	US	None	—	Gesneriaceae	HI; U.S.A. (HI)

TABLE 10.1

Endangered and threatened plant species, February 2016 [CONTINUED]

Common name	Scientific name	Species group	Federal listing status[a]	U.S. or U.S./foreign listed	Recovery plan date	Recovery plan stage[b]	Family	Current distribution
Ha'iwale	*Cyrtandra limahuliensis*	Flowering plants	T	US	08/23/98	F	Gesneriaceae	HI; U.S.A. (HI)
Ha'iwale	*Cyrtandra munroi*	Flowering plants	E	US	09/29/95	F	Gesneriaceae	HI; U.S.A. (HI)
Ha'iwale	*Cyrtandra oenobarba*	Flowering plants	E	US	06/17/10	O	Gesneriaceae	HI; U.S.A. (HI)
Ha'iwale	*Cyrtandra oxybapha*	Flowering plants	E	US	None	—	Gesneriaceae	HI;
Ha'iwale	*Cyrtandra polyantha*	Flowering plants	E	US	08/10/98	F	Gesneriaceae	HI; U.S.A. (HI)
Ha'iwale	*Cyrtandra sessilis*	Flowering plants	E	US	None	—	Gesneriaceae	HI; U.S.A. (HI)
Ha'iwale	*Cyrtandra subumbellata*	Flowering plants	E	US	08/10/98	F	Gesneriaceae	HI; U.S.A. (HI)
Ha'iwale	*Cyrtandra tintinnabula*	Flowering plants	E	US	05/11/98	F	Gesneriaceae	HI; U.S.A. (HI)
Ha'iwale	*Cyrtandra viridiflora*	Flowering plants	E	US	08/10/98	F	Gesneriaceae	HI; U.S.A. (HI)
Haha	*Cyanea acuminata*	Flowering plants	E	US	08/10/98	F	Campanulaceae	HI; U.S.A. (HI)
Haha	*Cyanea asarifolia*	Flowering plants	E	US	08/23/98	F	Campanulaceae	HI; U.S.A. (HI)
Haha	*Cyanea asplenifolia*	Flowering plants	E	US	None	—	Campanulaceae	HI;
Haha	*Cyanea calycina*	Flowering plants	E	US	None	—	Campanulaceae	HI; U.S.A. (HI)
Haha	*Cyanea copelandii ssp. copelandii*	Flowering plants	E	US	09/26/96	F	Campanulaceae	HI; U.S.A. (HI)
Haha	*Cyanea copelandii ssp. haleakalaensis*	Flowering plants	E	US	07/10/99	F	Campanulaceae	HI; U.S.A. (HI)
haha	*Cyanea crispa*	Flowering plants	E	US	08/10/98	F	Campanulaceae	HI; U.S.A. (HI)
Haha	*Cyanea dolichopoda*	Flowering plants	E	US	06/17/10	O	Campanulaceae	HI; U.S.A. (HI)
Haha	*Cyanea dunbarii*	Flowering plants	E	US	None	—	Campanulaceae	HI; U.S.A. (HI)
haha	*Cyanea duvalliorum*	Flowering plants	E	US	None	—	Campanulaceae	HI; U.S.A. (HI)
Haha	*Cyanea eleeleensis*	Flowering plants	E	US	06/17/10	O	Campanulaceae	HI; U.S.A. (HI)
Haha	*Cyanea glabra*	Flowering plants	E	US	07/10/99	F	Campanulaceae	HI; U.S.A. (HI)
Haha	*Cyanea grimesiana ssp. grimesiana*	Flowering plants	E	US	12/10/02	F	Campanulaceae	HI; U.S.A. (HI)
Haha	*Cyanea grimesiana ssp. obatae*	Flowering plants	E	US	08/10/98	F	Campanulaceae	HI; U.S.A. (HI)
Haha	*Cyanea hamatiflora ssp. carlsonii*	Flowering plants	E	US	09/26/96	F	Campanulaceae	HI; U.S.A. (HI)
Haha	*Cyanea hamatiflora ssp. hamatiflora*	Flowering plants	E	US	12/10/02	F	Campanulaceae	HI; U.S.A. (HI)
Haha	*Cyanea humboldtiana*	Flowering plants	E	US	08/10/98	F	Campanulaceae	HI; U.S.A. (HI)
Haha	*Cyanea kolekoleensis*	Flowering plants	E	US	06/17/10	O	Campanulaceae	HI; U.S.A. (HI)
Haha	*Cyanea koolauensis*	Flowering plants	E	US	08/10/98	F	Campanulaceae	HI; U.S.A. (HI)
Haha	*Cyanea kuhihewa*	Flowering plants	E	US	06/17/10	O	Campanulaceae	HI; U.S.A. (HI)
Haha	*Cyanea kunthiana*	Flowering plants	E	US	None	—	Campanulaceae	HI; U.S.A. (HI)
Haha	*Cyanea lanceolata*	Flowering plants	E	US	None	—	Campanulaceae	HI; U.S.A. (HI)
Haha	*Cyanea lobata*	Flowering plants	E	US	07/29/97	F	Campanulaceae	HI; U.S.A. (HI)
Haha	*Cyanea longiflora*	Flowering plants	E	US	08/10/98	F	Campanulaceae	HI; U.S.A. (HI)
Haha	*Cyanea macrostegia ssp. gibsonii*	Flowering plants	E	US	09/29/95	F	Campanulaceae	HI; U.S.A. (HI)
haha	*Cyanea magnicalyx*	Flowering plants	E	US	None	—	Campanulaceae	HI;
Haha	*Cyanea mannii*	Flowering plants	E	US	05/20/98	F	Campanulaceae	HI; U.S.A. (HI)
haha	*Cyanea maritae*	Flowering plants	E	US	None	—	Campanulaceae	HI;
Haha	*Cyanea marksii*	Flowering plants	E	US	None	—	Campanulaceae	HI;
haha	*Cyanea mauiensis*	Flowering plants	E	US	None	—	Campanulaceae	HI;
Haha	*Cyanea mceldowneyi*	Flowering plants	E	US	07/29/97	F	Campanulaceae	HI; U.S.A. (HI)
Haha	*Cyanea munroi*	Flowering plants	E	US	None	—	Campanulaceae	HI;
haha	*Cyanea obtusa*	Flowering plants	E	US	None	—	Campanulaceae	HI;
Haha	*Cyanea pinnatifida*	Flowering plants	E	US	08/10/98	F	Campanulaceae	HI; U.S.A. (HI)
Haha	*Cyanea procera*	Flowering plants	E	US	05/20/98	F	Campanulaceae	HI; U.S.A. (HI)
Haha	*Cyanea recta*	Flowering plants	T	US	08/23/98	F	Campanulaceae	HI; U.S.A. (HI)
Haha	*Cyanea remyi*	Flowering plants	E	US	09/20/95	F	Campanulaceae	HI; U.S.A. (HI)
Haha	*Cyanea rivularis*	Flowering plants	E	US	08/23/98	F	Campanulaceae	HI; U.S.A. (HI)
Haha	*Cyanea shipmanii*	Flowering plants	E	US	05/11/98	F	Campanulaceae	HI; U.S.A. (HI)
Haha	*Cyanea st.-johnii*	Flowering plants	E	US	08/10/98	F	Campanulaceae	HI; U.S.A. (HI)
Haha	*Cyanea stictophylla*	Flowering plants	E	US	05/11/98	F	Campanulaceae	HI; U.S.A. (HI)
Haha	*Cyanea superba*	Flowering plants	E	US	08/10/98	F	Campanulaceae	HI; U.S.A. (HI)
Haha	*Cyanea truncata*	Flowering plants	E	US	08/10/98	F	Campanulaceae	HI; U.S.A. (HI)

TABLE 10.1

Endangered and threatened plant species, February 2016 [CONTINUED]

Common name	Scientific name	Species group	Federal listing status[a]	U.S. or U.S./foreign listed	Recovery plan date	Recovery plan stage[b]	Family	Current distribution
Haha	Cyanea undulata	Flowering plants	E	US	05/31/94	F	Campanulaceae	HI; U.S.A. (HI)
Haha nui	Cyanea horrida	Flowering plants	E	US	None	—	Campanulaceae	
Hairy Orcutt grass	Orcuttia pilosa	Flowering plants	E	US	03/07/06	F	Poaceae	CA; U.S.A. (CA)
Hairy rattleweed	Baptisia arachnifera	Flowering plants	E	US	03/19/84	F	Fabaceae	GA; U.S.A. (GA)
Haiwale	Cyrtandra ferripilosa	Flowering plants	E	US	None	—	Gesneriaceae	
Haiwale	Cyrtandra nanawaleensis	Flowering plants	E	US	None	—	Gesneriaceae	
Haiwale	Cyrtandra paliku	Flowering plants	E	US	06/17/10	0	Gesneriaceae	HI; U.S.A. (HI)
Haiwale	Cyrtandra wagneri	Flowering plants	E	US	None	—	Gesneriaceae	HI;
Hala pepe	Pleomele fernaldii	Flowering plants	E	US	None	—	Agavaceae	HI; U.S.A. (HI)
Hala pepe	Pleomele forbesii	Flowering plants	E	US	None	—	Agavaceae	HI; U.S.A. (HI)
Hala pepe	Pleomele hawaiiensis	Flowering plants	E	US	09/26/96	F	Asparagaceae	HI; U.S.A. (HI)
Harperella	Ptilimnium nodosum	Flowering plants	E	US	03/05/91	F	Apiaceae	AL, AR, GA, MD, NC, OK, SC, VA, WV; U.S.A. (WV, SC, NC, MD, GA, AR, AL)
Harper's beauty	Harperocallis flava	Flowering plants	E	US	09/14/83	F	Liliaceae	FL; U.S.A. (FL)
Hartweg's golden sunburst	Pseudobahia bahiifolia	Flowering plants	E	US	None	—	Asteraceae	CA; U.S.A. (CA)
Hau kuahiwi	Hibiscadelphus giffardianus	Flowering plants	E	US	05/11/98	F	Malvaceae	HI; U.S.A. (HI)
Hau kuahiwi	Hibiscadelphus hualalaiensis	Flowering plants	E	US	09/26/96	F	Malvaceae	HI; U.S.A. (HI)
Hau kuahiwi	Hibiscadelphus woodii	Flowering plants	E	US	08/23/98	F	Malvaceae	HI; U.S.A. (HI)
Hawaiian bluegrass	Poa sandvicensis	Flowering plants	E	US	09/20/95	F	Poaceae	HI; U.S.A. (HI)
Hawaiian gardenia (=Na'u)	Gardenia brighamii	Flowering plants	E	US	09/30/93	F	Rubiaceae	HI; U.S.A. (HI)
Hawaiian vetch	Vicia menziesii	Flowering plants	E	US	05/18/84	F	Fabaceae	HI; U.S.A. (HI)
Hayun lagu (=(Guam), Tronkon guafi (Rota)	Serianthes nelsonii	Flowering plants	E	US	02/02/94	F	Fabaceae	GU, MP; Western Pacific Ocean-U.S.A. (Guam, MP-Rota)
Heau	Exocarpos luteolus	Flowering plants	E	US	09/20/95	F	Santalaceae	HI; U.S.A. (HI)
Heliotrope milk-vetch	Astragalus montii	Flowering plants	T	US	09/27/95	D	Fabaceae	UT; U.S.A. (UT)
Heller's blazingstar	Liatris helleri	Flowering plants	T	US	01/28/00	RF(1)	Asteraceae	NC; U.S.A. (NC)
Hickman's potentilla	Potentilla hickmanii	Flowering plants	E	US	08/19/04	F	Rosaceae	CA; U.S.A. (CA)
Hidden Lake bluecurls	Trichostema austromontanum ssp. compactum	Flowering plants	T	US	None	—	Lamiaceae	CA; U.S.A. (CA)
Highlands scrub hypericum	Hypericum cumulicola	Flowering plants	E	US	05/18/99	F	Hypericaceae	FL; U.S.A. (FL)
Higo chumbo	Harrisia portoricensis	Flowering plants	T	US	11/12/96	F	Cactaceae	PR; Endemic to Puerto Rico. Currently known from Mona Island, Monito Island, Desecheo NWR and Caja de Muertos; U.S.A. (PR)
Higuero de sierra	Crescentia portoricensis	Flowering plants	E	US	09/23/91	F	Bignoniaceae	PR; U.S.A. (PR)
Hillegrand's reedgrass	Calamagrostis hillebrandii	Flowering plants	E	US	None	—	Poaceae	HI;
Hilo ischaemum	Ischaemum byrone	Flowering plants	E	US	09/26/96	F	Poaceae	HI; U.S.A. (HI)
Hinckley oak	Quercus hinckleyi	Flowering plants	T	US	09/30/92	F	Fagaceae	TX; U.S.A. (TX)
Ho'awa	Pittosporum napaliense	Flowering plants	E	US	06/17/10	0	Pittosporaceae	HI; U.S.A. (HI)
Hoffmann's rock-cress	Arabis hoffmannii	Flowering plants	E	US	09/26/00	F	Brassicaceae	CA; U.S.A. (CA)
Hoffmann's slender-flowered gilia	Gilia tenuiflora ssp. hoffmannii	Flowering plants	E	US	09/26/00	F	Polemoniaceae	CA; U.S.A. (CA)
Holei	Ochrosia kilaueaensis	Flowering plants	E	US	09/26/96	F	Apocynaceae	HI; U.S.A. (HI)
Holmgren milk-vetch	Astragalus holmgreniorum	Flowering plants	E	US	09/29/06	F	Fabaceae	AZ, UT; U.S.A. (UT, AZ)
Holy Ghost ipomopsis	Ipomopsis sancti-spiritus	Flowering plants	E	US	09/26/02	F	Polemoniaceae	NM; U.S.A. (NM)
Honohono	Haplostachys haplostachya	Flowering plants	E	US	09/20/93	D	Lamiaceae	HI; U.S.A. (HI)
Hoover's spurge	Chamaesyce hooveri	Flowering plants	T	US	03/07/06	F	Euphorbiaceae	CA, OR; U.S.A. (CA)
Houghton's goldenrod	Solidago houghtonii	Flowering plants	T	US/foreign	09/17/97	F	Asteraceae	MI, NY, Canada (Ont.); U.S.A. (MI), Canada (Ont.)
Howell's spectacular thelypody	Thelypodium howellii spectabilis	Flowering plants	T	US	06/03/02	F	Brassicaceae	OR; U.S.A. (OR)
Howell's spineflower	Chorizanthe howellii	Flowering plants	E	US	09/29/98	F	Polygonaceae	CA; U.S.A. (FL)
Huachuca water-umbel	Lilaeopsis schaffneriana var. recurva	Flowering plants	E	US/foreign	None	—	Apiaceae	AZ; U.S.A. (AZ), Mexico
Hulumoa	Korthalsella degeneri	Flowering plants	E	US	None	—	Santalaceae	HI; U.S.A. (HI)
Ihi'ihi	Marsilea villosa	Ferns and allies	E	US	04/18/96	F	Marsileaceae	HI; U.S.A. (HI)
Indian Knob mountain balm	Eriodictyon altissimum	Flowering plants	E	US	09/28/98	F	Hydrophyllaceae	CA; U.S.A. (CA)
Ione (incl. Irish Hill) buckwheat	Eriogonum apricum (incl. var. prostratum)	Flowering plants	E	US	None	—	Polygonaceae	CA; U.S.A. (CA)

TABLE 10.1

Endangered and threatened plant species, February 2016 [CONTINUED]

Common name	Scientific name	Species group	Federal listing status[a]	U.S. or U.S./foreign listed	Recovery plan date	Recovery plan stage[b]	Family	Current distribution
Ione manzanita	*Arctostaphylos myrtifolia*	Flowering plants	T	US	None	—	Ericaceae	CA; U.S.A. (CA)
Island barberry	*Berberis pinnata ssp. insularis*	Flowering plants	E	US	09/26/00	F	Berberidaceae	CA; U.S.A. (CA)
Island bedstraw	*Gaium buxifolium*	Flowering plants	E	US	09/26/00	F	Rubiaceae	CA; U.S.A. (CA)
Island malacothrix	*Malacothrix squalida*	Flowering plants	E	US	09/26/00	F	Asteraceae	CA; U.S.A. (CA)
Island phacelia	*Phacelia insularis ssp. insularis*	Flowering plants	E	US	09/26/00	F	Hydrophyllacae	CA; U.S.A. (CA)
Island rush-rose	*Helianthemum greenei*	Flowering plants	T	US	09/26/00	F	Cistaceae	CA; U.S.A. (CA)
Jesup's milk-vetch	*Astragalus robbinsii var. jesupi*	Flowering plants	E	US	11/21/89	F	Fabaceae	NH, VT; U.S.A. (VT, NH)
Johnson's seagrass	*Haophila johnsonii*	Flowering plants	T	US	10/04/02	F	Hydrocharitaceae	FL; U.S.A. (FL)
Jones cycladenia	*Cycladenia humilis var. jonesii*	Flowering plants	T	US	12/30/08	O	Apocynaceae	AZ, UT; U.S.A. (UT, AZ)
Kamakahala	*Labordia cyrtandrae*	Flowering plants	E	US	08/10/98	O	Loganiaceae	HI; U.S.A. (HI)
Kamakahala	*Labordia helleri*	Flowering plants	E	US	06/17/10	O	Loganiaceae	HI; U.S.A. (HI)
Kamakahala	*Labordia lydgatei*	Flowering plants	E	US	05/31/94	F	Loganiaceae	HI; U.S.A. (HI)
Kamakahala	*Labordia pumila*	Flowering plants	E	US	06/17/10	O	Loganiaceae	HI; U.S.A. (HI)
Kamakahala	*Labordia tinifolia var. lanaiensis*	Flowering plants	E	US	07/10/99	F	Loganiaceae	HI; U.S.A. (HI)
Kamakahala	*Labordia tinifolia var. wahiawaensis*	Flowering plants	E	US	09/20/95	F	Loganiaceae	HI; U.S.A. (HI)
Kamakahala	*Labordia triflora*	Flowering plants	E	US	07/10/99	F	Loganiaceae	HI; U.S.A. (HI)
Kamanomano	*Cenchrus agrimonioides*	Flowering plants	E	US	12/10/02	F	Poaceae	HI; U.S.A. (HI)
Kauai hau. kuahiwi	*Hibiscadelphus distans*	Flowering plants	E	US	06/05/96	F	Malvaceae	HI; U.S.A. (HI)
Kauila	*Cotubrina oppositifolia*	Flowering plants	E	US	09/26/96	F	Rhamnaceae	HI; U.S.A. (HI)
Kaulu	*Pteralyxia kauaiensis*	Flowering plants	E	US	09/20/95	F	Apocynaceae	HI; U.S.A. (HI)
Kaulu	*Pteralyxia macrocarpa*	Flowering plants	E	US	None	—	Apocynaceae	HI; U.S.A. (HI)
Kearney's blue-star	*Amsonia kearneyana*	Flowering plants	E	US	05/24/93	F	Apocynaceae	AZ; U.S.A. (AZ)
Keck's checker-mallow	*Sidalcea keckii*	Flowering plants	E	US	None	—	Malvaceae	CA; U.S.A. (CA)
Kentucky glade cress	*Leavenworthia exigua laciniata*	Flowering plants	T	US	None	—	Brassicaceae	KY;
Kenwood Marsh checker-mallow	*Sidalcea oregana ssp. valida*	Flowering plants	E	US	None	—	Malvaceae	CA; U.S.A. (CA)
Kern mallow	*Eremalche kernensis*	Flowering plants	E	US	09/30/98	F	Malvaceae	CA; U.S.A. (CA)
Key tree cactus	*Pilosocereus robinii*	Flowering plants	E	US/foreign	05/18/99	F	Cactaceae	CA, FL; U.S.A. (FL), Cuba
Kincaid's lupine	*Lupinus sulphureus ssp. kincaidii*	Flowering plants	T	US	06/29/10	F	Fabaceae	OR, WA; U.S.A. (WA, OR)
Kic'ele	*Kadua coriacea*	Flowering plants	E	US	07/29/97	F	Rubiaceae	HI; U.S.A. (HI)
Kiponapona	*Phyllostegia racemosa*	Flowering plants	E	US	09/26/96	F	Lamiaceae	HI; U.S.A. (HI)
Kneeland Prairie penny-cress	*Thlaspi californicum*	Flowering plants	E	US	08/14/03	F	Brassicaceae	CA; U.S.A. (CA)
Knieskern's beaked-rush	*Rhynchospora knieskernii*	Flowering plants	T	US	09/29/93	F	Cyperaceae	NJ; U.S.A. (NJ, DE)
Knowlton's cactus	*Pediocactus knowltonii*	Flowering plants	E	US	03/29/85	F	Cactaceae	CO, NM; U.S.A. (NM, CO)
Ko'oko'olau	*Bidens amplectens*	Flowering plants	E	US	None	—	Asteraceae	HI; U.S.A. (HI)
Ko'oko'olau	*Bidens campylotheca pentamera*	Flowering plants	E	US	None	—	Asteraceae	HI;
Ko'oko'olau	*Bidens campylotheca waihoiensis*	Flowering plants	E	US	None	—	Asteraceae	HI;
Ko'oko'olau	*Bidens conjuncta*	Flowering plants	E	US	None	—	Asteraceae	HI;
Ko'oko'olau	*Bidens micrantha ctenophylla*	Flowering plants	E	US	07/29/97	F	Asteraceae	HI; U.S.A. (HI)
Ko'oko'olau	*Bidens micrantha ssp. kalealaha*	Flowering plants	E	US	09/26/96	F	Asteraceae	HI; U.S.A. (HI)
Ko'oko'olau	*Bidens wiebkei*	Flowering plants	E	US	09/29/95	F	Asteraceae	HI; U.S.A. (HI)
Ko'oloa'ula	*Abutilon menziesii*	Flowering plants	E	US	10/27/09	O	Malvaceae	HI; U.S.A. (HI)
Kodachrome bladderpod	*Lesquerella tumulosa*	Flowering plants	E	US	12/10/02	F	Brassicaceae	UT; U.S.A. (UT)
Kohe malama malama o kanaloa	*Kanaloa kahoolawensis*	Flowering plants	E	US	12/10/02	F	Fabaceae	HI; U.S.A. (HI)
Koholapehu	*Dubautia latifolia*	Flowering plants	E	US	09/20/95	F	Asteraceae	HI; U.S.A. (HI)
Koki'o	*Kokia drynarioides*	Flowering plants	E	US	05/06/94	F	Malvaceae	HI; U.S.A. (HI)
Koki'o	*Kokia kauaiensis*	Flowering plants	E	US	08/23/98	F	Malvaceae	HI; U.S.A. (HI)
Koki'o ke'oke'o	*Hibiscus arnottianus ssp. immaculatus*	Flowering plants	E	US	08/28/13	F	Malvaceae	HI; U.S.A. (HI)
Koki'o ke'oke'o	*Hibiscus waimeae ssp. hannerae*	Flowering plants	E	US	08/23/98	F	Malvaceae	HI; U.S.A. (HI)
Kolea	*Myrsine juddii*	Flowering plants	E	US	08/10/98	F	Primulaceae	HI; U.S.A. (HI)
Kolea	*Myrsine knudsenii*	Flowering plants	E	US	06/17/10	O	Primulaceae	HI; U.S.A. (HI)
Kolea	*Myrsine linearifolia*	Flowering plants	T	US	09/20/95	F	Primulaceae	HI; U.S.A. (HI)
Kolea	*Myrsine mezii*	Flowering plants	E	US	06/17/10	O	Primulaceae	HI; believed to be extinct; U.S.A. (HI)

TABLE 10.1

Endangered and threatened plant species, February 2016 [CONTINUED]

Common name	Scientific name	Species group	Federal listing status[a]	U.S. or U.S./foreign listed	Recovery plan date	Recovery plan stage[b]	Family	Current distribution
Kolea	*Myrsine vaccinioides*	Flowering plants	E	US	None	—	Primulaceae	HI;
Kookoolau	*Bidens hillebrandiana ssp. hillebrandiana*	Flowering plants	E	US	None	—	Asteraceae	HI;
Kopa	*Hedyotis schlechtendahliana var. remyi*	Flowering plants	E	US	07/10/99	F	Rubiaceae	HI; U.S.A. (HI)
Kopiko	*Psychotria grandiflora*	Flowering plants	E	US	06/17/10	O	Rubiaceae	HI; U.S.A. (HI)
Kopiko	*Psychotria hobdyi*	Flowering plants	E	US	06/17/10	O	Rubiaceae	HI; U.S.A. (HI)
Kral's water-plantain	*Sagittaria secundifolia*	Flowering plants	T	US	08/12/91	F	Alismataceae	AL, GA; U.S.A. (GA, AL)
Kuahiwi laukahi	*Plantago hawaiensis*	Flowering plants	E	US	05/11/98	F	Plantaginaceae	HI; U.S.A. (HI)
Kuahiwi laukahi	*Plantago princeps*	Flowering plants	E	US	07/10/99	F	Plantaginaceae	HI; U.S.A. (HI)
Kuawawaenohu	*Schiedea lychnoides*	Flowering plants	E	US	08/23/98	F	Caryophyllaceae	HI; U.S.A. (HI)
Kuenzler hedgehog cactus	*Echinocereus fendleri var. kuenzleri*	Flowering plants	E	US	03/28/85	F	Cactaceae	NM; U.S.A. (NM)
Kula wahine noho	*Isodendrion pyrifolium*	Flowering plants	E	US	05/11/98	F	Violaceae	HI; U.S.A. (HI)
Kulu'i	*Nototrichium humile*	Flowering plants	E	US	08/10/98	F	Amaranthaceae	HI; U.S.A. (HI)
La Graciosa thistle	*Cirsium loncholepis*	Flowering plants	E	US	None	—	Asteraceae	CA; U.S.A. (CA)
Laguna Beach liveforever	*Dudleya stolonifera*	Flowering plants	T	US	None	—	Crassulaceae	CA; U.S.A. (CA)
Lake County stonecrop	*Parvisedum leiocarpum*	Flowering plants	E	US	03/07/06	F	Crassulaceae	CA; U.S.A. (CA)
Lakela's mint	*Dicerandra immaculata*	Flowering plants	E	US	05/18/99	F	Lamiaceae	FL; U.S.A. (FL)
Lakeside daisy	*Hymenoxys herbacea*	Flowering plants	T	US/foreign	09/19/90	F	Asteraceae	IL, MI, OH; Canada (Ont.); U.S.A. (OH, MI, IL), Canada (Ont.)
Lanai sandalwood (='iliahi)	*Santalum haleakalae var. lanaiense*	Flowering plants	E	US	09/29/95	F	Santalaceae	HI; U.S.A. (HI)
Lane Mountain milk-vetch	*Astragalus jaegerianus*	Flowering plants	E	US	None	—	Fabaceae	CA; U.S.A. (CA)
Large-flowered fiddleneck	*Amsinckia grandiflora*	Flowering plants	E	US	09/29/97	F	Boraginaceae	CA; U.S.A. (CA)
Large-flowered skullcap	*Scutellaria montana*	Flowering plants	T	US	05/15/96	F	Lamiaceae	GA, TN; U.S.A. (TN, GA)
Large-flowered woolly meadowfoam	*Limnanthes floccosa ssp. grandiflora*	Flowering plants	E	US	03/22/13	F	Limnanthaceae	OR; U.S.A. (OR)
Large-fruited sand-verbena	*Abronia macrocarpa*	Flowering plants	E	US	09/30/92	F	Nyctaginaceae	TX; U.S.A. (TX)
Last Chance townsendia	*Townsendia aprica*	Flowering plants	T	US	08/20/93	F	Asteraceae	UT; U.S.A. (UT)
Lau'ehu	*Panicum niihauense*	Flowering plants	E	US	07/10/99	F	Poaceae	HI; U.S.A. (HI)
Laulihilihi	*Schiedea stellarioides*	Flowering plants	E	US	08/23/98	F	Caryophyllaceae	HI; U.S.A. (HI)
Layne's butterweed	*Senecio layneae*	Flowering plants	T	US	08/30/02	F	Asteraceae	CA; U.S.A. (CA)
Leafy prairie-clover	*Dalea foliosa*	Flowering plants	E	US	09/30/96	F	Fabaceae	AL, IL, TN; U.S.A. (TN, IL, AL)
Lee pincushion cactus	*Coryphantha sneedii var. leei*	Flowering plants	T	US	03/21/86	F	Cactaceae	NM; U.S.A. (NM)
Leedy's roseroot	*Rhodiola integrifolia ssp. leedyi*	Flowering plants	T	US	09/25/98	F	Crassulaceae	MN, NY, SD; ; U.S.A. (NY, MN)
Lehua makanoe	*Lysimachia daphnoides*	Flowering plants	E	US	06/17/10	O	Primulaceae	HI; U.S.A. (HI)
Lewton's polygala	*Polygala lewtonii*	Flowering plants	E	US	05/18/99	F	Polygalaceae	FL; U.S.A. (FL)
Liliwai	*Acaena exigua*	Flowering plants	E	US	07/29/97	F	Rosaceae	HI; U.S.A. (HI)
Little Aguja (=Creek) pondweed	*Potamogeton clystocarpus*	Flowering plants	E	US	06/20/94	F	Potamogetonaceae	TX; U.S.A. (TX)
Little amphianthus	*Amphianthus pusillus*	Flowering plants	T	US	07/07/93	F	Scrophulariaceae	AL, GA, SC; U.S.A. (SC, GA, AL)
Lloyd's Mariposa cactus	*Echinomastus mariposensis*	Flowering plants	T	US/foreign	04/13/90	F	Cactaceae	TX; Mexico-Coahuila; U.S.A. (TX), Mexico (Coahuila)
Lo'ulu	*Pritchardia kaalae*	Flowering plants	E	US	08/10/98	F	Arecaceae	HI; U.S.A. (HI)
Lo'ulu	*Pritchardia lanigera*	Flowering plants	E	US	None	—	Arecaceae	HI;
Lo'ulu	*Pritchardia maideniana*	Flowering plants	E	US	09/26/96	F	Arecaceae	HI; U.S.A. (HI)
Lo'ulu	*Pritchardia munroi*	Flowering plants	E	US	05/20/98	F	Arecaceae	HI; U.S.A. (HI)
Lo'ulu	*Pritchardia napaliensis*	Flowering plants	E	US	08/23/98	F	Arecaceae	HI; U.S.A. (HI)
Lo'ulu	*Pritchardia remota*	Flowering plants	E	US	03/31/98	F	Arecaceae	HI; U.S.A. (HI)
Lo'ulu	*Pritchardia schattaueri*	Flowering plants	E	US	09/26/96	F	Arecaceae	HI; U.S.A. (HI)
Lo'ulu	*Pritchardia viscosa*	Flowering plants	E	US	08/23/98	F	Arecaceae	HI; U.S.A. (HI)
Loch Lomond coyote thistle	*Eryngium constancei*	Flowering plants	E	US	03/07/06	F	Apiaceae	CA; U.S.A. (CA)
Lompoc yerba santa	*Eriodictyon capitatum*	Flowering plants	E	US	None	—	Hydrophyllaceae	CA; U.S.A. (CA)
Longspurred mint	*Dicerandra cornutissima*	Flowering plants	E	US	07/01/87	F	Lamiaceae	FL; known to occur in scrub habitat in Marion County, Florida (includes sites at the Cross Florida Greenway, along I-75, and on private lands in Marion Oaks and Ocala Waterway Estates);; U.S.A. (FL)
Louisiana quillwort	*Isoetes louisianensis*	Ferns and allies	E	US	09/30/96	F	Isoetaceae	AL, LA, MS; U.S.A. (MS, LA)
Lyon's pentachaeta	*Pentachaeta lyonii*	Flowering plants	E	US	09/30/99	F	Asteraceae	CA; U.S.A. (CA)

TABLE 10.1

Endangered and threatened plant species, February 2016 [CONTINUED]

Common name	Scientific name	Species group	Federal listing status[a]	U.S. or U.S./foreign listed	Recovery plan date	Recovery plan stage[b]	Family	Current distribution
Lyrate bladderpod	Lesquerella lyrata	Flowering plants	T	US	10/17/96	F	Brassicaceae	AL; U.S.A. (AL)
Ma'oli oli	Schiedea apokremnos	Flowering plants	E	US	08/23/98	F	Caryophyllaceae	HI; U.S.A. (HI)
Ma'oli oli	Schiedea hawaiiensis	Flowering plants	E	US	None	—	Caryophyllaceae	HI;
Ma'oli oli	Schiedea kealiae	Flowering plants	E	US	08/10/98	F	Caryophyllaceae	HI; U.S.A. (HI)
MacFarlane's four-o'clock	Mirabilis macfarlanei	Flowering plants	T	US	06/30/00	RF(1)	Nyctaginaceae	ID, OR; U.S.A. (OR, ID)
Maguire primrose	Primula maguirei	Flowering plants	T	US	09/27/90	F	Primulaceae	UT; U.S.A. (UT)
Mahoe	Alectryon macrococcus	Flowering plants	E	US	07/29/97	F	Sapindaceae	HI; U.S.A. (HI)
Makou	Peucedanum sandwicense	Flowering plants	T	US	09/20/95	F	Apiaceae	HI; U.S.A. (HI)
Malheur wire-lettuce	Stephanomeria malheurensis	Flowering plants	E	US	03/21/91	F	Asteraceae	OR; U.S.A. (OR)
Mancos milk-vetch	Astragalus humillimus	Flowering plants	E	US	12/20/89	F	Fabaceae	CO, NM; U.S.A. (NM, CO)
Mann's bluegrass	Poa mannii	Flowering plants	E	US	09/20/95	F	Poaceae	HI; U.S.A. (HI)
Many-flowered navarretia	Navarretia leucocephala ssp. plieantha	Flowering plants	E	US	03/07/06	F	Polemoniaceae	CA; U.S.A. (CA)
Mapele	Cyrtandra cyaneoides	Flowering plants	E	US	08/23/98	F	Gesneriaceae	HI; U.S.A. (HI)
Marcescent dudleya	Dudleya cymosa ssp. marcescens	Flowering plants	T	US	09/30/99	F	Crassulaceae	CA; U.S.A. (CA)
Marin dwarf-flax	Hesperolinon congestum	Flowering plants	T	US	09/30/98	F	Linaceae	CA; U.S.A. (CA)
Mariposa pussypaws	Calyptridium pulchellum	Flowering plants	T	US	None		Portulacaceae	CA; U.S.A. (CA)
Marsh sandwort	Arenaria paludicola	Flowering plants	E	US	09/28/98	F	Caryophyllaceae	CA; U.S.A. (WA, OR, CA)
Mat-forming quillwort	Isoetes tegetiformans	Ferns and allies	E	US	07/07/93	F	Isoetaceae	GA; U.S.A. (GA)
Maui remya	Remya mauiensis	Flowering plants	E	US	07/29/97	F	Asteraceae	HI; U.S.A. (HI)
Mauna Loa (=Ka'u) silversword	Argyroxiphium kauense	Flowering plants	E	US	11/21/95	F	Asteraceae	HI; U.S.A. (HI)
McDonald's rock-cress	Arabis macdonaldiana	Flowering plants	E	US	02/28/84	F	Brassicaceae	CA, OR; U.S.A. (CA)
Mead's milkweed	Asclepias meadii	Flowering plants	T	US	09/22/03	F	Asclepiadaceae	IA, IL, IN, KS, MO, WI: U.S.A. (WI, MO, KS, IN, IL, IA)
Mehamehame	Flueggea neowawraea	Flowering plants	E	US	07/10/99	F	Phyllanthaceae	HI; U.S.A. (HI)
Menzies' wallflower	Erysimum menziesii	Flowering plants	E	US	09/29/98	F	Brassicaceae	CA; U.S.A. (CA)
Mesa Verde cactus	Sclerocactus mesae-verdae	Flowering plants	T	US	03/30/84	F	Cactaceae	CO, NM; U.S.A. (NM, CO)
Metcalf Canyon jewelflower	Streptanthus albidus ssp. albidus	Flowering plants	E	US	09/30/98	F	Brassicaceae	CA; U.S.A. (CA)
Mexican flannelbush	Fremontodendron mexicanum	Flowering plants	E	US	None	—	Sterculiaceae	CA; U.S.A. (CA), Mexico
Miccosukee gooseberry	Ribes echinellum	Flowering plants	T	US/foreign	None		Saxifragaceae	FL, SC; U.S.A. (SC, FL)
Michaux's sumac	Rhus michauxii	Flowering plants	E	US	04/30/93	F	Anacardiaceae	GA, NC, SC, VA; U.S.A. (VA, SC, NC, GA)
Michigan monkey-flower	Mimulus michiganensis	Flowering plants	E	US	09/17/97	F	Scrophulariaceae	MI; U.S.A. (MI)
Minnesota dwarf trout lily	Erythronium propullans	Flowering plants	E	US	12/16/87	F	Liliaceae	MN; U.S.A. (MN)
Missouri bladderpod	Physaria filiformis	Flowering plants	E	US	04/07/88	F	Brassicaceae	AR, MO; U.S.A. (MO, AR)
Mohr's Barbara's buttons	Marshallia mohrii	Flowering plants	T	US	11/26/91	F	Asteraceae	AL, GA; U.S.A. (GA, AL)
Monterey clover	Trifolium trichocalyx	Flowering plants	E	US	08/19/04	F	Fabaceae	CA; U.S.A. (CA)
Monterey gilia	Gilia tenuiflora ssp. arenaria	Flowering plants	E	US	09/29/98	F	Polemoniaceae	CA; U.S.A. (CA)
Monterey spineflower	Chorizanthe pungens var. pungens	Flowering plants	T	US	09/29/98	F	Polygonaceae	CA; U.S.A. (CA)
Morefield's leather flower	Clematis morefieldii	Flowering plants	E	US	05/03/94	F	Ranunculaceae	AL, TN; U.S.A. (AL)
Morro manzanita	Arctostaphylos morroensis	Flowering plants	T	US	09/28/98	F	Ericaceae	CA; U.S.A. (CA)
Mountain golden heather	Hudsonia montana	Flowering plants	T	US	09/14/83	F	Cistaceae	NC; U.S.A. (NC)
Mountain sweet pitcher-plant	Sarracenia rubra ssp. jonesii	Flowering plants	E	US	08/13/90	F	Sarraceniaceae	NC, SC; U.S.A. (SC, NC)
Munz's onion	Allium munzii	Flowering plants	E	US	None		Liliaceae	CA; U.S.A. (CA)
Na'ena'e	Dubautia herbstobatae	Flowering plants	E	US	08/10/98	F	Asteraceae	HI; U.S.A. (HI)
Na'ena'e	Dubautia imbricata imbricata	Flowering plants	E	US	06/17/10	O	Asteraceae	HI; U.S.A. (HI)
Na'ena'e	Dubautia pauciflorula	Flowering plants	E	US	05/31/94	F	Asteraceae	HI; U.S.A. (HI)
Na'ena'e	Dubautia plantaginea magnifolia	Flowering plants	E	US	06/17/10	O	Asteraceae	HI; U.S.A. (HI)
Na'ena'e	Dubautia plantaginea ssp. humilis	Flowering plants	E	US	07/10/99	F	Asteraceae	HI; U.S.A. (HI)
Na'ena'e	Dubautia waialealae	Flowering plants	E	US	06/17/10	O	Asteraceae	HI; U.S.A. (HI)
Naenae	Dubautia kalalauensis	Flowering plants	E	US	06/17/10	O	Asteraceae	HI; U.S.A. (HI)
Naenae	Dubautia kenwoodii	Flowering plants	E	US	06/17/10	O	Asteraceae	NC; U.S.A. (NC)
Nani wai'ale'ale	Viola kauaiensis var. wahiawaensis	Flowering plants	E	US	08/23/98	F	Violaceae	HI; U.S.A. (HI)
Nanu	Gardenia mannii	Flowering plants	E	US	08/10/98	F	Rubiaceae	HI; U.S.A. (HI)
Napa bluegrass	Poa napensis	Flowering plants	E	US	None	—	Poaceae	CA; U.S.A. (CA)

TABLE 10.1

Endangered and threatened plant species, February 2016 [CONTINUED]

Common name	Scientific name	Species group	Federal listing status[a]	U.S. or U.S./foreign listed	Recovery plan date	Recovery plan stage[b]	Family	Current distribution
Navajo sedge	Carex specuicola	Flowering plants	T	US	09/24/87	F	Cyperaceae	AZ, UT; U.S.A. (UT, AZ)
Navasota ladies'-tresses	Spiranthes parksii	Flowering plants	E	US	09/21/84	F	Orchidaceae	TX; U.S.A. (TX)
Neches River rose-mallow	Hibiscus dasycalyx	Flowering plants	T	US	None	—	Malvaceae	TX;
Nehe	Lipochaeta fauriei	Flowering plants	E	US	08/23/98	F	Asteraceae	HI; U.S.A. (HI)
Nehe	Lipochaeta kamolensis	Flowering plants	E	US	07/29/97	F	Asteraceae	HI; U.S.A. (HI)
Nehe	Lipochaeta lobata var. leptophylla	Flowering plants	E	US	08/10/98	F	Asteraceae	HI; U.S.A. (HI)
Nehe	Lipochaeta micrantha	Flowering plants	E	US	08/23/98	F	Asteraceae	HI; U.S.A. (HI)
Nehe	Lipochaeta waimeaensis	Flowering plants	E	US	08/23/98	F	Asteraceae	HI; U.S.A. (HI)
Nehe	Melanthera tenuifolia	Flowering plants	E	US	08/10/98	F	Asteraceae	HI; U.S.A. (HI)
Nellie cory cactus	Coryphantha minima	Flowering plants	E	US	09/20/84	F	Cactaceae	TX; U.S.A. (TX)
Nelson's checker-mallow	Sidalcea nelsoniana	Flowering plants	T	US	06/29/10	F	Malvaceae	OR, WA; U.S.A. (WA, OR)
Nevin's barberry	Berberis nevinii	Flowering plants	E	US	None	—	Berberidaceae	CA; U.S.A. (CA)
Nichol's Turk's head cactus	Echinocactus horizonthalonius var. nicholii	Flowering plants	E	US	04/14/86	F	Cactaceae	AZ; U.S.A. (AZ)
Nioi	Eugenia koolauensis	Flowering plants	E	US	08/10/98	F	Myrtaceae	HI; U.S.A. (HI)
Nipomo Mesa lupine	Lupinus nipomensis	Flowering plants	E	US	None	—	Fabaceae	CA; U.S.A. (CA)
No common name	Abutilon eremitopetalum	Flowering plants	E	US	09/29/95	F	Malvaceae	HI; U.S.A. (HI)
No common name	Abutilon sandwicense	Flowering plants	E	US	08/10/98	F	Malvaceae	HI; U.S.A. (HI)
No common name	Achyranthes mutica	Flowering plants	E	US	07/10/99	F	Amaranthaceae	HI; U.S.A. (HI)
No common name	Adiantum vivesii	Ferns and allies	E	US	01/17/95	F	Adiantaceae	PR; U.S.A. (PR)
No common name	Agave eggersiana	Flowering plants	E	US	None	—	Agavaceae	VI;
No common name	Amaranthus brownii	Flowering plants	E	US	03/31/98	F	Amaranthaceae	HI; U.S.A. (HI)
No common name	Aristida chaseae	Flowering plants	E	US	07/31/95	F	Poaceae	PR; Endemic to Puerto Rico; U.S.A. (PR)
No common name	Asplenium diellafalcatum	Ferns and allies	E	US	08/10/98	F	Aspleniaceae	HI; U.S.A. (HI)
No common name	Asplenium dielmannii	Ferns and allies	E	US	06/17/10	O	Aspleniaceae	HI; U.S.A. (HI)
No common name	Asplenium dielpallidum	Ferns and allies	E	US	08/23/98	F	Aspleniaceae	HI; U.S.A. (HI)
No common name	Asplenium fragile insulare	Ferns and allies	E	US	04/10/98	F	Aspleniaceae	HI; U.S.A. (HI)
No common name	Asplenium unisorum	Ferns and allies	E	US	08/10/98	F	Aspleniaceae	HI; U.S.A. (HI)
No common name	Auerodendron pauciflorum	Flowering plants	E	US	09/29/97	F	Rhamnaceae	PR; Endemic to Puerto Rico; U.S.A. (PR)
No common name	Bonamia menziesii	Flowering plants	E	US	07/10/99	F	Convolvulaceae	HI; U.S.A. (HI)
No common name	Calyptranthes thomasiana	Flowering plants	E	US/foreign	09/30/97	F	Myrtaceae	VI; U.S. Virgin Islands and British Virgin Islands
No common name	Catesbaea melanocarpa	Flowering plants	E	US	08/18/05	F	Rubiaceae	PR, VI; U.S.A. (VI, PR), Antigua, Barbuda, Guadalupe
No common name	Chamaecrista glandulosa var. mirabilis	Flowering plants	E	US	05/12/94	F	Fabaceae	PR; Endemic to Puerto Rico; U.S.A. (PR)
No common name	Cordia bellonis	Flowering plants	E	US	10/01/99	F	Boraginaceae	PR; Endemic to Puerto Rico; U.S.A. (PR)
No common name	Cranichis ricartii	Flowering plants	E	US	07/15/96	F	Orchidaceae	PR; Endemic to Puerto Rico; U.S.A. (PR)
No common name	Cyanea profuga	Flowering plants	E	US	None	—	Campanlaceae	HI; Believed to be extinct
No common name	Cyanea purpurellifolia	Flowering plants	E	US	None	—	Campanulaceae	HI; Believed to be extinct; U.S.A. (HI)
No common name	Cyperus fauriei	Flowering plants	E	US	09/26/96	F	Cyperaceae	HI; U.S.A. (HI)
No common name	Cyperus pennatiformis	Flowering plants	E	US	07/10/99	F	Cyperaceae	HI;
No common name	Cyrtandra gracilis	Flowering plants	E	US	None	—	Gesneriaceae	HI; Believed to be extinct; U.S.A. (HI)
No common name	Cyrtandra waiolani	Flowering plants	E	US	None	—	Gesneriaceae	HI; Believed to be extinct; U.S.A. (HI)
No common name	Daphnopsis hellerana	Flowering plants	E	US	08/07/92	F	Thymelaeaceae	PR; U.S.A. (PR)
No common name	Delissea rhytidosperma	Flowering plants	E	US	08/23/98	F	Campanulaceae	HI; U.S.A. (HI)
No common name	Delissea undulata	Flowering plants	E	US	09/26/96	F	Campanulaceae	HI; U.S.A. (HI)
No common name	Dendrobium guamense	Flowering plants	T	US	None	—	Orchidaceae	HI;
No common name	Diplazium molokaiense	Ferns and allies	E	US	04/10/98	F	Woosiaceae	HI; U.S.A. (HI)
No common name	Doryopteris angelica	Ferns and allies	E	US	06/17/10	O	Pteridaceae	HI; U.S.A. (HI)
No common name	Doryopteris takeuchii	Ferns and allies	E	US	None	—	Pteridaceae	HI; U.S.A. (HI)
No common name	Elaphoglossum serpens	Ferns and allies	E	US	01/17/95	F	Lomariopsidaceae	PR; Endemic to Puerto Rico; U.S.A. (PR)
No common name	Eugenia bryanii	Flowering plants	E	US	None	—	Myrtaceae	HI;
No common name	Eugenia woodburyana	Flowering plants	E	US	10/06/98	F	Myrtaceae	PR; Endemic to Puerto Rico; U.S.A. (PR)
No common name	Festuca molokaiensis	Flowering plants	E	US	None	—	Poaceae	HI; U.S.A. (HI)
No common name	Geocarpon minimum	Flowering plants	T	US	07/26/93	F	Caryophyllaceae	AR, LA, MO, TX; U.S.A. (MO, LA, AR, TX)

TABLE 10.1

TABLE 10.1

Endangered and threatened plant species, February 2016 [CONTINUED]

Common name	Scientific name	Species group	Federal listing status[a]	U.S. or U.S./foreign listed	Recovery plan date	Recovery plan stage[b]	Family	Current distribution
No common name	*Gesneria pauciflora*	Flowering plants	T	US	10/06/98	F	Gesneriaceae	PR; Endemic to Puerto Rico; U.S.A. (PR)
No common name	*Gonocalyx concolor*	Flowering plants	E	US	None	—	Ericaceae	PR;
No common name	*Gouania hillebrandii*	Flowering plants	E	US	07/16/90	F	Rhamnaceae	HI; U.S.A. (HI)
No common name	*Gouania meyenii*	Flowering plants	E	US	08/10/98	F	Rhamnaceae	HI; U.S.A. (HI)
No common name	*Gouania vitifolia*	Flowering plants	E	US	08/10/98	F	Rhamnaceae	HI; U.S.A. (HI)
No common name	*Hesperomannia arborescens*	Flowering plants	E	US	08/10/98	F	Asteraceae	HI; U.S.A. (HI)
No common name	*Hesperomannia arbuscula*	Flowering plants	E	US	08/10/98	F	Asteraceae	HI; U.S.A. (HI)
No common name	*Hesperomannia lydgatei*	Flowering plants	E	US	05/31/94	F	Asteraceae	HI; U.S.A. (HI)
No common name	*Ilex sintenisii*	Flowering plants	E	US	07/31/95	F	Aquifoliaceae	PR; Endemic to Puerto Rico. Known from the El Yunque National Forest; U.S.A. (PR)
No common name	*Kadua degeneri*	Flowering plants	E	US	08/10/98	F	Rubiaceae	HI;
No common name	*Kadua parvula*	Flowering plants	E	US	08/10/98	F	Rubiaceae	HI;
No common name	*Kadua st.-johnii*	Flowering plants	E	US	09/20/95	F	Rubiaceae	HI; U.S.A. (HI)
No common name	*Keysseria (=Lagenifera) erici*	Flowering plants	E	US	06/17/10	O	Asteraceae	HI; U.S.A. (HI)
No common name	*Keysseria (=Lagenifera) helenae*	Flowering plants	E	US	06/17/10	O	Asteraceae	HI; U.S.A. (HI)
No common name	*Lepanthes eltoroensis*	Flowering plants	E	US	07/15/96	F	Orchidaceae	PR; Endemic to Puerto Rico. Known from El Yunque National Forest; U.S.A. (PR)
No common name	*Leptocereus grantianus*	Flowering plants	E	US	07/26/95	F	Cactaceae	PR; Endemic to the Culebra island; U.S.A. (PR)
No common name	*Lipochaeta venosa*	Flowering plants	E	US	05/23/94	F	Asteraceae	HI; U.S.A. (HI)
No common name	*Lobelia koolauensis*	Flowering plants	E	US	08/10/98	F	Campanulaceae	HI; U.S.A. (HI)
No common name	*Lobelia monostachya*	Flowering plants	E	US	08/10/98	F	Campanulaceae	HI; U.S.A. (HI)
No common name	*Lobelia niihauensis*	Flowering plants	E	US	08/10/98	F	Campanulaceae	HI; U.S.A. (HI)
No common name	*Lobelia oahuensis*	Flowering plants	E	US	08/10/98	F	Campanulaceae	HI; U.S.A. (HI)
No common name	*Lyonia truncata var. proctorii*	Flowering plants	E	US	07/31/95	F	Ericaceae	PR; Encemic to Sierra Bermeja, Puerto Rico; U.S.A. (PR), Endemic to Sierra Bermeja, located in the southwest corner of Puerto Rico.
No common name	*Lysimachia filifolia*	Flowering plants	E	US	09/20/95	F	Primulaceae	HI; U.S.A. (HI)
No common name	*Lysimachia iniki*	Flowering plants	E	US	06/17/10	O	Primulaceae	HI; U.S.A. (HI)
No common name	*Lysimachia lydgatei*	Flowering plants	E	US	07/29/97	F	Primulaceae	HI; U.S.A. (HI)
No common name	*Lysimachia maxima*	Flowering plants	E	US	None		Primulaceae	HI; U.S.A. (HI)
No common name	*Lysimachia pendens*	Flowering plants	E	US	06/17/10	O	Primulaceae	HI; U.S.A. (HI)
No common name	*Lysimachia scopulensis*	Flowering plants	E	US	06/17/10	O	Primulaceae	HI; U.S.A. (HI)
No common name	*Lysimachia venosa*	Flowering plants	E	US	06/17/10	O	Primulaceae	HI; U.S.A. (HI)
No common name	*Maesa walkeri*	Flowering plants	T	US	None		Myrsinaceae	
No common name	*Miracarpus maxwelliae*	Flowering plants	E	US	10/06/98	F	Rubiaceae	PR; Endemic to Puerto Rico; U.S.A. (PR)
No common name	*Miracarpus polycladus*	Flowering plants	E	US/foreign	10/06/98	F	Rubiaceae	PR; Netherlands Antilles (Saba); Puerto Rico and Netherlands Antilles (Saba); U.S.A. (PR), Saba, Anegada Island
No common name	*Myrcia paganii*	Flowering plants	E	US	09/29/97	F	Myrtaceae	PR; Endemic to Puerto Rico; U.S.A. (PR)
No common name	*Neraudia angulata*	Flowering plants	E	US	08/10/98	F	Urticaceae	HI; U.S.A. (HI)
No common name	*Neraudia ovata*	Flowering plants	E	US	09/26/96	F	Urticaceae	HI; U.S.A. (HI)
No common name	*Neraudia sericea*	Flowering plants	E	US	07/10/99	F	Urticaceae	HI; U.S.A. (HI)
No common name	*Nervilia jacksoniae*	Flowering plants	T	US	None		Orchidaceae	
No common name	*Nesogenes rotensis*	Flowering plants	E	US	05/03/07	F	Verbenaceae	MP; Western Pacific Ocean-U.S.A. (Commonwealth of the Northern Mariana Islands)
No common name	*Osmoxylon mariannense*	Flowering plants	E	US	05/03/07	F	Araliaceae	MP; Western Pacific Ocean-U.S.A. (Commonwealth of the Northern Mariana Islands)
No common name	*Phyllanthus saffordii*	Flowering plants	E	US	None	—	Phyllanthaceae	HI;
No common name	*Phyllostegia bracteata*	Flowering plants	E	US	None	—	Lamiaceae	HI;
No common name	*Phyllostegia floribunda*	Flowering plants	E	US	None		Lamiaceae	HI; U.S.A. (HI)
No common name	*Phyllostegia glabra var. lanaiensis*	Flowering plants	E	US	09/29/95	F	Lamiaceae	HI; U.S.A. (HI)
No common name	*Phyllostegia haliakalae*	Flowering plants	E	US	None		Lamiaceae	
No common name	*Phyllostegia hirsuta*	Flowering plants	E	US	08/10/98	F	Lamiaceae	HI; U.S.A. (HI)

Common name	Scientific name	Species group	Federal listing status[a]	U.S. or U.S./foreign listed	Recovery plan date	Recovery plan stage[b]	Family	Current distribution
No common name	*Phyllostegia hispida*	Flowering plants	E	US	09/26/96	F	Lamiaceae	HI; U.S.A. (HI)
No common name	*Phyllostegia kaalaensis*	Flowering plants	E	US	08/10/98	F	Lamiaceae	HI; U.S.A. (HI)
No common name	*Phyllostegia knudsenii*	Flowering plants	E	US	09/20/95	F	Lamiaceae	HI; U.S.A. (HI)
No common name	*Phyllostegia mannii*	Flowering plants	E	US	09/26/96	F	Lamiaceae	HI; U.S.A. (HI)
No common name	*Phyllostegia mollis*	Flowering plants	E	US	08/10/98	F	Lamiaceae	HI; U.S.A. (HI)
No common name	*Phyllostegia parviflora*	Flowering plants	E	US	07/10/99	F	Lamiaceae	HI; U.S.A. (HI)
No common name	*Phyllostegia pilosa*	Flowering plants	E	US	None	—	Lamiaceae	HI; U.S.A. (HI)
No common name	*Phyllostegia renovans*	Flowering plants	E	US	06/17/10	O	Lamiaceae	HI; U.S.A. (HI)
No common name	*Phyllostegia velutina*	Flowering plants	E	US	09/26/96	F	Lamiaceae	HI; U.S.A. (HI)
No common name	*Phyllostegia waimeae*	Flowering plants	E	US	09/20/95	F	Lamiaceae	HI; U.S.A. (HI)
No common name	*Phyllostegia warshaueri*	Flowering plants	E	US	09/26/96	F	Lamiaceae	HI; U.S.A. (HI)
No common name	*Phyllostegia wawrana*	Flowering plants	E	US	09/20/95	F	Lamiaceae	HI; U.S.A. (HI)
No common name	*Pittosporum halophilum*	Flowering plants	E	US	None	—	Pittosporaceae	HI;
No common name	*Pittosporum hawaiiense*	Flowering plants	E	US	None	—	Pittosporaceae	HI;
No common name	*Platanthera holochila*	Flowering plants	E	US	07/10/99	F	Orchidaceae	HI; U.S.A. (HI)
No common name	*Platydesma cornuta cornuta*	Flowering plants	E	US	None	—	Rutaceae	HI; U.S.A. (HI)
No common name	*Platydesma cornuta decurrens*	Flowering plants	E	US	None	—	Rutaceae	HI; U.S.A. (HI)
No common name	*Platydesma remyi*	Flowering plants	E	US	None	—	Rutaceae	HI;
No common name	*Poa siphonoglossa*	Flowering plants	E	US	09/20/95	F	Poaceae	HI; U.S.A. (HI)
No common name	*Polyscias bisattenuata*	Flowering plants	E	US	06/17/10	O	Araliaceae	HI; U.S.A. (HI)
No common name	*Polyscias flynnii*	Flowering plants	E	US	06/17/10	O	Araliaceae	HI; U.S.A. (HI)
No common name	*Polyscias lydgatei*	Flowering plants	E	US	None	—	Araliaceae	HI; U.S.A. (HI)
No common name	*Polyscias racemosa*	Flowering plants	E	US	09/20/95	F	Araliaceae	HI; U.S.A. (HI)
No common name	*Polystichum calderonense*	Ferns and allies	E	US	01/17/95	F	Dryopteridaceae	PR; Endemic to Puerto Rico; U.S.A. (PR)
No common name	*Pteris lidgatei*	Flowering plants	E	US	04/10/98	F	Adiantaceae	HI; U.S.A. (HI)
No common name	*Remya kauaiensis*	Flowering plants	E	US	09/20/95	F	Asteraceae	HI; U.S.A. (HI)
No common name	*Remya montgomeryi*	Flowering plants	E	US	09/20/95	F	Asteraceae	HI; U.S.A. (HI)
No common name	*Sanicula mariversa*	Flowering plants	E	US	08/10/98	F	Apiaceae	HI; U.S.A. (HI)
No common name	*Sanicula purpurea*	Flowering plants	E	US	12/10/02	O	Apiaceae	HI; U.S.A. (HI)
No common name	*Schiedea attenuata*	Flowering plants	E	US	06/17/10	O	Caryophyllaceae	HI; U.S.A. (HI)
No common name	*Schiedea diffusa ssp. macraei*	Flowering plants	E	US	None	—	Caryophyllaceae	HI; U.S.A. (HI)
No common name	*Schiedea haleakalensis*	Flowering plants	E	US	07/29/97	F	Caryophyllaceae	HI; U.S.A. (HI)
No common name	*Schiedea helleri*	Flowering plants	E	US	08/23/98	F	Caryophyllaceae	HI;
No common name	*Schiedea hookeri*	Flowering plants	E	US	07/10/99	F	Caryophyllaceae	HI; U.S.A. (HI)
No common name	*Schiedea jacobii*	Flowering plants	E	US	None	—	Caryophyllaceae	HI; U.S.A. (HI)
No common name	*Schiedea kaalae*	Flowering plants	E	US	08/10/98	F	Caryophyllaceae	HI; U.S.A. (HI)
No common name	*Schiedea kauaiensis*	Flowering plants	E	US	09/20/95	F	Caryophyllaceae	HI; U.S.A. (HI)
No common name	*Schiedea laui*	Flowering plants	E	US	None	—	Caryophyllaceae	HI; U.S.A. (HI)
No common name	*Schiedea lydgatei*	Flowering plants	E	US	09/26/96	F	Caryophyllaceae	HI; U.S.A. (HI)
No common name	*Schiedea membranacea*	Flowering plants	E	US	09/20/95	F	Caryophyllaceae	HI; U.S.A. (HI)
No common name	*Schiedea nuttallii*	Flowering plants	E	US	12/10/02	F	Caryophyllaceae	HI; U.S.A. (HI)
No common name	*Schiedea obovata*	Flowering plants	E	US	08/10/98	F	Caryophyllaceae	HI; U.S.A. (HI)
No common name	*Schiedea salicaria*	Flowering plants	E	US	None	—	Caryophyllaceae	HI;
No common name	*Schiedea sarmentosa*	Flowering plants	E	US	None	—	Caryophyllaceae	HI;
No common name	*Schiedea spergulina var. leiopoda*	Flowering plants	E	US	09/20/95	F	Caryophyllaceae	HI; U.S.A. (HI)
No common name	*Schiedea spergulina var. spergulina*	Flowering plants	T	US	09/20/95	F	Caryophyllaceae	HI; U.S.A. (HI)
No common name	*Schiedea trinervis*	Flowering plants	E	US	08/10/98	F	Caryophyllaceae	HI; U.S.A. (HI)
No common name	*Schiedea verticillata*	Flowering plants	E	US	03/31/98	F	Caryophyllaceae	HI; U.S.A. (HI)
No common name	*Schiedea viscosa*	Flowering plants	E	US	09/20/95	F	Caryophyllaceae	HI;
No common name	*Schoepfia arenaria*	Flowering plants	T	US	01/10/92	F	Olacaceae	PR; Endemic to Puerto Rico; U.S.A. (PR)
No common name	*Silene alexandri*	Flowering plants	E	US	09/26/96	F	Caryophyllaceae	HI; U.S.A. (HI)
No common name	*Silene hawaiiensis*	Flowering plants	T	US	09/26/96	F	Caryophyllaceae	HI; U.S.A. (HI)

TABLE 10.1

Eadangered and threatened plant species, February 2016 [CONTINUED]

Common name	Scientific name	Species group	Federal listing status[a]	U.S. or U.S./foreign listed	Recovery plan date	Recovery plan stage[b]	Family	Current distribution
No common name	*Silene lanceolata*	Flowering plants	E	US	09/26/96	F	Caryophyllaceae	HI; U.S.A. (HI)
No common name	*Silene perlmanii*	Flowering plants	E	US	08/10/98	F	Caryophyllaceae	HI; U.S.A. (HI)
No common name	*Spermolepis hawaiiensis*	Flowering plants	E	US	07/10/99	F	Apiaceae	HI; U.S.A. (HI)
No common name	*Stenogyne angustifolia angustifolia*	Flowering plants	E	US	09/20/93	D	Lamiaceae	HI;
No common name	*Stenogyne bifida*	Flowering plants	E	US	05/20/98	F	Lamiaceae	HI; U.S.A. (HI)
No common name	*Stenogyne campanulata*	Flowering plants	E	US	09/20/95	F	Lamiaceae	HI; U.S.A. (HI)
No common name	*Stenogyne cranwelliae*	Flowering plants	E	US	None	—	Lamiaceae	HI;
No common name	*Stenogyne kanehoana*	Flowering plants	E	US	08/10/98	F	Lamiaceae	HI; U.S.A. (HI)
No common name	*Stenogyne kauaulaensis*	Flowering plants	E	US	None	—	Lamiaceae	HI;
No common name	*Stenogyne kealiae*	Flowering plants	E	US	06/17/10	O	Lamiaceae	HI; U.S.A. (HI)
No common name	*Tabernaemontana rotensis*	Flowering plants	T	US	None	—	Apocynaceae	GU, MP;
No common name	*Tectaria estremerana*	Ferns and allies	E	US	01/17/95	F	Dryopteridaceae	PR; Endemic to Puerto Rico; U.S.A. (PR)
No common name	*Ternstroemia subsessilis*	Flowering plants	E	US	07/31/95	F	Theaceae	PR; Endemic to Puerto Rico. Known from El Yunque National Forest; U.S.A. (PR)
No common name	*Tetramolopium arenarium*	Flowering plants	E	US	09/26/96	F	Asteraceae	HI; U.S.A. (HI)
No common name	*Tetramolopium filiforme*	Flowering plants	E	US	08/10/98	F	Asteraceae	HI; U.S.A. (HI)
No common name	*Tetramolopium lepidotum ssp. lepidotum*	Flowering plants	E	US	08/10/98	F	Asteraceae	HI; U.S.A. (HI)
No common name	*Tetramolopium remyi*	Flowering plants	E	US	09/29/95	F	Asteraceae	HI; U.S.A. (HI)
No common name	*Tetramolopium rockii*	Flowering plants	T	US	09/26/96	F	Asteraceae	HI; U.S.A. (HI)
No common name	*Thelypteris inabonensis*	Ferns and allies	E	US	01/17/95	F	Thelypteridaceae	PR; Endemic to Puerto Rico; U.S.A. (PR)
No common name	*Thelypteris verecunda*	Ferns and allies	E	US	01/17/95	F	Thelypteridaceae	PR; Endemic to Puerto Rico; U.S.A. (PR)
No common name	*Thelypteris yaucoensis*	Ferns and allies	E	US	01/17/95	F	Thelypteridaceae	PR; Endemic to Puerto Rico; U.S.A. (PR)
No common name	*Tinospora homosepala*	Algae	E	US	None	—	Menispermaceae	
No common name	*Trematolobelia singularis*	Flowering plants	E	US	08/10/98	F	Campanulaceae	HI; U.S.A. (HI)
No common name	*Tuberolabium guamense*	Flowering plants	T	US	None	—	Orchidaceae	PR; British Virgin Islands (Anegada Island)
No common name	*Varronia rupicola*	Flowering plants	T	US/foreign	None	—	Boraginaceae	PR; Endemic to Sierra Bermeja, Puerto Rico; U.S.A. (Endemic to PR)
No common name	*Vernonia proctorii*	Flowering plants	E	US	07/31/95	F	Asteraceae	
No common name	*Vigna o-wahuensis*	Flowering plants	E	US	07/10/99	F	Fabaceae	HI; U.S.A. (HI)
No common name	*Viola helenae*	Flowering plants	E	US	05/31/94	F	Violaceae	HI; U.S.A. (HI)
No common name	*Viola lanaiensis*	Flowering plants	E	US	09/29/95	F	Violaceae	HI; U.S.A. (HI)
No common name	*Viola oahuensis*	Flowering plants	E	US	08/10/98	F	Violaceae	HI; U.S.A. (HI)
No common name	*Wikstroemia villosa*	Flowering plants	E	US	None	—	Thymelaeaceae	HI;
No common name	*Xylosma crenatum*	Flowering plants	E	US	09/20/95	F	Salicaceae	HI; U.S.A. (HI)
Nohoanu	*Geranium arboreum*	Flowering plants	E	US	07/29/97	F	Geraniaceae	HI; U.S.A. (HI)
Nohoanu	*Geranium hanaense*	Flowering plants	E	US	None	—	Geraniaceae	HI;
Nohoanu	*Geranium hillebrandii*	Flowering plants	E	US	None	—	Geraniaceae	HI;
Nohoanu	*Geranium kauaiense*	Flowering plants	E	US	06/17/10	O	Geraniaceae	HI; U.S.A. (HI)
Nohoanu	*Geranium multiflorum*	Flowering plants	E	US	07/29/97	F	Geraniaceae	HI; U.S.A. (HI)
North Park phacelia	*Phacelia formosula*	Flowering plants	E	US	03/21/86	F	Hydrophyllaceae	CO; U.S.A. (CO)
Northeastern bulrush	*Scirpus ancistrochaetus*	Flowering plants	E	US	08/25/93	F	Cyperaceae	MA, MD, NH, NY, PA, VA, VT, WV; U.S.A. (WV, VT, VA, PA, NY, NH, MD, MA)
Northern wild monkshood	*Aconitum noveboracense*	Flowering plants	T	US	09/23/83	F	Ranunculaceae	IA, NY, OH, WI; U.S.A. (WI, OH, NY, IA)
Oahu wild coffee (=kopiko)	*Psychotria hexandra ssp. oahuensis*	Flowering plants	E	US	None	—	Rubiaceae	HI; U.S.A. (HI)
Oha	*Delissea subcordata*	Flowering plants	E	US	08/10/98	F	Campanulaceae	HI; U.S.A. (HI)
Ohai	*Sesbania tomentosa*	Flowering plants	E	US	07/10/99	F	Fabaceae	HI; U.S.A. (HI)
Okeechobee gourd	*Cucurbita okeechobeensis ssp. okeechobeensis*	Flowering plants	E	US	05/18/99	F	Cucurbitaceae	FL; U.S.A. (FL)
Olulu	*Brighamia insignis*	Flowering plants	E	US	08/23/98	F	Campanulaceae	HI; U.S.A. (HI)
Opuhe	*Urera kaalae*	Flowering plants	E	US	08/10/98	F	Urticaceae	HI; U.S.A. (HI)
Orcutt's spineflower	*Chorizanthe orcuttiana*	Flowering plants	E	US	None	—	Polygonaceae	CA; U.S.A. (CA)
Osterhout milkvetch	*Astragalus osterhoutii*	Flowering plants	E	US	09/30/92	F	Fabaceae	CO; U.S.A. (CO)

TABLE 10.1

Endangered and threatened plant species, February 2016 [CONTINUED]

Common name	Scientific name	Species group	Federal listing status[a]	U.S. or U.S./foreign listed	Recovery plan date	Recovery plan stage[b]	Family	Current distribution
Otay mesa-mint	Pogogyne nudiuscula	Flowering plants	E	US/foreign	09/03/98	F	Lamiaceae	CA; Mexico (B.C.); U.S.A. (CA), Mexico (Baja California)
Otay tarplant	Deinandra (=Hemizonia) conjugens	Flowering plants	T	US/foreign	12/07/04	F	Asteraceae	CA; U.S.A. (CA), Mexico
Pa'iniu	Astelia waialealae	Flowering plants	E	US	06/17/10	O	Liliaceae	HI; U.S.A. (HI)
Pagosa skyrocket	Ipomopsis polyantha	Flowering plants	E	US	01/23/13	O	Polemoniaceae	CO; U.S.A. (CO)
Palapalai aumakua	Dryopteris crinalis var. podosorus	Ferns and allies	E	US	06/17/10	O	Dryopteridaceae	HI; U.S.A. (HI)
Pallid manzanita	Arctostaphylos pallida	Flowering plants	T	US	08/24/15	F	Ericaceae	CA; U.S.A. (CA)
Palma de manaca	Calyptronoma rivalis	Flowering plants	T	US	06/25/92	F	Arecaceae	PR; Puerto Rico and Hispaniola (Dominican Republic); U.S.A. (PR)
Palmate-bracted bird's beak	Cordylanthus palmatus	Flowering plants	E	US	09/30/98	F	Scrophulariaceae	CA; U.S.A. (CA)
Palo colorado	Ternstroemia luquillensis	Flowering plants	E	US	07/31/95	F	Theaceae	PR; Endemic to Puerto Rico. Known from El Yunque National Forest and Maricao Commonwealth Forest; U.S.A. (PR)
Palo de jazmin	Styrax portoricensis	Flowering plants	E	US	07/31/95	F	Styracaceae	PR; Endemic to Puerto Rico; U.S.A. (PR)
Palo de nigua	Cornutia obovata	Flowering plants	E	US	08/07/92	F	Verbenaceae	PR; Endemic to Puerto Rico; U.S.A. (PR)
Palo de ramon	Banara vanderbiltii	Flowering plants	E	US	03/15/91	F	Flacourtiaceae	PR; Endemic to Puerto Rico; U.S.A. (PR), endemic to Puerto Rico. Some individuals has been planted in Florida.
Palo de rosa	Ottoschulzia rhodoxylon	Flowering plants	E	US	09/20/94	F	Icacinaceae	PR; Endemic to Puerto Rico; U.S.A. (PR), Dominican Republic
Pamakani	Tetramolopium capillare	Flowering plants	E	US	07/29/97	F	Asteraceae	HI; U.S.A. (HI)
Pamakani	Viola chamissoniana ssp. chamissoniana	Flowering plants	E	US	08/10/98	F	Violaceae	HI; U.S.A. (HI)
Papala	Charpentiera densiflora	Flowering plants	E	US	06/17/10	O	Amaranthaceae	HI; U.S.A. (HI)
Papery whitlow-wort	Paronychia chartacea	Flowering plants	T	US	05/18/99	O	Caryophyllaceae	FL; U.S.A. (FL)
Parachute beardtongue	Penstemon debilis	Flowering plants	T	US	01/23/13	O	Plantaginaceae	CO; U.S.A. (CO)
Pariette cactus	Sclerocactus brevispinus	Flowering plants	T	US	04/14/10	O	Cactacea	UT; S. brevispinus is restricted to one population in a 29,000-hectare (ha) (72,000-acre (ac)) area located in the Pariette Draw along the Duchesne–Uintah County boundary (RANA 2009). Land ownership within the range of the species includes Bureau of and Management (BLM), Ute Tribe, State of Utah, and private land, with the majority of the species' known population occurring on BLM and Ute Tribal lands (Service 2009). Some individuals have been found in marginal habitats outside of the main population areas. More information is needed to better map the species' range in these areas.; U.S.A. (UT)
Parish's daisy	Erigeron parishii	Flowering plants	T	US	09/30/97	D	Asteraceae	CA; U.S.A. (CA)
Paudedo	Hedyotis megalantha	Flowering plants	E	US	None	—	Rubiaceae	HI; U.S.A. (HI)
Pauoa	Ctenitis squamigera	Ferns and allies	E	US	04/10/98	F	Aspleniaceae	HI; U.S.A. (HI)
Pecos (=puzzle, =paradox) sunflower	Helianthus paradoxus	Flowering plants	T	US	09/15/05	F	Asteraceae	NM, TX; U.S.A. (TX, NM)
Pedate checker-mallow	Sidalcea pedata	Flowering plants	E	US	07/31/98	F	Malvaceae	CA; U.S.A. (CA)
Peebles Navajo cactus	Pediocactus peeblesianus var. peeblesianus	Flowering plants	E	US	03/30/84	F	Cactaceae	AZ; U.S.A. (AZ)
Peirson's milk-vetch	Astragalus magdalenae var. peirsonii	Flowering plants	T	US	None	—	Fabaceae	CA; U.S.A. (CA)
Pelos del diablo	Aristida portoricensis	Flowering plants	E	US	05/16/94	F	Poaceae	PR; Endemic to Puerto Rico; U.S.A. (PR)
Pendant kihi fern	Adenophorus periens	Ferns and allies	E	US	12/10/02	F	Polypodiaceae	HI; U.S.A. (HI)
Penland alpine fen mustard	Eutrema penlandii	Flowering plants	T	US	08/31/93	O	Brassicaceae	CO; U.S.A. (CO)
Penland beardtongue	Penstemon penlandii	Flowering plants	E	US	09/30/92	F	Scrophulariaceae	CO; U.S.A. (CO)
Pennell's bird's-beak	Cordylanthus tenuis ssp. capillaris	Flowering plants	E	US	09/30/98	F	Scrophulariaceae	CA; U.S.A. (CA)
Persistent trillium	Trillium persistens	Flowering plants	E	US	03/27/84	F	Liliaceae	GA, SC; U.S.A. (SC, GA)
Peter's Mountain mallow	Iliamna corei	Flowering plants	E	US	09/28/90	F	Malvaceae	VA; U.S.A. (VA)
Pigeon wings	Clitoria fragrans	Flowering plants	T	US	05/18/99	F	Fabaceae	FL; U.S.A. (FL)
Pilo	Hedyotis mannii	Flowering plants	E	US	09/26/96	F	Rubiaceae	HI; U.S.A. (HI)
Pilo kea lau li'i	Platydesma rostrata	Flowering plants	E	US	06/17/10	O	Rutaceae	HI; U.S.A. (HI)
Pima pineapple cactus	Coryphantha scheeri var. robustispina	Flowering plants	E	US/foreign	None	—	Cactaceae	AZ; Mexico (Sonora); U.S.A. (AZ), Mexico (Sonora)
Pine Hill ceanothus	Ceanothus roderickii	Flowering plants	E	US	08/30/02	F	Rhamnaceae	CA; U.S.A. (CA)
Pine Hill flannelbush	Fremontodendron californicum ssp. decumbens	Flowering plants	E	US	08/30/02	F	Sterculiaceae	CA; U.S.A. (CA)

TABLE 10.1

Endangered and threatened plant species, February 2016 [CONTINUED]

Common name	Scientific name	Species group	Federal listing status[a]	U.S. or U.S./foreign listed	Recovery plan date	Recovery plan stage[b]	Family	Current distribution
Pismo clarkia	*Clarkia speciosa ssp. immaculata*	Flowering plants	E	US	09/28/98	F	Onagraceae	CA; U.S.A. (CA)
Pitcher's thistle	*Cirsium pitcheri*	Flowering plants	T	US/foreign	09/20/02	F	Asteraceae	IL, IN, MI, WI; Canada (Ont.); U.S.A. (WI, MI, IL, IN), Canada (Ont.)
Pitkin Marsh lily	*Lilium pardalinum ssp. pitkinense*	Flowering plants	E	US	None	—	Liliaceae	CA; U.S.A. (CA)
Po`e	*Portulaca sclerocarpa*	Flowering plants	E	US	09/26/96	F	Portulacaceae	HI; U.S.A. (HI)
Pondberry	*Lindera melissifolia*	Flowering plants	E	US	09/23/93	F	Lauraceae	AL, AR, GA, MO, MS, NC, SC; U.S.A. (SC, NC, MS, MO, LA, GA, FL, AR, AL)
Popolo	*Cyanea solanacea*	Flowering plants	E	US	None	—	Campanulaceae	HI;
Popolo ku mai	*Solanum incompletum*	Flowering plants	E	US	12/10/02	F	Solanaceae	HI; U.S.A. (HI)
Prairie bush-clover	*Lespedeza leptostachya*	Flowering plants	T	US	10/06/88	F	Fabaceae	IA, IL, MN, WI; U.S.A. (WI, MN, IL, IA)
Presidio clarkia	*Clarkia franciscana*	Flowering plants	E	US	09/30/98	F	Onagraceae	CA; U.S.A. (CA)
Presidio manzanita	*Arctostaphylos hookeri var. ravenii*	Flowering plants	E	US	08/08/03	F	Ericaceae	CA; U.S.A. (CA)
Price's potato-bean	*Apios priceana*	Flowering plants	T	US	02/10/93	F	Fabaceae	AL, IL, KY, MS, TN; U.S.A. (TN, MS, KY, IL, AL)
Pu`uka`a	*Cyperus trachysanthos*	Flowering plants	E	US	12/10/02	F	Cyperaceae	HI; U.S.A. (HI)
Pua `ala	*Brighamia rockii*	Flowering plants	E	US	05/20/98	F	Campanulaceae	HI; U.S.A. (HI)
Purple amole	*Chlorogalum purpureum*	Flowering plants	T	US	None	—	Liliaceae	CA; U.S.A. (CA)
Pygmy fringe-tree	*Chionanthus pygmaeus*	Flowering plants	E	US	05/18/99	F	Oleaceae	FL; U.S.A. (FL)
Red Hills vervain	*Verbena californica*	Flowering plants	T	US	None	—	Verbenaceae	CA; U.S.A. (CA)
Relict trillium	*Trillium reliquum*	Flowering plants	E	US	01/31/91	F	Liliaceae	AL, GA, SC; U.S.A. (SC, GA, AL)
Roan Mountain bluet	*Hedyotis purpurea var. montana*	Flowering plants	E	US	05/13/96	F	Rubiaceae	NC, TN, VA; U.S.A. (TN, NC)
Robust spineflower	*Chorizanthe robusta var. robusta*	Flowering plants	E	US	12/20/04	F	Polygonaceae	CA; U.S.A. (CA)
Rock gnome lichen	*Gymnoderma lineare*	Lichens	E	US	09/30/97	F	Cladoniaceae	NC, SC, TN, VA; U.S.A. (TN, NC)
rough popcornflower	*Plagiobothrys hirtus*	Flowering plants	E	US	09/25/03	F	Boraginaceae	OR; U.S.A. (OR)
Rough-leaved loosestrife	*Lysimachia asperulaefolia*	Flowering plants	E	US	04/19/95	F	Primulaceae	NC, SC; U.S.A. (SC, NC)
Round-leaved chaff-flower	*Achyranthes splendens var. rotundata*	Flowering plants	E	US	10/05/93	D	Amaranthaceae	HI; U.S.A. (HI)
Rugel's pawpaw	*Deeringothamnus rugelii*	Flowering plants	E	US	04/05/88	F	Annonaceae	FL; Known to occur in pine flatwoods at Tiger Bay State Forest, on county conservation lands, and on private lands, all within Volusia County, Florida.; U.S.A. (FL)
Running buffalo clover	*Trifolium stoloniferum*	Flowering plants	E	US	06/27/07	RF(1)	Fabaceae	AR, IN, KY, MO, OH, WV; U.S.A. (WV, OH, MO, KY, KS, IN, IL, AR)
Ruth's golden aster	*Pityopsis ruthii*	Flowering plants	E	US	06/11/92	F	Asteraceae	TN; U.S.A. (TN)
Sacramento Mountains thistle	*Cirsium vinaceum*	Flowering plants	T	US	09/27/93	F	Asteraceae	NM; U.S.A. (NM)
Sacramento Orcutt grass	*Orcuttia viscida*	Flowering plants	E	US	03/07/06	F	Poaceae	CA; U.S.A. (CA)
Sacramento prickly poppy	*Argemone pleiacantha ssp. pinnatisecta*	Flowering plants	E	US	08/31/94	F	Papaveraceae	NM; U.S.A. (NM)
Salt marsh bird's-beak	*Cordylanthus maritimus ssp. maritimus*	Flowering plants	E	US/foreign	12/06/85	F	Scrophulariaceae	CA; Mexico-Baja California; U.S.A. (CA), Mexico Baja California
San Benito evening-primrose	*Camissonia benitensis*	Flowering plants	T	US	09/21/06	F	Onagraceae	CA; U.S.A. (CA)
San Bernardino bluegrass	*Poa atropurpurea*	Flowering plants	E	US	None	—	Poaceae	CA; U.S.A. (CA)
San Bernardino Mountains bladderpod	*Lesquerella kingii ssp. bernardina*	Flowering plants	E	US	09/30/97	D	Brassicaceae	CA; U.S.A. (CA)
San Clemente Island bush-mallow	*Malacothamnus clementinus*	Flowering plants	E	US	01/26/84	F	Malvaceae	CA; U.S.A. (CA)
San Clemente Island indian paintbrush	*Castilleja grisea*	Flowering plants	T	US	01/26/84	F	Scrophulariaceae	CA; U.S.A. (CA)
San Clemente Island larkspur	*Delphinium variegatum ssp. kinkiense*	Flowering plants	E	US	01/26/84	F	Ranunculaceae	CA; U.S.A. (CA)
San Clemente Island lotus (=broom)	*Acmispon dendroideus var. traskiae (=Lotus d. ssp. traskiae)*	Flowering plants	T	US	01/26/84	F	Fabaceae	CA; U.S.A. (CA)
San Clemente Island woodland-star	*Lithophragma maximum*	Flowering plants	E	US	01/26/84	F	Saxifragaceae	CA; U.S.A. (CA)
San Diego ambrosia	*Ambrosia pumila*	Flowering plants	E	US/foreign	None	—	Asteraceae	CA; U.S.A. (CA), Mexico
San Diego button-celery	*Eryngium aristulatum var. parishii*	Flowering plants	E	US	09/03/98	F	Apiaceae	CA; U.S.A. (CA), Mexico
San Diego mesa-mint	*Pogogyne abramsii*	Flowering plants	E	US	09/03/98	F	Lamiaceae	CA; U.S.A. (CA)
San Diego thornmint	*Acanthomintha ilicifolia*	Flowering plants	T	US/foreign	None	—	Lamiaceae	CA; U.S.A. (CA), Mexico
San Francisco lessingia	*Lessingia germanorum (=L.g. var. germanorum)*	Flowering plants	E	US	08/08/03	F	Asteraceae	CA; U.S.A. (CA)
San Francisco Peaks ragwort	*Packera franciscana*	Flowering plants	T	US	10/05/87	F	Asteraceae	AZ; U.S.A. (AZ)
San Jacinto Valley crownscale	*Atriplex coronata var. notatior*	Flowering plants	E	US	None	—	Chenopodiaceae	CA; U.S.A. (CA)
San Joaquin adobe sunburst	*Pseudobahia peirsonii*	Flowering plants	T	US	None	—	Asteraceae	CA; U.S.A. (CA)

TABLE 10.1

Endangered and threatened plant species, February 2016 (CONTINUED)

Common name	Scientific name	Species group	Federal listing status[a]	U.S. or U.S./foreign listed	Recovery plan date	Recovery plan stage[b]	Family	Current distribution
San Joaquin Orcutt grass	Orcuttia inaequalis	Flowering plants	T	US	03/07/06	F	Poaceae	CA; U.S.A. (CA)
San Joaquin wooly-threads	Monolopia (= Lembertia) congdonii	Flowering plants	E	US	09/30/98	F	Asteraceae	CA; U.S.A. (CA)
San Mateo thornmint	Acanthomintha obovata ssp. duttonii	Flowering plants	E	US	09/30/98	F	Lamiaceae	CA; U.S.A. (CA)
San Mateo woolly sunflower	Eriophyllum latilobum	Flowering plants	E	US	09/30/98	F	Asteraceae	CA; U.S.A. (CA)
San Rafael cactus	Pediocactus despainii	Flowering plants	E	US	12/06/07	O	Cactaceae	UT; U.S.A. (UT)
Sandlace	Polygonella myriophylla	Flowering plants	E	US	05/18/99	F	Polygonaceae	FL; U.S.A. (FL)
Sandplain gerardia	Agalinis acuta	Flowering plants	E	US	09/20/89	F	Scrophulariaceae	CT, MA, MD, NY, RI; The current range for this species extends northward from Maryland to Massachusetts, specifically within each of these five states (Maryland, New York, Connecticut, Rhode Island, and Massachusetts). ; U.S.A. (RI, NY, MD, MA, CT)
Santa Ana River woolly-star	Eriastrum densifolium ssp. sanctorum	Flowering plants	E	US	None	—	Polemoniaceae	CA; U.S.A. (CA)
Santa Barbara Island liveforever	Dudleya traskiae	Flowering plants	E	US	06/27/85	F	Crassulaceae	CA; U.S.A. (CA)
Santa Clara Valley dudleya	Dudleya setchellii	Flowering plants	E	US	09/30/98	F	Crassulaceae	CA; U.S.A. (CA)
Santa Cruz cypress	Cupressus abramsiana	Conifers and cycads	E	US	09/26/98	F	Cupressaceae	CA; U.S.A. (CA)
Santa Cruz Island bush-mallow	Malacothamnus fasciculatus var. nesioticus	Flowering plants	E	US	09/26/00	F	Malvaceae	CA; U.S.A. (CA)
Santa Cruz Island dudleya	Dudleya nesiotica	Flowering plants	T	US	09/26/00	F	Crassulaceae	CA; U.S.A. (CA)
Santa Cruz Island fringepod	Thysanocarpus conchuliferus	Flowering plants	E	US	09/26/00	F	Brassicaceae	CA; U.S.A. (CA)
Santa Cruz Island malacothrix	Malacothrix indecora	Flowering plants	E	US	None	—	Asteraceae	CA; U.S.A. (CA)
Santa Cruz Island rockcress	Sibara filifolia	Flowering plants	T	US	None	—	Brassicaceae	CA; U.S.A. (CA)
Santa Cruz tarplant	Holocarpha macradenia	Flowering plants	T	US	09/30/99	F	Asteraceae	CA; U.S.A. (CA)
Santa Monica Mountains dudleya	Dudleya cymosa ssp. ovatifolia	Flowering plants	T	US	09/26/00	F	Crassulaceae	CA; U.S.A. (CA)
Santa Rosa Island manzanita	Arctostaphylos confertiflora	Flowering plants	E	US	04/22/94	F	Ericaceae	CA; U.S.A. (CA)
Schweinitz's sunflower	Helianthus schweinitzii	Flowering plants	E	US	04/22/94	F	Asteraceae	NC, SC; U.S.A. (SC, NC)
Scotts Valley polygonum	Polygonum hickmanii	Flowering plants	E	US	09/28/98	F	Polygonaceae	CA; U.S.A. (CA); vicinity of the City of Scotts Valley.
Scotts Valley spineflower	Chorizanthe robusta var. hartwegii	Flowering plants	E	US	09/28/98	F	Polygonaceae	CA; U.S.A. (CA)
Scrub blazingstar	Liatris ohlingerae	Flowering plants	E	US	05/18/99	F	Asteraceae	FL; U.S.A. (FL)
Scrub buckwheat	Eriogonum longifolium var. gnaphalifolium	Flowering plants	T	US	06/20/96	RF(1)	Polygonaceae	FL; U.S.A. (FL); Xeric sandy ridges of central Florida
Scrub lupine	Lupinus aridorum	Flowering plants	E	US	06/20/96	RF(1)	Fabaceae	FL; U.S.A. (FL); Xeric sandy ridges of central Florida
Scrub mint	Dicerandra frutescens	Flowering plants	E	US	05/18/99	F	Lamiaceae	FL; U.S.A. (FL)
Scrub plum	Prunus geniculata	Flowering plants	E	US	06/20/96	RF(1)	Rosaceae	FL; U.S.A. (FL); Xeric, sandy ridges of central Florida.
Sea bean	Mucuna sloanei persericea	Flowering plants	E	US	None	—	Fabaceae	
Seabeach amaranth	Amaranthus pumilus	Flowering plants	T	US	11/12/96	F	Amaranthaceae	DE, NC, NJ, NY, SC, VA; U.S.A. (VA, SC, RI, NY, NJ, NC, MD, MA, DE)
Sebastopol meadowfoam	Limnanthes vinculans	Flowering plants	E	US	12/11/14	D	Limnanthaceae	CA; U.S.A. (CA)
Sensitive joint-vetch	Aeschynomene virginica	Flowering plants	T	US	09/29/95	F	Fabaceae	MD, NC, NJ, VA; U.S.A. (VA, PA, NC, NJ, MD, DE)
Sentry milk-vetch	Astragalus cremnophylax var. cremnophylax	Flowering plants	E	US	09/28/06	F	Fabaceae	AZ; U.S.A. (AZ)
Shale barren rock cress	Arabis serotina	Flowering plants	E	US	08/15/91	F	Brassicaceae	VA, WV; U.S.A. (WV, VA)
Shivwits milk-vetch	Astragalus ampullarioides	Flowering plants	E	US	09/29/06	F	Fabaceae	UT; U.S.A. (UT)
Short-leaved rosemary	Conradina brevifolia	Flowering plants	E	US	05/18/99	F	Lamiaceae	FL; U.S.A. (FL)
Short's bladderpod	Physaria globosa	Flowering plants	E	US	None	—	Brassicaceae	IN, KY, TN;
Short's goldenrod	Solidago shortii	Flowering plants	E	US	05/25/88	F	Asteraceae	IN, KY; U.S.A. (KY)
Showy Indian clover	Trifolium amoenum	Flowering plants	E	US	None	—	Fabaceae	CA; Known extant only in cultivation; U.S.A. (CA)
Showy stickseed	Hackelia venusta	Flowering plants	E	US	12/12/07	F	Boraginaceae	WA; U.S.A. (WA)
Shrubby reed-mustard	Schoenocrambe suffrutescens	Flowering plants	E	US	09/14/94	F	Brassicaceae	UT; Shrubby reed-mustard occurs in three meta-populations in Uintah and Duchesne Counties:
Siler pincushion cactus	Pediocactus (= Echinocactus, = Utahia) sileri	Flowering plants	T	US	04/14/86	F	Cactaceae	AZ, UT; U.S.A. (UT, AZ)
Slender Orcutt grass	Orcuttia tenuis	Flowering plants	T	US	03/07/06	F	Poaceae	CA, OR; U.S.A. (CA)
Slender rush-pea	Hoffmannseggia tenella	Flowering plants	E	US	09/13/88	F	Fabaceae	TX; U.S.A. (TX)
Slender-horned spineflower	Dodecahema leptoceras	Flowering plants	E	US	None	—	Polygonaceae	CA; U.S.A. (CA)
Slender-petaled mustard	Thelypodium stenopetalum	Flowering plants	E	US	07/31/98	F	Brassicaceae	CA; U.S.A. (CA)

TABLE 10.1

Endangered and threatened plant species, February 2016 [CONTINUED]

Common name	Scientific name	Species group	Federal listing status[a]	U.S. or U.S./foreign listed	Recovery plan date	Recovery plan stage[b]	Family	Current distribution
Small whorled pogonia	Isotria medeoloides	Flowering plants	T	US/foreign	11/13/92	RF(1)	Orchidaceae	CT, DE, GA, IL, MA, ME, MI, MO, NC, NH, NJ, NY, OH, PA, RI, SC, TN, VA, WV; Canada (Ont.); U.S.A. (WV, VT, VA, TN, SC, RI, PA, NY, NJ, NH, NC, MO, MI, ME, MD, MA, IL, GA, DE, DC, CT), Canada (Ont.)
Small-anthered bittercress	Cardamine micranthera	Flowering plants	E	US	07/10/91	F	Brassicaceae	NC, VA; U.S.A. (VA, NC)
Small's milkpea	Galactia smallii	Flowering plants	E	US	05/18/99	F	Fabaceae	FL; U.S.A. (FL)
Smooth coneflower	Echinacea laevigata	Flowering plants	E	US	04/18/95	F	Asteraceae	GA, NC, SC, VA; U.S.A. (VA, SC, PA, NC, MD, GA)
Snakeroot	Eryngium cuneifolium	Flowering plants	E	US	05/18/99	F	Apiaceae	FL; U.S.A. (FL)
Sneed pincushion cactus	Coryphantha sneedii var. sneedii	Flowering plants	E	US	03/21/86	F	Cactaceae	NM, TX; U.S.A. (TX, NM)
Soft bird's-beak	Cordylanthus mollis ssp. mollis	Flowering plants	E	US	02/26/14	F	Scrophulariaceae	CA; U.S.A. (CA)
Soft-leaved paintbrush	Castilleja mollis	Flowering plants	E	US	09/26/00	F	Scrophulariaceae	CA; U.S.A. (CA)
Solano grass	Tuctoria mucronata	Flowering plants	E	US	03/07/06	F	Poaceae	CA; U.S.A. (CA)
Sonoma alopecurus	Alopecurus aequalis var. sonomensis	Flowering plants	E	US	None	—	Poaceae	CA; U.S.A. (CA)
Sonoma spineflower	Chorizanthe valida	Flowering plants	E	US	09/29/98	F	Polygonaceae	CA; U.S.A. (CA)
Sonoma sunshine	Blennosperma bakeri	Flowering plants	E	US	12/11/14	D	Asteraceae	CA; U.S.A. (CA)
South Texas ambrosia	Ambrosia cheiranthifolia	Flowering plants	E	US	None	—	Asteraceae	TX; U.S.A. (TX)
Southern mountain wild-buckwheat	Eriogonum kennedyi var. austromontanum	Flowering plants	T	US	None	—	Polygonaceae	CA; U.S.A. (CA)
Spalding's catchfly	Silene spaldingii	Flowering plants	T	US	10/12/07	F	Caryophyllaceae	ID, MT, OR, WA; U.S.A. (WA, MT, ID, OR), Canada (B.C.)
Spreading avens	Geum radiatum	Flowering plants	E	US	04/28/93	F	Rosaceae	NC, TN; U.S.A. (TN, NC)
Spreading navarretia	Navarretia fossalis	Flowering plants	T	US/foreign	09/03/98	F	Polemoniaceae	CA; Mexico (Baja California); U.S.A. (CA), Mexico (Baja California)
Spring Creek bladderpod	Lesquerella perforata	Flowering plants	E	US	09/08/06	F	Brassicaceae	TN; U.S.A. (TN)
Spring-loving centaury	Centaurium namophilum	Flowering plants	T	US	09/28/90	F	Gentianaceae	NV; U.S.A. (NV, CA)
Springville clarkia	Clarkia springvillensis	Flowering plants	T	US	None	—	Onagraceae	CA; U.S.A. (CA)
St. Thomas prickly-ash	Zanthoxylum thomasianum	Flowering plants	E	US/foreign	04/05/88	F	Rutaceae	PR, VI; Puerto Rico and Virgin Islands; U.S.A. (VI, PR)
Star cactus	Astrophytum asterias	Flowering plants	E	US	11/06/03	F	Cactaceae	TX; U.S.A. (TX), Mexico
Steamboat buckwheat	Eriogonum ovalifolium var. williamsiae	Flowering plants	E	US	09/20/95	F	Polygonaceae	NV; U.S.A. (NV)
Stebbins' morning-glory	Calystegia stebbinsii	Flowering plants	E	US	08/30/02	F	Convolvulaceae	CA; U.S.A. (CA)
Suisun thistle	Cirsium hydrophilum var. hydrophilum	Flowering plants	E	US	02/26/14	F	Asteraceae	CA; U.S.A. (CA)
Swamp pink	Helonias bullata	Flowering plants	T	US	09/30/91	F	Liliaceae	DE, GA, MD, NC, NJ, SC, VA; U.S.A. (VA, SC, NY, NJ, NC, MD, GA, DE)
Telephus spurge	Euphorbia telephioides	Flowering plants	T	US	06/22/94	F	Euphorbiaceae	FL; U.S.A. (FL)
Tennessee yellow-eyed grass	Xyris tennesseensis	Flowering plants	E	US	06/24/94	F	Xyridaceae	AL, GA, TN; U.S.A. (TN, GA, AL)
Terlingua Creek cat's-eye	Cryptantha crassipes	Flowering plants	E	US	04/05/94	F	Boraginaceae	TX; U.S.A. (TX)
Texas avenia	Avenia limitaris	Flowering plants	E	US/foreign	06/25/14	D	Sterculiaceae	TX; U.S.A. (TX), Mexico
Texas golden gladecress	Leavenworthia texana	Flowering plants	E	US	None	—	Brassicaceae	TX;
Texas poppy-mallow	Callirhoe scabriuscula	Flowering plants	E	US	03/29/85	F	Malvaceae	TX; U.S.A. (TX)
Texas prairie dawn-flower	Hymenoxys texana	Flowering plants	E	US	04/13/90	F	Asteraceae	TX; U.S.A. (TX)
Texas snowbells	Styrax texanus	Flowering plants	E	US	07/31/87	F	Styracaceae	TX; U.S.A. (TX)
Texas trailing phlox	Phlox nivalis ssp. texensis	Flowering plants	E	US	03/28/95	F	Polemoniaceae	TX; U.S.A. (TX)
Texas wild-rice	Zizania texana	Flowering plants	E	US	02/14/96	RF(1)	Poaceae	TX; U.S.A. (TX)
Thread-leaved brodiaea	Brodiaea filifolia	Flowering plants	T	US	None	—	Liliaceae	CA; U.S.A. (CA)
Tiburon jewelflower	Streptanthus niger	Flowering plants	E	US	09/30/98	F	Brassicaceae	CA; U.S.A. (CA)
Tiburon mariposa lily	Calochortus tiburonensis	Flowering plants	T	US	09/30/98	F	Liliaceae	CA; U.S.A. (CA)
Tiburon paintbrush	Castilleja affinis ssp. neglecta	Flowering plants	E	US	09/30/98	F	Scrophulariaceae	CA; U.S.A. (CA)
Tiny polygala	Polygala smallii	Flowering plants	E	US	05/18/99	F	Polygalaceae	FL; U.S.A. (FL)
Tobusch fishhook cactus	Sclerocactus brevihamatus ssp. tobuschii	Flowering plants	E	US	03/18/87	F	Cactaceae	TX; U.S.A. (TX)
Todsen's pennyroyal	Hedeoma todsenii	Flowering plants	E	US	01/31/01	RF(2)	Lamiaceae	NM; U.S.A. (NM)
Triple-ribbed milk-vetch	Astragalus tricarinatus	Flowering plants	E	US	None	—	Fabaceae	CA; U.S.A. (CA)
Ufa-halomtano	Heritiera longipetiolata	Flowering plants	E	US	None	—	Sterculiaceae	GU, MP;
Uhi uhi	Mezoneuron kavaiense	Flowering plants	E	US	05/06/94	F	Fabaceae	HI; U.S.A. (HI)

TABLE 10.1

Endangered and threatened plant species, February 2016 (CONTINUED)

Common name	Scientific name	Species group	Federal listing status[a]	U.S. or U.S./foreign listed	Recovery plan date	Recovery plan stage[b]	Family	Current distribution
Uinta Basin hookless cactus	Sclerocactus wetlandicus	Flowering plants	T	US	04/14/10	O	Cactaceae	UT; Sclerocactus wetlandicus is found primarily within Uintah County, Utah, along the Green River and its tributaries. The potential range of the species is approximately 186,159 hectares (ha) (460,009 acres (ac)), with 56 percent of this area on Federal land, 28 percent on tribal lands, and the remainder on private or State lands (Service 2009).; U.S.A. (UT)
Umtanum Desert buckwheat	Eriogonum codium	Flowering plants	T	US	None	—	Polygonaceae	WA;
Ute ladies'-tresses	Spiranthes diluvialis	Flowering plants	T	US	09/21/95	D	Orchidaceae	CO, ID, MT, NE, NV, UT, WA, WY; U.S.A. (WY, WA, UT, NV, NE, MT, ID, CO)
Uvillo	Eugenia haematocarpa	Flowering plants	E	US	09/11/98	F	Myrtaceae	PR; U.S.A. (PR)
Vahl's boxwood	Buxus vahlii	Flowering plants	E	US	04/28/87	F	Buxaceae	PR, VI; Extirpated from St. Croix, VI; Puerto Rico and St Croix; U.S.A. (VI, PR)
Vail Lake ceanothus	Ceanothus ophiochilus	Flowering plants	T	US	None	—	Rhamnaceae	CA; U.S.A. (CA)
Vandenberg monkeyflower	Diplacus vandenbergensis	Flowering plants	E	US	None	—	Phrymaceae	CA; U.S.A. (CA)
Ventura Marsh milk-vetch	Astragalus pycnostachyus var. lanosissimus	Flowering plants	E	US	None	—	Fabaceae	CA; U.S.A. (CA)
Verity's dudleya	Dudleya verityi	Flowering plants	T	US	09/30/99	F	Crassulaceae	CA; U.S.A. (CA)
Vine Hill clarkia	Clarkia imbricata	Flowering plants	E	US	07/27/15	D	Onagraceae	CA; U.S.A. (CA)
Virginia round-leaf birch	Betula uber	Flowering plants	T	US	09/24/90	RF(2)	Betulaceae	VA; U.S.A. (VA)
Virginia sneezeweed	Helenium virginicum	Flowering plants	T	US	10/02/00	D	Asteraceae	MO, VA; U.S.A. (VA, MO)
Virginia spiraea	Spiraea virginiana	Flowering plants	T	US	11/13/92	F	Rosaceae	GA, KY, NC, OH, TN, VA, WV; U.S.A. (WV, VA, TN, PA, OH, NC, KY, GA)
Wahane	Pritchardia aylmer-robinsonii	Flowering plants	E	US	None	—	Arecaceae	HI; U.S.A. (HI)
Walker's manioc	Manihot walkerae	Flowering plants	E	US/foreign	12/12/93	F	Euphorbiaceae	TX; U.S.A. (TX), Mexico
Water howellia	Howellia aquatilis	Flowering plants	T	US	09/24/96	D	Campanulaceae	CA, ID, MT, OR, WA; U.S.A. (WA, OR, MT, ID, CA)
Wawae'iole	Huperzia mannii	Ferns and allies	E	US	07/29/97	F	Lycopodiaceae	HI; U.S.A. (HI)
Wawae'iole	Huperzia nutans	Ferns and allies	E	US	08/10/98	F	Lycopodiaceae	HI;
Webber Ivesia	Ivesia webberi	Flowering plants	T	US	None	—	Rosaceae	CA, NV;
Welsh's milkweed	Asclepias welshii	Flowering plants	T	US	09/30/92	F	Asclepiadaceae	AZ, UT; U.S.A. (UT, AZ)
Wenatchee Mountains checkermallow	Sidalcea oregana var. calva	Flowering plants	E	US	09/30/04	F	Malvaceae	WA; U.S.A. (WA)
West Indian walnut (=Nogal)	Juglans jamaicensis	Flowering plants	E	US/foreign	12/09/99	F	Juglandaceae	PR; Puerto Rico, Cuba, Dominican Republic and Haiti; U.S.A. (PR); Cuba, Hispaniola
Western lily	Lilium occidentale	Flowering plants	E	US	03/31/98	F	Liliaceae	CA, OR; U.S.A. (OR, CA)
Western prairie fringed orchid	Platanthera praeclara	Flowering plants	T	US/foreign	09/30/96	F	Orchidaceae	IA, KS, MN, MO, ND, NE, SD; Canada (Man.); U.S.A. (SD, OK, NE, ND, MO, MN, KS, IA), Canada (Man.)
Wheeler's peperomia	Peperomia wheeleri	Flowering plants	E	US	11/26/90	F	Piperaceae	PR; Endemic to Puerto Rico; U.S.A. (PR), British Virgin Island and Dutch West Indies
White birds-in-a-nest	Macbridea alba	Flowering plants	T	US	06/22/94	F	Lamiaceae	FL; U.S.A. (FL)
White bladderpod	Lesquerella pallida	Flowering plants	E	US	10/16/92	F	Brassicaceae	TX; U.S.A. (TX)
White Bluffs bladderpod	Physaria douglasii ssp. tuplashensis	Flowering plants	T	US	None	—	Brassicaceae	WA;
White irisette	Sisyrinchium dichotomum	Flowering plants	E	US	04/10/95	F	Iridaceae	NC, SC; U.S.A. (NC)
White sedge	Carex albida	Flowering plants	E	US	None	—	Cyperaceae	CA; U.S.A. (CA)
White-haired goldenrod	Solidago albopilosa	Flowering plants	T	US	09/28/93	F	Asteraceae	KY; U.S.A. (KY)
White-rayed pentachaeta	Pentachaeta bellidiflora	Flowering plants	E	US	09/30/98	F	Asteraceae	CA; U.S.A. (CA)
Whorled sunflower	Helianthus verticillatus	Flowering plants	E	US	None	—	Asteraceae	AL, GA, TN;
Wide-leaf warea	Warea amplexifolia	Flowering plants	E	US	02/17/93	F	Brassicaceae	FL; Known to occur in the high pine (or sandhill) habitat on the Lake Wales Ridge in Lake, Orange, Osceola, and Polk Counties in Florida; U.S.A. (FL)
Willamette daisy	Erigeron decumbens	Flowering plants	E	US	06/29/10	F	Asteraceae	OR; U.S.A. (OR)
Willowy monardella	Monardella viminea	Flowering plants	E	US/foreign	None	—	Lamiaceae	CA; U.S.A. (CA), Mexico
Winkler cactus	Pediocactus winkleri	Flowering plants	T	US	12/06/07	O	Cactaceae	UT; U.S.A. (UT)
Wireweed	Polygonella basiramia	Flowering plants	E	US	05/18/99	F	Polygonaceae	FL; U.S.A. (FL)
Wright fishhook cactus	Sclerocactus wrightiae	Flowering plants	E	US	12/24/85	F	Cactaceae	UT; U.S.A. (UT)

TABLE 10.1

Endangered and threatened plant species, February 2016 [CONTINUED]

Common name	Scientific name	Species group	Federal listing status[a]	U.S. or U.S./foreign listed	Recovery plan date	Recovery plan stage[b]	Family	Current distribution
Yadon's piperia	*Piperia yadonii*	Flowering plants	E	US	08/19/04	F	Orchidaceae	CA; U.S.A. (CA)
Yellow larkspur	*Delphinium luteum*	Flowering plants	E	US	None	—	Ranunculaceae	CA; U.S.A. (CA)
Yreka phlox	*Phlox hirsuta*	Flowering plants	E	US	09/21/06	F	Polemoniaceae	CA; U.S.A. (CA)
Zapata bladderpod	*Lesquerella thamnophila*	Flowering plants	E	US	08/25/04	F	Brassicaceae	TX; U.S.A. (TX), Mexico
Zuni fleabane	*Erigeron rhizomatus*	Flowering plants	T	US	09/30/88	F	Asteraceae	AZ, NM; Entire

[a]E = Endangered; T = Threatened.
[b]D = Draft; F = Final; RF = Final revision; O = Other.

SOURCE: Adapted from "Generate Species List," in *Environmental Conservation Online System Species Reports*, U.S. Department of the Interior, U.S. Fish and Wildlife Service, February 2016, http://ecos.fws.gov/tess_public/pub/adHocSpeciesForm.jsp (accessed February 17, 2016), and "Listed FWS/Joint FWS and NMFS Species and Populations with Recovery Plans (Sorted by Listed Entity)," in *Recovery Plans Search*, U.S. Department of the Interior, U.S. Fish and Wildlife Service, February 2016, http://ecos.fws.gov/tess_public/pub/speciesRecovery.jsp?sort=1 (accessed February 17, 2016)

TABLE 10.2

The 10 listed plant species with the highest expenditures under the Endangered Species Act, fiscal year 2014

Ranking	Species	Population	Expenditure
1	Seagrass, Johnson's (*Halophila johnsonii*)	Entire	$3,060,149
2	Goldfields, Contra Costa (*Lasthenia conjugens*)	Entire	$1,178,969
3	Bird's beak, palmate-bracted (*Cordylanthus palmatus*)	Entire	$739,666
4	Ladies'-tresses, Ute (*Spiranthes diluvialis*)	Entire	$604,734
5	Milk-vetch, Lane Mountain (*Astragalus jaegerianus*)	Entire	$587,350
6	Catchfly, Spalding's (*Silene spaldingii*)	Entire	$587,187
7	Skyrocket, Pagosa (*Ipomopsis polyantha*)	Entire	$543,032
8	Lupine, Kincaid's (*Lupinus sulphureus ssp. kincaidii*)	Entire	$491,893
9	Monkeyflower, Vandenberg (*Mimulus fremontii var. vandenbergensis*)	Entire	$490,797
10	Bush-mallow, San Clemente Island (*Malacothamnus clementinus*)	Entire	$439,067

SOURCE: Adapted from "Table 2. Species Ranked in Descending Order of Total FY 2014 Reported Expenditures, Not Including Land Acquisition Costs," in *Federal and State Endangered and Threatened Species Expenditures: Fiscal Year 2014*, U.S. Department of the Interior, U.S. Fish and Wildlife Service, March 2, 2016, http://www.fws.gov/endangered/esa-library/pdf/20160302_final_FY14_ExpRpt.pdf (accessed March 9, 2016)

properties and reproductive mechanisms. This taxonomy is part of the broader science known as phylogenetic systematics, which studies the evolutionary relationships between living organisms. In the future the systematics approach is expected to be used to classify all life-forms.

In general, plants are assigned to the same taxonomic levels that are used to classify animals. This hierarchical structure includes kingdom, phylum, class, order, family, genus, and species. Beneath the species level, plants can be classified into subspecies, just as in animal taxonomy. There is an additional classification for plants at this level called variety (abbreviated as "var."). Varieties are subgroups with unique differences between them. For example, the invasive species known as kudzu has the scientific name *Pueraria montana*. There are two varieties: *Pueraria montana* var. *lobata* and *Pueraria montana* var. *montana*. The *lobata* variety is commonly found in the United States, whereas the *montana* variety is not.

Plant taxonomy also includes additional taxa (groups) between kingdom and phylum called subkingdom, superdivision, and division that distinguish between broad categories of plants. The subkingdom level distinguishes between vascular and nonvascular plants. Within vascular plants, there are two superdivisions: seed plants and seedless plants. Seed plants are divided into various divisions, the largest of which is flowering plants.

The USFWS uses five broad categories for plant types: algae, conifers and cycads, ferns and allies, lichens, and flowering plants.

Algae

Algae are simple plant organisms ranging in size from microscopic to seaweeds. As of April 2016, only one alga was listed under the ESA—*Tinospora homosepala*. It has no common name. The USFWS (https://www.gpo.gov/fdsys/pkg/FR-2015-10-01/pdf/2015-24443.pdf) notes that the alga was listed in October 2015 and given

an endangered status. It is found on the island of Guam in the south Pacific.

Conifers and Cycads

Conifers are cone-bearing, woody plants. Most are trees; only a few species are shrubs. Common tree types include cedar, cypress, fir, pine, redwood, and spruce. Cycads are unusual plants often mistaken for palms or ferns. They have thick, soft trunks and large, leaflike crowns. Cycads are found in tropical or semitropical regions. Their rarity makes them popular with collectors. As of February 2016, only four conifers or cycads were listed under the ESA. (See Table 10.1.)

The Santa Cruz cypress (*Cupressus abramsiana*) and the gowen cypress (*Cupressus goveniana*) are conifers found only in Southern California. The Santa Cruz cypress was listed as endangered, and the gowen cypress was listed as threatened. Both species are imperiled because they have a limited range of distribution and are threatened by alteration and loss of habitat.

The fadang is a tropical cycad found in Guam and other islands in the South Pacific. According to the USFWS (https://www.gpo.gov/fdsys/pkg/FR-2015-10-01/pdf/2015-24443.pdf), it was once quite common but is being obliterated by a nonnative insect called the cycad aulacaspis scale. The Florida torreya (*Torreya taxifolia*) is also a cycad. This scrubby tree is extremely rare and is found only on the bluffs along the Apalachicola River in the Florida Panhandle. An unknown disease virtually wiped out the species in the wild during the 1950s. Thus, it has been given an endangered listing.

Ferns and Allies

According to the International Union for Conservation of Nature (IUCN), in *Red List of Threatened Species Version 2015.4* (November 2015, http://www.iucnredlist.org/about/summary-statistics), there are approximately 12,000 described species considered to be ferns and

FIGURE 10.2

Range of Johnson's seagrass

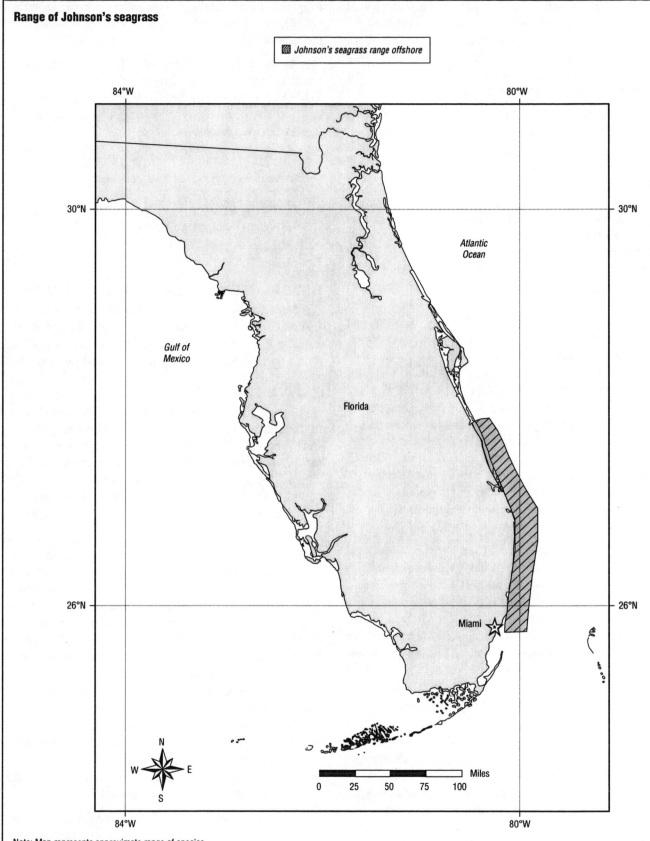

Note: Map represents approximate range of species.
Offshore distances are approximate.

SOURCE: "Johnson's Seagrass Range," in *Johnson's Seagrass Range Map*, U.S. Department of Commerce, National Oceanic and Atmospheric Administration, National Marine Fisheries Service, December 2007, http://www.nmfs.noaa.gov/pr/pdfs/rangemaps/johnsonsseagrass.pdf (accessed February 18, 2016)

allies. Ferns are an abundant and diverse plant group and are associated mostly with tropical and subtropical regions. In general, these plants are characterized by stems with long protruding leaves called fronds. Fern allies are plants with similar life cycles to ferns but without their stem or leaf structure. Examples of fern allies include club mosses and horsetails.

As of February 2016, 31 fern and fern ally species were listed under the ESA. (See Table 10.1.) Nearly all were endangered.

Lichens

Lichens are not truly plants. Scientists place them in the fungi kingdom, instead of the plant kingdom. Lichens are plantlike life-forms composed of two separate organisms: a fungus and an alga. In *Red List of Threatened Species Version 2015.4*, the IUCN indicates that 17,000 described lichens are known to science. Biologists believe there are up to 4,000 lichen species in the United States. They are found in many different habitats and grow extremely slowly. Some lichens look like moss, whereas others appear more like traditional plants with a leafy or blade structure. Lichens do not have a "skin" to protect them from the atmosphere. As a result, they are highly sensitive to air contaminants and have disappeared from many urban areas, presumably because of air pollution. Lichens are most predominant in undisturbed forests, bogs, and wetlands, particularly in California, Florida, Hawaii, the Appalachians, and the Pacific Northwest. They are commonly found on rocky outcroppings. Lichens provide a foodstuff for some animals and are used by some bird species in nest building.

As of February 2016, two lichen species were listed under the ESA: rock gnome lichen (*Gymnoderma lineare*) and Florida perforate cladonia (*Cladonia perforata*). (See Table 10.1.) Both were classified as endangered. During the 1970s rock gnome lichen was virtually wiped out in the Great Smoky Mountains National Park in Tennessee because of overzealous collecting by scientists. Florida perforate cladonia is found only in rosemary scrub habitats in portions of Florida. It is endangered because of loss or degradation of those habitats.

Flowering Plants

Flowering plants are vascular plants with flowers (clusters of specialized leaves that participate in reproduction). The flowers of some species are large and colorful, whereas others are extremely small and barely noticeable to humans. In *Red List of Threatened Species Version 2015.4*, the IUCN indicates that there are 268,000 described flowering plants. Biologists estimate that 80% to 90% of all plants on the earth are flowering plants.

As shown in Table 2.7 in Chapter 2, five flowering plants have been delisted under the ESA due to recovery:

Robbins' cinquefoil (2002), Eggert's sunflower (2005), Maguire daisy (2011), Tennessee purple coneflower (2011), and Johnston's fankenia (2016), which is found in parts of Texas and Mexico (see Figure 10.3.)

As of February 2016, 860 flowering plants were listed as endangered or threatened under the ESA. (See Table 10.1.) They come from a variety of taxonomic groups and are found in many different habitats. Some of the largest families represented are:

- Asteraceae (asters, daisies, and sunflowers)
- Brassicaceae (mustard and cabbage)
- Campanulaceae (bellflowers)
- Fabaceae (legumes and pulses)
- Lamiaceae (mints)

GEOGRAPHICAL BREAKDOWN OF PLANTS

Most threatened and endangered plant species in the United States are concentrated in specific areas of the country. Hawaii, California, and the Southeast (particularly Florida) are home to the majority of listed plant species.

Hawaiian Plants

Figure 10.4 shows the eight major islands that make up the state of Hawaii. The island of Oahu is home to the state's capital, Honolulu. Oahu, however, is not the largest of the islands. That distinction goes to the island labeled "Hawaii," which is commonly called "the Big Island." In the following discussion, the term *Hawaii* refers to the entire state.

According to the USFWS, in the press release "48 Kaua'i Species Protected under Endangered Species Act" (March 10, 2010, http://www.fws.gov/pacificislands/news%20releases/Kauai48ListingNR031010.pdf), Hawaii has the most endangered and threatened species of any state in the country. Because of its isolation from continental land masses, many of the species found in Hawaii exist nowhere else in the world. In fact, an estimated 90% of Hawaiian plant species are endemic. Because of large-scale deforestation and habitat destruction on the islands, Hawaii is home to more threatened and endangered plants than any other state in the nation. The USFWS (http://ecos.fws.gov/tess_public/pub/adHocSpeciesForm.jsp) reports that as of April 2016, there were more than 350 listed plant species in Hawaii. Nearly all are flowering plants and have an endangered listing.

Hawaiian plants have suffered from the introduction of invasive predators such as cows, pigs, and insects, as well as from the loss of critical pollinators with the decline of many species of native birds and insects. According to Marie M. Bruegemann, in "A Plan for Hawaiian Plants and Their Ecosystems" (*Endangered Species Bulletin*, vol. 28, no. 4, July–December 2003), 100 of Hawaii's 1,500

FIGURE 10.3

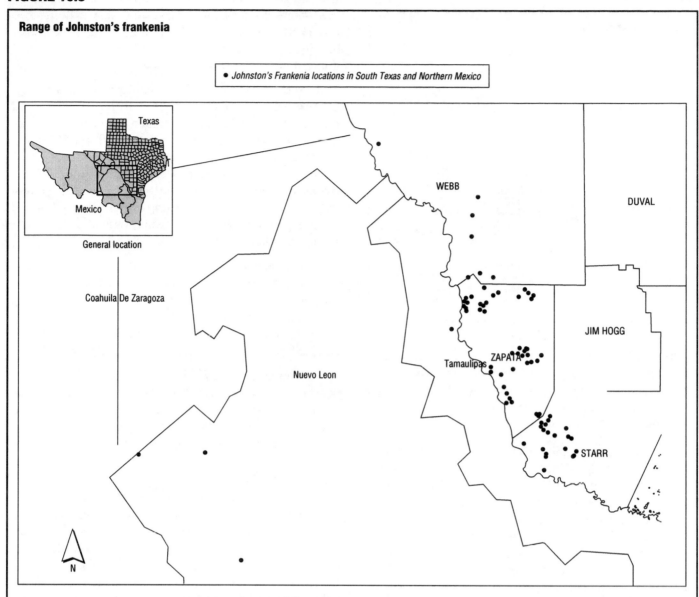

Range of Johnston's frankenia

- Johnston's Frankenia locations in South Texas and Northern Mexico

SOURCE: "Figure 1. Johnston's Frankenia Locations in South Texas and Northern Mexico," in *Post-Delisting Monitoring Plan for Johnston's Frankenia (Frankenia johnstonii)*, U.S. Department of the Interior, U.S. Fish and Wildlife Service, Corpus Christi Ecological Services Field Office, 2016, http://ecos.fws.gov/docs/species/doc4753.pdf (accessed February 19, 2016)

known plant species are believed to have become extinct since the islands were inhabited by humans.

The USFWS has developed more than a dozen recovery plans for imperiled Hawaiian plants. Many of the plans cover multiple species that are found in the same ecosystem or habitat type.

Californian Plants

The USFWS (https://ecos.fws.gov/tess_public/reports/ad-hoc-species-report-input) reports that as of April 2016 California was home to 183 ESA-listed plants, including several types of checker-mallow, dudleya, evening primrose, grass, jewelflower, larkspur, manzanita, milk-vetch, paintbrush, rock-cress, spineflower, and thistle.

MILK-VETCH. Milk-vetch is an herbaceous perennial flowering plant that is found in various parts of the world. It received its common name during the 1500s because of a belief among European farmers that the plant increased the milk yield of goats. As of April 2016, 11 species of milk-vetch were listed as threatened or endangered in California.

Peirson's milk-vetch is a plant with a long history of litigation and controversy in California. It is found in only one small area of Imperial County in the southern part of the state. This area is the Imperial Sand Dunes Recreation Area (ISDRA), which is managed by the U.S. Bureau of Land Management (BLM). ISDRA has a remote and barren landscape that is dominated by huge

FIGURE 10.4

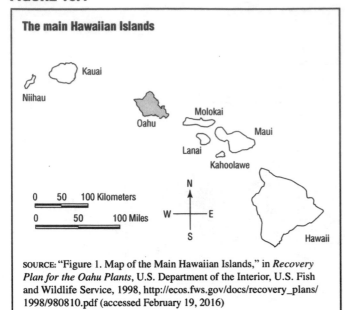

The main Hawaiian Islands

Niihau

Kauai

Oahu

Molokai

Lanai

Maui

Kahoolawe

Hawaii

0   50   100 Kilometers

0   50   100 Miles

N
W — E
S

SOURCE: "Figure 1. Map of the Main Hawaiian Islands," in *Recovery Plan for the Oahu Plants*, U.S. Department of the Interior, U.S. Fish and Wildlife Service, 1998, http://ecos.fws.gov/docs/recovery_plans/1998/980810.pdf (accessed February 19, 2016)

rolling sand dunes—the Algodones Dunes, the largest sand dune fields in North America. ISDRA covers 185,000 acres (75,000 ha) and is a popular destination for off-highway vehicle (OHV) riders, receiving more than 1 million visitors annually.

In 1998 Peirson's milk-vetch was designated a threatened species by the USFWS because of the threat of destruction by OHVs and other recreational activities at ISDRA. The agency decided not to designate critical habitat at that time, fearing the remaining plants would be subject to deliberate vandalism. The BLM was sued by conservation groups and accused of not consulting with the USFWS about the threats to Peirson's milk-vetch before establishing a management plan for ISDRA. In 2000, in response to that lawsuit, the BLM closed more than a third of ISDRA to OHV use.

In October 2001 a petition to delist the species was submitted on behalf of the American Sand Association, the San Diego Off-Road Coalition, and the Off-Road Business Association. A month later two lawsuits were filed against the USFWS by conservation organizations challenging the agency's decision not to designate critical habitat for the species. Under court order, the USFWS proposed critical habitat in 2003.

In August 2004 the USFWS (http://www.fws.gov/policy/library/2004/04-17575.html) issued a final designation of critical habitat for Peirson's milk-vetch that encompassed 21,836 acres (8,837 ha) of ISDRA. This was less than half of the acreage originally proposed. The reduction was made after an economic analysis revealed that closure of ISDRA areas to OHV use would have a negative impact on local businesses. In February 2008 the USFWS (http://edocket.access.gpo.gov/2008/pdf/08-545.pdf) issued a new

final designation of critical habitat that included 12,105 acres (4,899 ha), substantially less area than was designated in 2004. The new designation excluded acreage because of the "disproportionately high economic and social impacts" of including it in the critical habitat.

In June 2004 the USFWS completed a status review that was triggered by the 2001 delisting proposal and found that the species should remain listed as threatened. In 2005 the original petitioners and additional OHV and motorcycle associations submitted a new petition to delist Peirson's milk-vetch. In a 90-day finding the USFWS announced that the petition did present adequate information indicating that delisting might be warranted. However, in July 2008 the agency issued a 12-month finding that delisting was not warranted.

In September 2008 the USFWS (http://ecos.fws.gov/docs/five_year_review/doc1995.pdf) completed a five-year status review of Peirson's milk-vetch in which the agency recommended no changes to the species' threatened listing under the ESA. The USFWS noted that OHV activity remained the "primary threat" to the plant's survival.

In April 2012 the USFWS (http://www.gpo.gov/fdsys/pkg/FR-2012-04-27/pdf/2012-10212.pdf) provided notice that it was initiating a five-year review of dozens of western species including the Peirson's milk-vetch. As of April 2016, the results of the review had not been released.

Southeastern Plants

As of April 2016, the USFWS (https://ecos.fws.gov/tess_public/reports/ad-hoc-species-report-input) indicated that the southeastern states contained more than 172 threatened and endangered plant species listed under the ESA. The most common families are the Asteraceae (asters, daisies, and sunflowers), Fabaceae (legumes and pulses), and Lamiaceae (mints).

FLORIDIAN PLANTS. Approximately 50 of the threatened and endangered plant species listed under the ESA are found only in Florida. They include multiple species of mint, pawpaw, rosemary, and spurge.

Many of Florida's imperiled plants are found in the southern part of the state—the only subtropical ecological habitat in the continental United States. The majority of native plant species located in the bottom half of the southern Florida ecosystem originated from the tropics.

In May 1999 the USFWS published *South Florida Multi-species Recovery Plan* (http://pbadupws.nrc.gov/docs/ML1219/ML12193A340.pdf), which covered 68 species, including 35 plant species. In late 2006 an implementation schedule for many, but not all, of the species in the plan was issued. The *South Florida Multi-species Recovery Plan* is considered a landmark plan because it was one of the first recovery plans to focus on an ecosystem approach to recovery, rather than on a species-by-species approach.

TABLE 10.3

Foreign endangered and threatened plant species, February 2016

Common name	Scientific name	Species group	Federal listing status*	Current distribution
Guatemalan fir (=pinabete)	*Abies guatemalensis*	Conifers and cycads	T	Mexico, Honduras, Guatemala, El Salvador
Chilean false larch	*Fitzroya cupressoides*	Conifers and cycads	T	Chile, Argentina
Costa Rican jatropha	*Jatropha costaricensis*	Flowering plants	E	Costa Rica

*T = Threatened. E = Endangered.

SOURCE: Adapted from "Generate Species List," in *Environmental Conservation Online System Species Reports*, U.S. Department of the Interior, U.S. Fish and Wildlife Service, February 2016, http://ecos.fws.gov/tess_public/pub/adHocSpeciesForm.jsp (accessed February 17, 2016)

THREATENED AND ENDANGERED FOREIGN SPECIES OF PLANTS

In *Red List of Threatened Species Version 2015.4*, the IUCN indicates that there were 11,233 species of threatened plants (including flowering plants, gymnosperms, ferns and allies, mosses, and green and red algae) and 35 species of lichens, mushrooms, and brown algae in 2015. Habitat loss is the primary reason for the threatened status of the vast majority of IUCN-listed plants.

The IUCN notes that 310,442 flowering plants, gymnosperms, ferns and allies, mosses, and green and red algae and 52,280 species of lichens, mushrooms, and brown algae are known and described around the world.

As of February 2016, the USFWS listed only three totally foreign species of plants as threatened or endangered under the ESA. (See Table 10.3.) All three are found in Mexico or in Central or South America.

IMPORTANT NAMES AND ADDRESSES

Alaska Fisheries Science Center
National Oceanic and Atmospheric Administration
U.S. Department of Commerce
7600 Sand Point Way NE, Bldg. 4
Seattle, WA 98115
(206) 526-4000
FAX: (206) 526-4004
E-mail: afsc.webmaster@noaa.gov
URL: http://www.afsc.noaa.gov/

AmphibiaWeb
Museum of Vertebrate Zoology
University of California
3101 Valley Life Sciences Bldg.
Berkeley, CA 94720-3160
(510) 642-3567
FAX: (510) 643-8238
E-mail: supportamphibiaweb@berkeley
.edu
URL: http://amphibiaweb.org/

Bureau of Land Management
1849 C St. NW, Rm. 5665
Washington, DC 20240
(202) 208-3801
FAX: (202) 208-5242
URL: http://www.blm.gov/

Bureau of Reclamation
1849 C St. NW
Washington, DC 20240-0001
(202) 513-0501
FAX: (202) 513-0309
URL: http://www.usbr.gov/

Center for Biological Diversity
PO Box 710
Tucson, AZ 85702-0710
(520) 623-5252
1-866-357-3349
FAX: (520) 623-9797
E-mail: center@biologicaldiversity.org
URL: http://www.biologicaldiversity
.org/

Center for Plant Conservation
15600 San Pasqual Valley Rd.
Escondido, CA 92027-7000
(760) 796-5686
E-mail: cpc@sandiegozoo.org
URL: http://www.centerforplantconser
vation.org/

Congressional Research Service
Library of Congress
101 Independence Ave. SE
Washington, DC 20540
(202) 707-5000
URL: http://www.loc.gov/crsinfo/

Convention on International Trade in Endangered Species of Wild Fauna and Flora Secretariat
International Environment House
11 Chemin des Anémones
Geneva, CH-1219, Switzerland
(011-41-22) 917-81-39/40
FAX: (011-41-22) 797-34-17
E-mail: info@cites.org
URL: http://www.cites.org/

Defenders of Wildlife
1130 17th St. NW
Washington, DC 20036
(202) 682-9400
1-800-385-9712
E-mail: defenders@mail.defenders.org
URL: http://www.defenders.org/

Earth System Research Laboratory
National Oceanic and Atmospheric Administration
325 Broadway
Boulder, CO 80305-3337
URL: http://www.esrl.noaa.gov/gmd/

Ecosystems—Wildlife: Terrestrial and Endangered Resources Program
U.S. Geological Survey
12201 Sunrise Valley Dr.
Reston, VA 20192

(703) 648-4050
URL: http://www.usgs.gov/ecosystems/

Environmental Defense Fund
1875 Connecticut Ave. NW, Ste. 600
Washington, DC 20009
1-800-684-3322
URL: http://www.edf.org/

Goddard Institute for Space Studies
National Aeronautics and Space Administration
2880 Broadway
New York, NY 10025
(212) 678-5500
URL: http://www.giss.nasa.gov/

Greenpeace U.S.A.
702 H St. NW, Ste. 300
Washington, DC 20001
(202) 462-1177
1-800-722-6995
FAX: (202) 462-4507
E-mail: info@wdc.greenpeace.org
URL: http://www.greenpeace.org/usa/

Heritage Foundation
214 Massachusetts Ave. NE
Washington, DC 20002-4999
(202) 546-4400
URL: http://www.heritage.org/

International Union for Conservation of Nature
Rue Mauverney 28
Gland, 1196, Switzerland
(011-41-22) 999-0000
FAX: (011-41-22) 999-0002
E-mail: mail@iucn.org
URL: http://www.iucn.org/

International Whaling Commission
The Red House
135 Station Rd.
Impington, CB24 9NP, United Kingdom
(011-44-1223) 233-971

FAX: (011-44-1223) 232-876
URL: http://iwc.int/home

Land Trust Alliance
1660 L St. NW, Ste. 1100
Washington, DC 20036
(202) 638-4725
FAX: (202) 638-4730
E-mail: info@lta.org
URL: http://www.lta.org/

National Association of Home Builders
1201 15th St. NW
Washington, DC 20005
1-800-368-5242
URL: http://www.nahb.com/

National Audubon Society
225 Varick St.
New York, NY 10014
(212) 979-3000
FAX: (212) 979-3188
URL: http://www.audubon.org/

National Forest Service
U.S. Department of Agriculture
1400 Independence Ave. SW
Washington, DC 20250-1111
1-800-832-1355
URL: http://www.fs.fed.us

National Marine Fisheries Service
National Oceanic and Atmospheric Administration
1315 East-West Hwy.
Silver Spring, MD 20910
(301) 713-2379
FAX: (301) 713-2384
URL: http://www.nmfs.noaa.gov/

National Marine Mammal Laboratory
Alaska Fisheries Science Center
National Oceanic and Atmospheric Administration
7600 Sand Point Way NE F/AKC3
Seattle, WA 98115-6349
(206) 526-4045
FAX: (206) 526-6615
E-mail: nmml.information@noaa.gov
URL: http://www.afsc.noaa.gov/nmml/

National Ocean Service
National Oceanic and Atmospheric Administration
1305 East-West Hwy.
Silver Spring, MD 20910
(301) 713-3010
URL: http://oceanservice.noaa.gov/

National Park Service
1849 C St. NW
Washington, DC 20240
(202) 208-6843
URL: http://www.nps.gov/

National Wildlife Federation
11100 Wildlife Center Dr.
Reston, VA 20190
1-800-822-9919
URL: http://www.nwf.org/

National Wildlife Health Center
U.S. Geological Survey
6006 Schroeder Rd.
Madison, WI 53711-6223
(608) 270-2400
FAX: (608) 270-2415
URL: http://www.nwhc.usgs.gov/

National Wildlife Refuge System
U.S. Fish and Wildlife Service
1-800-344-9453
URL: http://www.fws.gov/refuges/

Natural Resources Defense Council
40 W. 20th St.
New York, NY 10011
(212) 727-2700
FAX: (212) 727-1773
E-mail: nrdcinfo@nrdc.org
URL: http://www.nrdc.org/

Nature Conservancy
4245 N. Fairfax Dr., Ste. 100
Arlington, VA 22203-1606
(703) 841-5300
1-800-628-6860
URL: http://nature.org/

Northeast Fisheries Science Center
National Oceanic and Atmospheric Administration
166 Water St.
Woods Hole, MA 02543-1026
(508) 495-2000
FAX: (508) 495-2258
URL: http://www.nefsc.noaa.gov/

Northern Prairie Wildlife Research Center
U.S. Geological Survey
8711 37th St. SE
Jamestown, ND 58401
(701) 253-5500
FAX: (701) 253-5553
URL: http://www.npwrc.usgs.gov/

Northwest Fisheries Science Center
National Oceanic and Atmospheric Administration
2725 Montlake Blvd. East
Seattle, WA 98112
(206) 860-3200
FAX: (206) 860-3217
URL: http://www.nwfsc.noaa.gov/

Pacific Legal Foundation
National Litigation Center
930 G St.
Sacramento, CA 95814
(916) 419-7111
FAX: (916) 419-7747
URL: http://www.pacificlegal.org/

Sierra Club
85 Second St., Second Floor
San Francisco, CA 94105
(415) 977-5500
FAX: (415) 977-5797
E-mail: information@sierraclub.org
URL: http://www.sierraclub.org/

TRAFFIC North America—Regional Office
1250 24th St. NW
Washington, DC 20037
(202) 293-4800
FAX: (202) 775-8287
E-mail: tna@wwfus.org
URL: http://www.traffic.org/

United Nations Environment Programme
United Nations Ave., Gigiri
PO Box 30552
Nairobi, 00100, Kenya
(011-254-20) 7621234
E-mail: unepinfo@unep.org
URL: http://www.unep.org/

U.S. Army Corps of Engineers
441 G St. NW
Washington, DC 20314-1000
(202) 761-0011
URL: http://www.usace.army.mil/

U.S. Department of Justice
Environment and Natural Resources Division
Law and Policy Section
950 Pennsylvania Avenue NW
Washington, DC 20530-0001
(202) 514-2701
E-mail: webcontentmgr.enrd@usdoj.gov
URL: http://www.justice.gov/enrd/

U.S. Fish and Wildlife Service
Endangered Species Program
5275 Leesburg Pike
Falls Church, VA 22041
(703) 358-2171
URL: http://www.fws.gov/endangered/

U.S. Government Accountability Office
441 G St. NW
Washington, DC 20548
(202) 512-3000
E-mail: contact@gao.gov
URL: http://www.gao.gov/

Water Resource Center
U.S. Environmental Protection Agency
1200 Pennsylvania Ave. NW
Washington, DC 20460
URL: http://water.epa.gov/aboutow/ownews/wrc/

Western Ecological Research Center
U.S. Geological Survey
3020 State University Dr.
Modoc Hall, Rm. 4004
Sacramento, CA 95819
(916) 278-9485

FAX: (916) 278-9475
URL: http://www.werc.usgs.gov/

WildEarth Guardians
516 Alto St.
Santa Fe, NM 87501
(505) 988-9126
FAX: (505) 213-1895

E-mail: info@wildearthguardians.org
URL: http://www.wildearthguardians.org/
site/PageServer

Wilderness Society
1615 M St. NW
Washington, DC 20036
(202) 833-2300

1-800-843-9453
URL: http://www.wilderness.org/

World Wildlife Fund
1250 24th St. NW
Washington, DC 20037-1193
(202) 293-4800
URL: http://www.worldwildlife.org/

RESOURCES

A leading source of information on endangered species is the U.S. Fish and Wildlife Service (USFWS), an agency of the U.S. Department of the Interior. The USFWS oversees the endangered species list. Its comprehensive website (http://www.fws.gov/endangered/) includes news stories on threatened and endangered species, information about laws protecting endangered species, regional contacts for endangered species programs, and a searchable database called the Threatened and Endangered Species System (http://ecos.fws.gov/tess_public/) with information on all listed species. Each listed species has an information page that provides details regarding the status of the species (whether it is listed as threatened or endangered and in what geographic area), *Federal Register* documents pertaining to listing, information on habitat conservation plans and national wildlife refuges pertinent to the species, and, for many species, links to descriptions of biology and natural history. Particularly informative are the recovery plans published for many listed species. These recovery plans detail the background research on the natural history of endangered species and list measures that should be adopted to aid in conservation.

The USFWS also maintains updated tables of the number of threatened and endangered species by taxonomic group, as well as lists of threatened and endangered U.S. species. The agency publishes the bimonthly *Endangered Species Bulletin*, which provides information on new listings, delistings, and reclassifications, besides news articles on endangered species. Finally, the USFWS prints an annual report on expenditures that have been made under the Endangered Species Act.

The National Marine Fisheries Service (NMFS) is responsible for the oversight of threatened and endangered marine animals and anadromous fish. The NMFS is a division of the National Oceanic and Atmospheric Administration (NOAA), which also operates the National Marine Mammal Laboratory, the Northeast Fisheries Science Center, and the Northwest Fisheries Science Center. NOAA's National Ocean Service is an excellent source of information about marine creatures.

The U.S. Geological Survey (USGS) performs research on many imperiled animal species. Data sheets on individual species are available from the USGS National Wildlife Health Center. Other important USGS centers include the Western Ecological Research Center, the Northern Prairie Wildlife Research Center, the Nonindigenous Aquatic Species information resource at the Center for Aquatic Resource Studies (http://nas.er.usgs.gov/), and the Ecosystems—Wildlife: Terrestrial and Endangered Resources Program.

Information on federal lands and endangered species management can be found via the National Wildlife Refuge System, the National Park Service, and the National Forest Service. Information on water quality in the United States is available via the U.S. Environmental Protection Agency (https://www.epa.gov/science-and-technology/water-science). Information on wetlands can be found at the USFWS's National Wetlands Inventory (http://www.fws.gov/wetlands/).

Data and information related to global warming are available from the National Aeronautics and Space Administration's Goddard Institute for Space Studies and from NOAA's Earth System Research Laboratory, Global Monitoring Division.

Other federal agencies that proved useful for this book were the U.S. Department of Justice's Environment and Natural Resources Division, which defends the federal government in court cases involving environmental laws, such as the Endangered Species Act, and the U.S. Army Corps of Engineers, which maintains the National Inventory of Dams. The U.S. Government Accountability Office and the Congressional Research Service publish a number of reports that assess the policies and effectiveness of the Endangered Species Program.

The International Union for Conservation of Nature (IUCN) provides news articles on a wide array of worldwide conservation issues and maintains the *Red List of Threatened Species* (http://www.iucnredlist.org/about/summary-statistics). This site includes an extensive database of information on IUCN-listed threatened species. Species information that is available includes the Red List endangerment category, the year the species was assessed, the countries in which the species is found, a list of the habitat types the species occupies, major threats to continued existence, and current population trends. Brief descriptions of ecology and natural history and of conservation measures for protecting listed species are also available. Searches can also be performed by taxonomic group, Red List categories, country, region, or habitat.

The Convention on International Trade in Endangered Species of Wild Fauna and Flora (CITES) provides information on international trade in endangered species. It includes a species database of protected flora and fauna in the three CITES appendixes, as well as information on the history and aims of the convention and its current programs.

Many private organizations are dedicated to the conservation of listed species and their ecosystems. Readers with interest in a particular endangered species are advised to conduct Internet searches to locate these groups. The Save the Manatee Club, which focuses on West Indian manatees, and Bat Conservation International, which focuses on protection of imperiled bat species, are only two of many examples.

BirdLife International provides diverse resources on global bird conservation. It is an association of nongovernmental conservation organizations that has nearly 2.8 million members worldwide.

AmphibiaWeb (http://amphibiaweb.org/) provides detailed information on global amphibian declines. It maintains a watch list of recently extinct and declining species, discusses potential causes of amphibian declines and deformities, and provides detailed information on amphibian biology and conservation. AmphibiaWeb also sponsors a discussion board where readers can submit questions regarding amphibians.

TRAFFIC (http://www.traffic.org/) was originally founded to help implement the CITES treaty, but it now addresses diverse issues in the wildlife trade. It is a joint wildlife trade monitoring organization of the World Wildlife Fund and the IUCN. TRAFFIC publishes several periodicals and report series on the wildlife trade, including the *TRAFFIC Bulletin*.

The International Whaling Commission provides information on whaling regulations, whale sanctuaries, and other issues that are associated with whales and whaling. The Center for Biological Diversity plays a major role in the petition and listing process under the Endangered Species Act and conducts scientific investigations regarding imperiled species.

A useful historical resource was *The Endangered Species Act at Thirty: Renewing the Conservation Promise* (Dale D. Goble, J. Michael Scott, and Frank W. Davis, eds., 2006). The Gallup Organization provided information related to public polls that have been conducted in recent years concerning environmental issues.

Information Plus sincerely thanks all the previously mentioned organizations for the valuable information they provided.

INDEX

Lawsuits
  bull trout, 62
  Endangered Species Act, 18
  Environment and Natural Resources
    Division, 31
  Equal Access to Judgment Act, 30
  overprotection lawsuits, 30–31
  Peirson's milk-vetch protection, 180
  polar bear protection, 36
  by private organizations and individuals,
    13, 29
  riders to appropriations bills, 35
  sea turtle protection, 98
  snail darters, 56
  wolves, protection of, 111
Least terns, 131, 132(*f*8.3)
Leatherback sea turtle, 97, 98(*f*6.9)
Legislation
  Alaska National Interest Lands
    Conservation Act, 11
  appropriations bills riders, 35, 111, 146
  Consolidated and Further Continuing
    Appropriations Act, 35
  Consolidated Appropriations Act, 35
  Endangered Species Conservation Act, 17
  Endangered Species Preservation Act, 17
  Equal Access to Judgment Act, 30
  Evading the Endangered Species Act, 37
  Federal Agriculture Improvement and
    Reform Act, 11
  Marine Mammal Protection Act, 26,
    39–40, 52
  Marine Turtle Protection Act (Florida),
    99
  National Defense Authorization Act, 35,
    146
  See also Endangered Species Act
Lepidoptera. *See* Butterflies, moths, and
  skippers
Leporidae family. *See* Rabbits
Lesser prairie chicken, 35
Lewis, Meriwether, 116
Lichens, 178
Lighting, beach, 99
Lincoln County, MT, 110
Linnaeus, Carolus, 1
Listed species, protections and actions for,
  23–28
Listing considerations, 20*t*
Listing process, Endangered Species Act,
  19–23, 21*f*
Little Tennessee River, 31
Lizards, 94, 99–100, 100(*f*6.13)
Loggerhead sea turtles, 93, 97, 98(*f*6.9)
Logging, 127, 130
Longleaf pine forests, 95, 96
Louisiana, 98
Louisiana black bears, 108
Lucas, Frank, 35, 146
Lynx, 113–114, 114*t*

M

Magazine Mountain shagreen, 75
Maguire daisy, 178
Mammals. *See* Marine mammals; Terrestrial
  mammals
Manatees and dugongs, 40, 49–51, *51f*
Marbled murrelets, 132, *132(f*8.4)
Marine and anadromous fish, 65*t*–66*t*
  Endangered Species Act, 64
  Pacific salmonids, 66–72, 67*f*, 68*f*, 69*f*
  sawfish, 73, 73*f*, 73*t*
  steelhead, 67*f*, 72, 72*f*
Marine Mammal Health and Stranding
  Response Program, 43–44
Marine Mammal Protection Act, 26, 39–40,
  52
Marine mammals, 41*t*
  dolphins and porpoises, 45
  expenditures under the Endangered
    Species Act, 42*t*
  manatees and dugongs, *51f*
  Marine Mammal Protection Act, 39–40
  polar bears, 51–53
  role of, 39
  sea otters, 46–48, 49*f*, 50(*f*3.8)
  seals and sea lions, 45–46, 46*f*, 47*f*, 48*f*,
    69–70
  sonar, 31
  whales, 43*f*, 44*t*
Marine Turtle Protection Act (Florida), 99
Marineland, 39
Metamorphosis, 87, 91, 147
Methane, 15
Mexican wolves, 111
Midwestern United States, 108
Migration
  Convention on the Conservation of
    Migratory Species of Wild Animals,
    14
  Pacific salmonid, 66–67
Migratory birds
  shore birds, 131
  songbirds, 129
  whooping cranes, 133
Milk-vetch, 179–180
Mississippi sandhill crane, 133
Mobile, AL, 96
Mobile Area Water and Sewer System, 96
Modoc sucker, 30
Mojave Desert, 94–95
Mollusks. *See* Clams and mussels; Snails
Monito geckos, 100, 100(*f*6.13)
Monito Island, 100
Montana, 36, 110
Moose, 111
Moths. *See* Butterflies, moths, and skippers
Mussels. *See* Clams and mussels
Mustelidae family. *See* Sea otters

N

Naming conventions, 1–2
National Abnormal Amphibian Program, 92
National Association of Home Builders v.
  Defenders of Wildlife, 31
National Defense Authorization Act, 35,
  146
National Marine Fisheries Service (NMFS)
  abalone, 80–81
  candidate species, 23*t*
  critical habitat, 26
  delisting, 28–29
  emergency listing, 23
  Endangered Species Act, 17, 27
  Environment and Natural Resources
    Division, 31
  evolutionarily significant units, 19
  marine and anadromous fish, 64
  marine mammals, 40
  numbers of endangered and threatened
    species, 6
  Pacific salmonids, 68, 70
  plants, 155
  private-party petitions, 29
  proposed species list, 25*t*
  recovery plans, 27
  right whales, 43
  sea turtles, 97–98, 99
  snails, 80
National Oceanic and Atmospheric
  Administration (NOAA)
  corals, 84–85
  invasive mussels, 78–79
  Right Whale Sighting Advisory System,
    44
National Park Service (NPS)
  conservation, 9–10
  Endangered Species Act, 17
  Interagency Grizzly Bear Committee,
    110
  sea turtles, protection of, 99
National parks, 6
National Petroleum Reserve, 11
National Snow and Ice Data Center, 53
National Stone, Sand, and Gravel
  Association, 37
National Wilderness Preservation System, 9
National Wildlife Refuge Association, 14
National Wildlife Refuge (NWR) System, 9,
  10*t*–11*t*
Native Americans, 45, 110
Natural disasters, 14, 93
Natural Resources Conservation Service,
  11, 12, 37
Natural Resources Defense Council, Winter
  v., 31
Natural stressors, 14
Nature Conservancy, 13
Nesting habitat, sea turtle, 99
New listings and politics, 34